BUILDING A CENTURY OF PROGRESS

BUILDING
A CENTURY
OF PROGRESS

THE ARCHITECTURE OF
CHICAGO'S 1933–34
WORLD'S FAIR

LISA D. SCHRENK

UNIVERSITY OF
MINNESOTA PRESS
MINNEAPOLIS
LONDON

This book is supported by a grant from the
Graham Foundation for Advanced Studies in the
Fine Arts and by a grant from Norwich University.

Every effort has been made to obtain permission to reproduce
the illustrations in this book. If any acknowledgment has not been
included, we encourage copyright holders to notify the publisher.

Design and composition by Yvonne Tsang
at Wilsted & Taylor Publishing Services

Published by the University of Minnesota Press
111 Third Avenue South, Suite 290
Minneapolis, MN 55401-2520
http://www.upress.umn.edu

LIBRARY OF CONGRESS CATALOGING-IN-PUBLICATION DATA

Schrenk, Lisa Diane.
Building a century of progress : the architecture of
Chicago's 1933–34 World's Fair / Lisa D. Schrenk.
p. cm.
Includes bibliographical references and index.
ISBN 978-0-8166-4836-8 (hc : alk. paper)
1. Century of Progress International Exposition (1933–1934 : Chicago, Ill.)—
Buildings. 2. Exhibition buildings—Illinois—Chicago—History—20th century.
3. Chicago (Ill.)—Buildings, structures, etc. I. Title.
NA6750.C45C467 2007
720.9773'1109043—dc22   2007009547

Printed in the United States of America on acid-free paper

The University of Minnesota is an
equal-opportunity educator and employer.

12 11 10 09 08 07   10 9 8 7 6 5 4 3 2 1

For my parents

ANN AND LORENZ SCHRENK

for sharing with me
their interest in history
and passion for research

CONTENTS

ACKNOWLEDGMENTS

My fascination with the Century of Progress International Exposition began with a paper written for a seminar on Frank Lloyd Wright and Modernism at the University of Texas at Austin. While exploring Wright's conceptual designs for the second Chicago World's Fair, an interest in the larger scope of the exposition quickly developed. This, and a conspicuous lack of secondary sources on the event, led to the decision to further study the architecture of the fair for my doctoral dissertation, resulting in hundreds of hours spent digging through archives and the acquisition of a growing collection of exposition memorabilia.

Numerous people contributed energy, expertise, materials, and support to make possible the completion of this book. I am profoundly grateful to Anthony Alofsin, who first suggested that I explore the architecture of A Century of Progress. The advice I received from John Clarke, Richard Cleary, Linda Henderson, Jeffrey Meikle, and Danilo Udovicki-Selb while investigating the topic as a graduate student at the University of Texas was invaluable. More recently, Art Schaller, Daniel Doz, Arne Aho, Wendy Cox, and other colleagues at Norwich University all contributed in a variety of ways. Students at Norwich in my own seminars on the architecture of Frank Lloyd Wright, Chicago, and international expositions have offered thought-provoking insights and interpretations contributing to my own understanding of the fair.

The preparation of this book has greatly benefited from the guidance provided by my editors, Pieter Martin and Katie J. Houlihan, and the staff at the University of Minnesota Press. Particular thanks go to the book's copy editor, Kathy Delfosse. Her meticulous work has significantly improved the final result. Daniel Ochsner's design eye helped to give the layout of the book its striking quality, matching the incredible imagery produced for the exposition. Carol Ann Krinsky of New York

University, Katherine Solomonson of the University of Minnesota, Kevin Harrington of the Illinois Institute of Technology, and Robert Rydell of Montana State University enhanced this work by generously sharing their scholarly advice.

I particularly would like to thank John Holabird Jr., the late William Keck, Virgil and Mildred Barnes, both now deceased, and Betty Pulchalski, who took the time to recall their personal experiences at A Century of Progress. John Holabird Jr., William Keck, James Morrow, and Guy Walton kindly shared original documents from the exposition. Additional assistance on this book was provided by Patricia Bakunas and the other curators in Special Collections at the University of Illinois, Chicago; Piriya Metcalfe and Bryan McDaniel at the Chicago History Museum (formerly the Chicago Historical Society); Mary Woolever and Kim Krueger in the Ryerson and Burnham Library at the Art Institute of Chicago; Deborah Ahlers, Lisa Allard, Ellen Hall, Tammy Hunt, and Annette Wicklund at the Kreitzberg Library, Norwich University; Melissa Miller and Rick Watson at the Harry Ransom Humanities Research Center at the University of Texas at Austin; Jim Quigel at the Historical Collections and Labor Archives, Pennsylvania State University; Jennifer Masengarb at the Chicago Architectural Foundation; Bennett Johnson, president of the Chicago Art Deco Society; John Ferry of the Estate of R. Buckminster Fuller; Bruce Laverty at the Athenaeum of Philadelphia; Irene Falconer at the Aaron Galleries, Chicago; Josh Gartler, at Posters Plus, Chicago; John C. Blew of Bell, Boyd, and Lloyd, Chicago; Julie Tozer and Gerald Beasley at the Avery Architectural and Fine Arts Library, Columbia University; Lindsey MacAllister at the Museum of Science and Industry, Chicago; Bruce Brooks Pfeiffer and Margo Stipe at the Taliesin Archives in Scottsdale, Arizona; Judy Hansen and the other staff members of the Fine Arts Library, University of New Mexico; Lynne Farrington in Special Collections, University of Pennsylvania; Jerry Hills and Karine Luetgert at the Masonite Corporation, West Chicago; and Barbara Klingbeil of Roberts and Schaefer Company.

I am especially indebted to my family and friends, whose assistance and encouragement were crucial to the completion of this work. My parents, Ann and Lorenz Schrenk, not only provided love and guidance but also computer, photocopying, and editorial support; my sister, Janet Schrenk, furnished editing assistance, and she and my brother, Stephen Schrenk, contributed computer advice. Many friends offered support, shelter, and helpful input. They include Sue Allen, Andrew Bellcourt, Tom Browne, Dale Burzacott, Roger and Donna Christy, Megan Granda Bahr, Elaine Harrington, Dana Hutt, Karen Hyde, Ellen McCumsey, Jerry McManus, Aliene and Clarke O'Byrne, Jan Roberg, Gerry Schrenk, Janet and Carl Weis, Jennifer Wheeler, and Mark Witzling. A special thank you goes to my husband, Steven Weis, for his computer assistance and, more important, for his love, support, and boundless patience. Sometimes one does need a rocket scientist.

BUILDING A CENTURY OF PROGRESS

THE FUTURE BEGINS

*Pseudo-classical architecture
washed behind the ears . . .
pretty cardboard pictures of
ancient wall masses.*

FRANK LLOYD WRIGHT,
in the *New Republic*

On a warm evening in late May 1933, an enormous crowd gathered along the Chicago lakefront to await the magnificent grand opening of a long-heralded event that offered a chance for respite from the disheartening economic conditions that were gripping the nation.[1] The Century of Progress International Exposition was marketed as a beacon of hope that a better future based on modern developments in science and technology was just around the corner. In 1893, as the city held its first world's fair, over 200 trillion miles away on the star Arcturus tiny atoms of helium were rapidly fusing together. As they merged, the atoms emitted massive amounts of energy that immediately began speeding through the vastness of space. Forty years later, as the hoards packed the Chicago shoreline, a small fraction of that energy reached Earth.[2] Using telescopes and recently developed photoelectric cells, scientists at four different astronomical observatories simultaneously captured some of that well-traveled energy. They transformed the dim pulses, said to be fainter than the rays of a candle, into a stream of electrical current. This power was then sent racing along miles of telegraph wire to the site along Lake Michigan where the expectant crowd had assembled.[3]

As the sun began to set, dark clouds started building to the south. A few light raindrops fell. The music of a symphony orchestra playing in the background heightened anticipation among the crowd.[4] Finally, as the last rays of natural light began to disappear behind the silhouetted skyscrapers to the west, an amplified voice rang out. "Harvard, are you ready?" "Yes," was the transmitted reply. A red glow of neon dramatically darted across a billboard-sized map of the eastern half of the United States. "Is Allegheny ready?" "Ready." "Is Illinois ready?" "Yes." "Yerkes?" "Let's go."[5] Soon other large, red neon tubes began flashing on, each one

Hall of Social Sciences (detail).

I

marking the arrival of an electric signal from an observatory. At precisely 9:15 p.m. the final tube glowed a brilliant crimson, setting off a generator positioned in the center of the sign. The hum of its motor grew louder and louder until enough energy was produced to throw a switch that turned on a searchlight at the top of a modern fair pavilion located nearby. The sharp beacon of light slowly circled the surrounding area. To the crowd's astonishment, as the beam fell onto each of the newly constructed fair pavilions, the building burst into a brilliant, multihued extravaganza of light and fireworks. A Century of Progress was officially open.[6]

THE SETTING

Fifteen months before the spectacular opening ceremony of the Century of Progress International Exposition, a group of prominent designers had gathered at a symposium to celebrate the recent opening of an architectural exhibition of photographs and models located on the twelfth floor of the Heckscher Building in New York City. Included among the scheduled speakers were local architects Harvey Wiley Corbett and Raymond Hood.[7] The two designers were unusually busy at the time despite the harsh economic conditions that had placed many of their colleagues on the list of the unemployed. Both were heavily engaged in designing two of the largest architectural projects under way in the United States—Rockefeller Center in New York City and the world's fair located 800 miles to the west in Chicago. The symposium and the related New York architectural show, Modern Architecture—International Exhibition, were sponsored by the recently established Museum of Modern Art (MoMA).[8]

While the exhibit initially attracted only minimal critical attention, the show's catalog and a related book significantly influenced the way later architects and historians perceived the development of modern architecture in the United States. These publications offered a clear definition of modern architecture based on the aesthetic characteristics of contemporary, progressive European building design that was both easy to understand and easy to illustrate. That noted members of the German architectural diaspora of the mid-1930s were soon teaching at major American schools of design helped ensure that the ideology promoted in the show eventually became the standard framework through which modern architecture in the United

FIG. I.1. Diagram of how energy from the star Arcturus lit the Century of Progress International Exposition on opening day. From Charles Schwarz, "Light Rays from Arcturus Beam Brightly," *Chicago Daily News*, 22 May 1933.

BRIDGING CHASM OF FORTY YEARS BY LIGHT FROM ARCTURUS

IMPULSE FROM STAR ARCTURUS CAPTURED BY POWERFUL TELESCOPES TO TURN ON LIGHTING SYSTEM OF THE WORLD FAIR.
General view of the crowd assembled last night in the court of honor of the Hall of Science to await the instant when the lights were turned on. The star Arcturus is 40 light years away and its rays have been traveling to the earth since the Columbian exposition in 1893. The fair grounds soon after this picture was taken was transformed into a radiant array of lights.

States was interpreted. Conceived primarily in formal terms, the definition put forth in the New York exhibition, however, encompassed only a small segment of the progressive architecture produced in the United States during the late 1920s and early 1930s.

FIG. I.2. Opening-night lighting ceremony in the courtyard of the Hall of Science. From "Impulse from Star Captured by Powerful Telescopes to Turn on Lighting System of the World Fair," *Chicago Tribune,* 27 May 1933.

After the First World War, prominent American architects increasingly addressed current social and technological issues in their work. Awareness of the need to find designs appropriate to the modern age provided a source of creativity, as well as uncertainty, among many designers. Architects and critics engaged in lively debates concerning the definition of modern architecture and the future direction of building design. This discourse reflected the development of diverse architectural ideologies and forms that ranged from Beaux-Arts classicism to streamlining.

In contrast to the MoMA exhibition, the Century of Progress International Exposition presented a more comprehensive manifestation of the complexity of modern architecture during the years between the two world wars. In part it directly responded to major aspects of the culture in which it was created. The fair's built environment celebrated the latest developments in science and technology while exploiting recently introduced concepts of spectacle for large public gatherings. At the same time, it responded to both the pervasive effects of the Great Depression and the growing presence of a government-supported consumer culture. Most significantly, however, the architecture of the 1933–34 Chicago World's Fair reflected the underlying goal among its designers to create a distinctively American modern architecture that was clearly relevant to the times. The result was an extraordinary fairground comprised of pavilions that presented a wide range of innovative designs.

THE CENTURY OF PROGRESS INTERNATIONAL EXPOSITION

In 1928 Chicago's city officials designated three and a half miles of newly reclaimed land along the shore of Lake Michigan directly south of the central business district as the site for the Century of Progress International Exposition. The white, porticoed temples of recently completed neoclassical buildings, including the Field Museum, the Shedd Aquarium, and Soldier Field, framed the northern end of the site. Along with the masonry office towers of the city's central business district, these historically derived buildings provided a largely monochromatic backdrop, reminiscent of the neoclassical pavilions of the first Chicago World's Fair, contrasting sharply with the brightly colored, modern exhibition buildings and festive banners that soon covered the fairgrounds (Plate 1).

FIG. I.3. Bird's-eye view of south end of the fairgrounds with transportation pavilions in the foreground. Postcard from collection of author.

Architects produced a wide variety of building designs for A Century of Progress, reflecting the desire among event organizers not only to celebrate past cultural developments but also to predict advances. The past was represented by re-creations of identifiable historic buildings, quaint ethnic

A CENTURY OF PROGRESS
CHICAGO, 1933

In the foreground—
GOODYEAR'S LANDING FIELD

settings, and seductive midway carnival attractions. Dominating the fairgrounds, however, were over fifty large, colorful modern exhibition halls, futuristic model houses, and progressive foreign buildings that sharply contrasted with the neoclassical character of previous American world's fairs. Major pavilions at A Century of Progress reflected the latest trends in modern architecture, ranging from the silver-and-gold Illinois Host Building, with decorative features derived from the Exposition Internationale des Arts Décoratifs et Industriels Modernes held in 1925 in Paris, to the curved, streamlined facade of the Crane Company Building. Several of the earliest-constructed pavilions, including the Hall of Science, which formed the centerpiece of the fair, and the Electrical Building, were decorated with panels of bas-relief sculpture containing stylized, allegorical figures representing the sciences. Many other buildings, including most of the corporate pavilions, such as the Chrysler Building, had only large letters spelling out the company's name across unadorned facades. Pavilions, such as the Time and Fortune Building and the Havoline Thermometer, strove for more immediate corporate recognition by including colossal reproductions of their products or related items as part of their buildings' designs. Several other companies commissioned exhibition halls constructed out of their own modern products. For example, the jewel-like Owens-Illinois Glass-Block Building consisted of a tower and two wings built out of their new colorful glass bricks. In the center of the fairgrounds, the Home and Industrial Arts Exhibit included an enticing display of modern houses that attracted long lines of curious homemakers. These full-scale model designs featured innovations in residential living developed in the studios of progressive designers and in the headquarters of American corporations. Almost all the fair buildings, regardless of their aesthetic design and function, incorporated innovative building materials and construction techniques. A comprehensive color scheme, created by Joseph Urban, articulated the individual exterior planes of the major buildings through the use of vivid hues while unifying the diverse fair pavilions. At night, blazing, dramatic lighting effects created an enchanting spectacle best viewed from the massive Skyride that towered above the fairgrounds.

THE ROLE OF INTERNATIONAL EXPOSITIONS IN THE DEVELOPMENT OF MODERN ARCHITECTURE

The Century of Progress International Exposition presented an ideal opportunity for prominent architects to work together on a large event that could publicize their modern architectural ideas. The cooperative arrangement for the participating designers was similar to that of recent contemporary housing exhibitions in Germany and Austria, such as the Weissenhofsiedlung held in Stuttgart in 1927, sponsored by progressive European design organizations.[9] Many American architects wrote to fair organizers asking if they could contribute designs to the Chicago

Stuttgart Weissenhof Siedlung

exposition, hoping to illustrate their own ideas through actual buildings at a time when few major construction projects were under way in the United States.[10] Fair organizers rejected most of these requests. Several architects, including Frank Lloyd Wright, were not deterred and used the exposition to promote their design ideas by creating novel conceptual plans for the fair or criticizing the event in architectural publications or in the popular press.

The important role of international expositions in promoting architectural ideas did not commence in 1933. Beginning with the first international exposition, held in 1851 in London, these events have presented innovative ideas in architectural design to large numbers of people. The colossal Crystal Palace, built in 1851 to house the Great Exhibition of the Works of Industry of All Nations, demonstrated to the public the capabilities of iron and glass construction, as well as the benefits of prefabrication and mass production.[11] Other expositions also used building designs to illustrate technological and aesthetic developments, such as the potential of iron construction in the erection of the Eiffel Tower at the 1889 Exposition Universelle in Paris. Small display rooms and pavilions exhibiting avant-garde designs had also appeared at world's fairs. For example, the German Exhibit Building at the Louisiana Purchase Exposition held in St. Louis, Missouri, in 1904 contained an ornate court from the *Summer Residence of an Art Lover* by Joseph Maria Olbrich and a reading room by Peter Behrens. New ideas in architecture appeared not only in full-scale designs but also in displays of drawings and related objects, such as the presentation of art nouveau designs at the 1900 Exposition Universelle in Paris and again four years later at the St. Louis

FIG. I.4 *(top facing)*. Illinois Host Building with art deco detailing. Kaufmann and Fabry, photographers.
FIG. I.5 *(below facing)*. Time and Fortune Building. Kaufmann and Fabry, photographers.
FIG. I.6 *(above)*. Weissenhofsiedlung housing exhibition, Stuttgart, Germany, 1927. Postcard from collection of author.

fair.[12] Innovative buildings designed for expositions held just prior to the 1933–34 Chicago fair were also significant in the development of architectural ideas. The angular building forms and bas-relief decorations that permeated the 1925 Exposition Internationale des Arts Décoratifs et Industriels Modernes in Paris strongly influenced designers in both Europe and the United States, as did later modern fair buildings, such as Mies van der Rohe's elegant German Pavilion built for the 1929 exposition in Barcelona.

Some world's fair designers looked to historical forms for inspiration. For example, while the World's Columbian Exposition had included Louis Sullivan's colorful and organically ornamented Transportation Building, the commanding presence of the white, neoclassical pavilions that dominated the fair's Court of Honor helped pave the way for a tremendous wave of neoclassical designs at later expositions and in large institutional buildings throughout the United States. These classical designs continued to be popular among civic leaders right up to the opening of A Century of Progress.

Re-creations of picturesque ethnic villages and historical landmarks were major features at many world's fairs, beginning with the 1867 Paris Exposition

FIG. I.7. Reading room by Peter Behrens in the German arts and crafts exhibit at the 1904 Louisiana Purchase Exposition in St. Louis. From *Descriptive Catalogue of the German Arts and Crafts and the Universal Exposition, St. Louis* (St. Louis, Mo.: Imperial German Commission, 1904), 2.

FIG. I.8. Ethnic villages at A Century of Progress, with Midget Village to the left and the Old English Village to the right. Kaufmann and Fabry, photographers.

Universelle. While visitors greatly enjoyed a sense of fantasy as they shopped in "Bavarian" hamlets, ate among "Indian" temples, or were entertained in "African" jungles, these attractions typically served underlying purposes, including promoting various facets of commerce, nationalism, colonialism, and eugenics. Through the construction of historic national villages and monuments that reduced a nation's identity to easily readable iconographic symbols, participating countries could reinterpret their own or their colonies' pasts to fit specific political agendas.[13] However, in the case of the Chicago fair, most of the historic villages and monuments (many financed and designed by local underemployed architects and built primarily as investments) served predominantly for entertainment. Like the nearby neoclassical museums, these buildings provided a contrasting background to what fairgoers experienced in the modern exhibition halls and futuristic model residences.

AMERICAN ARCHITECTURE DURING THE EARLY 1930S

No other building project in the United States during the early 1930s promoted modern architecture as broadly as the second Chicago World's Fair. The plurality of the designs produced for the exposition reflected the great breadth of aesthetic forms that appeared in American architecture during the years between the two world wars. Many of the most prominent designers in the country who had received their educations at the École des Beaux-Arts continued to design in the neoclassical style that had dominated the earlier Columbian Exposition. A number of their colleagues, however, preferred creating neo-Gothic forms that recalled the great cathedrals and universities of Europe. Some academically educated designers, including Bertram Goodhue and Paul Cret, allowed context to guide their choice of a specific stylistic vocabulary for a given commission. By the 1930s, however, historical designs were often modernized by eliminating all but austere hints of the basic decorative elements that defined a traditional style. The 1925 Exposition Internationale des Arts Décoratifs et Industriels Modernes had in part advocated a machine-age aesthetic that reflected the rise of jazz and the quickening pace of life during the Roaring Twenties. Its influence could be found in the use of sleek, angular, abstract forms by many American architects, including Ely Jacques Kahn, who favored producing designs that clearly reflected the changing times.[14] The ideas and projects of prominent European designers, such as those who had exhibited at the Weissenhofsiedlung in 1927, were highlighted in architectural journals and influenced American architects searching for more efficient building forms. These included both European immigrants, such as William Lescaze and Richard Neutra, and native-born designers like George Frederick Keck. A few architects who rejected traditional forms, such as Frank Lloyd Wright and Buckminster Fuller, developed their own, more personal, styles of modern architecture.

In the early 1930s, thousands of architects, irrespective of their design ideologies, joined construction workers and others in the building trades among the unemployed as construction starts plummeted because of the Great Depression. The only other large-scale architectural project under way at this time in the United States was Rockefeller Center, a corporate complex consisting of thirteen tall office towers covering three blocks in New York City.[15] Almost all American architects not at work on Rockefeller Center or A Century of Progress found themselves confined to designing projects on paper or to promoting their ideas at professional meetings or through the written word in trade publications. Architectural exhibitions also provided a means for exchanging new design ideas without the prohibitive cost of construction. The most historically influential of these exhibits was MoMA's 1932 Modern Architecture—International Exhibition.

The exhibition (commonly known as the International Style Show) was curated by Henry-Russell Hitchcock and Philip Johnson and consisted of photographs, models, and plans of contemporary architectural designs.[16] For the show, the curators selected buildings that typically included flat, unadorned facades that appear starkly white in the large black-and-white photographs that lined the beige gallery walls like priceless paintings.[17] Relying on a formalist approach to art history, Hitchcock and Johnson focused on the aesthetic qualities of the chosen works while omitting many issues that strongly influenced modern architecture, particularly those that involved social, economic, and technological factors.[18] The selected buildings, used to illustrate the curators' definition of modern architecture, showed three major characteristics: an expression of volume over mass and solidity; a sense of regularity as opposed to rigid symmetry; and a reliance for visual interest on the inherent beauty of materials and proportions, as opposed to applied ornament.[19]

The exhibit prominently featured buildings by progressive European architects who had participated in the Weissenhofsiedlung exposition in Germany, including Le Corbusier, Gropius, Oud, and Mies van der Rohe.[20] To fulfill a mandate made by the board of directors of MoMA, which stipulated that 50 percent of the show be devoted to American architecture, Hitchcock and Johnson also included works by Frank Lloyd Wright, Howe and Lescaze, Raymond Hood, Richard Neutra, and the Bowman Brothers.[21] In comparison to the European buildings, these designs revealed significant diversity in the work of forward-looking American architects.

While the MoMA show attracted 33,000 visitors during its six-week run in New York, the ideas expounded in the exhibition were primarily disseminated through the publication of a related book by Hitchcock and Johnson, *The International Style: Architecture since 1922*, that later became widely read in American schools of architecture.[22] Free from the desires of the museum's board of directors, the authors of *The International Style* included a different selection of illustrations from those in either the exhibit catalog or the show. The curators replaced images that did not support their stylistic interpretation of

FIG. I.9. Section of International Style Show dedicated to Le Corbusier, 1932. Digital image copyright The Museum of Modern Art; licensed by SCALA / Art Resource, NY.

modern architecture (including most of the buildings by American designers) with photographs that projected stronger illustrations of specific aesthetic qualities.[23] As a result, their presentation of the International Style became both more visually oriented and more restrictive in its formal guidelines, ultimately giving preference to an exclusive collection of mainly European monuments. These buildings eventually became accepted by many twentieth-century academics as the major icons of modern architecture. The book's limited formal definition of modern architecture, however, contrasted sharply with what was concurrently being put forward by many prominent architects in the United States, including those participating in the design of the Century of Progress International Exposition.

THE DEFINITION OF MODERN ARCHITECTURE IN THE UNITED STATES

Clearly understanding what was meant by the term *modern architecture* became a major objective among prominent American designers and critics during the late 1920s and early 1930s. The phrase was not precisely defined and was therefore adaptable to different ideologies during these years.[24] Although American architects often looked to their European counterparts for inspiration and direction, many realized the need for solutions that could better meet the specific demands of their own country. The disparate political and economic situations in Europe (still struggling to recover from the First World War) and in the United States (experiencing unprecedented prosperity) during the 1920s contributed greatly to differences between developing ideas about modern architecture by progressive American and European designers. For example, many European architects, trying to move beyond the recent events of the war, rejected the past and searched for revolutionary change. Americans, meanwhile, who only recently had become cognizant of their own cultural history, typically did not feel as strongly about the need to divorce modern architecture completely from the past and, instead, often saw it more as an outgrowth from previous developments and the next logical step in the evolution of building design.

While progressive European architects focused on creating new idealistic solutions to reflect the social reforms taking place in their countries, their American counterparts were often more focused on meeting the more tangible needs of industry and commerce. In 1964 Sibyl Moholy-Nagy, architectural historian and wife of Bauhaus master Laszlo Moholy-Nagy, commented on American architects' more pragmatic view of modern design. Although dealing with growing corporate agendas, American architects were free of ties to the radical political and social ideologies developing in Europe. Looking back on modern architecture during this period, she stated:

For the American designer functionalism meant, and still means, building as economically and as technologically as possible, with minimal consideration of personal or aesthetic principles. To the diaspora architects [those displaced primarily by the rise of National Socialism in Germany in the 1930s] functionalism meant pure ideology, visualizing self-evident truths of ethical, aesthetic, and social *Weltanschauung.*[25]

The acceptance of a variety of aesthetic styles in the United States to meet the needs of rapidly growing urban centers did not preclude debate on the definition of the term *modern architecture.* Its meaning continued to evolve during the 1920s and early 1930s both in practice and in rhetoric, as architects were acutely aware that they were in a transitional period in building design.[26] What direction American architecture should take was a favorite topic of discussion at architectural meetings and in both professional and popular periodicals. Central to much of the deliberation was a growing desire to formulate a more precise understanding of modern architecture.

In the early 1920s the term *modern architecture* changed from referring primarily to all forms of contemporary building design, including those that exhibited historical characteristics, to serving as a catchphrase for recent designs that were not considered historical or traditional. This reflected a growing division in American architecture between designers and critics who favored time-tested traditional styles and those who eschewed eclectic architecture in favor of new forms they felt to be more relevant to the era. By the end of the decade, many designers began separating modern architecture from a stylistic definition and instead viewed progressive building design as that which exhibited an integral use of new construction materials and processes while meeting modern needs. The result was a wide range of architectural forms produced by prominent designers in the United States prior to the dramatic reduction of all construction starts in the early 1930s as the country slipped deeper into the Depression.

THE ARCHITECTURAL SETTING FOR THE EXPOSITION

The designers who were eventually selected to serve on the Century of Progress International Exposition's official architectural commission realized that the event offered a rare design opportunity, as they were able to develop and present their ideas without having to deal with the difficult clients, zoning rules, skeptical bankers, or restrictive programs that often dictated more permanent building projects. The long and winding exposition site along the Lake Michigan shore, as well as financial limitations resulting from the Great Depression, provided both inspiration and guidance for the committee members. A lack of a rigid building code allowed exposition architects to break away from conventional standards. The knowledge that the buildings were going to be short-lived and set outside the everyday world offered the designers the freedom to experiment. They were able to specify new building materials, processes, and forms without having to be concerned that their buildings would lose value over time as styles changed or experimental construction materials failed. Extensive publicity and large attendance figures ensured an attentive audience that included not only other architects and designers but also thousands of potential future clients.

The need for organizers to present a distinctively modern fair both influenced the character of the exhibits on display, as will be seen in chapter 1, and strongly affected the architectural designs for the event. After years dominated by revival and eclectic forms, many academically trained designers, including members of the fair's architectural commission, began rejecting traditional Beaux-Arts planning and historical styles in favor of new machine-age designs.[27] The major pavilions at the Chicago exposition clearly reflected this departure from the past through the application of modern materials, in the use of laborsaving construction methods, in the incorporation of decorative color and lighting, and in the introduction of a variety of new forms. These changes developed from the exposition architects' desire to make the pavilions reflect current progressive ideas in building design, as well as from five related circumstances: (1) recent developments in the building industry, (2) the ephemeral nature of the exposition, (3) the depressed state of the economy, (4) the need to compete with other novel forms of mass entertainment, and (5) the conditions of the specific site. Each of these factors served as a catalyst for the introduction and promotion of a wide variety of new ideas in architecture and construction at the fair. Innovations included the adoption of newly available building materials and structural systems, the incorporation of experimental construction processes, the introduction of new architectural forms and concepts in decoration, and the display of novel ideas in interior living.

The temporary character of the Chicago fair demanded maximum economy in construction.[28] Costs for a building slated to last only about a year could not be amortized over decades as was done with more permanent construction. Unlike most previous expositions, the event received no government subsidies to offset expenses. Costs, passed on to the exhibitors through rentals for display spaces, had to be kept at affordable levels. This forced fair organizers to keep the square-foot cost of exhibit space close to that of the 1893 World's Columbian Exposition. Labor costs, however, had increased approximately eightfold; the cost of materials, between two- and fivefold.[29]

The realities of the bleak economic situation during the Great Depression further affected the situation. Labor was readily available, but financing for large, elaborate projects was difficult to find.[30] The exposition architects not only had to eliminate several elaborate features from the early fair designs, including an airport

and the Tower of Water (a skyscraper-scaled fountain), but they were also forced to carry out, in the words of one of the engineers for the event, the "utilization of the utmost economy."[31] As a result, they found themselves with no other alternative than to rely on recently available, inexpensive building materials and processes that required minimal labor.[32]

The depressed economy also contributed to a backdrop that contrasted sharply with the dreamlike world within the gates of the fairgrounds, a world reminiscent of the exhilarating energy of the days before the stock market crash, when the exposition was first being planned. The event offered visitors hope for a better tomorrow by presenting buildings that contained innovations intended to make living easier and more enjoyable. While not everyone left the fairgrounds desiring a futuristic steel or glass house like those on exhibit, many people did go away excited about the new products they had seen on display and, more importantly, with the belief that an economic recovery was just beyond the horizon. The exposition, in fact, played a significant role in initiating Chicago's economic revival, particularly for the city's building industry, by generating hundreds of desperately needed jobs during the

FIG. I.10. Hall of Social Science, showing the Radio Entrance, with bas-relief symbolizing modern radio and its applied uses, designed by Alfonso Iannelli, and sculpted pylons on the north side of building, representing the God of Fire, the God of Light, the Goddess of Night, and the God of Storm, designed by Leo Friedlander. Kaufmann and Fabry, photographers.

FIG. I.11. Bird's-eye rendering of the Tower of Water proposed for the 1933 Century of Progress International Exposition, Ralph Walker, architect. Voorhees, Gmelin, and Walker Photographs. From Ryerson and Burnham Archives, The Art Institute of Chicago. Digital file copyright The Art Institute of Chicago.

construction of the fair and hundreds more after the start of the event in positions ranging from carpenters to building-products demonstrators.

The need to compete with ever-more-available mass cultural outlets, in particular radio and motion pictures, meant that the exposition had to present an even greater spectacle than those of earlier world's fairs to attract the large numbers of visitors necessary to guarantee financial and popular success. No longer did people need to travel great distances to experience new ideas and different cultures. A visit to the local atmospheric movie house or the purchase of a family radio receiver provided a window onto the world from the comfort of home or neighborhood. From the start, fair organizers understood that they had to market the exposition as offering something even more extravagant to the public.

Fortunately, advances in transportation, which made traveling long distances quicker and more comfortable, made it possible for large numbers of out-of-town fairgoers to reach A Century of Progress with relative ease. New streamlined trains and airplanes, and the fact that Chicago was a major transportation hub situated in the center of the country, meant that the journey to the exposition could often be completed in hours instead of days. The dramatic rise of automobile ownership during the 1920s and steadily improving road conditions allowed many people to forgo public transportation in favor of traveling to the event in their own cars. The location of the fairgrounds, near streetcar and rail lines, and surrounded by land available for large parking lots, contributed to the relative ease of reaching the site.

Factors regarding the specific location of the exposition led fair architects to experiment with new materials and building techniques. According to Allen D. Albert, an organizer of the exposition, the biggest thrill for the members of the architectural commission at their first official meeting was finding out that the site of the exposition would be on new, man-made land placed under the jurisdiction of the South Park Commission and not the City of Chicago. This meant that the designers did not have to comply with the city's strict building code.[33] Instead, they initially only had to observe the authority of the state fire marshal.[34] While public safety and insurance underwriters' requirements necessitated that some form of building restrictions would eventually have to be put in place, a code did not officially go into effect until December 1932, well after the construction of several major pavilions.[35] The incorporation of this building code, written to meet the specific requirements of the exposition, granted designers greater freedom than codes typically allowed for the safe construction of more permanent buildings.

FIG. I.12. "World's Largest Parking Lot," located immediately west of the fairgrounds. Postcard from collection of author.

We parked our car in this world's largest parking lot
HERBERG-WEBSTER PHOTO   BETWEEN 16th AND 26th STS. ON COLUMBUS DRIVE

The special code enabled the architects and builders to use inexpensive, yet innovative, materials, such as plywood and wallboards. It also allowed them to eliminate unnecessary windows and benefit from the efficiencies of prefabrication. In some cases, after conclusive testing proved their short-term safety, the code even allowed the use of products felt inappropriate for permanent construction.[36] It additionally permitted the presence of slightly higher maximum structural stresses than were normally acceptable for regular buildings. This made possible the construction of the lighter wall sections deemed necessary because of the site's unstable soil conditions (Plate 2).[37]

One aspect of the building code that significantly contributed to the increase in experimental building was the elimination of ancillary fireproofing. Fair organizers decided that it would be less costly to replace a building and its contents after a major fire than to fireproof it in the first place. This dramatically lowered initial construction costs. To avoid a major catastrophe, architects specified incombustible interior materials and slow-burning exterior products, such as gypsum board. The designers also avoided the use of any materials with the potential to create significant quantities of smoke or fumes. Additional safety measures included the careful protection of electrical transformers and the incorporation of numerous exits for rapid egress during an emergency.[38]

As one of the few major architectural events to take place in the United States during the early 1930s, the Century of Progress International Exposition played a significant role in stimulating the field of design at a time when architects were attempting to respond to a rapidly changing world. The fair designers' search for an appropriate definition of modern architecture for the event led to the creation of distinctive aesthetic forms that, in addition to being free from obvious precedents, incorporated new fundamental principles of design. The mixed reception of the exposition pavilions by architects, critics, and the general public reflected the diversity of design ideologies in American architecture during the years the fair was planned and built, as well as the growing role of professional and popular publications in promoting new ideas. The story of the architecture of the 1933–34 Chicago World's Fair provides insight into these and other consequential issues, most specifically the impact of the Great Depression and the growing role of a corporate consumer culture on American architecture.

ONE

SCIENCE FINDS—
INDUSTRY APPLIES—
MAN CONFORMS

With trumpet blasts and speeches which were literally heard round the world, Chicago yesterday hurled the challenge of A Century of Progress in the face of more than three years of depression. A strip of land 500 feet wide, three and a half miles long, dredged from the bottom of Lake Michigan, set with such buildings as have never been seen outside the sketch-books of dreaming architects, glowing with colors that have not before been so massed, even in ancient cities and under Oriental skies—here is Chicago's defiant embodiment of its belief that mankind does go forward and that the best is yet to come.

R.L. DUFFUS, "The Fair: A World of Tomorrow"

The elaborately staged opening-night lighting ceremony clearly illustrated to the world that A Century of Progress was unlike any international exposition held before. By the 1930s the traditional primary goal of world's fairs—to communicate new ideas, technological developments, and political agendas—had, to a large extent, been outgrown. The financial fiasco of the Sesquicentennial International Exposition held in Philadelphia in 1926 confirmed for many leading businessmen and politicians at the time that international expositions had lost their sense of purpose in the modern age.[1] The delivery of information to the general public could typically be accomplished much more efficiently through radio, newsreels, and other modern means of communication.[2]

With the failure of Philadelphia's exposition fresh on their minds, the board of trustees for the Chicago fair realized that an entirely new character and structure was essential if the event were to achieve cultural and financial success.[3] In their attempt to create a seductively grand spectacle that would appeal to Americans in a growing age of consumerism, the organizers traveled throughout the United States and Europe to examine a wide variety of museums and exhibitions that featured new concepts of display. Their destinations ranged from the Deutsches Museum in Munich, Germany, one of the first museums of science and industry, to an exhibition sponsored by the Baltimore and Ohio (B&O) Railroad that highlighted the progress of transportation in the United States.[4] The great popularity of these events clearly illustrated to the Chicago planners that an exposition that featured recent advances in science and industry offered the greatest potential for success.[5]

Fair organizers eventually arrived at a carefully crafted central focus for their event—the betterment of mankind through advances in scientific technology. The concept of modern human progress, emphasized in the final title for the event, was popularized during this period in writings by a number of prominent Americans ranging from Charles Beard to Henry Ford to Watson Davis.[6] This scientific theme reflected a major shift in American society. The underlying basis of national economic growth was evolving from land acquisition and individual entrepreneurship, which had shaped the country in the nineteenth century, to an elaborate technology-based consumer culture that developed from an increasingly complex twentieth-century institutional network made up of business corporations, government agencies, private foundations, and educational institutions.[7] To emphasize the shift of the country's pioneering spirit from the open countryside of the West to the laboratories of universities, corporations, and government agencies, fair organizers planned to highlight the latest advances in scientific technology through novel forms of entertainment. While presenting new developments to the public had been central to the basic concept of world's fairs since the introduction of international expositions in 1851, uniting the wide variety of exhibits and activities at such an event through a central scientific theme was first carried out at A Century of Progress.

Many of the specific features of the Chicago fair were developed by event organizers after visits to major international expositions held in Europe between 1929 and 1931.[8] Records indicate that they observed everything from the design of exhibits to the type of gravel used for pedestrian pathways. The planners applied modern underlying principles to every possible aspect of the Chicago fair. These included a focus on the practical uses of science, an emphasis on the present and future over the past, the theatrical exhibition of manufacturing processes and products as opposed to static displays, the presentation of new, faster forms of transportation, the organization of exhibits cooperatively, by industry rather than by individual competing companies, and the dominant use of private resources instead of public funding to finance and promote the event.

BIRTH OF THE FAIR

Captain Myron E. Adams, a minister and social service worker, first presented the idea to hold a fair to celebrate Chicago's centennial to the city's mayor, William Dever, in a letter dated 17 August 1923.[9] He recommended that Chicago sponsor "the greatest Centennial Exhibit in the world" in either 1933, the 100th anniversary of the city's incorporation as a village, or 1937, Chicago's centennial of officially

becoming a city. Adams expressed his hope that the event would provide the incentive for carrying out needed civic improvements, including un-realized elements in Daniel Burnham Sr.'s earlier City Beautiful plans.[10] Other potential benefits of the celebration suggested by Adams would be an increase in Chicagoans' civic pride and greater worldwide attention for the city. He went on to propose several fundamental ideas that were even-tually adopted, most significantly, that the exposition be situated on man-made land located along the lakefront immediately south of the Loop.[11]

FIG. 1.1. Bird's-eye view of the 1931 Exposition Coloniale Internationale in Paris. Reproductions of Angkor Wat and other ethnic buildings are shown in the foreground and the modern Metropolitan section appears in the distance. Postcard from collection of author.

Public interest in a second Chicago exposition quickly grew as early support-ers began contacting leading citizens, civic institutions, and newspapers. In March 1926 the Chicago City Council officially approved studying the idea of hosting another world's fair.[12] This gave Mayor Dever the authority to appoint a committee of 150 citizens to begin planning an event to commemorate Chicago's 100th an-niversary. However, when William Hale Thompson was elected mayor of the city in 1927, some of Chicago's leading men in finance expressed their concern to him that the event would be a monetary failure. In August of that year, Mayor Thomp-son announced that no world's fair would be held, and plans for the centennial exposition were officially dropped.[13]

A group of prominent citizens led by Charles S. Peterson, city treasurer of Chicago, would not let the idea of a second world's fair slip away so easily.[14] They informed Mayor Thompson that canceling the plans for a centennial exposi-tion had resulted in great public disappointment. A lively public meeting, held on

13 December 1927, demonstrated to the new mayor how widespread citizen support for a fair was.[15] Some advocates recalled the advantages the city had received from the World's Columbian Exposition, while others extolled the potential positive effects of uniting the loyal citizens of Chicago behind a large, visible event. The fair's potential to improve the city's reputation was also mentioned.[16] This proved to be a strong selling point, as Chicago's image had been considerably tarnished during Prohibition through publicity regarding bootlegging and related criminal activities in the city.[17] Persuaded by the supporters' arguments, Mayor Thompson restarted the planning process, and on 5 January 1928 a not-for-profit corporation of eighty trustees, chosen from among the city's leading businessmen, was established to hold "a World's Fair in Chicago in the year 1933."[18] Rufus C. Dawes, the brother of Charles G. Dawes, vice president of the United States under Calvin Coolidge, became president of the Chicago Second World's Fair Centennial Celebration Corporation.[19] Other officers included Charles S. Peterson as vice president, Daniel H. Burnham Jr. as secretary, George Woodruff as treasurer, and Arthur Anderson as comptroller.[20] Major Lenox Lohr, an army engineer, was hired as general manager. To become an official world's fair, however, formal sponsorship from the U.S. government was needed. Vice President Dawes submitted the necessary proposal to Congress on behalf of the exposition's corporation. On 5 February 1929, a joint resolution passed authorizing the president of the United States to invite the nations of the world to participate in the second Chicago World's Fair.[21]

Although plans went forward, the 1933 Chicago exposition still had not received support from those citizens and government officials who continued to worry about the event's potential financial risks. The inability of the Sesquicentennial Exposition to attract sufficient visitors to pay for the event continued to be cited as proof that international fairs were obsolete. Fortunately, the planning and administration of the Century of Progress International Exposition was placed in the hands of highly competent people who fully believed in the fair. In a remarkably harmonious fashion, these men managed to produce a successful event appropriate to the modern era.

A SHIFT IN FOCUS: THE SERVICE OF SCIENCE

According to fair organizers, the original purpose of the event was to celebrate the centennial anniversary of the founding of Chicago.[22] The city, which had consisted of little more than a small village of "log cabins and framed shacks" around Fort Dearborn in 1833, would have the opportunity to show off its rapid development into a world-class city.[23] The organizers quickly realized, however, that this theme alone could not attract enough international, or even national, interest to guarantee a successful exposition. Consequently, they decided to change the scope of the fair in two significant ways.

The first and most important modification resulted in the unification of every aspect of the exposition around a central scientific theme. This concept distinguished the Chicago fair from earlier American expositions,which, despite often being held to commemorate a specific event, typically projected a jumble of messages and ideas to fair visitors. The second change broadened the focus of the fair geographically and temporally by emphasizing both current and potential future scientific advances from around the world.

The exposition's new official name and motto reflected the evolution of its theme. The initial desire to highlight past accomplishments of the City of Chicago was embodied in the exposition's early titles. The Second World's Fair Centennial Celebration was renamed the Chicago's World's Fair Centennial Celebration in 1928.[24] But by the beginning of July 1929, fair trustees had once again changed the name, this time to A Century of Progress, appropriately reflecting the fair's emphasis on mankind's continuing scientific developments.[25] In a similar vein, the different mottoes for the exposition also expressed the evolution of the event's focus. The original slogan for the fair, I Will, borrowed from the earlier Columbian Exposition, instilled in people the belief that Chicago, which had faced and conquered several major difficulties during its brief history, could rise above the Great Depression.[26] After the decision was made to emphasize the practical uses of scientific developments, a second slogan, Science Finds—Industry Applies—Man Conforms, was introduced. This carefully constructed motto was perceived as being more appropriate to the era as it reflected the growing role of the scientist in modern culture and the prevalent belief at the time in man's ability to conquer nature through advances in scientific technology. The new slogan was also more encompassing and better represented the desire of fair organizers to promote the prevailing agenda of leading American policy makers, who believed that a stronger national economy would result if scientists, industrialists, and consumers worked in unison with government toward common goals.

The growth of public interest in scientific developments during the 1920s was a major factor in selecting a theme for the fair. This increase was due in part to the greater availability of technical information and products, such as automobiles, radios, and talking movies, as disposable income and free time increased for many Americans during the decade. The success of *Popular Mechanics* and *Scientific American,* magazines that made scientific advances understandable for the general reader, reflected the rise in public fascination with new technology. As with these publications, the basic objectives of the fair were to increase public appreciation of the importance of the sciences to modern life and to present industry as the offspring of science and technology.[27]

The idea to focus the exposition on science's service to humanity was first suggested to the fair's executive committee early in the planning process by George E. Hale.[28] Hale was a leading astrophysicist and founder of the National Research

Council, an organization set up in 1916 to provide scientific and technical advice to the U.S. military. Later, after the end of the First World War, the council stimulated forward-looking research by promoting cooperation among scientists in both academia and industry.[29] Hale proclaimed Chicago to be the only major city in the world whose entire life was contained in the preceding 100 years of unprecedented advances in science.[30] To realize the potential of a scientific theme for the fair, Rufus Dawes appointed National Research Council members to the Scientific Advisory Committee to A Century of Progress.[31] Its first meeting, held in June 1929, focused on seven areas of science to be featured at the fair: mathematics, astronomy, physics, chemistry, biology, geology, and medicine.[32] Thirty-three individual subcommittees were created consisting of over 400 "eminent men throughout the United States in all the departments of natural science."[33] These scientists unselfishly provided advice regarding the content of the basic science exhibits, and suggested ways to present scientific displays to the public in a comprehendible and engaging fashion.[34] The success of the Scientific Advisory Committee was readily apparent during the exposition, as illustrations of the effects of science on everyday life pervaded the event.

Fair organizers realized it was imperative that the scientific exhibits appeal to academics and the public alike. They encouraged exhibitors to create displays that would be both understandable and entertaining to an average twelve-year-old.[35] Complex ideas and applications were broken down and presented in simple language. The organizers hoped that by stressing the influence of scientific progress and its effects on daily life through the creation of popular exhibits, the general public would receive a "deeper appreciation of the service of science to society" and, as a result, would be willing to support scientific research.[36]

Exhibits of the basic sciences, such as a demonstration of the motion of molecules, were located in the Hall of Science.[37] Other more practical applications of recent scientific advances, including demonstrations of the latest in communication technology, were placed in the Electrical and General Exhibits buildings. Fair organizers also sought to include less obvious illustrations of how scientific progress influenced everyday life. For example, many of the exhibits in the Hall of Social Science revolved around the "social consequences" of scientific achievement.[38] Even celebrations—such as the dramatic lighting of the fair at the opening ceremony, which was repeated nightly—were envisioned to present scientific lessons to the public.

While the first part of the slogan Science Finds—Industry Applies—Man Conforms clearly reflected the main theme of the exposition, fair organizers had constructed the rest of the phrase just as carefully. They saw the event as an important opportunity to lift Chicago, if not the whole country, from the depths of the Great Depression by encouraging

FIG. 1.2. Poster advertising A Century of Progress. The personification of Chicago's I Will spirit stands on top of the earth framed by figures representing science and industry. Buildings of the city's past, present, and future are shown in the background. Courtesy of Poster Plus, Chicago, www.posterplus.com.

APRIL
25 CENTS
POPULAR MECHANICS MAGAZINE
PROGRESS
Thirtieth Anniversary Issue

collaboration among the government, scientists, and industries. As a result, corporations and professional organizations played a prominent role in the presentation of new technology at the fair. World's fairs had always included exhibits highlighting commercial products, but A Century of Progress was the first international exposition at which corporations had such a dominant presence. Industry was most visibly represented by large corporate pavilions throughout the fairgrounds, such as those erected by Sears, Roebuck and Company, Armour and Company, and Johns-Manville.

The major aim of many industry-sponsored exhibits was to encourage public spending by generating a perceived need for mass-produced products. At the time of the fair, many pro-business writers were promoting the idea that recessions were caused by underconsumption and that the most efficient way out of poor economic situations was to increase consumer spending.[39] It was believed that if corporations applied the innovative technologies being developed in the scientists' laboratories, greater efficiencies could be achieved. If people then conformed by buying into the changes these advances offered, the result was sure to be a stronger economy for the emerging consumer culture. Including *Man Conforms* in the slogan also reflected a growing belief among American policy makers that widespread consumption of mass-produced goods was not only a democratic right but also an effective way to blur the lines

FIG. 1.3 *(facing).* April 1932 cover of *Popular Mechanics.* The personification of progress leads onward men representing industry, science, and government. FIG. 1.4 *(above).* A demonstration of the production of McCormick-Deering binder twine in the International Harvester Company exhibit. Postcard from collection of author.

FIG. 1.5. Sears-Roebuck Building, with streamlines across facade. Kaufmann and Fabry, photographers.

dividing various ethnic groups and separating blue- and white-collar workers. The outcome, they projected, would be a larger and more homogenized middle class and, consequently, a significant reduction in labor and class tensions.[40] Fair organizers believed that promoting a modern scientific ethos would increase the general population's interest in the technology behind the growing number of modern, factory-made items available for purchase, thus amplifying the demand for those products.

The encompassing scientific theme helped set A Century of Progress apart from previous expositions. It unified many otherwise dissimilar aspects of the fair, including architecture, and became a clear marketing device that drew both exhibitors and the public to an event that was perceived as new, modern, and exciting. More important and lasting, however, was its legacy, which was to help equate the scientific with the modern in the minds of millions of American consumers.

PAST AND PRESENT TO THE FUTURE

While Hale's original idea to incorporate a dominant scientific theme into the exposition was initially limited to past and current developments, fair organizers almost immediately decided to expand this theme by highlighting the potential of future advances in the sciences.[41] The concept of evolutionary development prevalent in intellectual circles at the time permeated many facets of the exposition.

A series of scientific books, for example, published by the Williams and Wilkins Company of Baltimore in connection with A Century of Progress included a volume that explored "the past 100 years of ideas in evolution."[42] Another book in the series, by Fay-Cooper Cole, the chair of the Anthropology Department at the University of Chicago, examined the "long road from savagery to civilization."[43] Chronological exhibits that presented human development in North America beginning with cave life and ending with modern America were found throughout the fairgrounds.[44] One popular display from the 1934 fair season illustrated how archaeologists learned from human refuse. Located next to an exhibit on Chicago's past urban development, a diorama showed a cross-section of a city dump. Layers of waste from the preceding forty years provided evidence of the way America's garbage mirrored influential scientific and cultural advances since the time of the World's Columbian Exposition.[45] In the oldest stratum, a crumpled gramophone horn, parts of an antique carpet sweeper, and a typewriter could be found. A newer layer labeled 1923 contained a Hupmobile radiator, signifying the rise of the automobile, while the great increase in the number of glass bottles in the most recent layer divulged the recent repeal of Prohibition.[46]

The educational exhibits commonly presented progress in a chronological framework through which current and future advances could be measured; the fair organizers also encouraged illustrations of evolutionary developments on many less obvious levels. The concept was expressed architecturally, not only through re-creations at the exposition of significant historical buildings, such as Abraham Lincoln's log cabin and a series of

FIG. 1.6. Diorama of a city dump with stratum dates identified by the appearance of items that reflect scientific and cultural advances in the decades since the 1893 World's Columbian Exposition. From *Official Guide Book of the World's Fair of 1934* (Chicago: Cuneo Press, 1934), 92.

FIG. 1.7. Reproduction of Abraham Lincoln's birthplace, one of the many historical buildings at A Century of Progress. Kaufmann and Fabry, photographers.

traditional ethnic villages, but also by the contrast between the modern pavilions and the surrounding neoclassical civic buildings.[47]

As the country slipped further into the Depression, public interest in the future grew. Many Americans, trying to escape the hardships and uncertainties of the current devastating economic situation, fantasized about the potential technological marvels of the future—a practice that continued throughout the 1930s with the rise of motion pictures, radio shows, and comic strips about such heroes as Flash Gordon and Buck Rogers. The fair offered not only a brief respite from the troubles of daily life but also a sense of hope fostered by images of a better tomorrow.

The official guidebook encouraged visitors to examine the recent scientific developments on exhibit while imagining future advances. The guide paradoxically looked to the past by using the first Chicago fair to illustrate the way progress would continue into the future. It quoted one observer at the time of the 1893 fair as saying that the World's Columbian Exposition had "everything . . . that was undreamed of 25 years ago." He went on prophetically to exclaim:

You have here [at the World's Columbian Exposition] the culmination of invention and science. . . . if we should have another exhibit twenty-five years from now, the probability is that not one of the things which seem so wonderful, will then be valued. They will have been superseded by inventions so much more useful, that it is barely within the compass of any man's mind to conceive of what the future has in store for us.[48]

The discoveries of X-rays, electrons, and the radioactivity of uranium all within three years of the close of the Columbian Exposition supported his point.

Domestic life provided one of the easiest ways for fairgoers to relate to the potential future effects of scientific developments. Eleven full-scale model residences in the Home and Industrial Arts Exhibit illustrated the possibilities of newly introduced scientific technology.[49] These houses were constructed with the latest in interior fashion and technological devices; some features, such as television, were yet to be fully developed.[50] The forward-looking dwellings, such as the House of Tomorrow and the Masonite House, came to be among the most popular features of the exposition.[51] The numerous published articles discussing the model residential display, with titles such as "Tomorrow's Housing," "Chicago and Tomorrow's House?" and "Beautiful Houses of Today and Tomorrow," reflected a growing interest among the American public in the possibilities of future modern living.[52]

Prefair publicity about the futuristic model residences and other exposition pavilions attracted over a million people to the fairgrounds in the months prior to opening day.[53] Drawn by a desire to obtain a glimpse of the upcoming exposition, visitors became fascinated by the construction of

FIG. 1.8. The Masonite House. Built to highlight the many uses of Masonite products to fair visitors, it was one of a series of model modern homes on exhibit at the fair. From Dorothy Raley, *A Century of Progress Homes and Furnishings* (Chicago: M. A. Ring, 1934), 90.

the unusual buildings. Mesmerized, they witnessed workers assembling prefabricated components made of modern building materials in an efficient, factory-like
manner. Capitalizing on people's innate interest in viewing processes, fair organizers highlighted the concept of production in a wide range of exhibition displays at
A Century of Progress.

MOVEMENT: PROCESS OVER PRODUCT

With the rise of motion pictures and radio in the 1920s, the general public was becoming increasingly sophisticated in their preferences in cultural entertainment.
Movies and the introduction of more rapid forms of transportation led Americans
to desire a faster pace of life. The official logo of the fair, with its energetic lines
representing the path of light from Arcturus rapidly traveling through the present and on toward the future, reflected this growing
craving for speed. No longer were rows of idle machines, cases of dead specimens, or static displays of
manufactured goods, the sights that had dominated
previous exhibitions, adequate to attract and retain
the modern fairgoer's attention.[54] More dramatic displays and more spectacular forms of transportation
were needed.

FIG. 1.9. Logo for A Century of Progress,
representing the light from Arcturus speeding
through space. From *Color Beauties of A
Century of Progress, Chicago, 1933* (Chicago:
Exposition Publications and Novelties, 1933).

During their visits to European expositions, the
Chicago fair planners realized that still exhibits were
dead exhibits. At the Exposition Internationale de la
Grande Industrie, Sciences, et Applications, Art Wallon Ancien held in Liège in 1930, they noted that an
expensive relief map showing the locations of Belgium's sugar works received little attention, whereas
an old-fashioned caramel-wrapping machine drew
continuous crowds of fascinated onlookers. An exhibit that illustrated soap making from raw materials
to commercially packaged goods was one of the most
popular displays.[55] It became clear to the fair organizers that incorporating motion into exhibits would be
the key to attracting and maintaining the interest of
fairgoers in Chicago. "People like to see wheels go
'round," according to the fair's general manager Lenox
Lohr at the opening of the exposition. "There is motion or the suggestion of movement—progress—in all
exhibits."[56]

Educating the public to the benefits of the growing commercial nature of American culture was a major underlying goal of many of the corporate exhibits. While the products of industry were well known to consumers, the processes of their creation typically remained mysterious. The fair planners believed that Americans, like their European counterparts, would find great interest in displays illustrating the development of modern manufactured goods.[57] Wherever possible, exhibits would show the evolution or production of a product by incorporating motion to catch and retain the viewers' attention. Using action-filled exhibits illustrating production processes was not new at the 1933 fair, but Chicago's organizers were the first to make the concept of production the main focus of as many exhibits as possible. This included the creation of assembly-line displays that highlighted the influence of scientific progress on modern life, even on such mundane consumer products as the tin can.

Over 5 million people visited the American Can Company exhibit in 1934 to view a display that fairgoers voted the most popular demonstration at the fair that year.[58] The captivating exhibit helped eliminate old misconceptions about packaged foods and made the can a symbol of the impact scientific progress could have on the welfare of millions of people of all classes throughout the civilized world. Unlike most of the exhibits that told the chronological story of the creation of a commodity, the American Can display worked backward, from the consumer to the product, in its attempt to illustrate the benefits of tin cans.[59]

The highlight of the exhibit was the canning machine. Mesmerized visitors watched intently as the elaborate machine with its numerous moving parts churned out little tin-can banks decorated with printed images of the exposition buildings. Well over a million fairgoers waited in long lines to push a button to start the machine that then produced their own colorful, commemorative tin can.[60] For some fairgoers, carrying out this simple act was emotionally overwhelming. According to a contemporary article, one in forty visitors to the exhibit "completely lost courage at the critical moment and had to have the machine operated for them."[61] Walter Benjamin argued in his treatise "The Work of Art in the Age of Mechanical Reproduction" (1936) that the authenticity or aura of an artistic object is destroyed through its mechanical reproduction, but these mass-produced items maintained their authentic meaning by serving as individual reminders of the exposition experience, particularly for those who had participated in the actual ceremony creating their own souvenirs (Plate 3).[62]

Elaborate industrial exhibits that demonstrated the creation of modern products on assembly lines could be found throughout the fairgrounds. After the repeal of Prohibition, for example, those interested could watch a production line of young women in starched uniforms bottling spirits in the streamlined Hiram Walker and Sons' Canadian Club Café.[63] General Motors drew huge crowds to their pavilion to witness the complete manufacturing process of Chevrolets. From a second-story balcony a fifth of a mile long, up to 1,000 visitors at once could observe the 200 workmen below complete each step of the assembly process over and over again as they produced a steady stream of automobiles that upon completion were driven away under their own power.[64] Not to be outdone, Firestone installed a fully equipped modern tire factory in their pavilion to demonstrate how bales of rubber from the company's plantations in Liberia were transformed into vulcanized tires packaged and ready for final inspection.[65]

Other transportation exhibits also incorporated elements of motion beyond assembly lines. One of the most popular attractions at the fair was the stage show *Wings of a Century*. Using Lake Michigan as a backdrop and with an animated soundtrack and a cast of 150 actors, the elaborate production took an evolutionary approach to highlight developments in transportation. Familiar stories in American history, such as that of the golden-spike transcontinental railroad ceremony at Promontory Point, Utah, were presented chronologically. The start of the show, which presented Native Americans on horseback and in canoes, was relatively slow-paced, but excitement grew as each faster and more powerful form of transportation was introduced. The grand finale displayed a dazzling tableau of modern vehicles, featuring the latest models of automobiles, streamlined locomotives, and airplanes.[66]

FIG. 1.10. Assembly line of young women bottling spirits in the Hiram Walker and Sons building. Postcard from collection of author.

Special events reinforced the drama of the final scene of the *Wings of a Century* by offering even more spectacular illustrations of speed and modern technology. One of the most exciting was the arrival of the *Burlington Zephyr* (later known as the *Pioneer Zephyr*), which reached the fairgrounds to great fanfare on opening day 1934. The train had just com-

BOTTLING LINE AT THE HIRAM WALKER EXHIBIT, 16TH ST. BRIDGE IN NORTH LAGOON—CENTURY OF PROGRESS—1934

BOTTLING "CANADIAN CLUB" AND LONDON DRY GIN

pleted its first major excursion, a record-setting nonstop run from Denver to Chicago. Heavily advertised, the event generated extensive publicity for the locomotive, as well as for A Century of Progress, as huge crowds lined the tracks along the 1,000-mile journey to witness the sleek, streamlined, stainless-steel train zip by.[67] An even more dazzling event was the arrival of Italo Balbo, the renowned Italian aviator, and his armada of seaplanes on 15 July 1933 after a nonstop trans-Atlantic crossing, a highlight of the exposition and a significant feat of fascist propaganda.[68]

More thrilling for many fairgoers was the chance to experience novel forms of modern transportation firsthand. One of the most dramatic ways of doing this was to ride the mammoth Skyride. The attraction consisted of the world's second largest suspension bridge, with a span of 1,850 feet.[69] Visitors could travel either to the top of one of the two 620-foot-tall towers or between them in double-decker, streamlined rocket cars that offered ever-changing airplanelike views of the magnificent architectural precinct below (Plate 4).

Planners had initially wanted to provide moving sidewalks and escalators to facilitate pedestrian travel between pavilions, but these devices were eliminated as budgets tightened with the faltering economy. Instead, fairgoers walked or hired old-fashioned jinrikishas or roller chairs, or they rode in one of the modern open-sided Greyhound "Intra-Fair Auto-Liners." Although the buses looked sleek and fast, they moved through the fairgrounds at a leisurely pace.

Children were just as enamored with motion as were their parents. Young

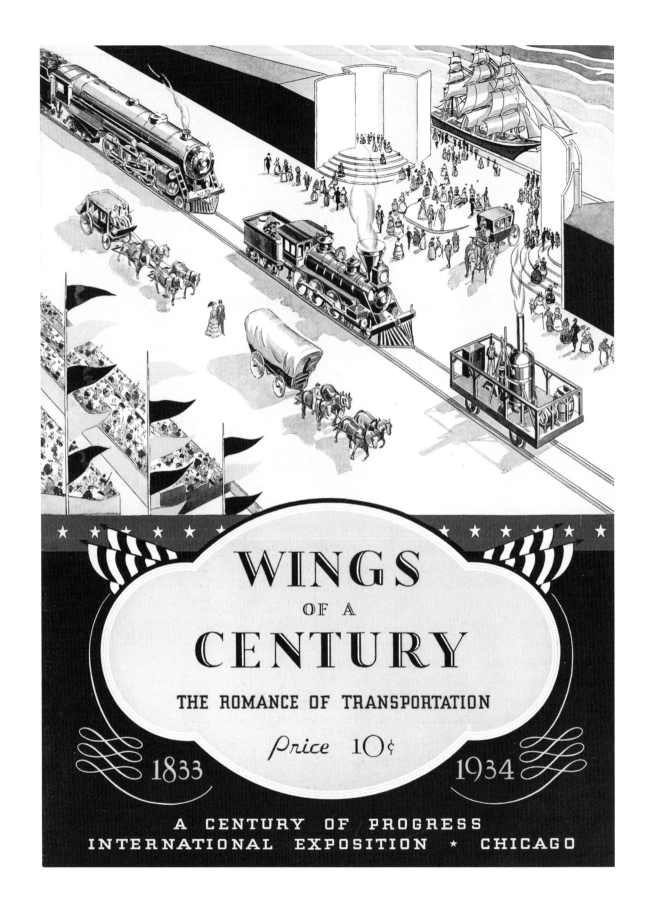

WINGS
OF A
CENTURY

THE ROMANCE OF TRANSPORTATION

Price 10¢

1833   1934

A CENTURY OF PROGRESS
INTERNATIONAL EXPOSITION ★ CHICAGO

visitors could experience the excitement of speed at Enchanted Island, a special amusement area geared specifically for the more than 2 million children expected to attend the exposition during the first season. For a small fee, young fairgoers could be left for the day at this real-life fairyland, which featured massive storybook figures (including characters from the *Wizard of Oz*), a house constructed of over 5 million marbles, and the Magic Mountain Slide, which was topped by a romantic castle. For those daring enough, there were miniature automobiles and a railway train to ride. The more adventurous could fly through the air while seated at the controls of one of the rocket ships that orbited around a central pole. The modern fascination with speed was even reflected in the design of Tony, the forty-five-foot-high boy that topped the coaster wagon–shaped Radio Flyer Pavilion, dramatically leaning forward as if he were racing down a hill (Plate 5).

FIG. 1.12 *(facing)*. Program cover for the elaborate *Wings of a Century* transportation stage show. From *Wings of a Century: The Romance of Transportation,* brochure produced by A Century of Progress, Inc., 1933, from collection of author.

FIG. 1.13 *(above)*. Streamlined Greyhound Intra-Fair Auto-Liners in front of the General Motors Building in 1934. Kaufmann and Fabry, photographers.

PARTICIPATION OF INDUSTRY

To enable visitors to develop a broader understanding of recent advances in transportation and other areas of technology, organizers grouped exhibits by industry or field of science around a central thematic display. Organizing individual displays thematically was not new. At the 1867 Exposition Universelle in Paris, the main exhibition hall, the large oval Galerie des Machines constructed on the Champ de Mars, was laid out in seven concentric galleries. Each ring featured a specific type of product ranging from machinery to the fine arts. Individual nations were assigned slices of the building, with each country's location dictated by its physical placement on earth. This allowed fairgoers to view all the exhibits from a specific field or country with relative ease.[70]

Designers working in the Chicago exposition's Applied Science and Industry Division strove to develop a more flexible, yet still cohesive, thematic organizational system to help increase fairgoers' comprehension. They arranged displays pertaining to a specific area around a general focal exhibit. As at the 1867 exposition, this created a logical, albeit less obvious, structure.[71] Each branch of science or industry was presented as a unified assembly, and not, as had been the case at previous expositions, as groups of competing individual businesses.[72] In fact, fair organizers specifically rejected the previous practice of placing exhibitors in direct competition with each other for major awards. Instead, they persuasively encouraged cooperative, industry-wide displays and awarded certificates of participation to all exhibitors.

While the fair organization financed some of the general displays, the exhibits department of the Chicago fair asked major trade and industry associations, as well as professional scientific societies and leading corporations, to sponsor collective exhibits that presented the "problems, services, and needs" of a specific thematic area.[73] Some trade organizations became enthusiastic participants in the central displays, but others, because of sharp competition among members of individual industries or poor financial conditions, were unwilling or unable to present a united front.[74] Realizing the tremendous potential gains from promoting their industry as a whole, many large corporations readily accepted the invitation to sponsor a general exhibit. Corporations gained the opportunity to present a gesture of goodwill to the public, as well as to receive prominent publicity. In an attempt to create a feeling of unity among all participants of an individual field and to provide greater support for the industry-wide exhibits, fair organizers attempted to discourage displays that featured specific finished products.[75] Instead, they preferred that exhibitors demonstrate the production of items or the presentation of ideas that related to the field in general. While many of the thematic exhibits were located in the Hall of Science and the General Exhibits Building, the fair continued a long-standing practice of constructing individual pavilions to house exhibits pertaining to specific fields and industries, including electricity, dairy production, and home design. In the case of the transportation industries, the central focus was the massive Travel and Transport Building. The equally substantial corporate pavilions for the major automobile manufacturers, including General Motors, the Chrysler Cor-

poration, and, in 1934, the Ford Motor Company, surrounded this pavil-ion.[76] The spectacular pageant *Wings of a Century* served as the dramatic centerpiece of the area devoted to the transportation industries, drawing huge numbers of visitors to the far south end of the fairgrounds.

FIG. 1.14. The Chrysler Building, one of many large corporate pavilions at the fair. From *Architectural Forum* 59 (July 1933): 43.

MEDICAL SECTION

The medical section in the Hall of Science offers a more representative example of the fair's displays. The Chicago exposition was promoted as the first interna-tional fair to include a major section devoted specifically to medicine.[77] William Allen Pusey, a trustee of the exposition and former head of the American Medical Association, and Eben J. Carey, dean of the Medical School at Marquette Univer-sity, directed the planning of the health displays.[78] They, along with a board of twenty-five advisers, sought exhibits from all over the world that would simply yet dramatically depict the tremendous strides that man had made during the past cen-tury in detecting, determining the causes of, treating, and preventing human and animal diseases.[79] The scientists grouped the exhibits into three classifications: Scientific, Industrial, and Popular, which directly corresponded to the three parts of the fair's slogan, Science Finds—Industry Applies—Man Conforms.[80] The indi-vidual displays were chosen for their ability to illustrate the basic scientific facts in medicine, their application in the practice of medicine, and the "arts and sci-ences which produce the chemicals and instruments that are used in the practice of medicine."[81] According to Pusey, these selection criteria were adhered to throughout the planning process, and as a result the medical section presented a unified front that attracted great interest among the visitors.[82]

The guidebook to the medical science exhibits laid out specific objectives in regard to choosing and developing displays that were directly applicable to the fair's other thematic areas. The planners designed exhibits to be "seen by the greatest number of persons in the shortest amount of time and with the least amount of effort" by incorporating an efficient layout that integrated the individual parts of the exhibit into the larger whole.[83] In addition to avoiding long, technical words and using various approaches to arouse public curiosity, they encouraged retention of information through association and the repetition of details.

Instead of static displays of the latest medical gadgets, the major exhibits presented action scenes. In many of the displays, including models on loan from the German Hygiene Museum in Dresden, fairgoers could pull levers or push buttons to activate explanatory demonstrations.[84] Other exhibits incorporated moving pictures, including one that illustrated the first operation in which ether was used as an anesthetic. Sound, meanwhile, provided additional interest in a dental exhibit titled *The Talking Tooth*.[85] A series of real human embryos, illustrating the week-by-week development of fetuses, integrated elements of time and evolution without actually using motion.

Central to the medical exhibits was the Transparent Man, a life-size model of the human body with a clear acetate skin. Taking advantage of the recent excitement over the marvels of X-rays, the exhibit demonstrated the ability to see inside solid forms.[86] All organs could be viewed and il-

FIG. 1.15. Crowd of fairgoers viewing a series of real human fetuses in the Medical Exhibits area of the Hall of Science. The exhibit illustrated the progress of early human development. From Eben J. Carey, *Medical Science Exhibits: A Century of Progress* (Chicago: A Century of Progress, 1936), 116.

luminated in turn, providing a feeling of action to the stationary figure. Young men assigned to the area as guides used the Transparent Man to give demonstrations of anatomy and physiology. Nearby, cross sections from two preserved human bodies, one sliced vertically and the other horizontally, helped illustrate how internal organs fit together.[87] These widely publicized sensational exhibits attracted thousands of fairgoers of all ages and backgrounds to the medical section every day. Not surprisingly, many children found the scientific exhibits in the Hall of Science more interesting than even the dramatic Skyride or the wondrous pint-size amusements at Enchanted Island.[88]

FIG. 1.16. Young fair guide in uniform presenting a demonstration of the Transparent Man to a group of fascinated schoolchildren. From Eben J. Carey, *Medical Science Exhibits: A Century of Progress* (Chicago: A Century of Progress, 1936), xxii.

In the exhibits and displays of the Medical Section, past developments formed a backdrop on which to project recent and future advances. The American Medical Association sponsored a presentation on the history of medical progress over the preceding 100 years that set the stage for envisioning future advances in medicine. In this display, the procedures of the saddleback doctor of the nineteenth century formed a backdrop against which current technical equipment and methods were highlighted.[89] A vivid display of Native American medicines, amulets, and charms suggested that modern medicine was superior to that of the past because the procedures and medications were based on science.[90] To make the exhibit understandable to the largest number of people, written descriptions were avoided wherever possible. Instead, information was disseminated primarily by dioramas, transparencies, mechanical devices, and sound apparatuses.[91]

The designers produced the medical section to be educational for both scholars and a general audience.[92] Demonstrations and displays were aimed at young adults in the hope that most of the viewers could grasp a basic understanding of the illustrated principles. Popular lectures given during the fair also helped make recent medical advances understandable to lay visitors.[93]

These new concepts of display and of methods for transmitting information, which were repeated in other areas throughout the fairgrounds, contributed to A Century of Progress's triumph as a successful modern exposition. The event would never have been realized, however, had it not been for one other significant aspect, revolutionary in the operation of American world's fairs—the avoidance of direct government funding. The fair's organizers accomplished this by using creative financing to raise revenue and by attracting free publicity.

FINANCING THE EXPOSITION

The underwriting of international expositions by local and national governments, both in the United States and abroad, was a widespread practice.[94] In America, the World's Columbian Exposition, the Louisiana Purchase Exposition, and the Panama-Pacific International Exposition each received between 4 million and 6 million dollars in support from local, state, and national governments.[95] In contrast, the Century of Progress International Exposition sought no direct government funding. Instead, it sold gold notes (official IOUs, backed by gold) and various forms of memberships in the exposition. Charging exhibitor and concessionaire booth fees, a practice used at trade expositions but not common to previous world's fairs, raised additional revenue.[96] The avoidance of government support became crucial to the financial success of the exposition especially after the stock market crash in 1929, when public funds would have surely evaporated.

Before the president of the United States could officially invite other countries of the world to the Chicago exposition, the fair corporation was required to raise 5 million dollars.[97] Former vice president Charles G. Dawes headed the campaign to acquire needed funds.[98] He issued 10 million dollars in gold notes of A Century of Progress that were secured by 40 percent of the income from gate receipts and guaranteed by wealthy citizens of Chicago, including Julius Rosenwald of Sears, Roebuck and Company, Robert McCormick of the *Chicago Tribune*, Philip K. Wrigley of chewing-gum fame, and Dawes himself.[99] Issued on 28 October 1929 (one day prior to Black Tuesday of the stock market crash), $12,176,000 in guarantees was secured by the middle of November.[100] More than 50 percent of the notes were committed to the guarantors themselves by the summer of 1929.[101] These funds financed the early operations of the exposition and the construction of the first major exhibition pavilions, including the Hall of Science, the Travel and Transport Building, and the Electrical Building.[102] The use of notes helped boost financial support within the fair organization. Contractors accepted over 2.5 million dollars in gold notes in lieu of cash, and all employees of the exposition received part of their salary in notes.[103] This provided the incentive for a great number of people to make sure the exposition was a financial success.

Selling memberships in the exposition raised additional early funds. Founding memberships that cost $1,000 each and sustaining memberships that cost $50 apiece allowed many Chicago citizens to become investors in the exposition.[104] Fifty-six sustaining memberships and 286 founding memberships raised approximately $272,000 by the opening of the fair. In return for the membership, Chicagoans received both the feeling that they were loyally supporting their city and the authority to deduct the amount of the membership from their taxable income.[105]

In February 1928, the financiers of the exposition introduced an even more accessible investment opportunity. To raise general awareness of the event and increase available funds, the fair corporation sold World's Fair Legion certificates to the general public. Costing five dollars apiece, they could be exchanged at the start of the exposition for ten admission tickets. The fair corporation sold over 118,000 of these memberships, raising well over a half a million dollars in additional revenue.[106]

Advance tickets and season passes were also made available. By the start of the exposition the fair corporation had sold approximately 3.4 million admission tickets.[107] In addition to producing necessary funds, the advance sales raised confidence that in spite of the Great Depression, the fair would go on.

After the installation of a fence around the site in June 1932, fair organizers began charging people ten cents to enter the grounds. Income raised from the public's desire to preview the fair site and the construction of the pavilions supplied needed revenue for financing the early policing and maintenance of the buildings and grounds. Some of the amusements completed early were also opened to the public. The full-scale reproduction of Fort Dearborn, for example, opened its doors on 16 May 1931, two years before the official start of the fair. So many people paid the twenty-five-cent entry fee to visit the fort that the attraction had paid for itself by the time the exposition officially opened.[108]

Fees charged exhibitors and concessionaires at the exposition contributed greatly toward making the event a reality despite the devastating financial blow of the stock market crash. By opening day, the fair had received about 3 million dollars from the sale of space to exhibitors.[109] Buildings erected by the U.S. government and such private companies as General Motors, Firestone, and Time–Fortune

FIG. 1.17 *(above)*.
Reenactment with troops
in the full-scale model of
Chicago's Fort Dearborn.
From Acme Photo.
FIG. 1.18 *(facing)*. Poster
advertising the Canadian
Pacific Railway's special
fares to A Century of
Progress. Courtesy of
Poster Plus, Chicago,
www.posterplus.com.

generated an additional 3 million dollars. Because most commitments by exhibitors were made prior to the final design of the buildings, planners could scale specific exhibit areas for the exact needs of each industry or corporation, thereby avoiding the expense of constructing unsalable space. When the books finally closed on the exposition after the completion of demolition work in 1936, a profit of $160,000 remained. This placed the Century of Progress International Exposition in the unique position of being the first major exposition to turn a profit.[110]

PROMOTING THE EXPOSITION

Another change from most previous expositions that helped keep the event financially sound was the elimination of funds for advertising.[111] The Century of Progress's Committee on Public Information, and later its Department of Promotion, became adept at obtaining free publicity.[112] Initially, the Department of Promotion had to overcome the belief among many potential supporters that world expositions were passé. The organizers of the exposition used the offer of five-dollar fair memberships not only to raise funds but also to generate excitement. By spending only a few dollars, anyone could become part owner of the exposition. The tremendous success in selling these memberships to the citizens of Chicago helped squelch much of the initial opposition to the event.[113]

The Department of Promotion realized early on that if it could not attract

significant public attention through press releases highlighting the exciting plans and enticing stories of the exposition, then it would be hopeless to try to capture the public's interest through paid advertising. To disseminate information on the fair's activities, they used a wide range of modern methods.[114] In addition to promoting the event in newsreels, broadcasters transmitted radio announcements from a studio in the fair's Administration Building. A speakers' bureau showed colorized slides of the exposition pavilions during lectures to various community groups. Railroads and steamship lines mailed over 1 million brochures that contained illustrations and facts about the exposition to potential fairgoers encouraging them to travel to the event by public forms of transportation.[115] According to *Time* magazine, thousands of people from the East and West coasts traveled by rail to the fair each week.[116] Air traffic records were shattered during the first week of the exposition. Even with extra planes pressed into service, airlines reported long waiting lists on their Chicago routes during the two fair seasons.[117]

Stories about A Century of Progress were published in newspapers throughout the world and in a wide assortment of scholarly journals, trade publications, and monthly magazines. These periodicals ranged from *Painters Magazine and Paint and Wall Paper Dealer* to *Colliers*, from *Constructor* to *Redbook*, and from *Farmers' Elevator Guide* to *Sibley Journal of Engineering*. Advertisements that included images from the exposition provided additional publicity in newspapers and magazines. The July 1933 issue of *Architectural Forum*, for example, contained "A Special Advertising Section for A Century of Progress," displaying advertisements placed by companies with products used in the construction of the fair buildings.

Despite the availability of various modern forms of promotion, word of mouth was the most powerful advertising method for A Century of Progress. Postcards, letters, and other kinds of reminiscences indicate that after people returned home they shared with family and friends their experiences at the colorful, futuristic fair. Souvenirs from the event, most decorated with images of the pavilions, including ashtrays, bracelets, pennants, and booklets, also illustrated to the uninitiated that the second Chicago World's Fair was an event not to be missed.

The exposition organizers oversaw a fair that was successful not only in turning a profit, while being both educational and entertaining for its audience, but also in fulfilling a belief, which continues in part even to this day among many Americans, that any question raised can eventually be answered through scientific study. The general underlying concepts introduced by the fair trustees in their attempt to produce a successful modern exposition also came to be incorporated into the design and construction process of the architecture for the event. As with the general organizers, the designers on the fair's official architectural commission struggled with their role in creating the first specifically modern American international exposition.

TWO

DESIGNING THE CITY
OF COLOR AND DELIGHT

*The architecture of the world is undergoing
a great change. It has shown those signs that
indicate the birth of a great fresh impulse. The
architects of the Chicago World's Fair Centennial
Celebration of 1933 intend that the buildings
of the Fair shall express the beauty of form and
detail of both national and the international
aspects of this new creative movement.*

JOHN HOLABIRD

The need to present a distinctly modern exposition not only influenced the character of the exhibits on display but also strongly affected the architectural designs for A Century of Progress. The failure of the recent Sesquicentennial International Exposition warned of what not to attempt stylistically in Chicago. Neoclassical pavilions like those of the first Chicago exposition's "White City" would be neither viewed as appropriate nor received favorably by the exposition organizers and contemporary architectural critics.[1] They required an even more spectacular event that would dramatically express in its physical form the current progressive trends in architecture.

The difficulty the designers faced in attempting to produce an appropriate setting for a modern fair stemmed largely from the ambiguous state of progressive architecture in the United States. The issues regarding modern building design raised by the architectural commissioners during the planning phase closely echoed those discussed by their colleagues in contemporary trade publications. Most prominent were the potential impacts of a wide variety of new building products and construction techniques, and the emerging debates over the definition of modern architecture.

THE DEBATES OVER MODERN ARCHITECTURE

By the mid-1920s European designers were using the term *modern architecture* to define a form of functional building that incorporated new technology in an

attempt to meet social, economical, and political needs. American architects, meanwhile, typically continued to use the phrase more traditionally, as a reference to all forms of contemporary building design, including those that exhibited historical characteristics.[2] The words *modernistic* and *moderne* began to be used on both sides of the Atlantic to describe recently introduced, nonhistorical architecture, in particular those buildings with forms similar to designs exhibited in Paris at the Exposition Internationale des Arts Décoratifs et Industriels Modernes in 1925.[3] Only near the end of the decade, with the increased coverage of innovative European designs in American architectural periodicals, did *modern architecture* become a catchphrase for recent designs that were not considered historical or traditional in the United States. This reflected a growing division between the (usually older) designers who relied on traditional design vocabularies and principles to guide their work and those who shunned historical plans and details in favor of developing new forms. George Edgell, dean of the School of Architecture at Harvard University, described this battle in his book *The American Architecture of To-Day*, published in 1928, when he wrote:

> The whole question of modernism in American architecture is under dispute. . . . To the modernist the conservative is an unimaginative beast in

a treadmill, monotonously turning over lifeless repetitions of the master-pieces of the past. To the classicist, the designer in a modernistic man-ner is but a charlatan bent upon being new for the advertising that new-ness brings and ruining architecture by his obliviousness to all the lessons which the past can teach.[4]

Architectural critic Lewis Mumford first alluded to this ideological division in 1924 in his book *Sticks and Stones*, in which he ridiculed traditionalists for pro-ducing insincere and imitative designs, such as the neoclassical pavilions created for the 1893 World's Columbian Exposition.[5] In contrast, he saw modern architec-ture as "an establishment [of technical developments] devoted to the manufactur-ing of light, the circulation of air, the maintenance of a uniform temperature, and the vertical transportation of its occupants," a concept he continued to favor in fol-lowing years.[6] By divorcing what distinguished a building as modern from stylistic characteristics, Mumford encouraged readers to accept a variety of different formal solutions as modern architecture.

Not all architects, however, agreed with Mumford's concept of modern archi-tecture. The strong tradition of styles in the United States led some designers, like many of the architects who were producing art deco designs, to search for a contemporary style based on decorative characteristics. They typically viewed modern architecture as the next step in the continual evolution of building design. Like previous architectural styles—such as the Italianate, the Second Empire, the Eastlake—the modern style would serve, perhaps

FIG. 2.2. Gate of Honor at the 1925 Exposition Internationale des Arts Décoratifs in Paris. Postcard from collection of author.

I.— EXPOSITION INTERNATIONALE DES ARTS DÉCORATIFS — PARIS - 1925
PORTE d'HONNEUR (par Henry Favier et André Ventre, Architectes, réalisée par Edgard Brandt, maître ferronnier)

only briefly, as the favorite architectural form until another new style, fitting the next phase of society's development, took its place.

The battle between traditionalists and modernists culminated with a debate at the Sixty-third Convention of the American Institute of Architects (AIA) in 1930. George Howe took the side of the modernists, C. Howard Walker represented the traditionalists, Earl H. Reed Jr. provided a voice for the "Wrightians," and Ralph Walker spoke for the "neo-traditional-modernists." During the debate, Howe, a Philadelphian, attacked the "grab-bag" styles of the traditionalists. C. Howard Walker, a Bostonian who taught architectural history, likened modern architecture to Pandora's box and warned that "a cult of elimination of everything that is not strictly utilitarian is a callow conception." Reed, from Chicago, echoed a stern warning by Louis Sullivan against Beaux-Arts classicism and pleaded for the continuation of the progressive midwestern tradition of Sullivan and Frank Lloyd Wright. And Ralph Walker, a leading proponent of art deco skyscraper designs, rejected the belief that American architects should look toward the work of engineers and Europeans for guidance. He denounced the perceived need for a formula for modern architecture and instead called for greater individualism.[7]

The lack of consensus over the definition of modern architecture created great confusion for both architects and the public. As Raymond Hood pointed out in a 1929 *Architectural Forum* article, while many people understood that art had "gone modern," few people knew what "going modern" really meant.[8] Continuing shifts in the debates over the definition only added to the confusion. By late 1930, the disputes regarding modern architecture no longer pitted traditionalists against modernists (the traditionalists had all but lost). Debates instead raged between those who considered modern architecture a style that incorporated a defined design vocabulary and those who, like Mumford, saw it as a set of principles set apart from a specific formal style. While Hood felt that most people favored the stylistic definition, he believed that modern design must result from honest attempts by architects to meet functional needs irrespective of visual forms.[9]

Other progressive designers and critics shared Hood's view, but they also stressed the use of building materials and processes. Louis Leonard, a graduate of the École des Beaux-Arts and an architect in the office of Walker and Weeks in Cleveland, considered the use of new materials to be the quintessence of modern design. In an *American Architect* article titled "What Is Modernism?" he traced his belief back to the nineteenth-century French theorist Eugène Emmanuel Viollet-le-Duc, who had stated that architecture must be truthful in its programmatic requirements, as well as in its expression of materials and methods of construction. The creation of an appropriate style, according to Leonard, would then follow automatically.[10]

With the growing awareness of the devastating effects of the stock market crash and with the continuing influence of ideas from Europe, many American architects soon began viewing modern architecture as building designs that met current social needs through the use of new materials and processes. Beaux-Arts-trained architect John F. Harbeson of Philadelphia wrote a series of articles published in *Pencil Points* beginning in 1930 titled "Design in Modern Architecture." The first article in the series, "What Is Modern?" interpreted modern architecture as "architecture which attempts to solve the problems resulting from modern social conditions, by modern methods of construction, and using the materials and resources we can now command."[11] With the arrival of the Great Depression, conscious concern for social issues grew among architects in the United States. Leopold Arnaud, future dean of the School of Architecture at Columbia University, described the inherent role of these issues in modern architecture in his 1932 *American Architect* article "The Evolution of a New Architecture" when he wrote, "Good architecture is today what it has always been: current social requirements truthfully expressed in current building materials and methods. . . . It is the marriage of the traditional with the experimental, which produces the healthy child, modernism."[12]

Arnaud denounced Hitchcock and Johnson's MoMA exhibition for avoiding these larger issues in their formal definition of modern architecture. He stressed how mistaken the curators were in their assumption that one single style, however flexible, could fulfill building needs throughout the world. The promotion of uniformity in modern building design without taking into consideration the nationality, topography, or climate of a given place, Arnaud concluded, should not and could not be allowed.[13]

Spurred on by the necessity to house a modern world's fair on a limited budget, fair organizers knew that creating an appropriate environment for the event would be a difficult challenge. The development of the overall design scheme, which eventually reflected a definition of modern architecture similar to Arnaud's, was a slow evolutionary process that took place over the course of several years. The first step in that process was to select a group of prominent and competent designers to serve on the exposition's architectural commission.

THE SELECTION PROCESS FOR THE ARCHITECTURAL COMMISSION

The exposition officers for A Century of Progress relegated decisions regarding the design of the site plan and major buildings to an official architectural commission that was established on 21 February 1928.[14] The process of selecting architects for the committee spawned a great controversy among many local professionals, similar to the one that had developed during the first Chicago World's Fair. In early 1890 a strong feeling spread among local progressive designers that Daniel Burnham Sr., head of the architectural commission for the World's Columbian Exposition, had sold out to prominent, neoclassical, East Coast architects, such as McKim, Mead, and White, by giving them a majority of the important building commissions for the 1893 fair. This view continued to grow in the years after the event as designers and critics began to fully comprehend the role of the White City designs in creating the immense popularity of neoclassical buildings in the United States over the next four decades. Most affected were the progressive Midwest architects, including Louis Sullivan and his followers, who found their aesthetic ideologies all but ignored. These designers, attempting to express the democratic ideas on which the United States was founded, had specifically avoided classical ornament and instead relied on a design vocabulary based on geometric and naturalistic forms. Sullivan, keenly aware of the Columbian Exposition's influence on later architecture, helped ferment a growing backlash against neoclassicism in the 1920s when in 1924 he prophesied that the Columbian Exposition would "set American architectural development back fifty years."[15]

By the mid-1920s, Chicago's architects were witnessing the realization of Sullivan's pronouncement. Underrepresented in the major architectural publications, which were primarily headquartered on the East Coast, these designers searched for other ways of promoting their innovative ideas. They understood the importance that a successful second Chicago World's Fair could have in helping the city regain its position at the center of American architectural development. The potential impact of a major exposition on the direction of architectural design had been made clear to them by the sharp rise in popularity of *moderne* forms immediately after the 1925 Exposition Internationale des Arts Décoratifs et Industriels Modernes.[16]

Many Chicago architects strongly believed that they should be given the authority to decide the design of a world's fair located in their hometown. However, the legacy of the city's frontier roots and the perception that its culture was inferior to New York's contributed to a lack of confidence in the local designers' ability, even by Chicago's own elite establishment. The board of trustees' decision to choose two prominent East Coast designers, Paul Philippe Cret and Raymond Hood, to help select members for the architectural commission clearly reflected this lack of faith.[17]

Both Cret and Hood were widely respected Beaux-Arts-trained designers. The former, a nationally recognized architect and professor at the University of Pennsylvania, designed buildings that strongly reflected the lessons of his formal schooling.[18] Cret stressed the importance of the plan in his design process and emphasized a sense of axial organization in his work. At the same time, the formal characteristics of his designs responded strongly to the functional and emotional needs of the building's users. By the time he became involved in planning the Chicago exposition, Cret's architecture had begun to reveal his desire to balance the classically derived ornament favored at the École des Beaux-Arts with the functionality of modernism. This typically resulted in the combination of an axial plan and austere classical decoration, as can be seen in his design for the Folger Shakespeare Library (1929) built in Washington, D.C.[19] While basic classical elements are still present on the facade of the library, Cret reduced them to mere shadows of the historical forms from which they were derived. Flat pilasters without capitals recall fluted columns, while a simple band suggests a cornice.

Hood, a New York architect well known for his skyscraper designs, had a significant tie to the midwestern city, having won the Chicago Tribune Tower Competition with John Mead Howells in 1922.[20] Their neo-Gothic entry, complete with flying buttresses, reflects the pervasive use of historical forms at the time. The great publicity resonating from the competition contributed to Hood's growing national reputation and led to several commissions for other skyscrapers, including the Daily News (1929) and the McGraw-Hill (1931) buildings in New York City. Both these office towers illustrate Hood's pragmatic view of modern design. He had little use for discussions regarding aesthetics in contemporary architecture, stating that he designed the Tribune Tower, as well as his American Radiator Building (1924), "in the 'vertical' style or what is called 'Gothic' simply because I happen to make them so."[21]

Like Cret, Hood felt that modern building design offered a sense of honesty and efficiency in meeting functional needs. The success of a

FIG. 2.3. Folger Shakespeare Library in Washington, D.C., designed by Paul Cret. Photograph by author.

FIG. 2.4. Chicago Tribune Tower, designed by Howells and Hood, 1922–25. Photograph by author.

building, Hood wrote, lay not in its stylistic form but in the degree of satisfaction of its occupants, its economic soundness, and its acceptability to the public—all things that were contingent on the adequacy of the building's plan.[22] Major commissions in Hood's career illustrate a development away from the classical Beaux-Arts forms of his school projects toward the clean lines of modernism as he grew to eschew stylistic restrictions.

The selection process for the exposition's architectural commission involved the creation of three separate lists, each of approximately fifty candidates. Hood and Cret produced the first list, Allen D. Albert (who was serving at the time as President Dawes's assistant) created the second, and a group of architects whose clients included members of the exposition's board of trustees generated the third. Albert recalled that his list included primarily older, well-established architects, while the other two lists, evidently almost identical in composition, contained the names of a number of younger designers.[23] Approximately thirty architects appeared on all three lists.[24]

Three specific criteria were then weighed in choosing the commission members:

1. The eminence of each architect as a designer
2. The merit of his designing as tested by buildings that had stood long enough to be deliberately judged
3. The ability of the architect to cooperate with others.[25]

Based on these factors, Arthur Brown Jr., Harvey Wiley Corbett, and Louis Ayres were chosen to join Hood and Cret on the commission.[26] This initial committee revealed a strong East Coast bias. Brown, a designer in San Francisco, constituted the lone member from outside the New York or Philadelphia areas. To help balance the committee and avoid an outcry from local designers, fair organizers asked the initial members to select three or four architects from Chicago. As a result, Edward Bennett, John Holabird, and Hubert Burnham joined the commission on 14 March 1928. All three had close professional or personal ties to members of the official building committee for the first Chicago World's Fair.[27]

Even with the careful selection of designers, great apprehension existed about the composition of the commission and the ability of eight prominent architects to work together as a team. This concern was directly expressed in the omission of America's most notorious and temperamental architect, Frank Lloyd Wright. Although widely respected for his ideas on modern architecture by those selecting the committee, Wright had been specifically excluded because of his renowned inability to work cooperatively with other architects.[28]

Without Wright, the commission lacked an important figure in the rise of modern American architecture. Other prominent designers, however, did contribute to

FIG. 2.5. Members of the Architectural Commission behind an early model of the fairgrounds showing the Tower of Water in the center of the lagoon. On the wall behind the architects are preliminary renderings of fair pavilions, including one of the Travel and Transport Building (probably rendered by Hugh Ferriss), located above Paul Cret. From left to right: Holabird, Brown, Cret, Corbett, Bennett (back), Walker (front), Burnham (back), and Hood (front). From Avery Architectural and Fine Arts Library, Columbia University.

the design process by serving as consultants to the committee. Industrial designer Norman Bel Geddes and architectural renderer Hugh Ferriss both worked briefly for the commission early in the planning process. They did not, however, participate in the final design of the exposition.[29] The committee added other consultants as needed, including theater designer Joseph Urban, who created the color scheme for the exposition, and Ferruccio Vitale, who oversaw the landscape design.[30]

While all the primary members of the architectural commission had received some form of Beaux-Arts training, they did not always hold the same views regarding recent ideological developments in their chosen field.[31] Some members of the committee saw themselves as modernists, whereas others favored more traditional design forms; thus the commissioners mirrored the current debate in American architecture over the proper direction of progressive building design in the United States.

Raymond Hood expressed his concern regarding potential conflicts between members of these two groups on the commission. In a letter to Paul Cret, he stated that the committee might find itself equally divided between "conservatives," those designers favoring the tested value of revival forms, and "modernists," those more interested in current design trends.[32] The division, he feared, might lead to long fruitless discussions. In his letter, Hood identified the conservatives as Bennett, Brown, Ayres, and Burnham and the modernists as Holabird, Corbett, Cret, and himself. As it turned out, the solution to the problem lay in the refusal by Ayres (a prominent New York architect) to join the commission. This provided Hood and Cret the opportunity to recommend Ralph T. Walker, a member of the modern camp, as a replacement.[33] Appointing other progressives, such as Geddes and Ferriss, as consultants further guaranteed a modernist leaning.

Although labeled a modernist, Walker, a participant in the AIA debate on modern architecture in 1930, strongly opposed the unadorned functional designs of prominent progressive European designers, like those highlighted by Hitchcock and Johnson in the International Style Show. He observed that "most of the so-called modern European architecture, although extremely economical, is far from pleasing in appearance."[34] Walker wrote in 1928 that "the fundamental spiritual and intellectual needs of man can never be satisfied with the thin, austere design of the engineer-architect, which, while perfectly honest, fails to take into consideration the thoughts or emotions of anyone other than a 'Robot.'"[35] Instead, he favored more creative uses of recently introduced materials, such as cast stone, as the stimulus for a new architecture consisting of an "infinite variety of complex forms and an intricate meaning."[36]

Many other progressive American architects and critics, including several other members of the architectural commission, shared Walker's opinion. Cret, for example, pointed out that, in reality, functionalism had little to do with the actual design process of many architects who considered themselves modernists. He referred to the work of progressive architects who repudiated all ornament as "nudist architecture," and he strongly believed that architecture was a "Fine Art and not just a minor branch of engineering." "Civilizations," Cret wrote, "are measured by their effort to rise above the primary stage of usefulness."[37] Corbett, agreeing with his colleagues, challenged architects to aspire to design buildings that would both "work successfully as a machine *and* at the same time be beautiful to look at" (emphasis added).[38]

For the more conservative designers on the commission, the exposition presented the necessary impetus for them to move away from the architectural ideology and vocabulary of their schooling and examine new materials, design processes, and forms. Although some critics of the fair, such as Frank Lloyd Wright, labeled the commissioners a "breed of eclectics," as a group they considered themselves to be innovative designers.[39] Corbett wrote in an article in *The Architect and Engineer* that even though he, Bennett, Brown, and Cret were older men, they still had new ideas for the design of a modern world's fair.[40]

The commissioners were in an ideal position to design an aesthetically successful modern exposition in part because they were well informed on current trends in architecture, not only in their own country but also abroad. Most had

witnessed firsthand the works of progressive architects in Europe and had attended
many of the recent European international expositions. According to Chicago architectural writer Alfred Granger, the fair architects had "come home from Paris
[after visiting the 1931 Exposition Coloniale Internationale] inspired by the effects
achieved through the use of new materials, new forms and the possibilities of electric lighting and wished the forthcoming exposition in '33 to be wholly 'modern'
in every respect."[41]

DEFINING A MODERN FAIR

With the decision made to create an exposition that would present a vision of modern architecture to the world, the commissioners knew they had to reach a clear
consensus regarding what they meant by *modern*. Lively discussions took place
at early meetings of the architectural commission over what constituted modern
architecture as each member proffered his own individual ideas on building design.
Like the American architectural community at large, the commission was divided:
Some of the commissioners, most notably John Holabird, initially felt that modern
architecture formed another step in an evolutionary development of architectural
styles. Others saw it more as a set of design principles based on issues of purpose
and function set apart from style. Cret, for example, wrote in 1931, "Modernism is
something much deeper than this or that formula or ornamentation. Ornamentation is 'fashion,' it is only surface deep."[42] He went on to state that a skyscraper was
a modern structure regardless of its composition or mode of expression or "whatever kind of old cast-offs" it was clothed in, since it was a building type introduced
in the modern era.[43]

All three of the New Yorkers on the commission—Corbett, Hood, and Walker—
agreed that the skyscraper presented a major symbol of modern architecture. This
reflected the view held by many designers and critics in the 1920s that the one
truly American contribution to modern building design was the tall office building: a form that offered a clear visual representation of the abilities of current structural technology while symbolically expressing the important role of commerce
in a twentieth-century capitalistic society. Having promoted setback skyscraper
designs, the New York commissioners shared the view that a tall vertical tower
should form the centerpiece of A Century of Progress.

Edward Bennett and Arthur Brown Jr. still embraced the neoclassicism of the
City Beautiful movement, but Raymond Hood, like Cret, placed functional needs
ahead of aesthetics. Looking at each project as an individual problem needing its
own design solution, he candidly expressed his view on modern architecture in
the foreword to R. W. Sexton's book *American Apartment Houses, Hotels, and
Apartments*:

Modern architecture consists of studying our problems from the ground up, solving each point in the most logical manner, in the light of our present day knowledge. . . . Effort need not be centered on striving to create a new style, or on trying to develop an architecture that is distinctively American. We only need to do our building in a straightforward manner, meeting squarely every condition that presents itself, and the style and decoration will come of themselves.[44]

Although the commissioners' definitions varied, a statement from the first committee meeting, held in Chicago on 23 May 1928, reveals their early commitment to create a unified philosophical vision of modern architecture:

The architecture of the buildings and of the grounds of the Exposition of 1933 will illustrate in definite form the development of the art of architecture since the great Fair of 1893, not only as in America, but in the world at large. New elements of construction, products of modern invention and science, will be factors in the architectural composition. Artificial light, the tremendous progress of which has astonished all designers in recent years, will become an inherent component of the architectural composition. The extraordinary opportunities of the site for the use of water as an intrinsic element of the composition will be developed to the maximum.[45]

Holabird's desire to incorporate specific stylistic forms in order to create a modern exposition significantly different from previous fairs eventually lost out to an approach that focused more on new needs and new products for design solutions to those needs. The consensus to base aesthetic design decisions on the characteristics of recently developed building materials and processes, an idea shared by many progressive-minded colleagues, clearly contrasted with the more formal understanding of modern architecture put forth in the International Style Show. The Chicago exposition as built, however, did present to the public a visual language of modernism predominantly free of an overt classical language.

PRELIMINARY DESIGNS

At the inaugural meeting of the architectural commission, the committee members experienced the novelty of flying over the fairgrounds in an airplane. As they viewed the emerging man-made site, they discussed several preliminary exposition designs, which Edward Bennett had been asked to create at the time he joined the commission.[46] Like the City Beautiful plans for Chicago's lakefront that he and Daniel Burnham Sr. had produced years earlier, Bennett's designs clearly indicate a reliance on basic Beaux-Arts principles.

Several well-developed schemes by Bennett, dating from May to August 1928, illustrate strictly symmetrical plans recalling the Court of Honor at the 1893 Chicago World's Fair. A wide path running from a main entrance at Twenty-third Street across a large water basin to an airport projecting into Lake Michigan formed the major east–west axis. A second walkway beginning at the same location and heading south mirrored a similar path angling toward the north that terminated at the Shedd Aquarium. One design, dated 30 August 1928, presents a tall central tower framed by a series of large forward-projecting bays located immediately beyond the lagoon on the dominant axis. To the south an informal park balanced a more rigidly arranged northern area that incorporated Soldier Field and the recently constructed neoclassical museums nearby. Several of the major elements present in these early designs, including the projecting airport, the major entrance at Twenty-third Street, and the series of water basins, reappeared as major elements in later studies produced by the other committee members.

After returning to their respective offices to study problems specific to the site and to contemplate the general character of the fair, the commissioners reconvened on 5 December 1928.[47] They planned to combine the best elements from each of their individual schemes in arriving at a final design. Although not every architect presented drawings at this meeting, each contributed suggestions and expressed concerns about the basic physical form of the exposition.

Viewing A Century of Progress as a model for an ideal city, the commissioners incorporated innovative solutions in their early preliminary designs that they felt could improve the layout of a highly congested setting, whether a world's fair or a modern city. The commissioners were particularly interested in developing ways to facilitate efficient and safe

FIG. 2.6. Preliminary study of proposed exposition grounds, Bennett, Parsons, and Frost, consulting architects, 30 August 1928. From Edward H. Bennett Collection, Ryerson and Burnham Archives, The Art Institute of Chicago. Digital file copyright The Art Institute of Chicago.

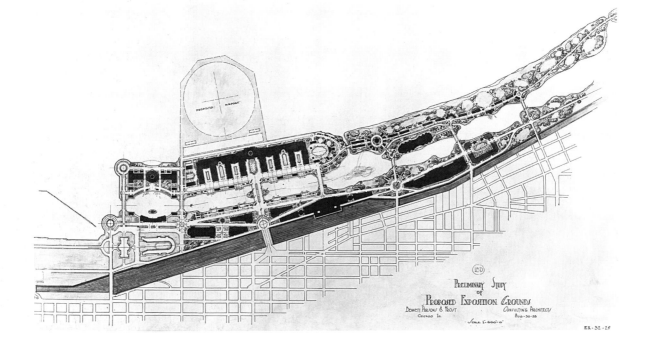

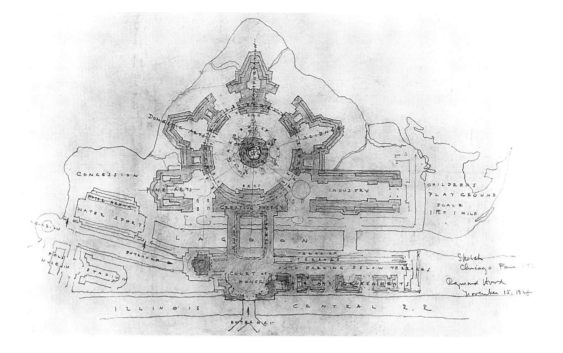

movement of large numbers of people though the fairgrounds. Several de-signs presented at this meeting included some form of mechanical trans-portation system reserved for people on foot in order to reduce perceived distances and weariness among visitors and to protect them from vehicu-lar traffic.[48] Hood's plan, typical of the commissioners' designs, included two circuits of moving sidewalks elevated above the ground. One spanned the lagoon connecting the Court of Honor near the main entrance to a central area labeled "Creative Energy." The second loop encircled a central island containing a massive electric generator identified as the "Volcano of Light" surrounded by the "Garden of Arts."[49] On a raised path, he felt, visitors could experience an exciting view of the fairgrounds while reaching their next des-tination with relative ease.

This desire to incorporate a raised walkway into the design grew out of the strong interest several committee members had in segregating different modes of transportation in order to relieve congestion in urban settings. Bennett had previ-ously incorporated multilevel roads in designs for Chicago that he presented to the Fifth National Conference on City Planning in 1913.[50] He continued to refine this idea in his later work as a consultant to the Chicago Planning Commission. Cor-bett, meanwhile, had experimented with separating pedestrians from motorized vehicles through the use of elevated walkways and multilevel roads beginning in the early 1920s while serving as a consultant to the Committee on the Regional

FIG. 2.7. Preliminary sketch of Chicago Fair, Raymond M. Hood, architect, 15 November 1928. From Edward H. Bennett Collection, Ryerson and Burnham Archives, The Art Institute of Chicago. Digital file copyright The Art Institute of Chicago.

Plan of New York and Its Environs.[51] In the late 1920s Walker, Hood, and Holabird teamed up to design an unrealized project for Terminal Park along Chicago's lakefront. The plan included segregated pathways specifically designated for rail, motor, and pedestrian traffic, as well as a marina for watercraft.[52]

Mechanical "people movers" had appeared at earlier expositions. A cart that traveled on two widely spaced elevated tracks inside the Galerie des Machines at the Paris exposition in 1889 offered fairgoers an aerial view of the exhibits inside the building. Eleven years later in the same city, a more practical application of moving sidewalks, known as the *trottoir roulant*, whisked people around the grounds of the 1900 Exposition Universelle.[53] The planners of the Columbian Exposition in 1893 had, in their design, featured movable sidewalks for transporting people between buildings, but because of complaints by pushchair concessionaires, the concept was relegated to an entertainment attraction located on a 2,500-foot pier projecting into Lake Michigan.[54] The innate public appeal of unusual transport systems is reflected in the skyrides, monorails, and other similar attractions incorporated into the designs of many later international expositions and other large fairs.

FIG. 2.8. The *trottoir roulant*, a moving sidewalk that encircled the fairgrounds, at the Paris Exposition in 1900. From *The Parisian Dream City: A Portfolio of Photographic Views of the World's Exposition at Paris* (St. Louis: Thompson Publishing Company, 1900), n.p.

The committee members' earlier experiences in creating designs for heavily populated urban settings contributed to a shared belief that most past expositions' sites had been too large.[55] They felt that spreading exhibition halls over vast areas of land would not only tire fairgoers out but also reduce the unified feel of the overall design scheme. Since there was

no thought of limiting the number of exhibitors at the Chicago fair, the obvious solution, from these architects' perspective, lay in the construction of multistoried buildings.

To reduce fairgoers' fatigue, most of the designers felt that the main entrance of multilevel pavilions should be located on an upper story, thereby allowing people to view exhibits while filtering downward through the buildings.[56] Fairgoers exiting a pavilion at ground level could take a ramp or escalator back to the roof, from which they could then travel on the movable sidewalks over connecting bridges to the next building. Ramps could also provide places for patrons to wait in line for entry into the pavilions. The commissioners believed that the changing vistas seen as one slowly walked up the ramps would make waiting in lines less tedious. Not all commissioners were in favor of the elaborate multistoried schemes. Brown, for example, believed that the ground presented the best level for circulation.[57]

After each member's ideas had been presented at the meeting, the commissioners produced a list of specific principles to be incorporated into the design of the fair:

- Multistoried buildings
- Both vertical and horizontal mechanical transportation systems
- A fine arts display at the Art Institute with mechanical transportation from the fairgrounds
- No automobile parking within the exposition
- Five million square feet of flexible exhibit space
- Provisions for making pageants easily viewable
- Water incorporated not only within the grounds but also throughout the buildings
- Artificial light used both for illumination inside the buildings and for decorative purposes, both night and day
- A major axis running parallel to the lakeshore and a minor cross-axis at Twenty-third Street
- An attempt to develop a substantially more economical type of fireproof construction for exposition use.[58]

The committee members took these principles into consideration while creating a new round of overall schemes for the fair. They then each brought a plan, sections, and a bird's-eye view of their designs to the third meeting of the commission, held on 21 January 1929.[59] Despite the modern principles the architects had promulgated, this round of designs revealed that most had not yet moved beyond the lessons of their formal training. Even the architects regarded the studies as "rather traditional developments of the best world's fair planning of earlier years."[60] The use of classical massing, masonry (or, for temporary structures, staff, a building material consisting of a mixture of plaster and sawdust), and strong axial, Beaux-Arts planning in all the schemes directly reflected the architects' traditional backgrounds. The designs blended well with the neoclassical forms of the recently completed Field Museum and Soldier Field adjacent to the fairgrounds, but they did not project the image of a modern fair.

As the architects examined these preliminary designs, four major ideas for the basic layouts emerged. The designers gave each form a descriptive title: "the Hole," which consisted of buildings surrounding a giant amphitheater; "the Cork," which included a dominant building or tower marking major and minor axes; "the Chain," which broke the site down into sections along the shoreline; and "the Vestibule," which contained a dominant water portal at the north end of the site.[61]

Arthur Brown and Hubert Burnham both presented "cork" schemes that featured elegant classical designs with colonnades and formal gardens suggestive of the Italian Renaissance. Brown's scheme, recalling his design for the neoclassical Horticultural Building at the Panama-Pacific International Exposition, included a domed tower marking the center of Northerly Island. Enclosed colonnaded buildings to each side surrounded large central courtyards containing formal gardens, and similar building compositions were repeated directly across the lagoon on the mainland.

Burnham's design also showed a strongly symmetrical scheme with a central tower on Northerly Island. Its lofty form, however, was more reminiscent of setback skyscrapers. Long colonnades enclosed the lagoon and divided it into a series of regularly shaped pools, the central one in the shape of a quatrefoil. The row of pools continued to the south as less formally shaped ponds. According to a caption for the plan published in *Pencil Points*, elevated moving sidewalks, which helped unify the design, would provide an "outstanding feature that would distinguish this exposition from previous ones."[62]

FIG. 2.9 *(top facing).* Preliminary study of proposed exposition grounds showing "cork" scheme, Hubert Burnham, architect, 20 January 1929. From Edward H. Bennett Collection, Ryerson and Burnham Archives, The Art Institute of Chicago. Digital file copyright The Art Institute of Chicago.
FIG. 2.10 *(below facing).* Perspective rendering of the Chicago World's Fair, showing "hole" scheme, Raymond M. Hood, architect, 18 January 1929. From Edward H. Bennett Collection, Ryerson and Burnham Archives, The Art Institute of Chicago. Digital file copyright The Art Institute of Chicago.

Raymond Hood's symmetrical "hole" scheme, meanwhile, recalled a variety of ancient classical cultures, revealing his lack of preference for a specific stylistic vocabulary. The design focused on a large aerial moving sidewalk in the shape of an elongated D. The flat side of the D, located along the Illinois Central Railway tracks, was to be an arrival platform for fair visitors. A wide staircase leading to a central water basin doubled as bleachers for large gatherings. The curve of the D, which projected into Lake Michigan, recalled Hellenistic sanctuaries. Processional stairways, similar to those at the ancient sites of Lindos and Kos, led up to a U-shaped building reminiscent of the Altar of Zeus at Pergamon. Classical domes topped each side of the building, and a central colonnade echoed the rows of Doric columns on Soldier Field located across the fairgrounds. A tall, massive obelisk marked the center of the plan; exhibit buildings stepped away to the north and the south.

PRELIMINARY STUDY
OF
PROPOSED EXPOSITION GROUNDS
HUBERT BURNHAM, ARCHT. JAN. 20, 1929

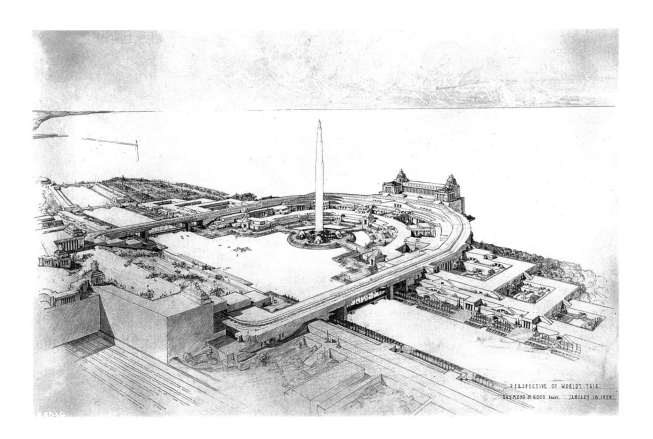

PERSPECTIVE OF WORLD'S FAIR
RAYMOND M. HOOD ARCHT. JANUARY 18, 1929

At the meeting, John Holabird stressed the need for an element of great height that could correspond to a modern office building as a central feature of the design. He felt that a colossal modern feature that dominated the exposition grounds would give the fair a dramatic, easily identified emblem, as the Eiffel Tower had at the Paris exposition in 1889. While Hood incorporated a central obelisk as the focal point in his design, every other architect on the commission included a tall building reminiscent of a setback skyscraper—a visual form clearly representative of the modern technological theme of the fair.[63]

In addition to incorporating major vertical elements, the designs took into consideration how the fair would appear from the air.[64] The presence of an airport as a major element in several of these early designs (and the inclusion of flying airplanes in some of the preliminary perspectives) indicates the rising popularity of the airplane at this time.[65] Excitement over air travel and enthusiasm for viewing the world from above led to the inclusion of both dirigible rides and the Skyride attraction. Souvenirs, including silver trays, postcards, and posters, often presented images of the whole fairgrounds as viewed from above. Some architects even considered how their buildings would appear from the sky. Albert Kahn, the architect of the Ford Building (1934), for example, designed the rotunda of the pavilion to look like a gigantic mechanical gear from the air.

The commissioners also addressed the fair organizers' desire to incorporate modern technology into the design of the exposition. The architects continued to investigate a variety of elaborate methods for moving fairgoers along the roofs of buildings and throughout the rest of the grounds. Noiseless electronic launches designed to follow a network of canals comprised just one of the novel ideas suggested as a means to move people between various areas of the site.[66]

The commissioners gathered the best details of the individual preliminary schemes to create an "accepted *parti*," or list of included elements, a common aspect of the design process taught at the École des Beaux-Arts.[67] The *parti* for the exposition design consisted of a dominant building celebrating scientific developments in the middle of the site, a water portal at the north end of the fairgrounds, an airport projecting into Lake Michigan, and moving sidewalks connecting the exhibition buildings.[68] The commissioners decided unanimously that the main pavilions should be three or four stories high, totaling 5 million square feet of space. They also agreed that the next round of submitted designs should be in black and white and should include a site plan, three sectional drawings, a bird's-eye perspective, and any additional drawings necessary to illustrate the basic design of included mechanical transportation systems.

Although the commissioners continued to follow the familiar Beaux-Arts approach to design, their fifth official meeting marked a major shift toward the creation of a modern fair. The seven architects present at the start of the meet-

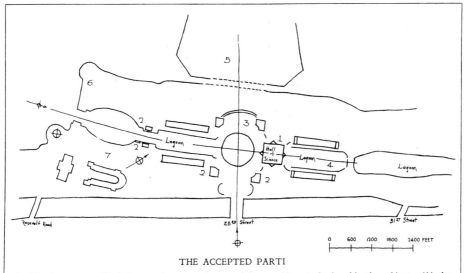

THE ACCEPTED PARTI

In this scheme are combined the more important elements of the several layouts developed by the architects: (1) the
Hall of Science, which is to stand over the lagoon and in height and architectural character to be the dominant of the
entire composition; (2) the Water Portal, which is to be the chief decorative feature of the entrances; (3) the axis
at 23rd Street; (4) the south lagoon; and (5) the proposed airport. This parti provides three main features: Nos.
2, 3 and 4, each of which is comparable with the Grand Basin of the Columbian Exposition of 1893, and is considerably larger. (6) Site of the proposed Horticultural Building, and (7) site of the proposed Festival Hall. These
two buildings, with the Stadium, the Field Museum, the Shedd Aquarium and the Planetarium north of the Water
Portal (No. 2) will comprise a monumental group of permanent buildings almost in the heart of Chicago.

ing (Hood arrived later) closely followed the agreed-on *parti* in their new series of preliminary plans.[69] They presented their designs next to a series of site plans of previous expositions and significant historical urban sites, such as St. Peter's in Rome and the Place de la Concorde in Paris.[70] Most of the schemes incorporated setback skyscraper forms for the central Hall of Science tower, but for the first time the architects began to depart from a classical style.[71] Many of the plans contained smaller secondary towers laid out symmetrically. Cret, Brown, and Walker all included two rows of small towers lining the lagoon to the north. Bennett, Corbett, and Burnham used secondary towers to mark the crossings of lesser axes in their designs. The dramatic use of exterior lighting in several of the schemes may have reflected the presence of the two recently hired consultants to the group—Norman Bel Geddes and Hugh Ferriss.[72]

Comments among the commissioners regarding the new designs were almost all positive and revolved around the minor variations in the schemes. For example, Brown stated that Corbett's design was clearly defined and came nearest to "establishing the hall of science as the radiation point for all the other points of the fair." Meanwhile, several of the architects described Holabird's composition as brilliant and commented on the fact that it afforded "a wonderful view of the tower."[73] After ladling numerous accolades on each other's work, the commissioners selected the most successful elements and began to incorporate them into a final draft of

FIG. 2.11. Drawing of the accepted *parti* illustrating the major elements for the preliminary designs of the fairgrounds presented at the fifth meeting of the architectural commission, held in early May 1929. From Allen D. Albert, "The Architecture of the Chicago World's Fair of 1933," *American Architect* 135 (5 April 1929): 421.

FIG. 2.12. Perspective rendering of Chicago World's Fair 1933 using *parti*, Arthur Brown Jr., architect. From Edward H. Bennett Collection, Ryerson and Burnham Archives, The Art Institute of Chicago. Digital file copyright The Art Institute of Chicago.

the preliminary plan, from which individual buildings could be designed. Their work, however, was disrupted by the late arrival of Raymond Hood.

Having arrived in Chicago from Europe during the evening of the first day of the fifth official meeting, Hood did not present his exposition scheme until the next morning. His design greatly startled the other architects, as he had ignored the given *parti*. Instead, his design included a diverse group of elements informally situated along either side of a long rectangular basin, highlighted by a massive setback tower located off center.[74] Hood did include an airport projecting into Lake Michigan, but only two minor axes provided access to it. On the north end of the grounds, a large ramp crisscrossed the water leading to a terrace that overlooked the grounds to the south. A series of X-shaped pylons flanked a long cascading fountain leading from the top of the terrace to the large basin.

Hood told his colleagues that he had come to the realization that "no matter how grand" the symmetrical preliminary plans appeared, they "were still monotonous."[75] He stated that he had been impressed with the "value of 'unfolding interest'" in the compositions of the recently held international expositions in Barcelona and Seville.[76] He realized that an informal layout would provide an element of flexibility by freeing the designers from a formal site plan. The shift from the use of axial symmetry to an emphasis solely on a sense of balance reflected a general transformation taking place in the minds of many progressive designers. This emphasis formed one of the three major principles of modern architecture as laid out by Hitchcock and Johnson in the International Style Show. Cret agreed with Hood and stressed that the exposition would be more modern with an asymmetrical site plan and, at the same time, would present a greater departure from earlier fairs. He also thought that Hood's design would allow the individuality of the various architects, painters, and sculptors to be expressed, providing a greater variety in the overall scheme.[77]

An additional benefit discussed by Hood was the ease in adapting an irregular layout to the site, thus allowing for the widest possible range of building treatments.[78] Serendipitously, an asymmetrical plan was better suited to the unstable financial times. It provided greater flexibility in the design, thus allowing exhibitors to be added or removed as financial resources changed. It also meant that buildings could be scaled for specific needs and functions without having to worry about directly addressing the designs of other structures nearby.

The committee members then took a vote to decide the commission's preferred individual plan. Corbett, a staunch supporter of a symmetrical layout, expressed his feeling that the committee should not even consider

FIG. 2.13. Bird's-eye view rendering of the Chicago World's Fair, Raymond M. Hood, architect. From Edward H. Bennett Collection, Ryerson and Burnham Archives, The Art Institute of Chicago. Digital file copyright The Art Institute of Chicago.

Hood's asymmetrical design since he had ignored the assigned elements of the *parti* and, thus, had not followed the established design rules. The rest of the commissioners quickly overruled Corbett's objections, and Hood's asymmetrical design won with five votes.[79] By carrying out this decision, the commissioners finally cut themselves "adrift from the past, breaking away from traditions of balance and symmetry and classical design."[80]

THE FINAL LAYOUT

The commissioners selected Cret to create the final preliminary layout for the exposition.[81] His scheme formed the backbone of the built design that emerged as A Century of Progress. Once the members of the architectural commission had established the basic site design, they divided the major elements of the fairgrounds among themselves. The irregular layout provided for easier partitioning of the grounds for individual assignments.[82]

During this period, the architectural commission made numerous changes to the overall design. Even prior to the stock market crash in October 1929, they had reduced the gross square footage of the major exposition buildings from 5 million to between 2.5 million and 3 million.[83] Not only were the last major vestiges of the members' Beaux-Arts planning jettisoned, but insufficient financial resources and a realization of the severity of the Depression resulted in the eventual elimination of several features central to earlier schemes owing to their financial, as well as design, impracticality.[84] The first major casualties were the moving sidewalks and the airport.[85] Elaborate water elements, including the colossal Tower of Water designed by Ralph Walker, also disappeared. A much smaller tower for the Hall of Science and the massive Skyride attraction replaced a towering fountain as the main focal point for the exhibition. The design and placement of the Electrical Building, the General Exhibits Building, and the Hall of Science also underwent major changes. In order to keep up with all these modifications, the committee relied on a design method favored by Hood.[86] They created a twenty-eight-foot-long clay model of the site on which the architects experimented with different arrangements of the major pavilions and other prominent design features.

The changes in location, size, and design of buildings, as well as the elimination of elements, resulted in the shuffling of individual assignments.[87] Even with all the alterations, the final layout for the exposition still recalled Cret's interpretation of Hood's asymmetrical concept for the fairgrounds. The design as built wound its way down the shore of Lake Michigan and along Northerly Island. Bridges connected the island with the coast, creating a large hourglass-shaped lagoon at the northern end of the grounds. Most of the major general exposition halls were located in this area. The designers placed ethnic structures and midway attractions primarily in the center of the fairgrounds and the children's area on Northerly Island. In addition to the Travel and Transport Building and automobile manufacturers' halls, situated at the southern end of the grounds were a reproduction of the Mayan Nunnery at Uxmal, Mexico, and a U.S. Army camp. Above everything hovered the giant Skyride.

HALL OF SCIENCE

An examination of the Hall of Science, the centerpiece of A Century of Progress, provides considerable insight into the design process for the major fair pavilions produced by the architectural commissioners. Designed by Paul Cret, the science pavilion went through at least four major stages reflecting the evolution of the commissioners' definition of modern architecture for the fair. In addition to aesthetic decisions occurring within the planning process of the exposition, outside circumstances, in particular the devastating economic situation, affected major decisions regarding its design.

As early as spring 1929, with the introduction of a scientific theme for the exposition, organizers expressed their desire for a large pavilion dedicated to the pure sciences as the main focal point of the fairgrounds.[88] At this time, the architectural commissioners specified that a tall science building be included at the center of the site in the accepted *parti.* A dominant visual landmark for the exposition, the central skyscraper would serve as a vivid illustration for the public of how advances in scientific technology were significantly affecting modern society. What was most pertinent for the commissioners, however, was to reinforce the perception that the skyscraper was the major icon of modern American architecture. The restrictions of the Great Depression and the decision to

FIG. 2.14. Final layout of A Century of Progress. "A Century of Progress," *Architectural Record* 73 (May 1933): 344.

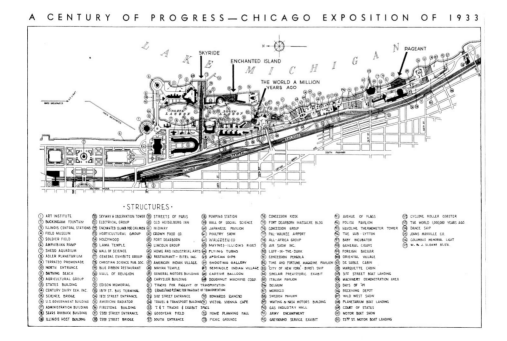

A CENTURY OF PROGRESS—CHICAGO EXPOSITION OF 1933

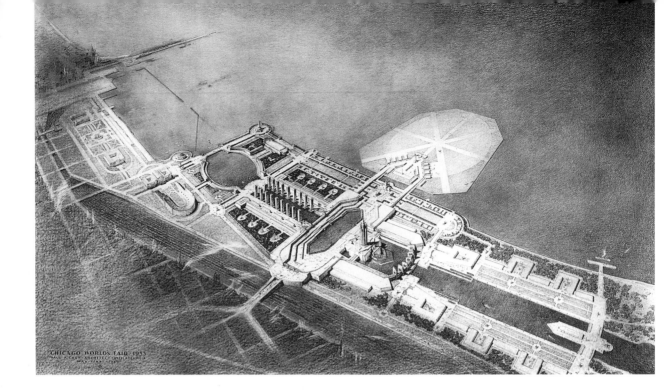

use inexpensive, prefabricated materials reduced the soaring "Temple of Pure Sciences" to a less prominent carillon tower located at the southwest corner of a large, two-story pavilion.

Cret's own preliminary site design based on the official *parti* illustrates the early development of several other major elements that he eventually incorporated into the final design for the Hall of Sciences. Like most of the schemes by the other commissioners, Cret's plan consisted of a massive setback skyscraper surrounded by water in the midst of a series of basins that ran parallel to the shoreline. Surface patterns and rows of columns at the top of the tower, as well as on the projecting wings of the pavilion, reveal the architect's preference for flattened classical forms. Cret designed the curved wings to each side of the tower to embrace visitors standing in front of the building. A series of rectangular flying buttresses lining a basin on the south side provided a backdrop for the tower. Cret used similar projecting pylons to decorate a curved wall at the main entrance in his final design. To the north of the pavilion in the preliminary design, tall piers lined a long, rectangular basin framing a main axis leading to the building. In the constructed design, banners provided a similar effect along the Avenue of Flags, the major axis that led to the building from the north. Cret maintained the pavilion's close relationship to the lagoon exhibited in this early design throughout his later schemes. However, as the commissioners began to realize the severe limitations on available funds, they decided to relocate the Hall of Science from the central lagoon site to a more solid piece of land immediately southeast of Soldier Field. As a result, the pavilion lost its strong axial relationship to the other major elements of the exposition visible in this and other early preliminary designs.

Untitled drawings illustrated several other early designs for the Hall of Science. A rendering labeled "30-1157-5" and signed "AK" shows figures relaxing along a basin of water surrounding a tall tower. The presence of the water suggests that the rendering dates from before the decision was made to move the building inland. The massive structure consists of an assemblage of vertical and horizontal elements, including four large columns that support a projecting terrace. A decorative band along the top of the first floor offers visual relief to the windowless base of the tower. On the upper levels, bands of glass alternating with projecting wall surfaces provide a sense of rhythm to the multistoried building. Its exact height is not apparent, as the structure continues upward beyond the top of the rendering.

The eventual decision not to construct a large skyscraper at the fair led Cret to significantly alter his design. A drawing rendered in a heavy style, signed by the architect and dated "3-12-'30," illustrates a courtyard surrounded by series of terraces to the east and a large hall with a trussed roof immediately to the west.[89] Cret joined the projecting wings of the Hall of Science to Corbett's General Exhibits Building, located immediately to the south, by a viaduct at an upper level and by less formal paths along the ground. The long arms of the U-shaped structure extend eastward to form bridges across the lagoon, uniting the science pavilion with Hood's

FIG. 2.16. Hall of Science, scheme 30-1157-5. Preliminary rendering of Hall of Science at 1933 Century of Progress International Exposition. From Edward H. Bennett Collection, Ryerson and Burnham Archives, The Art Institute of Chicago. Digital file copyright The Art Institute of Chicago.

Electrical Building on Northerly Island. These raised walkways reflect the commission's continuing desire to provide convenient pedestrian paths between buildings even after they had to eliminate the moving sidewalks.

A drawing labeled "30-1157-7" and published in the *T-Square Club Journal* presents a similar yet more refined design, on which the architect based his final layout. The towers of the General Exhibits Building on the far side of the pavilion are more prominent than in the previous design. A row of projecting bays lining the central wall of the courtyard give the facade an accordion-like appearance, recalling the entrance of the fair's Administration Building. For decoration, Cret combined the refined classical forms he favored with motifs reminiscent of the 1925 art deco exposition in Paris. He limited his ornamentation to specific areas on the facades, thereby allowing most of the wall surfaces to consist of flat unadorned planes—a practice common to most of the built pavilions for the Chicago fair, although, ironically, not to the final design of the Hall of Science.

In its built form, the Hall of Science maintained the U-shaped plan, but two other major elements were added—a raised circular entrance court on the north facade and a 176-foot-tall carillon tower on the southwest corner. Cret responded to the different functional needs of each face of the building by creating a design that presented four distinct elevations, with more complex compositions on the north and east facades. The grand Avenue of Flags led to the main entrance on the north side of the pavilion, which was reached by a long ramp that led to a large circular forecourt on the second level. A semicircular group of fifty-two-foot-tall pylons framed the court. Raised walkways provided access to other major exhibition halls

FIG. 2.17 *(below)*. Hall of Science, preliminary scheme dated "3-12-'30," Paul P. Cret, architect. The curve of Soldier Field is to the right and the General Exhibits Building is on the upper left. From Paul Philippe Cret Collection, Athenaeum of Philadelphia.

FIG. 2.18 *(above facing)*. Hall of Science, scheme 30-1157-7, with the repeating towers of the General Exhibits Building in background. Preliminary rendering of Hall of Science at 1933 Century of Progress International Exposition, Paul P. Cret, architect. From Edward H. Bennett Collection, Ryerson and Burnham Archives, The Art Institute of Chicago. Digital file copyright The Art Institute of Chicago.

FIG. 2.19 *(below facing)*. Bird's-eye view of the Hall of Science prior to the construction of neighboring pavilions. Postcard from collection of author.

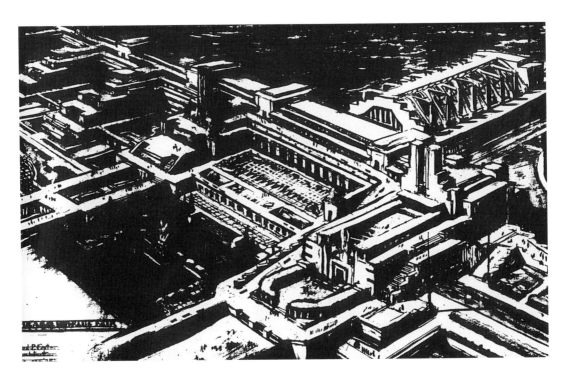

Aerial View of Hall of Science
A Century of Progress

to the east and south. An opening in the floor of the circular forecourt allowed visual access to a large rotunda below, in a fashion similar to the sunken plaza at New York City's Rockefeller Center, built soon after the completion of the Hall of Science. The large U-shaped court on the east side of the building, which opened toward the lagoon, was designed to hold up to 80,000 people during major events, such as the magnificent opening-night lighting ceremony and presentations by visiting dignitaries.[90] By terracing the building, Cret provided places for people to view featured events (in addition to seating set up in the courtyard) and allowed the pavilion to serve as a festive backdrop for major fair activities.

The exterior wallboard used in almost all the exhibition pavilions was not yet commercially available at the time of the science building's construction. Fair organizers chose instead to use sheets of prefabricated plywood and battens bolted to a steel frame.[91] Unlike on the unadorned facades of the other large pavilions, the construction workers laid out the plywood panels so that the battens formed interesting geometric patterns.[92] Additional visual interest was generated by retaining the undulating form of the center wall of the U-shaped court. Cret repeated this rhythmic pattern inside the pavilion with the incorporation of zigzag designs on the end walls of the building's main hall.

FIG. 2.20. Great Hall of the Hall of Science, showing zigzag pattern on back wall and recessed neon lighting on the ceiling. Kaufmann and Fabry, photographers.

Like most of the major exhibition pavilions, the final design of the Hall of Science contained no windows. The strict control of light levels and air quality this allowed was only made possible by recent improvements in lighting and mechanical technology. When visiting the artificially controlled spaces, fairgoers were subtly reminded of a major underlying theme of the event—the ability of man to overcome nature through advances in science and technology.

FIG. 2.21. North Court of the Hall of Science, with *Knowledge Combating Ignorance*, sculpture by John H. Storrs, in the foreground and bas-relief panels between the large pylons on the curving facade located behind. Kaufmann and Fabry, photographers.

This scientific theme was reinforced in the sculpture created for the pavilion. For example, John H. Storrs's freestanding *Knowledge Combating Ignorance*, located in a niche on the forecourt of the Hall of Science, portrayed a man empowered by scientific knowledge fearlessly glancing down at a large serpent representing ignorance wrapped around his leg. A second freestanding sculpture, *Science Advancing Mankind*, was located in the center of the lower plaza below the opening in the northern forecourt. Created by Louise Lentz Woodruff, the imposing, rectilinear robot protectively leaned over a man and a woman as it gently guided them to a future world made better through the latest advances in scientific technology.[93]

More common than freestanding sculptures at the exposition were bas-relief panels, which replaced the more traditional surface ornamentation on many of the early exhibition pavilions.[94] The panels typically contained figures in stylized forms, popularized by the Exposition Internationale des Arts Décoratifs et Industriels Modernes, that symbolically represented various aspects of science or modern

life. For example, the large pylons on the north court of the Hall of Science framed four panels of nude males holding attributes relating to physics, mechanical science, chemistry, and natural science. Panels with more abstract human forms also illustrating various areas of science, including medicine, zoology, and botany, decorated the base of the sculpture *Science Advancing Mankind.*

Color was a major decorative feature that greatly contributed to the creation of a festive atmosphere. Designer Joseph Urban, who was well versed in modern color theory, specified that white paint be used for the semicircular north court of the Hall of Science, with the recesses located between the pylons in blue and a few minor features highlighted in red. The use of blue and white continued around the lower level of the building in the form of horizontal stripes that in colorized photographs give the impression of rows of giant Lego building blocks. Orange on the upper level of the building emphasized the location of main entrances, while yellow dominated the southern wing of the U-shaped court. Blue on the north and east sides of the bell tower contrasted with the other two tower facades, which were painted white. To unite the pavilion with the General Exhibits Building, the bridge joining the two exhibition halls continued the white and blue colors used on the Hall of Science. The dominance of yellow and blue on the General Exhibits Building also contributed toward visually unifying the two pavilions (Plate 6).

At night dramatic lighting set the building vividly aglow. Earlier international expositions had demonstrated innovative uses of lighting, but their effects had been pale in comparison to the magnificent spectacle in the evening sky during the nightly reenactment of the opening-night lighting ceremony. The Hall of Science alone incorporated more wattage than was used for the entire World's Columbian Exposition.[95]

The designers had to select the placement of specific colors of neon and other forms of lighting to prevent inharmonious blending with the painted facades. They also faced the challenge of illuminating dark-colored walls, which tended to absorb large quantities of light. As a result, the designers scrapped a plan to alternate over 2,500 feet of red and blue vertical neon stripes on the carillon tower of the Hall of Science. Instead, blue was limited to the north and east sides of the tower, which were painted blue, and red was used on the white south and west walls. The beams of floodlights placed inside the buttresses on the north court reflected off the blue walls, giving the recesses a cool glow. To contrast with the blue light, 1,280 feet of bright-red neon indirectly lit the front of the pylons.[96] Supplemental lighting included sixty-six 1,000-watt floodlights beaming upward onto the building and six powerful searchlights shining down from the west tower of the Skyride.[97]

FIG. 2.23. Great U-shaped courtyard of the Hall of Science at night, showing lighting effects. Hedrich-Blessing, photographers. From Louis Skidmore, "The Hall of Science," *Architectural Forum* 57 (October 1932): 307.

The back wall of the U-shaped court displayed another novel example of festive lighting. The plywood panels that formed the V-shaped bays was perforated by an abstract geometric pattern that represented tree branches. A revolving shaft on which various-color projectors were mounted behind the silhouetted grilles produced vibrant color changes on the surfaces. The result was an undulating facade of continually shifting colors that drew fairgoers' attention to the building at night.

Cret's design for the Hall of Science, along with a group of Spanish Renaissance–style buildings he produced at approximately the same time for the University of Texas at Austin, illustrate his stylistic flexibility. He often stepped away from the stripped classical forms he favored in order to meet the needs of a specific setting, a request by a client, or a type of building material that required a different aesthetic vocabulary. While participation in the creation of the exposition had various levels of aesthetic and ideological impact on Cret and the other commissioners, it gave them the opportunity to develop innovative concepts of modern architecture in a fantastic setting where their ideas were experienced by many of their peers, along with millions of other fair visitors.

THREE

PREFABRICATED PALACES:
FORMAL DESIGNS OF THE PAVILIONS

*Children—Attention! The buildings you will see
at this fair are very different than those you are
used to, but they are the product of the times
in which you live. They have no windows
because we wish to have uniform light within,
by electricity. They have flat walls, no cornices
and no columns. They had to be like that, partly
because they are not built of stone or plaster but
are covered with various kinds of thin building
materials. They are to be painted in bright
colors. Will you like them? Perhaps. Should you
like them? Yes, if they are good buildings.*

EDWARD H. BENNETT

Early in the planning process fair organizers realized that to sell A Century
of Progress to potential investors and exhibitors they needed to present concrete
evidence that the exposition would go on
despite the nation's grim economic situation. In a dramatic demonstration that
they had no intention of even scaling
down the event, the organizers authorized construction of two major pavilions,
one at each end of the long and narrow fairgrounds, three years prior to opening
day.[1] The designs of the Administration Building, located at the north end of the
grounds, and the Travel and Transport Building, situated far to the south, gave
potential investors, as well as an inquisitive public, a hint of things to come.[2] The
350-foot-long E-shaped Administration Building, designed by the Chicago members of the architectural commission (Bennett, Holabird, and Burnham), was built
of recently introduced materials and illustrated new, low-cost trends in office and
factory construction.[3] The Travel and Transport Building, designed by the same architects, generated considerable publicity because of its peculiar form. Huge zigzag
steel walls, massive towers, and projecting support cables gave the pavilion's circular Railroad Hall the appearance of a colossal insect (Plate 7).[4] Its bizarre shape,
shocking to some and a curiosity to many, led critics to refer to the pavilion jok-
ingly as Dawes's Gas Tank, a dubious tribute to the president of the exposition.[5]
After one look at these two unusual buildings, it became clear that the exposition
architects had no interest in reincarnating the first Chicago World's Fair. They completely rejected the Beaux-Arts classicism of the World's Columbian Exposition in

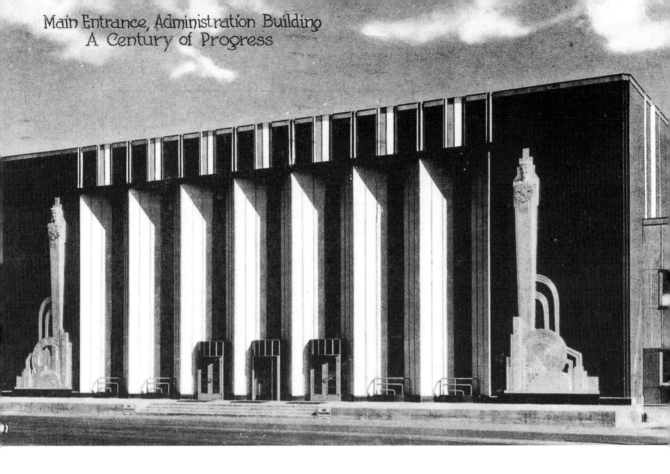

FIG. 3.1. Entrance of the Administration Building. Its accordion-like facade and abstract sculpture represent the role of science in a modern industrial society. Postcard from collection of author.

favor of innovative building designs more appropriate to the modern era. The result was a fairground filled with strange and fantastic pavilions.

Prior to the fair's construction, Allen D. Albert, then secretary to the architectural commission, commented that people were constantly asking him in what style the exposition would be built. Commissioner Harvey Wiley Corbett responded to this question by stating that "the 'style' of the world's fair would be the last thing determined and not the first." He wrote that instead of selecting a specific style, the exposition designs would be based on the nature of the exhibits, the contemplated attendance figures, the conditions of modern life, and new structural trends.[6]

The architects, steeped in the contemporary debate over whether modern architecture was a new style or a set of design principles free of a specific stylistic interpretation, eventually concluded that modern architecture should be defined as a set of principles. The implied division between the two views was not, however, sharply delineated in the minds of some of the commissioners. Shortly after the exposition's official opening, Corbett defended the pavilion designs in the professional journal *Architect and Engineer* primarily in formal terms.[7] He claimed that "in virtually all of its aspects this 1933 world's fair architecture is modern" because it depended on planes and surfaces for its character and effectiveness. He emphasized the lack of gingerbread effects, stating that he and his colleagues "[had] made a sincere effort toward simplicity in the design of the buildings on which they worked."[8] Instead of the ornate plaster decorations of the earlier Chicago exposition, Corbett wrote, the architects of the current fair had achieved interesting decorative effects by using various forms of colored light against the background of painted planes and surfaces—formal characteristics that the designers derived from a reliance on new materials and building techniques, functional needs, economic conditions, and current developments in the fine arts.[9]

The general physical character of the architecture for A Century of Progress underwent significant stylistic development during the designing and construction phases of the exposition; this development went well beyond departing from Beaux-Arts classicism. The architectural commissioners initially incorporated in their work formal characteristics that clearly echoed the ornate designs popularized at European expositions held in the mid-1920s. By 1931, however, the commissioners had rejected the use of applied sculptural reliefs and other decorative elements in favor of less ornate architectural forms that celebrated the modern building materials of which the pavilions were constructed. This was due both to the growing economic depression and to the influence of other designers who worked at the exposition once construction of the earliest pavilions was under way. To expedite implementation of the building designs, fair organizers created the Department of Works. Members included color consultant Joseph Urban and landscaper Ferruccio Vitale. Walter D'Arcy Ryan from General Electric became director of illumination. Daniel H. Burnham Jr., Hubert Burnham's brother, was hired as director of works (the same position his father had held forty years earlier at the World's Columbian Exposition), while Clarence W. Farrier, a city planning engineer, became his assistant.[10] Bert M. Thorud, the engineer of the Travel and Transport Building and later the Skyride, was employed as the fair's structural engineer.

Other architects hired to form a planning and construction staff included Louis Skidmore, as chief of design of the Works Department, and his brother-in-law, Nathaniel A. Owings, as supervisor of development. Owings also oversaw the organizational work for *Wings of a Century*, the Skyride, and other entertainment attractions run by the exposition corporation.[11] Skidmore and Owings, along with Otto Teegen, Joseph Urban's assistant, formed a committee known as "X," or the Little Architectural Commission. The X committee was responsible for approving the designs of non-fair-owned pavilions and exhibit displays.[12] As a result, Skidmore and Owings oversaw the design and construction of approximately fifty corporate pavilions and 600 individual displays.[13] Much of their work consisted of modernizing designs that arrived with "the concentration in the wrong direction," meaning an excess of ornate details, including "velvet drapes, gold tassels, corded railings and other trappings."[14]

AESTHETIC QUALITIES OF THE
EARLY EXPOSITION PAVILIONS

FIG. 3.2 *(above)*. Staff architects at work on designs for the fair in the Administration Building (i37696aa). Courtesy of Chicago History Museum.
FIG. 3.3 *(top facing)*. Palace of Liberal Arts at the 1926 Sesquicentennial Exposition, Philadelphia. Note the similarity of proportions to the center bay of the Administration Building at A Century of Progress, shown in Figure 3.1. Postcard from collection of author.
FIG. 3.4 *(below facing)*. Pavillon de la Maîtrise at the 1925 Exposition Internationale des Arts Décoratifs et Industriels Moderne, Paris. Note the similarity of the starburst design above the entrance to that on Railroad Hall of the Travel and Transport Building at A Century of Progress, shown in Plate 7. Postcard from collection of author.

The architects of the fair believed they were creating modern architecture by using new materials and ideas. Critics of the earliest pavilions, how-ever, justifiably accused the designers of covering the buildings' facades with features popularized by the 1925 Exposition Internationale des Arts Décoratifs et Industriels Moderne.[15] The first large exhibition halls showed strong stylistic ties to the decorative architecture of that earlier Paris expo-sition: angular, zigzag forms; flat, decorative surface patterns; and stylized, allegorical, relief sculptures.

Most, perhaps all, of the members of the architectural commission had traveled to the Exposition Internationale des Arts Décoratifs and had also visited many of the other international expositions held in France, Belgium, Spain, and Sweden between 1929 and 1931 as they searched for new design concepts that they could adapt for the Chicago fair.[16] Having rejected a classical vocabulary for A Century of Progress, the designers initially incorporated what they felt to be an appropriate modern language of architecture derived from the decorative forms that had graced many of the European exposition pavilions. For example, although the Chicago members of the architectural commission used the design of the Palace of Liberal Arts from the failed 1926 Sesquicentennial International Exposi-tion as a model for the massing of the entrance to the Administration

Building, its accordion-like facade consisted of vertical zigzag projections—forms similar to those on European fair buildings, such as the Polish Pavilion at the Exposition Internationale des Arts Décoratifs.[17] The Travel and Transport Building's Railroad Hall also incorporated undulating walls, as well as enormous starburst grilles that recalled similar designs located above the entrances of the Pavillon de la Maîtrise of the Galeries LaFayette department store at the 1925 Paris exposition.[18] An even more obvious example of a designer's use of earlier expositions as architectural pattern books was the massing and classical elements of the Christian Science Monitor Building's entrance. Its design was almost identical to that of the Swedish Pavilion in Paris, even featuring the same slender Ionic columns.[19]

The strong formal impact of the European expositions on the architecture of A Century of Progress was also revealed in the inclusion of similar stylized allegorical sculptures, which appeared in relief on the earliest fair buildings in Chicago. In attempting to capture the zeitgeist and, more directly, the theme of the event, the artists creating sculpture for the fair typically emphasized the machine and other aspects of modern technology more than their European colleagues had done. They included representations of urban skylines, gears, radio waves, and other scientific emblems reflecting recent technological developments. Like the freestanding sculpture *Science Advancing Mankind* at the Hall of Science, slender, abstract, herm figures with skyscrapers and gearlike forms at their feet flanked the entrance of the Administration Building, presenting complex iconographic messages regarding the role of science in modern industrial society.[20]

FIG. 3.5. Fair visitors being pushed in a roller chair in front of the Christian Science Monitor Building at A Century of Progress. Kaufmann and Fabry, photographers.

Raymond Hood worked closely with New York artist Gaston LaChaise to develop a design program of bas-relief sculptures for the exterior of the Electrical Building. The works, carried out by a group of prominent art-

Exposition Internationale des Arts Décoratifs. - Paris 1925.
28. Pavillon National de Suède. (Carl. S. Bergsten, architecte).

ists, celebrated the growing importance, both real and symbolic, of electrical power in modern life (Plate 8).[21] As part of the composition, Ulric H. Ellerhusen created two forty-foot-high relief panels, titled *Atomic Energy* and *Stellar Energy*, for either side of a waterfall of neon lights on the main facade.[22] Each panel included a large stylized figure with dramatic, curvilinear forms representing the powerful forces of energy (Plate 9). LaChaise himself sculpted a companion piece that stood over the entrance to the Communications Building. Titled *The Conquest of Time and Space*, the work was filled with images relating to man's recent discoveries regarding electricity, including an electric generator, a telescope, telegraph wires, and telephone cables. In the center of the panel a nude figure with a radio wave running between his outstretched arms symbolized the potential of man's ability to harness electrical power.[23]

The technological iconography continued at the Water Gate, a grand entrance located at the north end of the Electrical Building. It consisted of two massive pylons demarcating an imposing gateway. Sculptor Lee Lawrie placed geometric relief figures in linear registers representing light on one pylon and sound on the other.[24] Sphinxes, representing the unknowable, at the bases of both towers in heraldic composition contributed to the gate's hieroglyphic character and helped direct

FIG. 3.6. The Swedish Pavilion at the 1925 Exposition Internationale des Arts Décoratifs in Paris, with slender Ionic columns and proportions similar to those of the Christian Science Monitor Building at A Century of Progress, shown in Figure 3.5. Postcard from collection of author.

FIG. 3.7 *(above). The Conquest of Time and Space,* a relief sculpture by Gaston LaChaise, above the entrance to the Communications Building. Postcard from collection of author.
FIG. 3.8 *(facing). Water Gate,* designed by Lee Lawrie, on north end of Electrical Building, with figures representing sound and light decorating the pylons flanking the entrance. From Jewett E. Ricker, ed., *Sculpture: A Century of Progress, Chicago, 1933* (Chicago, 1933), booklet in Cererar Collection, University of Chicago Library, Special Collections Research Center.

visitors toward the entrance stairway. Although not themselves icons of technology, their inclusion reflected the rise in popularity of exotic Egyptian forms resulting from Howard Carter's widely publicized discovery of Tutankhamen's intact tomb in 1922. Three grotesques above the beasts on one pylon represented the sun, the moon, and artificial light. Similar figures on the other pier represented thunder, music, and a modern noisemaker, the telephone. Toward the top of each pylon, "genies" descended from the heavens with light and sound, while zigzag banding symbolized the airwaves in which light and sound travel.

Although not as dramatic or as iconographically complex, the sculpture on Edward Bennett and Albert Brown's U.S. Government Building was also imbued with obvious symbolic meaning. Three large figures, approximately twenty feet high, fronting massive triangular pylons represented the major branches of the federal government. Although they showed similar formal characteristics, a different sculptor created each: *Judicial* was created by Lorado Taft, *Legislature* by John H. Storrs, and *Executive* by Raoul Josset. Despite the abstract quality of the figures' garments, the classical forms of these works symbolically tied them to classical sculpture located on other government buildings in the United States and, less directly, to that found on civic and religious buildings in classical antiquity. The inclusion of these sculptures reflected the U.S. government's desire to demonstrate to the world its dedication to strong democratic principles at a time when communism and fascism were finding vocal and active supporters at home and abroad.[25]

Although the subject matter of the sculptures at the exposition typically related to the general scientific theme of the event (the U.S. Government Building being a notable exception), there was a sense of disunity between much of the sculpture and the architecture of the fair. With the exception of the Electrical Building, artists produced most of the decorative features for the major pavilions, including sculpture, color, and exterior lighting, well after the architects had completed the building designs. In the case of the Hall of Science, images of the pavilion, including on some postcards sold at the fair, show different sculptural forms (or no sculpture at all) from the artistic works that eventually appeared.

Cret had hoped that the addition of sculpture (as well the plantings and colored paint) would add charm to the Hall of Science—a quality that he found lacking in his own final design.[26] While sculpture did add interest to the pavilion, it also contributed a sense of dissonance. This aesthetic division between sculpture and building was a sign of a growing belief in architecture that not only historical decorations but all forms of applied ornament were out of place in the modern age. The impoverished state of the economy, and the resulting need to keep construction costs to a minimum during the early 1930s, accelerated the practice of eliminating inessential details and ornament in modern architecture. Following this trend, most of the architects who designed the later exhibition pavilions for A Century of Progress eschewed sculpture and decorative relief patterns.

AESTHETIC QUALITIES OF THE LATER EXPOSITION PAVILIONS

Required to produce low-cost pavilion designs, architects began relying more and more on the form of the buildings, along with colored paint and electric lighting, to create financially sound yet festive modern exhibition halls. The result was the emergence of a variety of different formal designs. One common solution was to feature the modern prefabricated materials of which the pavilions were constructed. In direct contrast, other buildings incorporated easily recognizable gigantic iconic forms that directly related to the mass-produced merchandise of the pavilion's corporate sponsor. A third group of buildings adhered to historical vocabularies. These landmarks and entertainment attractions, including a series of national and ethnic villages, often appeared to have been constructed out of traditional materials, but like the other fair structures, they were typically built of lighter and less expensive modern products. Another major aesthetic solution at the fair was streamlining, which directly reflected the increasing pace of modern life by borrowing the curving, aerodynamic forms of the latest vehicular designs.

The desire of fair organizers to maintain constant light levels in the interior display areas through the use of artificial light while keeping

FIG. 3.9. U.S. Government Building. The visible statues represent the executive branch (by Raoul Josset) to the left and the legislative branch (by John H. Storrs) to the right. The third figure, not visible in the photograph, represents the judicial branch (by Lorado Taft). Hedrich-Blessing, photographers. From "Nine Major Buildings, A Century of Progress, Chicago 1933," *Architectural Forum* 59 (July 1933): 19.

construction costs to a minimum led architects to eliminate window openings on the major buildings. This and the absence of decorative elements resulted in large unbroken spans of exterior wall surfaces. The smoothness of the prefabricated gypsum-board wall panels used in the construction of most of the major pavilions contributed to a general emphasis on volume in the designs as opposed to mass—a principle of modern architecture prominently featured in the International Style Show.

One exhibition hall that relied on its form and materials for aesthetic interest was the small Dairy Building (designed by Bennett, Parsons, and Frost), a stack of cubic forms topped by a tower. Instead of using significant applied ornamentation, the architects emphasized the junctions of the individual prefabricated panels to break up the large planes of the building's wall surfaces. Exhibition halls that similarly lacked applied decorative features included the large Gas Industries and Horticultural pavilions, as well as many less prominent buildings, such as the Swedish Pavilion, the Johns-Manville Building, and the German-American Restaurant (originally constructed as the Polish Pavilion). Without symbolic imagery on the exterior, signs became crucial in identifying these buildings. Large letters across their facades, spelling out the name of the country, the company, or the area of scientific research of the exhibits inside, served as the dominant design element. Neon lighting on the signs made it possible to identify the individual buildings at night.

FIG. 3.10. Dairy Building, with facades of large flat panels. Postcard from collection of author.

Designers of the second group of pavilions relied on representational shapes instead of large scripted labels to identify a building's purpose or sponsor. A number of architects designing secondary pavilions embraced

SWEDISH PAVILION
WORLD'S FAIR 1934

this functional expressionism to various degrees. The most literal interpretations included attention-getting corporate buildings designed as colossal representations of their products. Other pavilions contained elements that offered more symbolic clues to their function. Three of the most significant examples of direct functional representation at the Chicago fair included the Radio Flyer Pavilion, with its colossal boy riding a thirty-five-foot-long wagon-shaped building; the Havoline Building, topped by a 200-foot-tall thermometer that recorded the current temperature at the fairgrounds; and the Time and Fortune Building, which featured enormous magazine covers in its design. These gigantic "ducks" (as such buildings came to be called) at A Century of Progress were among the first major examples of colossal, iconic forms in modern building design.[27]

Several foreign pavilions offered more abstract representations of their underlying purpose. The architects of the Italian Pavilion (Mario de Renzi, Antonio Valent, and Adalberto Libera), for example, incorporated into their design dynamic forms that expressed the major political goal of the displays inside: to increase support for fascism among Americans.[28] The building consisted of easily recognizable symbols of Italy's recent transportation achievements, such as the thin, airplane wing–shaped horizontal canopy that hovered above the central entrance, and of its political ideology, most prominently an eighty-foot-high steel-and-prismatic-glass tower in the shape of a *fascio littorio*, the ancient Roman symbol of power and

FIG. 3.11. The Swedish Pavilion was labeled with large letters across its front facade. The yellow-and-blue exterior and nearby flag also helped fairgoers identify the building. The Doric colonnade of Soldier Field appears in the background. Kaufmann and Fabry, photographers.

authority adopted by Italian fascism (Plate 10).[29] Another abstract representation of a modern form of transportation appeared on the exterior of the Streets of Paris attraction. Visitors to the faux French street scene located inside, where Sally Rand entertained fairgoers, often wearing only her large fans, entered the complex over a gangway that led to a giant, squared-off steamship, complete with lifeboats and smokestacks. The nautical elements recalled the Atlantic Ocean voyage Americans would experience if they were to travel to the real streets of Paris.

The numerous ethnic villages at A Century of Progress presented additional examples of symbolic reductions in time, space, and cultural meaning though architectural forms. The reconstructions of landmarks and quaint historical village scenes had been a favorite form of entertainment at expositions since the nineteenth century. These stage sets served as backdrops for venues, like the Streets of Paris, where fair visitors could experience the foods, dances, and architecture of distant cultures and purchase ethnic souvenirs. By visiting a pseudo-Belgium, Mexico, or Morocco, fairgoers eliminated potential difficulties of experiencing un-

FIG. 3.12. Havoline Building, which recorded the current temperature on its 200-foot-high neon Thermometer Tower. Kaufmann and Fabry, photographers.

FIG. 3.13. Exterior of the Streets of Paris attraction, with elements recalling a steamship. Kaufmann and Fabry, photographers.

familiar cultures, but in return they received only a contrived view of the featured country.

Other pavilions at the Chicago fair exhibited even less obvious symbolic forms. The Ford Building, for example, expressed the mechanical side of automobile production through its large gear-shaped hall (Plate 11). The central rotunda of the U.S. Government Building echoed the original dome of the Capitol in Washington, D.C., and, along with the pavilion's sculpture, contributed to its symbolic representation of American democracy. While the form of the General Exhibits Building presented few clues to the pavilion's purpose, its row of identical towerlike entrance bays echoed the rhythm of the modern assembly-line production process used in the creation of many of the items displayed inside.[30]

Several other pavilions reflected a desire among some exposition designers to look toward the transportation industry for aesthetic inspiration. Engineers had recently identified the teardrop as the most efficient aerodynamic form. Its shape, a functional and an aesthetic symbol for the faster pace of modern life, was quickly incorporated into new designs for airplanes, trains, and automobiles. "Speedlines," groups of three horizontal bands, also began appearing on new vehicles. Designers soon began applying these symbolic forms even to stationary items, including buildings.

The eventual widespread popularity of streamlining in the United States was largely due to the writings of industrial designer Norman Bel Geddes, who

6. Market Place

promoted the use of these forms in numerous articles and in his 1932 treatise, *Horizons*. The appearance of similar forms at A Century of Progress was in part a result of Geddes's brief tenure as a consultant to the exposition's architectural commission. He had presented a series of unrealized theater and restaurant designs for the fair, designs that he later included in his book.[31]

During the construction of the exposition, designers in the United States were only beginning to explore the potential of streamlining in architecture. Most examples of streamlining present at the exposition in 1933 were fairly subtle and were primarily limited to the design of transportation vehicles, exhibitor booths, and souvenirs. The sixty open-sided Greyhound Intra-Fair Auto-Liners that moved visitors through the park provided one of the most conspicuous examples of streamlining at the exposition. The two-tone paint schemes on the rounded bus cabs helped produce the illusion of a sleek aerodynamic form. Additional examples of streamlined vehicles appeared above the fair, in the futuristic aluminum rocket cars that whisked visitors between "Amos" and "Andy," the two towers of the gigantic Skyride (Plate 12). Aerodynamic shapes also floated in the sky over the site. The Goodyear Company operated blimps that offered visitors bird's-eye views of the fairgrounds below, and the *Macon*, the world's largest dirigible, visited the fairgrounds in June 1933 (Plate 13). Streamlining in exhibition displays was limited mainly to the use of curved walls and groups of speedlines, as at the Union Carbide and Carbon exhibit in the Hall of Science.[32] Objects for sale at the exposition often exhibited streamlining. Speedlines framed an image of a setback skyscraper surrounded by a log cabin and a tepee on a round glass flask with "A Century of Progress 1833–1933" stamped on it.[33] Even the official logo of the fair, reproduced on countless souvenirs, brochures, and other objects, featured energetic, curving speedlines.

In architecture speedlines initially appeared as decorative features on rectilinear buildings. One example at the fair was the entrance overhangs on the otherwise angular Travel and Transport Building. More-characteristic curving streamlines were found above the sculptures over the north entrance of the Hall of Social Science and along the courtyard of the Electrical Building. The most fully streamlined building at the Chicago fair in 1933 was a small pavilion sponsored by the Crane Company. The walls of the rectangular exhibit hall curved around the building, while speedlines served as guidelines for sans-serif lettering that wrapped around the building above the first floor. On top of the building, a vertical plane with rounded corners formed a backdrop for large letters that spelled the word *Crane.*

The aerodynamic aesthetic of streamlining was more prevalent during the fair's second season. Three fully streamlined vehicles—the high-speed, lightweight, *Burlington Zephyr* and Union Pacific *M-10,000* trains and Buckminster Fuller's three-wheeled, teardrop-shaped Dymaxion Car Number Three—were popular with fairgoers.[34] Several of the new pavilions, including the Swift Bridge and Open Air Theatre, also presented streamlined designs. The smooth aerodynamic form of the Hiram Walker and Sons' Canadian Club Café, affectionately referred to as the Doodlebug, led a writer for *Architectural Forum* to proclaim that the design could have come directly from the boards of Erich

FIG. 3.15. The Crane Company Building featured sans-serif lettering and streamline detailing. Kaufmann and Fabry, photographers.

FIG. 3.16. The streamlined *Burlington Zephyr* on display next to Chicago, Burlington, and Quincy's fifty-year-old locomotive No. 35 in the transportation area at A Century of Progress in 1934. Postcard from collection of author.

Mendelsohn, the German expressionist architect known for his curving, aerodynamic building forms.[35] Those intent on viewing the bottling of whiskey or wishing to dine in the building's café passed through a screen of tall piers before reaching the teardrop-shaped building, which tapered to a curved end that projected 400 feet into the lagoon (Plate 14).

The symbolic representations in the pavilion designs at A Century of Progress, which ranged from the subtle to the blatant, reflected a major and growing division in mid-twentieth-century American architecture. Designers favoring an academic modernism strove to present an architecture intellectually symbolic of the current age, whereas those interested in promoting a more commercial brand of modernism preferred the creation of symbolic forms that the masses could easily comprehend. While many architects and the cultural elite in the United States continued to favor looking toward Europe for a more sophisticated language of modernism, the second Chicago World's Fair served as a major impetus for the acceptance of a variety of modern building forms.

THE USE OF COLOR AT THE EXPOSITION

With ornate detailing of buildings becoming both less affordable and less academically acceptable, architects searched for new methods of creating aesthetically interesting designs that would not detract from the formal character of the building. While the International Style Show emphasized the use of white and neutral colors in modern architecture, in the years prior to the MoMA exhibit many progressive architects in both Europe and the United States found color an ideal alternative to applied ornament.[36] Fair architects used strong colors to achieve greater interest and unity in the architecture of A Century of Progress.[37] Workers sprayed the buildings with gallons of brightly colored paint, creating an aesthetically exciting modern atmosphere at a relatively low cost. The vivid reds, greens, oranges, and blues contrasted sharply with the more subtle colors used at earlier fairs, such as the light cream that had dominated the Court of Honor at the Columbian Exposition and the pastels that had covered the pavilions of 1915 Panama-Pacific Exposition in San Francisco.

An article in *Painters Magazine and Paint and Wall Paper Dealer* stated that the "inspiration of a painted exposition came from the needs of the architecture, the demands of the age and the desire to illustrate to the public not only the compelling power of color, but certain truths in its usefulness to architecture and its aid to comfort."[38] This increased interest in the use of bright hues at the end of the 1920s was widespread and was shared by designers in many areas beyond architecture, including manufacturing. The author of an article published in *Business Week* in connection with the opening of the exposition predicted that the carefully derived color scheme of the fairgrounds would offer an "object lesson in the use of color" for many industries.[39]

In the spring of 1932 the architectural commissioners hired Joseph Urban to develop a comprehensive color scheme for the Chicago fair. While most American designers had little experience with the potential effects of vivid hues in architecture, Urban had recently designed the colorful New School for Social Research in New York City. Although trained as an architect, he was better known in the United States for his brilliant stage sets for the Boston Opera Company, the Metropolitan Opera in New York, and the Ziegfeld Follies and for his numerous movie sets.[40] Urban's ability to produce dramatic environments that provided a sense of escape made him an ideal candidate to create the exposition's color palette.

In producing the chromatic composition for the fair, Urban carefully studied the spatial relationships among the main buildings and then chose specific colors to heighten and enliven effects already achieved in the buildings' designs.[41] He treated the different facades of the pavilions as individual elements while unifying the structures into an overall composition. According to *Painters Magazine and Paint and Wall Paper Dealer*, this handling of color bore a "resemblance to contemporary European practice which expresses the space or volume enclosed by the buildings in terms of articulated exterior planes."[42]

As alluded to in the article, a number of progressive architects in the Netherlands and Germany had tested the ability of color to define space during the mid- and late 1920s. Their ideas developed out of a scientific approach to the use of color based on discoveries by A. H. Munsell and others at the turn of the century. At that time, both scientists and artists began to describe colors in terms of hue, value, and chroma. By the end of the decade, a number of European designers, in particular

Josef Albers at the Bauhaus, attempted to understand the effects of color in design through various forms of analytical study.

Dutch architect Gerrit Rietveld, in collaboration with his client Truus Schröder, experimented with new color concepts developed by de Stijl artists, including Piet Mondrian and Theo Van Doesburg, in his design for the Schröder House in Utrecht. Rietveld and Schröder used pure primary colors, grays, and black to accentuate the walls, window mullions, and railings, as well as to explode aesthetically the individual surface planes of the avant-garde residence. The interior of the house includes red floors, blue and black walls, and solid-colored window covers designed to hang on the walls during the day.

More than any other progressive European architect, German designer Bruno Taut experimented with vivid color planes that attained results similar to those Urban later achieved at the Chicago fair. One significant example of Taut's use of intense hues to accentuate individual surfaces was his contribution to the 1927 Weissenhofsiedlung in Stuttgart. His small single-family model house led one contemporary critic to exclaim that the colors came "right out of the paint-box."[43] The ceiling was bright yellow, one wall bright blue, another bright red, and a third bright green, while the floor was painted black. Similar colors accentuated the individual exterior facades of the house. Both American and European architectural journals published Taut's and Rietveld's designs, making it probable that Urban had become familiar with their work by the time he began creating the color scheme for the Chicago fair.

In the United States public interest in color grew during the years when the exposition was planned and built. This was to a large extent due to the increased selection of colors becoming available in mass-produced items as manufacturers began realizing the role color options could play in increasing consumer consumption. By the end of the 1920s the public was no longer limited to driving a black automobile or washing dishes in a white kitchen sink. Recent developments in plastics made it possible to offer a choice of colors for a wide range of products, including tumblers, poker chips, and inexpensive jewelry. According to *Business Week*, the brightly colored bathroom fixtures and kitchen utensils that had recently come on the market were a sign of modern times (Plate 15).[44]

The rise in color choices in commercial products and the inherent meaning behind certain hues were topics of a number of influential articles in these years, offering some insight into the growing relationship between academic science and industry. *Fortune* magazine published a major article, "Color in Industry," in February 1930, just months before construction began on the first buildings at the fairgrounds. The article described Americans' recent release from their "chromatic inhibitions" as manufacturers began marketing household objects in colors with romantic, foreign names such as T'ang red, orchid of Vincennes, royal Copenhagen blue, and Ming green. The use of color in industry, according to the author, was a matter not just of fashion but of utility. Proper selection of colors could help improve the

FIG. 3.18. Model house designed by Bruno Taut for the Weissenhofsiedlung in Stuttgart in 1927. Intense hues accentuate the individual surfaces. From Norman N. Rice, "Small House Construction: A Problem to Be Solved," *Architectural Forum* 55 (August 1931): 222.

"identification, attention, and standardization" of companies and their products.[45] By *standardization* the author meant the use of color to reinforce the traditional symbolic meanings of specific hues.

In order to understand the underlying connotations of various colors, scientists in these years began examining the potential psychological effect of color. By the time of the exposition's opening, Maud Maple Miles had been studying and preaching the psychological effects of color for at least a decade. She attempted to educate industry on the ability of certain colors to improve factory production, not only by enhancing light distribution in work spaces and creating greater efficiency by color-coordinating objects but also by improving the disposition and morale of employees.[46]

In a brochure highlighting the use of their paint at A Century of Progress, the American Asphalt Paint Company also discussed the psychological role of color. It claimed that when used intelligently, color "can induce happiness instead of sadness. It can produce alertness or drowsiness, comfort or discomfort, perfect vision or indistinctness. . . . Color amuses, fascinates or annoys, inspires or disheartens, excites or repels, exaggerates or undervalues."[47] To promote the benefits of using color paint in building, the American Asphalt Paint Company and other paint manufacturers pooled approximately a million dollars for advertising these ideas in 1933.[48]

The application of bright colors in American architecture lagged significantly behind their use in consumer goods. In 1928 Leon E. Stanhope, president of the Illinois Society of Architects, declared that color was "coming into building exteriors more and more frequently in Europe and in the business centers of American cities" as a replacement for expensive applied ornament.[49] However, even through the 1920s, architectural color resided primarily in plastic and in nonessential ornamentation.[50] A critic writing in the journal *Architect* in 1929 reported that the use of color was particularly timid in skyscrapers. He blamed the lack of color in architecture on clients, who he believed were "loath to embark on any very opulent use of color," as they wished to "play safe and do nothing that will knock their neighbors' eyes out."[51]

Unwilling clients, however, did not deserve all the blame. Acceptance of past taboos regarding the use of vivid color in architecture, particularly during the recent wave of neoclassicism, continued.[52] The author of an unsigned *Fortune* article exclaimed that although "color is itself ornament and may be applied boldly to the very structure of a skyscraper, [its use] is still held to be advanced and possibly dangerous thinking."[53] Some progressive designers believed that covering building materials with paint was dishonest and instead favored the use of products in their natural state. However, many of the new building materials used at the Chicago fair, such as gypsum board, could not stand up to rain or sun and hence were unsuitable for exterior use without a layer of paint or some other covering for protection against the elements.[54]

The writer of the *Fortune* article also proclaimed that, as of 1930, America had not yet witnessed a significant architectural effort that incorporated an unreserved use of color. The country had to wait three more years before experiencing the first major exploration into the potential of color in modern architecture at the Chicago fair. Joseph Urban's own New School for Social Research, however, did provide a hint of things to come. The seven-story building included black window spandrels, window frames, and brick. Inside the designer specified that the window frames and column surfaces on each floor be a different, vivid color. Yellow, green, and vermilion were visible from the exterior through large horizontal bands of windows.[55]

A major reason why architects had not previously specified the use of bold spans of bright hues in their designs was the lack of stability in colored paint. Most types of brightly colored paint available in the early 1930s began to fade as soon as they were exposed to the elements. The architectural commission eventually selected the most promising product for protecting the exteriors of the exposition buildings—a new type of casein paint produced by the American Asphalt Paint Company, chosen for its ability to maintain clear, bright hues on exterior wall surfaces for the full fair season.

In an article published in *World's Fair Weekly* (one of the official publications of A Century of Progress), Urban's assistant Otto Teegen gave three major reasons for the application of colored paint to the over 10.5 million square feet of wall surfaces.[56] First, color helped unify the individual exhibition halls into a cohesive design. Unlike the Columbian Exposition, with its predominantly classical building forms, the 1933 exposition included a wide range of building designs, which presented a chaotic composition. Teegen went on to assert that color made the flat surfaces of the pavilions more interesting, in particular those buildings without major decorative features. He also stated that it would help create a festive atmosphere.[57] His boss, Urban, hoped that providing an environment that contrasted sharply with the dingy gray buildings in the Chicago Loop would allow people to leave their everyday cares and troubles behind them while attending the exposition and "be conscious only of the joys of living."[58]

Urban's color scheme consisted of twenty-four of the "strongest, clearest, purest, [and] most direct pigments available," including brilliant blues, yellows, reds, and oranges, as well as greens, grays, black, silver, and gold.[59] Only 20 percent of the buildings' surfaces were white.[60] Additional color came from bright flags and banners, as well as from the thousands of people clothed in various hues moving through the fairgrounds (Plate 16).

Urban likened his use of color to that of keys and melodies in a musical composition. By specifying particular hues, he was able to tie groups of buildings together in color themes. He also carefully considered the orientation of the various facades in his color layout. Cool colors were favored for the north walls, neutral colors for the east and west walls, and warm colors for the south walls. Cool colors were also used to emphasize recesses (Plate 17).[61]

In a few instances the color choices had specific symbolic meanings. For example, the yellow-and-blue facades of the Swedish Pavilion recalled the colors of that country's flag. Owing to red's close association with communism, the architectural commissioners specifically rejected its use around the north lagoon near the U.S. Government Building.[62]

Saturated colors also appeared inside the exposition pavilions. Shepard Vogelgesang, an assistant to Urban, was responsible for the interior coloration. He selected colors based on practical considerations, such as whether the exhibit space needed to be dark or required ample light. Vogelgesang created what he referred to as the "follow the green line" concept, in which he gave colors specific symbolic meaning. For example, in the Hall of Science yellow indicated industrial exhibits; blue-red, the medical area; and turquoise-blue, the general science section.[63] The three colors came together in circulation areas, including at ramps and staircases.[64] In the Great Hall of the building, Vogelgesang specified white, light gray, electric blue, midnight blue, aluminum, and gold. Its vast ceiling contained stripes of dark blue to help conceal light fixtures (Plate 18).[65]

After Joseph Urban died in July 1933, Vogelgesang took over as head color consultant. When organizers decided to reopen the exposition for a second season, they hired Vogelgesang to develop a new color scheme that would give the fairgrounds a fresh and brilliant appearance by offering the public a new and different color spectacle.[66] The result was an exposition colored with larger spans of fewer hues. The palette consisted of eight new colors that ranged from orange-red to turquoise to a rich, sumptuous purple-red.[67]

Vogelgesang selected specific colors for various zones of the fairgrounds in his design. Each vista had a uniform color scheme. For the center of the fairgrounds by the Hall of Science the artist specified red and red-blue. Near the Agriculture Building, red and orange dominated. He favored blue and green around the General Exhibits Building, while red-orange denoted the horticultural area.[68]

Another major change to the color scheme was the increased use of white. In contrast to 1933, when approximately 20 percent of building surfaces had been painted white, somewhere between 35 and 38 percent received a coat of white paint in 1934.[69] It was generously used as a transitional color between the zones, as well as in the transportation area. Even the immense Travel and Transport Building, which had been painted red and black when initially constructed and then green for the opening of the exposition, was drained of its color. The official reason

for the increased use of white was that colored electric lights showed up better against it at night.[70] However, since white walls tend to wash out colored light, there must have been other reasons. One possible explanation was a waning interest in the use of brilliant colors in modern architecture by the mid-1930s.

FIG. 3.19. Railroad Hall of the Travel and Transport Building, with a fresh coat of white paint for the 1934 fair season. Kaufmann and Fabry, photographers.

Vogelgesang, well versed in the psychological effects of color, changed the hues of the flags and banners according to the day's temperature. He lined the Avenue of Flags with red banners on cool days and blue banners on warm days in an attempt to neutralize the psychological effects of the climate (Plates 19 and 20). In direct contrast to his predecessor, Vogelgesang favored cool colors on the warmer south sides of the pavilions and warmer colors in areas that were typically hidden in shadows.[71] He also took advantage of the ability of bright, warm colors to make objects appear closer. For example, red was substituted for blue on many of the buildings on Northerly Island to make it seem nearer to the mainland in the hope of encouraging more people to cross the lagoon and visit the pavilions located on the other side.[72]

The use of color at the fair successfully contributed to the creation of a unique and festive setting that helped separate the exposition from the everyday architecture of the surrounding city. Like the contemporary atmospheric and art deco movie theaters, the colorful fair offered a stimulating escape from the grim reality of the Depression. The application of paint also fulfilled the more practical purpose of providing an inexpensive method for weatherproofing exposed surfaces while offering a low-cost, modern way of decorating buildings without relying on the use of applied ornament. The exposition's color symphony did not end at sunset but continued into the evening through the extensive application of dramatic electric lighting effects that projected streams of various hues onto the pavilions and into the night sky.

INNOVATIVE LIGHTING AT THE FAIR

In addition to the spectacular nightly relighting of the fairgrounds from energy generated and amplified from the light of the star Arcturus, the exposition included such innovative lighting features as flashing or evolving patterns of color or intensity, which attracted attention through movement. The fair used more electric lighting than any single event up to this time. It also offered the first major decorative application of several recently developed forms of lighting, including neon and ultraviolet.

The 1933–34 Chicago World's Fair was not the first international event to demonstrate new technological developments in electricity and lighting. The Centennial International Exposition held in Philadelphia in 1876, for example, introduced the Welsbach gas burner to the public. The first major use of carbon-filament incandescent lighting took place at the 1893 World's Columbian Exposition, where strings of lights outlined buildings. The concept of "floodlighting," using pastel color transparencies and glass jewels to achieve wondrous effects, was introduced at the Panama-Pacific fair in 1915. Fourteen years later, at the Exposición Internacional de Barcelona, innovative colored lights swept over the fairgrounds in rhythmic cycles controlled from a central station, to great popular acclaim.[73]

The late 1920s and early 1930s were a time of creative development in exterior electric lighting. According to a 1933 article in *Literary Digest,* although the art of outdoor lighting was still in its infancy, the Chicago exposition marked a distinct advancement in its development.[74] Four months before the scheduled opening of the fair, organizers hired the General Electric Company and the Westinghouse Electric and Manufacturing Company to design the exterior lighting.[75] General Electric's Walter D'Arcy Ryan was placed in charge of overseeing the process.[76] In their attempt to determine the most appropriate and exciting lighting techniques, scientists carried out tests in laboratories located in the Administration Building.[77] As with color, a major goal in the application of decorative lighting was to consolidate the buildings into a unified whole.[78] Ryan also used lighting to increase the exposition's presence in the Chicago area by projecting moving beams of light into the evening sky to form colorful beacons that were visible for miles. Like a yard light attracting bugs, the beams attracted large crowds of visitors to the event.

Designers favored indirect lighting for almost all the illumination at the fair.

Lighting close to the ground was soft and diffused, while the lights on towers and piers radiated brilliantly. The effect was like that of a city on a misty morning when the tops of tall buildings are brightly lit by direct sunlight that has yet to reach the ground. Intense pools of light filled building recesses, which silhouetted projecting areas.[79] In an article describing the illumination of the exposition, published in *Architectural Forum*, Ryan identified six types of lighting incorporated into the event. They included street, path, and bridge lighting; exterior surface lighting; building outlining and decorative lighting; water lighting; spectacular lighting; and indoor lighting.[80]

Street lighting standards concealed or subdued their source wherever possible to avoid unnecessary glare and to prevent blocking views. All standards were required to be "simple, direct, and economical in design"; one example, a mushroom-shaped lamp with a translucent, colored Micarta shade, was used to illuminate minor roads, paths, and garden areas.[81]

FIG. 3.20. Various examples of lighting standards at the fairgrounds. From W. D'Arcy Ryan, "Lighting 'A Century of Progress,'" *Electrical Engineering* 53 (May 1934): 735.

The Chicago exposition presented one of the first major attempts to create dramatic effects by using floodlights to deliberately combine colored lighting with colored wall surfaces.[82] Designers found that floodlights close in color to the illuminated surfaces provided the best results.[83] Like the street lighting, the floodlights had concealed bulbs to prevent irritating glare. The step-back forms on some of the pavilions, particularly those with multilevel terraces, such as the Hall of Science, made it difficult to illuminate some building surfaces successfully. Workers created various types of screens and shields that harmonized with the pavilion designs to avoid views directly into exposed lights from elevated walkways and other raised platforms.

Outlining and decorating the pavilions with gaseous tubes, as on the Hall of Science, provided one of the most exciting and innovative uses of electric lighting at the exposition. According to Charles Borland, the general manager of Federal Electric Company (the firm responsible for providing the gaseous lighting), at the time organizers first began to discuss lighting the fair, no major installations of neon tubes for architectural illumination existed in the United States.[84] Claude Neon, a French firm that had patented the process of creating gaseous tubes in 1915, held a virtual monopoly on its manufacture. Prior to 1932, when the patent expired, the company was selling franchise licenses for $100,000 each plus royalties, making neon lighting prohibitively expensive. The technique for gaseous lighting had not even been introduced in the United States until 1923, and when it did appear it was limited primarily to advertising signs.[85] Interest in neon signs, however, grew significantly at the end of the 1920s, as did the number of craftsmen creating gaseous tubing without official licenses.

FIG. 3.21. Chrysler Building at night. Hedrich-Blessing, photographers (HB-01718-X). Courtesy of Chicago History Museum.

FOUNTAIN AND COURT OF ELECTRICAL GROUP

Fortunately for the fair designers, the patent expired just in time for the exposition, paving the way for A Century of Progress to present the first major application of gaseous tubes in architectural lighting.

FIG. 3.22. Morning Glory Fountain in front of the neon "waterfall" on the facade of the Electrical Building. Postcard from collection of author.

The neon tubing concealed in metal channels on the exterior of the fair's headquarters served as a model for the application of the more than 40,000 feet of gaseous lighting used to decorate major pavilions, including the Hall of Science, the Havoline Thermometer, and the U.S. Government, Agriculture, General Exhibits, General Motors, and Chrysler buildings.[86] One of the most striking examples of gaseous lighting at the exposition was the cascade "fountain" located on the facade of the Electrical Building. The initial plans called for a waterfall, but the cost of sending 90,000 gallons of water per minute down the facade of the building led Hood and the other designers to search for a more affordable alternative.[87] Electric lighting presented a less expensive, yet still appropriate, option for a decorative feature symbolizing the use of hydroelectric power.[88] The final design's seven fifty-five-foot-tall blue cascades incorporated over 4,600 feet of the reported 7,900–12,000 feet of gaseous tubing that decorated the pavilion.[89]

Water features presented another category of innovative lighting design at the exposition. Because of the relatively high cost of creating interesting water effects, only two major aquatic elements incorporating lighting were initially built. The first, the huge, seventy-foot-tall Morning Glory Fountain in front of the Electrical Building, contained 135 underwater floodlights that slowly changed color. The floodlights, along with 500 jets of water, guaranteed a brilliant evening show. The second, a large triple fountain in the lagoon, drew the attention of fairgoers by including constantly changing lights. While the outer two major water jets contained plain white lights, eight distinct, elaborate water effects, each lasting seventy-five seconds, took place in the central fountain, creating a ten-minute cycle of evolving hues.[90]

Ryan's category of spectacular lighting effects included two other major features that nighttime fairgoers could not miss. On the roof of the Electrical Building a huge white fan of seventeen movable, thirty-six-inch, incandescent searchlights projected 21 million candlepower of light into the evening sky. The result was the largest battery of incandescent searchlights employed for special effects up to that time.[91] Not to be outdone, at the south end of the grounds the Aurora Borealis show used cascading clouds of chemical vapor dropped from airplanes to reflect light emanating from a scintillator composed of twenty-four army-type searchlights similar to those used to light Niagara Falls.[92] The brightness of the lights equaled a staggering 1.440 billion candlepower. Trained attendants overseeing the searchlights changed color filters and positioned each beam in a prearranged schedule, creating a nightly show of fireless fireworks in the sky.[93] The result was not only an exciting culmination to a long day of overstimulation for visitors. It was also an important source of advertising for the event, as the fair designers once again relied upon motion to attract and hold the public's attention. In this case, the audience was located all over Chicago, as the ever-changing colorful glow in the sky could be seen for miles around (Plate 25).

In sharp contrast to the glass-walled Crystal Palace of 1851, the windowless buildings at the Chicago fair needed artificial lighting at all times. The chief benefit was that constant light levels could be maintained on the interior displays. Major hallways and exhibits were lit both by indirect lighting and by novel, decorative electrical features. The main lighting for the standard display areas consisted of aluminum reflectors and ground-glass discs secured to suspended ceilings with metal spring clips. Indirect lighting from backlit cutout signs on the fronts of exhibit space brightened the corridors.[94] Approximately 2,100 feet of red neon lined four setbacks along the grand staircase in the Electrical Building. The interior of the Great Hall in the Hall of Science contained 600 feet of blue and green tubing that stretched the full length of the room.[95]

Many of the exhibitors employed elaborate lighting effects that incorporated ever-changing color and light levels to draw attention to their displays. Westinghouse presented one of the liveliest demonstrations of novel lighting. Dedicated as a living monument to the company's founder, George Westinghouse, the display included eight columns composed of semicircular trays ten feet in diameter and four feet apart. Lit from within, they formed stacks of constantly changing colored discs. Under the columns, the word *Westinghouse* was spelled out in sheet metal letters lit from below. Floodlighting provided additional interest to this and many other exhibit areas.[96] In the Travel and Transport Building, a lamp that projected light onto the canvas-covered walls created gigantic color patterns that were synchronized to music. In the Owens-Illinois Glass-Block Building, colored gaseous

tubes, concealed behind a molded glass element, ran the entire length of the tower. On the interior, portable fixtures projected light onto the ceiling, providing indirect lighting to the pavilion's wings.[97] The result was an opulent, multicolor glass sensation.

Organizers promoted additions to the lighting program at the 1934 fair along with its new color scheme. According to C. W. Cutler, a lighting engineer, the night effects were notably brighter and offered more satisfying spectacles than during the previous year.[98] Fairgoers perceived the exposition as brighter not only because the total illumination of the event increased from approximately 21 billion to 30 billion candlepower, but also because more of the building surfaces were painted white, which reflected a larger percentage of that light.[99] Fair designers introduced additional novel lighting features in their attempt to draw the public back to the event. To help bring greater interest to the two towers of the Skyride, streamers of frosted white light bulbs that ended in bursts of red light were added to the connecting cables.[100] Two bands of neon tubing framed the observation platform windows on each tower.[101] At the north end of the fairgrounds, sixteen high-intensity arc searchlights were added to the Planetarium Bridge, which balanced the scintillator at the other end of the grounds.[102]

Connected to the Planetarium Bridge was a new fountain located in the North Lagoon—another major electrical feature introduced at the 1934 exposition. The

FIG. 3.23. The Westinghouse Company display featured novel lighting effects, including stacks of constantly changing colored discs. From *Official World's Fair in Pictures: Chicago 1933* (Chicago: Reuben H. Donnelley, 1933), n.p.

FIG. 3.24. Night photograph of the 150-foot-diameter water dome and Triple Fountain with the scintillator in the background. From Museum of Science and Industry, Chicago.

fountain's water jets culminated in a dome of water 150 feet in diameter. Underwater floodlights illuminated the entire 670-foot-long fountain. Jets sent approximately 68,000 gallons of water per minute into the air. Green, amber, red, blue, and white lights created an ever-changing colorful effect that could be controlled either automatically or manually (Plate 26).[103]

The most lavish new use of electric lighting at the exposition in 1934 was on the Ford Pavilion. Henry Ford, realizing he had made a major mistake in declining to participate the previous year, sponsored a magnificent new pavilion designed by Albert Kahn. The building required over 100 miles of electrical wire and used 7 billion candlepower, more than two-thirds of the brightness added to the fair in 1934.[104] The lighting design incorporated double rows of over 5,600 red, blue, and green fixtures on dimmers located inside three circular setbacks at the top of the gear-shaped rotunda.[105] For the first time, designers compensated for the loss in light intensity due to the colored surfaces by differentially increasing the wattage of the various colors of bulbs.[106] The Torch of Light, the most elaborate decorative lighting element in the Ford Building, consisted of twenty-four thirty-six-inch searchlights that together projected an intensity of 600 million candle-power into the night sky.

Other innovative types of lighting were also introduced at the fair in 1934. Westinghouse presented the first public demonstration of the high-pressure mercury-vapor lamp in its corporate display. More than 500 of the long tubular fixtures gave off an intense green-blue light in an exhibit that highlighted the fact that these lamps could provide twice as much light for the same power consumption as ordinary incandescent bulbs.[107] Another new type of lighting effect at the exposition used fluorescent paint in connection with gaseous tubes for floodlighting.[108] The novelty paint, developed by scientists connected with the fair, emitted a "weird glow" when electric light reflected from its surfaces.[109] The engineering staff of the Westinghouse exhibit also successfully demonstrated ultraviolet light. A Century of Progress press release predicted that "in the days immediately to come it [ultraviolet] will work magic in all of our homes."[110]

The groundbreaking forms of illumination offered dramatic alternatives to the elaborate show-stopping features, such as the massive Tower of Water, that had been eliminated from the plans because of financial constraints. More significantly, the electric features served as major landmarks for the fair during the evening hours. For the participating electric companies, the event offered the opportunity to demonstrate the potential of innovative lighting in architecture. The Federal Electric Company, for example, made a concerted effort to use the exposition to promote its gaseous tubes as a decorative feature of modern buildings. Robert Barclay, their director of research, provided "light-seeing" tours of the fairgrounds. According to an article published in the *Chicago Daily News*, those who took these tours were primarily architects, builders, and designers of business and domestic structures.[111]

Although early designs for the Chicago exposition followed popular stylistic developments in the field, the architects soon adopted new decorative forms, specifically appropriate for the temporary event, that incorporated innovative uses of color and electric lighting. They derived aesthetic features from the characteristics of new building materials and processes, and in doing so they created a financially feasible event at a time when few supplemental resources were available. Although the architectural commissioners did not promote their pavilion designs as models for everyday architecture, the fact that the buildings were viewed by millions of fairgoers helped increase public acceptance for their forms. While the exposition buildings varied widely, ranging from plain, box-shaped containers to huge, iconic forms, they were unified by the use of recently introduced building materials and techniques and by the seductive applications of color and light.

FOUR

BUILDING INNOVATIONS AT THE EXPOSITION

In addition to all our old familiar materials, with their respective developments, we now have a whole new world of synthetic and prefabricated materials—an ever-increasing group of ferrous and non-ferrous metals and their alloys, new products in the age-old field of ceramics and glass. We have new finishes—paints, varnishes, and nitrocellulose lacquers. Then there are the endless applications of new and old engineering ideas in structural products and in sanitation, heating, ventilation, air conditioning, refrigeration and illumination. Little wonder that in the practice of architecture it is beyond the power of any one individual to follow all of its branches.

JAMES B. NEWMAN, "The Architect and New Materials"

Driving the various formal designs of the architecture for the Century of Progress International Exposition was the incorporation of an amazing variety of new building products and processes. Many of the innovative ideas in building construction exhibited at the fair developed as the result of dramatic changes that took place during and after the First World War. The building materials division of the War Industries Board had established uniform specifications in the design of war-related building projects, and after the war commercial industries continued to standardize specifications as they adapted materials developed for the war to meet peacetime needs. Thus government and scientific technology played bigger roles in the building industry, and almost all aspects of construction, including carpentry, wiring, and plumbing, as well as building materials, came to be standardized. A need for a significant increase in efficiency in construction during the 1920s provided the impetus for the continuation of scientific development in the field. According to figures compiled by the National Research Council, approximately 300 companies employed 9,300 researchers in 1920. By the end of the decade, this number had increased sixfold.[1] Advances in experimental laboratories resulted in new structural techniques and in the introduction of numerous synthetic and prefabricated building products to meet the need for lighter and more durable facing materials.[2] Products that underwent mechanical manipulation during production, such

Rows of identical Quonset hut chicken coops in the
Poultry Farm exhibit (detail).

as plywood, Masonite Presdwood, and gypsum board, were both stronger and less expensive materials than those available naturally. The increase during the 1920s in scientific experiments in nonaesthetic aspects of building design, such as insulation and acoustical control, led to the development of new generations of products that invisibly contributed to improving the comfort of indoor living.

Even as construction starts significantly declined in the early 1930s, the number of newly available materials and methods of building continued to rise. This increase resulted from the need to lower costs for all types of construction through the use of products that could reduce installation labor and that weighed less to transport.[3] An article on mass-produced houses in *Fortune* declared 1933 the "natal-year of pre-fabrication" as designers began adapting mass-production concepts developed by the automobile manufacturers and other major commercial industries to building construction.[4] Many businesses, including steel corporations, cement companies, and raw material producers not traditionally connected to the building industry, viewed the tremendous urgency for decent affordable housing in these years as a huge untapped market with the potential to cure their own ailing finances.[5] Often these companies diverted large portions of their limited available resources to developing new building materials from the same raw materials they had used to manufacture other commercial goods prior to the collapse of the economy. Many of these products were introduced to the public at A Century of Progress. Included was an ever-growing group of ferrous and nonferrous metals and alloys, new types of ceramics and glass, and innovative synthetic materials. Companies also exhibited new finishing products, such as paints, varnishes, and lacquers, and countless new applications of more traditional materials.[6]

With the downturn of the economy after 1929, the building industry faced major changes. Many small companies disappeared, and those that did survive turned to new strategies for promoting their products. Some began placing eye-catching ads in popular magazines, such as *Good Housekeeping* and *Popular Mechanics*, in addition to continuing to advertise in trade journals. Architectural publications, which had fewer newly completed buildings to highlight during these years, greatly increased the number of pages dedicated to discussions of new building products and processes. An article in *Architectural Record* in April 1933, for example, contained detailed descriptions of recently introduced materials and methods in the building trades. The stated purpose of the piece was to enable designers to compare current methods and products for residential building.[7] *Architectural Forum* published a large article titled "New Materials and Methods in Country House Construction" in March 1933 that described recently introduced building products and methods.[8] It devoted over twenty pages of the June 1934 issue to information about dozens of different innovative man-made materials and products available to meet modern construction needs. The promotion of new construction materials and techniques at trade fairs and other expositions helped demonstrate the latest innovations in the building industry directly to the public, as well as to designers and builders. Although the fair was held at the nadir of the Depression, many firms took full advantage of A Century of Progress to promote the benefits of their modern building products and techniques.

DEVELOPMENTS IN STRUCTURAL SYSTEMS

Designers of the Chicago World's Fair looked toward new structural ideas for inspiration in the creation of novel, modern-looking buildings. Two major developments in roofing—thin concrete shells and suspended roofs—highlight the advances in structural systems introduced at the event. Both incorporated thin-membrane roofs able to span large distances. Other structural developments featured at the exposition included innovative low-cost pile footings, which offered a better alternative to spread footings (wide shallow footings, usually of reinforced concrete) on the relatively unstable fairground site, and a new system of steel framing, ideally suited to the thin-panel construction of most of the pavilions' facades.

The Travel and Transport Building presented the most prominent structural innovation at the Chicago fair. The massive pavilion, nearly 1,000 feet long, housed two enormous display halls. The first, which held exhibits relating to the steamship industry, was a rectangular space 220 feet long (large enough to hold a full-scale model of a steamship). The other, a colossal rotunda 206 feet in diameter and approximately 120 feet tall, was dedicated to railroad displays. The steamship area was roofed by three-hinged steel trusses.

FIG. 4.1. Travel and Transport Building, showing both the Railroad Hall and the linear Steamship Hall. Postcard from collection of author.

The structural design of the Railroad Hall was significantly more complex and aesthetically more interesting.[9] Designed to enclose a turntable displaying the latest in locomotive designs, the rotunda protruded from the main body of the pavilion, providing a visual focus for fairgoers and critics.[10] While newspapers and other publications were wrong in calling the space the largest domed interior in the world, the structure was significant for incorporating the first major suspended roof in the United States.[11] Instead of hiding the structural system behind an ornate facade, as had the architects of the neoclassical pavilions at the earlier Chicago exposition, the designers of the Travel and Transport Building proudly exhibited the structural system of the Railroad Hall in full view on the exterior. Incorporating technology originally used for the construction of tents and suspension bridges, a steel-paneled drum was secured by cables that traveled upward from the roof to the tops of twelve 150-foot-tall steel towers that encircled the hall. The cables then continued down to anchors at the outer edge of a broader, lower level of the building, giving the pavilion its insectlike form.[12]

FIG. 4.2. Structural details for the suspended roof of the Travel and Transport Building. From "Cable System to Support 200-Ft. Circular Roof," *Engineering News-Record* 106 (8 January 1931): 73.

The use of a suspended roof with structural towers placed along the outer wall eliminated the need for columns that would otherwise have interfered with the open interior space. A catenary deck hung from large cables that ran across the roof between the towers.[13] Placed on rocker bases, the towers were back-guyed by anchoring cables that traveled through

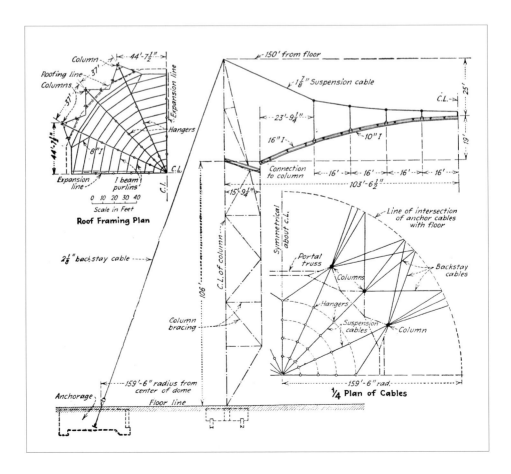

wing gusset plates at the tops of the columns to concrete counterweights below.[14] The designers took great care to ensure that the Railroad Hall could handle a major surge in live load.[15] Without the weight of a regular truss system, the dead load of the roof was extremely small. Increased stress from even a minimal amount of extra weight, such as the presence of snow, or a minor change in temperature or atmospheric pressure, stretched the cables, forcing the structure to shift.[16] Fortunately, the design of what came to be popularly known as the Breathing Dome allowed for significant expansion and contraction—as much as a six-foot change in the circumference of the roof and up to an eighteen-inch shift in height.[17]

According to Major Lenox Lohr, the manager of A Century of Progress, the initial concept for the suspended dome was first suggested during a meeting he attended with a group of engineers. In discussing the needs for a transportation pavilion, he asked how a roof could be supported over a large hall while still allowing the space underneath to be completely unobstructed. Someone, partly in jest, exclaimed, "skyhooks"—a close description of what was eventually used, as the towers located around the exterior of the Railroad Hall formed hooks for the cables that supported the roof.[18]

While the Travel and Transport Building provided the first example in the United States of a suspended system to support a domed structure, the structural concept had a long history.[19] In a paper presented to the Western Society of Engineers, Clarence W. Farrier, assistant director of works for the 1933–34 Chicago World's Fair, correctly pointed out that the basic concept of this type of system had been used for centuries.[20] At least as far back as the first century AD the Romans had incorporated suspended awnings called *velaria* to cover seating areas in ancient theaters and amphitheaters, including the Colosseum.[21] According to the exposition engineers, nineteenth-century circus tents provided the most direct source of inspiration in regard to scale and function.[22] Their large canvas roofs, usually supported by four tall masts placed toward the corners of the structure, were, as in the design of the Railroad Hall, stabilized by rigging staked into the ground beyond the perimeter of the structure.[23]

The development of suspended roof systems in more permanent modern buildings began in Europe during the first half of the nineteenth century. The designers of the Travel and Transport Building, and in particular its engineer Bert Thorud, undoubtedly knew about these buildings through engineering texts and journal articles. One such piece, "Large Roofs Suspended by Cables to Avoid Columns," published in *Engineering News-Record* in October 1921, documents the first known uses of suspended structural systems for buildings. It includes a theater in Stráznice, Moravia, designed by B. Schnirch in 1823–24, which is believed to have been the first suspended roof incorporated into a major permanent building in modern times.[24]

The architects of the Chicago exposition may have also been aware of the use of suspended roof systems in unrealized schemes for previous American fairs. The earliest recorded example, a submission by James Bogardus and his partner Hamilton Hoppin for the 1853 New York Exposition, is believed to have been the first proposed use of a suspended roof for a semipermanent building in the United States.[25] The design for this glass exposition palace included a circular amphitheater, approximately 400 feet in diameter, with a sheet-iron roof suspended by either rods or chains in a catenary curve supported from a central, cast-iron tower 300 feet high.[26] As in the major pavilions at the 1933–34 world's fair, supporters promoted this earlier, unbuilt exposition building as being able to be prefabricated and constructed out of reusable materials.[27] In 1890 E. S. Jennison published an unrealized design for the 1893 World's Columbian Exposition in which the whole fair was to be held under a gigantic suspended tent— a concept later promoted by Frank Lloyd Wright in an unbuilt scheme for A Century of Progress.[28] In Jennison's project, cables were to extend from a single central pylon 1,000 feet tall to form a round interior space 3,000 feet in diameter inside a structure of corrugated metal and glass.[29]

The Chicago members of the architectural commission who designed the Travel and Transport Building were well aware of a contemporary building design that contained a suspended structural system—Buckminster Fuller's Dymaxion House. The futuristic-looking, hexagonal dwelling consisted of a central mast from which the floors and roof were suspended. Soon after the inventor patented the design as the "4-D" model house in April 1928, it was published in the *Chicago Evening Post*. The first public exhibition of the Dymaxion House design was held in Chicago at Marshall Field's department store in 1929, within blocks of the local architectural

FIG. 4.3 *(below).* James Bogardus's proposed Crystal Palace design for the 1853 New York Exposition, which included a circular amphitheater with a suspended sheet-iron roof. From Benjamin Silliman Jr. and C. R. Goodrich, *The World of Science, Art, and Industry, Illustrated from Examples in the New-York Exhibition, 1853–54* (New York: G. P. Putnam and Company, 1854), 4. FIG. 4.4 *(facing).* Dymaxion House by Buckminster Fuller, featuring floors suspended from a central mast. Courtesy of the Estate of R. Buckminster Fuller.

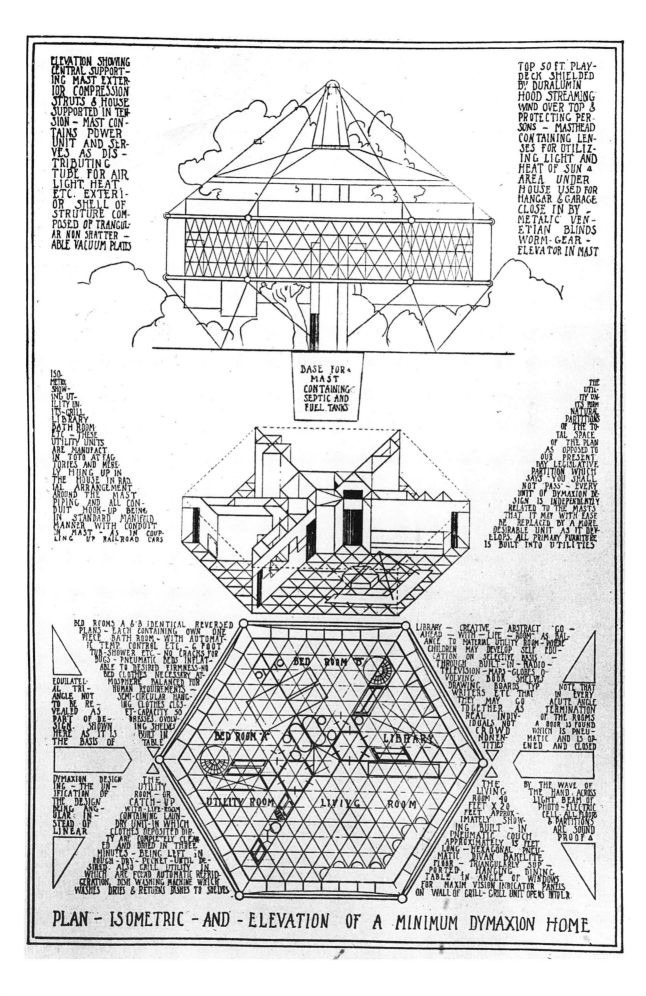

PLAN - ISOMETRIC - AND - ELEVATION OF A MINIMUM DYMAXION HOME

commissioners' downtown offices.[30] Chicagoans learned more about the ideas behind the house the following year when Fuller presented a lecture, titled "The Fundamentals of Dymaxion Design," at the Chicago Arts Club.[31]

The Railroad Hall of the Travel and Transport Building was not the only structure designed for A Century of Progress to incorporate post-and-tension technology. The creation of other buildings with similar structural systems reveals a growing interest in those concepts among architects and engineers. One unrealized project for the fair, a hockey arena, produced by Klekamp and Whitmore in 1932, included a roof composed of cables that traveled out from the center to points along the exterior wall. This resulted in a concave covering that sloped downward toward the center of the building (in contrast to the convex dome of the Travel and Transport Building). As in the design of the Railroad Hall, back-guys traveled from piers on top of the arena, but in this case to bollards situated beyond the roofed structure.[32]

The gigantic Skyride, which dominated the fairgrounds, also featured a suspended structural system.[33] Billed as the tallest man-made structure west of the Atlantic Ocean, the Skyride illustrated the post-and-tension principle used for the roof of the Travel and Transport Building's Railroad Hall.[34] The design incorporated over 100 miles of cable that ran like rays of the sun from each side of the tops of the towers to locations along lower horizontal cables. Located 210 feet above the lake, the lower cables held the double-decker rocket cars of aluminum, steel, and glass that traveled between the two large towers.[35] Additional cables stretched from both the 200-foot-high platforms and the peaks of the towers to counterweights and anchorages located approximately 600 feet behind each tower. The result was an elegant web of steel.[36]

With the Tower of Water eliminated from the final fair scheme, the Skyride filled the need for a dominant vertical element that could provide

FIG. 4.5. Preliminary drawings for the gigantic Skyride attraction. From William G. Grove, "Transporter Suspension Bridge to Thrill World's Fair Visitors," *Engineering News-Record* 109 (11 August 1932): 172.

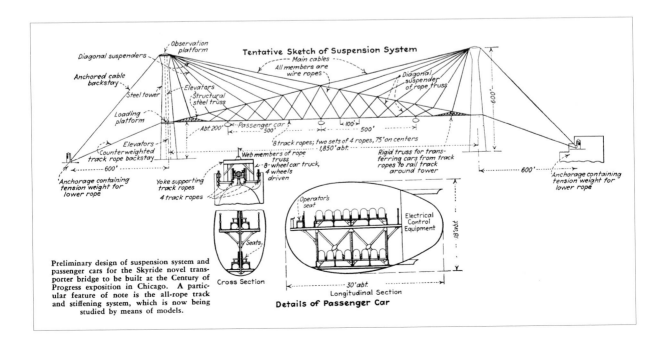

Preliminary design of suspension system and passenger cars for the Skyride novel transporter bridge to be built at the Century of Progress exposition in Chicago. A particular feature of note is the all-rope track and stiffening system, which is now being studied by means of models.

a symbolic landmark for the exposition.[37] It was originally designed to be located in the north and south lagoons, but the architectural commission moved the west tower just south of Soldier Field and the east tower north of the Electrical Building in the final site plan.[38] Orienting the Skyride in this direction gave fairgoers an additional means of reaching Northerly Island. The sleek steel-frame towers and the futuristic, streamlined cars passing above the fairgrounds presented a clear symbol of the fair's scientific theme. A major highlight for many fairgoers, the Skyride thrilled the more than 2.5 million people who rode on it during the 1933 fair season.[39]

Less conspicuous than either the Travel and Transport Building or the Skyride, the small building put up by the Brook Hill Farm Dairy introduced another innovative structural system to the American public: the thin-shell concrete roof.[40] Not built until the second season of the fair, the dairy, located at the far south end of the fairgrounds even beyond the transportation area, was easily overlooked. Its construction, however, was just as significant as that of the prominent suspended-steel structures. The Brook Hill Farm built its model dairy primarily to exhibit the latest advances in the "scientific production of milk."[41] Designed by architect Richard Philipp of Milwaukee and structural engineer John Ernst Kalinka from the Chicago engineering firm of Roberts and Schaefer, the concrete dairy consisted of a stable, a milking parlor, and a bottling plant.[42] Individual, hygienic stalls in the stable, each with its own sanitary drinking bowl, held thoroughbred Holstein and Guernsey cows.[43] According to a contemporary article published in *Concrete* magazine, the designers based their decision to use concrete as the primary building material for the dairy on factors of "economy, fire-safety and practicability."[44] The use of concrete—a product that could be easily washed and, unlike wood or other more porous materials, deterred the breeding of germs—helped guarantee an uncontaminated product.[45]

An official Century of Progress press release stated that the building was modeled after "the latest type of European airplane hangar."[46] At first glance the dairy building did look like a small multihangar terminal, with its row of barrel-vaulted bays and a windowless "air-traffic control" tower. Modern sans serif–type spelled out "Brook Hill Dairy" on each side of the tower, with dashes of horizontal speedlines located at the top and bottom. While the actual formal qualities were not as remarkable as those of other exposition pavilions, the use of concrete was. The roof of the building consisted of a series of five three-inch-thick concrete barrel vaults that spanned fourteen feet each.[47] A Haydite concrete mix (concrete that includes a lightweight aggregate in the mix), laid out with shovels on plywood forms and then screened and vibrated into place, left smooth-finished surfaces on both the tops and the exposed bottoms of the vaults.[48] The result was a hygienic, modern-looking building. The contiguous elliptical barrel-vaulted roof was the first

FIG. 4.6. Brook Hill Farm Dairy. From "New Fair Buildings," *Architectural Forum* 61 (July 1934): 30.

thin-shell structure to be constructed in the United States.[49] Additionally, the dairy had the distinction of featuring the first double curvature in a barrel-shaped concrete-shell roof anywhere in the world.[50]

Early developments of thin-shell concrete, as with the catenary roof of the Travel and Transport Building, had primarily taken place in Europe. In the early 1920s Franz Dischinger and Ulrich Finsterwalder, employees of Dyckerhoff-Widmann, an engineering firm located in Jena, Germany, solved the mathematical formulas for simple, geometric shell designs.[51] Soon Dischinger, along with Walther Bauersfeld of the Carl Zeiss Optical Company, was experimenting with concrete shells.[52] The engineers designed a structural concrete roof for the Jena Planetarium, the first modern astronomical theater. To create the eighty-two-foot-diameter dome, a thin layer of wet concrete was sprayed over a skeletal frame of reinforcement bars.[53] This technique, later used for the Brook Hill Farm Dairy building, became known as the Zeiss-Dywidag, or Z-D, process.[54] With the popular success of the Jena Planetarium, Dyckerhoff-Widmann found a niche in the building industry. They incorporated thin-shell concrete domes into the design of a dozen other planetariums in Germany and began designing domes for other purposes, including a hemisphere with an eighty-five-foot span for an electric light company in Frankfurt (1928).[55] In addition to domes, the company began to investigate the construction of barrel vaults for roofing square or rectangular spaces. A factory building for the Zeiss Company, constructed in 1924 in Jena, was probably the earliest building to incorporate a thin-shell concrete barrel vault.[56] The roof included skylight openings situated between reinforcing rods to create a decorative grille. This clearly illustrated one of the major benefits of concrete shells—that they could be perforated without sacrificing structural integrity. By the 1930s, employees at Dyckerhoff-Widmann had begun producing more complex geometrical forms of concrete shells. Their roof design for a large market hall in Leipzig (circa 1927) included two massive octagonal domes.[57] At 249 feet in diameter, they became the largest domes in the world.[58]

Back in the United States Kalinka and other engineers learned firsthand about reinforced shell construction from Anton Tedesko, a young engineer who had arrived in the country in the early 1930s from Germany as an agent for Dyckerhoff-Widmann.[59] In 1932 the company sold a license for its process of creating thin shells to Roberts and Schaefer, a Chicago firm that soon employed Tedesko as the engineer-manager of the Structural Department and later as vice president.[60]

The use of the Z-D system received much attention in the United States during the mid-1930s through articles on the construction of both the Brook Hill Farm Dairy at the Chicago fair and the concrete dome of the Hayden Planetarium at the American Museum of Natural History in

FIG. 4.7. Construction of the barrel-vaulted concrete roof of the Brook Hill Farm Dairy. From "Reinforced Concrete Shell Roof over Unobstructed Dairy Floor," *Concrete* 42 (July 1934): 4.

FIG. 4.8. Planetarium in Jena, Germany, with a roof constructed by the Zeiss-Dywidag process. Photograph by author.

New York City, built a few months after the dairy.[61] These articles appeared in publications with widely varied readers, including the *Journal of the American Concrete Institute, Engineering News-Record*, and *Popular Mechanics.* The authors of these articles promoted concrete shells as ideal solutions for roofing large, unobstructed spaces. They stressed that concrete construction was fireproof and eliminated the need for rafters, purlins, or heavy trusses. Advances in the construction of barrel vaults during these years, particularly in the development of reusable formworks, led to the creation of more cost-efficient designs.

Another major structural advance at the Chicago World's Fair was much less obvious to fairgoers than the suspended roof of the Travel and Transportation Building or even the small concrete-vaulted Brook Hill Farm Dairy building. The foundations of most of the pavilions at the exposition consisted of a new form of inexpensive pile footing. This allowed the relatively unstable man-made ground along the lakefront to support the construction of large exhibition halls (an advance only made possible by the use of new, lighter-weight materials for the modern pavilions). The new footing was the latest in a series of advances in foundation design that had taken place in Chicago since the Great Fire of 1871.[62] Although this innovative footing system was hidden from the millions of fair visitors, it received prominent attention from members of the construction industry through articles in *Architectural Forum, Architectural Record,* and *Engineering News-Record.*[63]

The fill that covered the site of the exposition averaged twenty to thirty feet deep and consisted of everything from high-quality sand to an assortment of refuse, rumored to include not only rubble from Chicago's Great Fire but also tons of tin cans and even an entire truckload of Kewpie dolls.[64] Test borings taken only fifteen feet apart disclosed that significant settling had occurred in some places while other sites, some immediately adjacent to the sinking locations, had risen.[65] The wide variations in readings prevented the establishment of a sound ground bearing value, which was required for the use of spread footings. This led to the adoption of the new pile-foundation system for all the large buildings on the fairgrounds except the Administration Building and the large columns supporting the cables for the suspended dome of the Travel and Transport Building.[66]

The designers of the fair witnessed a clear illustration of the potential problems of relying on a spread-foot foundation system at the site early in the design process when part of the foundation of the Administration Building failed. Because the building was located on a rise, well above water level, piles would have to have been unusually long to reach solid ground. Hence, the decision was made to use spread footings. After the start of construction, however, significant settling began to occur uniformly over the whole building except at the east end of the central wing of the pavilion's E-shaped footprint. There, where the total settlement reached eighteen inches, engineers had to install jacks in order to elevate the sagging section of the building.[67]

The use of pile footings prevented similar settling problems in other pavilions. The standard practice of incorporating a minimum of three piles under each column, however, would have resulted in prohibitively expensive foundations for the temporary buildings.[68] Because the structures were to be constructed out of new, lightweight panels, the engineers felt that

FIG. 4.9. Low-cost pile-foundation system developed for the Chicago exposition and used for most of the fair pavilions. From Bert M. Thorud, "Engineering Research and Building Construction," *Architectural Forum* 59 (July 1933): 65.

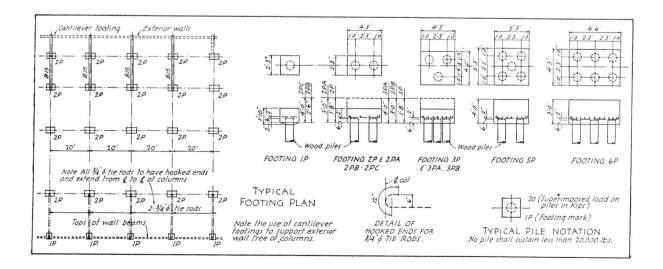

they could use fewer piles by creating a network of footings connected by tie-rods immediately below ground level.[69] Thus, most exterior columns sat above only one pile, while two piles typically supported the interior ones. A wall beam located between either the pile caps or the column bases provided additional stability.[70] The interconnection of exterior columns and reinforced concrete floors prevented wall footings from moving significantly inward. Further savings resulted from cantilevering concrete girders beyond the pilings, allowing wall and stair construction to be set away from the columns.[71]

In addition to structural innovations in roofing and foundations, much progress was made in the design of steel framing in these years.[72] The architects of the Chicago exposition demonstrated the benefits of new skeletal-frame structural systems, which replaced traditional wooden balloon framing, in connection with the standardized exterior panels used on most of the fair buildings. These modern wall panels, typically produced from factory-made materials—including asbestos-cement wallboard, precast gypsum board, plywood, metal siding, and laminated insulation board—were either bolted or clipped to the steel frames, thereby allowing for quick assembly and later for easy disassembly.

INNOVATIVE WALL MATERIALS

In the early 1920s, as industries adapted materials developed for the First World War to meet peacetime needs, they continued the transition to standardization that had begun during the war. Plywood, for example, favored as a paneled veneer for wartime airplane fuselages, eventually found acceptance for use in mass-produced furniture and, after the development of adequate waterproof glues, for standardized sheathing panels in residential and small commercial construction.[73]

The architectural commissioners for A Century of Progress incorporated many of these modern building materials, ranging from metal panels to gypsum board to processed wood products, into designs for the large exhibition pavilions. Unfettered by the limitations of a strict building code, other designers demonstrated the latest in residential building materials in the model houses on display in the Home and Industrial Arts Exhibit.[74] In fact, building-products manufacturers sponsored several of the residences specifically to highlight the practicability and value of their new products. The corporations worked hand in hand with the architects to create residences that embodied "scientific advancement in the elements of construction and design, furnishings and equipment."[75]

FIG. 4.10. Great Hall of the Hall of Science under construction. From Avery Architectural and Fine Arts Library, Columbia University.

During the initial stages of constructing the exposition, engineers held experiments at the fairgrounds to test potential new materials for use in the temporary exhibition halls.[76] The Celotex Company, for example, conducted tests of its insulating Cemesto-Board at the Travel and Transport

HALL OF SCIENCE
A CENTURY OF PROGRESS 1933

DATE 10-28-31   NEG. NO. 50

Building in 1931 in order to determine the material's suitability for the construction of pavilion walls.[77] These tests reflected a general trend toward developing new materials that could meet more than one major functional need—in this case, it could act both as a surfacing and an insulating material. Other experiments were set up to test two different systems of construction: the use of load-bearing walls and the employment of surface panels that were divorced from a structural framework.[78] The latter method proved, in most cases, to be more suitable to the specific needs of the exposition. As a result, the architectural commissioners favored the use of steel framing and new forms of factory-made wall panels for all the major pavilions at the fair.[79]

Architects typically incorporated a number of new products in their exposition designs, as demonstrated in the Administration Building, the first pavilion constructed for the event.[80] The local commissioners experimented with innovative materials for its structure, interior and outer walls, and other, less visible, parts of the building. Even prior to completion, the Administration Building drew great attention, particularly from architects, engineers, and builders interested in witnessing firsthand the application of new materials and design ideas.

The Chicago architects who designed the building specified Transite, a type of precast asbestos-cement wallboard, for the exterior of the pavilion and gypsum wallboard for the interior.[81] Both materials were attached to a structural steel frame with case-hardened screws. The sides of the building were insulated with Sprayo-Flake, an experimental mixture of emulsified asphalt, sodium silicate, and shredded paper, blown in between the walls with pneumatic guns, while Maizewood, a material consisting of

FIG. 4.11. Installation of Maizewood on the roof of the Administration Building. From "The Forum of Events: Products and Practices," *Architectural Forum* 58 (March 1933): 40.

processed cornstalks, insulated the roof.[82] Bands of standard factory sashes, with many of the vertical mullions removed, emphasized the horizontality of the building.[83] The architects also highlighted new forms of interior finishes. For instance, they specified covering the walls and ceiling of the Trustees' Dining Room with Flexwood, a veneer mounted on cloth and applied like wallpaper.[84]

In addition to asbestos-cement wallboard, the commissioners experimented with other factory-made materials for the paneled exteriors of the main pavilions. These included precast gypsum board, five-ply Douglas fir plywood, ribbed-metal siding, pressed-steel plates, and prefabricated, laminated insulation boards.[85] The architects selected prefabricated materials for each pavilion by assessing their strength and durability, ease of securing to framework, resistance to moisture absorption, relative resistance to combustion, weight, and availability.[86] They also considered the ease of dismantling and salvage value. After erecting the second and third major pavilions—the Travel and Transport Building, constructed of steel panels, and the Hall of Science, built of plywood—fair designers relied on gypsum board exterior siding for most of the remaining large exhibition pavilions. Although early gypsum board had had properties similar to the asbestos-cement wallboard used on the Administration Building, the more recently developed gypsum products favored by the designers were less costly and offered surfaces more suitable for painting.

The General Exhibits Building, designed by Corbett, was just one of the fair's many pavilions constructed of gypsum board.[87] A sandwich-panel system less expensive than plywood, gypsum board consists of a noncombustible gypsum plaster (ground calcium sulfate combined with water) covered in paper to make it appropriate for drywall construction.[88] Augustine Sackett took out the first patent for gypsum board in 1894 and four years later began producing a multilayered product to which plaster could be applied. In 1909 United States Gypsum Company took over the business and, by standardizing production, greatly increased the commercial availability of the material. The most significant advances in the development of gypsum wallboard took place in the 1920s, when United States Gypsum marketed several new products, including Sheetrock, which includes a finished surface.[89] Around 1931 the company introduced a new form of Sheetrock suitable for exterior use on temporary buildings, such as the exhibition halls.

Contractors specified half-inch Sheetrock for all exterior walls of the General Exhibits Building.[90] Corbett took advantage of the material in his design for the pavilion by highlighting the flatness of the panels' surfaces. He used vertical planes of the panels to form abstract "skyscraper setbacks" marking each of the building's four projecting entrances.[91] The Sheetrock he specified consisted of a standard gray newspaper stock paper on one side and a "standard wood fiber pulp paper with a close grained highly calendered surface in an ivory color" on the other side. The

construction contract for the pavilion stated that the Sheetrock was to be cut into standardized panels and primed with aluminum paint prior to arrival at the fairgrounds.[92] In addition to exterior walls, gypsum board was used for both the interior walls and the ceilings of the pavilion, as well as for most of the walls of the other fair buildings.[93] The relative lightness and ease of handling the material significantly sped construction, resulting in a major saving in labor costs. It also, according to Nathaniel Owings, provided the best surface yet developed for the application of paint.[94]

Prior to the availability of Sheetrock, the architectural commission studied the use of plywood, thin wood veneers joined together by adhesives, as a less expensive alternative to Transite for exterior pavilion walls.[95] The history of modern plywood began when John K. Mayo first patented a form of it in 1865. Late-nineteenth-century cabinetmakers used it for the bottoms of drawers and other nonvisible furniture parts.[96] It was not until the invention of the rotary cutter around 1890, however, that large sheets of laminated wood became readily available. Although the plywood industry initially developed slowly, production grew significantly during the First World War as the material became widely used in aircraft construction.[97]

The use of plywood in building developed dramatically around the time of the

FIG. 4.12 *(facing).* Trustees' Dining Room in the Administration Building, with walls and ceiling covered in Flexwood veneers, including Davis Leavitt's wall mural depicting industry. From commemorative photograph album of A Century of Progress presented to John Root, from collection of John Holabird Jr.

FIG. 4.13 *(above).* General Exhibits Building. Kaufmann and Fabry, photographers.

Chicago fair as a result of the development of stronger, more durable adhesives. Although casein glues introduced around 1900 provided the earliest water-resistant adhesives for plywood, the introduction of a German phenol-resin binder in 1931 made use of the material for exterior building construction practical.[98] The general promotion of prefabrication and the need for more cost-efficient building construction contributed to an increase in the sale of plywood during these years.[99]

The Administration Building provided a model for the structural design of Cret's Hall of Science, but plywood was specified in place of Transite for the exterior walls. The designers favored plywood over asbestos-cement boards as the laminated wood eliminated the need for weather stripping, expanded and contracted less with changes in climate, and was less expensive than Transite.[100] Additional advantages of plywood included its ease in handling, its relatively high insulation value, and its ideal surface for painting.[101] In constructing the Hall of Science, workers secured standardized four-by-eight-foot panels of half-inch, five-ply, laminated Douglas fir to wall studs with thin battens. Butt joints were used for vertical seams, and shiplap joints were used for horizontal connections. Battens allowed for expansion and contraction of the panels and created interesting patterns on the exterior facades. Designers specified plywood decking for the floors in the Hall of Science, as well as in the Electrical Building and a number of other major pavilions. Primarily functioning as a subflooring material, plywood cost approximately half as much as the metal decking previously used in the Administration and Travel and Transport buildings. The smooth face of the plywood provided an ideal base surface for a layer of Masonite inner-flooring, which was then covered by a finished flooring product.[102]

In addition to the Hall of Science, many of the stage-set building facades in the ethnic villages were constructed of plywood and other panel materials. The strength of plywood made it an ideal material for the cutout backdrops that lined the edges of these attractions.[103] The National Lumber Manufacturers' Association also used plywood in its design for a model residence as part of the Home and Industrial Arts Exhibit.[104]

Another model house demonstrated the versatility of Masonite, a recently introduced man-made wood-paneling product. W. H. Mason, founder of the Masonite Corporation, had discovered that a specific series of mechanical manipulations, which included exploding scrap wood chips into fibers, then heating and pressing them into standardized, shaped panels, could transform the waste of lumber production into a thin hardboard that was both stronger and less expensive than natural wood.[105] First produced in 1926, Masonite Presdwood was originally used primarily for insulation and not as a finished surface material because it did not resist moisture well. However, in 1931 the company introduced Tempered Presdwood, a water-resistant hardboard product for exterior use that was much denser and stronger than previous Masonite boards. While the company initially marketed Tempered Presdwood for the construction of concrete forms, it demonstrated the product's potential as an exterior building material through the construction of its Masonite House.[106]

Designed by Frazier and Raftery, the Masonite House featured products developed by the company. The exterior walls of the wood-frame residence consisted of Masonite Structural Insulation covered by Tempered Presdwood, which was then painted with thermolyzed tung-oil paint. Workmen glued the Presdwood panels to the insulation, which was then nailed to the wood studs. They then sealed the joints with strips of Masonite.[107] Walls consisted of Masonite Quartrboard, a material less dense than the Presdwood. Designers specified Masonite Temprtile for

FIG. 4.14. Entrance hall of the Masonite House. From Dorothy Raley, *A Century of Progress Homes and Furnishings* (Chicago: M. A. Ring, 1934), 94.

the kitchen and bathroom floors and Masonite Cushioned Flooring, promoted as a surface that defied indentation, for the remaining floors throughout the house.[108] Quartrboard was also installed under ceiling joists.[109] Interior walls of the Presdwood, left natural in part of the entrance hall and covered by a variety of materials elsewhere in the residence, created a comfortable appearance. Frazier and Raftery also featured Masonite in the house through the inclusion of Kitchenmaid cabinets that contained Presdwood parts and by the presence of four-by-four-inch tiles of the company's new tile-treated board on the bathroom walls.[110] Unlike in some of the other model houses, there was no preassembly of materials, but the Masonite boards were produced in large panels, which significantly reduced the need for on-site labor.[111]

The versatility of Masonite was well demonstrated at A Century of Progress; millions of feet of the product were specified for various functions.[112] Over 300,000 feet of Tempered Presdwood flooring covered the plywood subfloors in the Hall of Science and the Electrical Building.[113] Builders also used regular Presdwood in the interiors of many of the pavilions, including the reading room in the Time and Fortune Building, and in the Schlitz Garden and Mueller Pabst restaurants. The entire bridge of the Swift Bridge and Open Air Theatre was built of Masonite panels, as were all the ticket booths, more than 100 Orange Crush and Citrus Fruits stands, and numerous individual display booths. Masonite was also used for the sound chamber of forty-five loudspeakers and for every official sign. Engineers specified two and a half miles of Tempered Presdwood for structural panels lining the shore of Lake Michigan and for the fountain in the center of the lagoon.[114]

Another material that was used extensively at A Century of Progress was steel, one of the most popular modern building products in the early 1930s. Exposition designers specified steel for the external construction of several of the pavilions, as well as for structural framing for buildings throughout the fairgrounds. Suffering financial problems resulting from the Great Depression, steel manufacturers looked to construction to revitalize their struggling industry.[115] Steel was viewed by many architects and builders during this time as the modern substitute for lumber, being easy to fabricate, lightweight, and strong. In addition, it had salvage value and could resist the elements.[116]

The Chicago architectural commissioners specified narrow steel panels for construction of the Travel and Transport Building's exterior walls, including the giant drum of the Railroad Hall.[117] The vertical channels of twenty-gauge steel, initially designed for floor decking, were only six inches wide but ran up to eighty feet long.[118] The individual steel channels interlocked with each other on the interior and were then clipped to horizontal steel girders so as to present the appearance of a continuous smooth surface.[119] The sections of wall were fastened to a steel frame that also supported steel floor decks. Because of steel's extremely limited sound-

PLATE 1 *(previous page)*. Poster advertising A Century of Progress, featuring
the U.S. Government Building. Courtesy of Poster Plus, Chicago,
www.posterplus.com.

PLATE 2 *(top)*. The Home Planning Hall. Kaufmann and Fabry, photographers.

PLATE 3 *(bottom)*. Three of the more than 1 million souvenir cans produced at
the American Can Company exhibit. Photograph by author.

PLATE 4 *(top facing)*. Bird's-eye color rendering of the fairgrounds, showing the
Skyride at night. Postcard from collection of author.

PLATE 5 *(below facing)*. The Radio Flyer Pavilion, topped by Tony, a forty-five-
foot-high boy. Kaufmann and Fabry, photographers.

PLATE 6 *(right).* U-shaped courtyard of the Hall of Science in 1933. Image from collection of author.

PLATE 7 *(below).* The Railroad Hall of the Travel and Transport Building, painted green in 1933. Image from collection of author.

PLATE 8 *(top facing).* The multicolored Electrical Building in 1933. Postcard from collection of author.

PLATE 9 *(below facing).* Entrance court of Electrical Building, with relief sculptures of atomic and stellar energy and a neon fountain. Kaufmann and Fabry, photographers.

ELECTRICAL GROUP

COURT OF ELECTRICAL GROUP

PLATE 10 *(above).*
Italian Pavilion.
Kaufmann and Fabry,
photographers.
PLATE 11 *(right).*
Ford Building.
Kaufmann and Fabry,
photographers.
PLATE 12 *(facing).*
Bird's-eye view from
the Skyride. Postcard
from collection
of author.

approved as of September 1, 1932
A Century of Progress
Rufus C. Dawes
President

© H. M. Pettit.

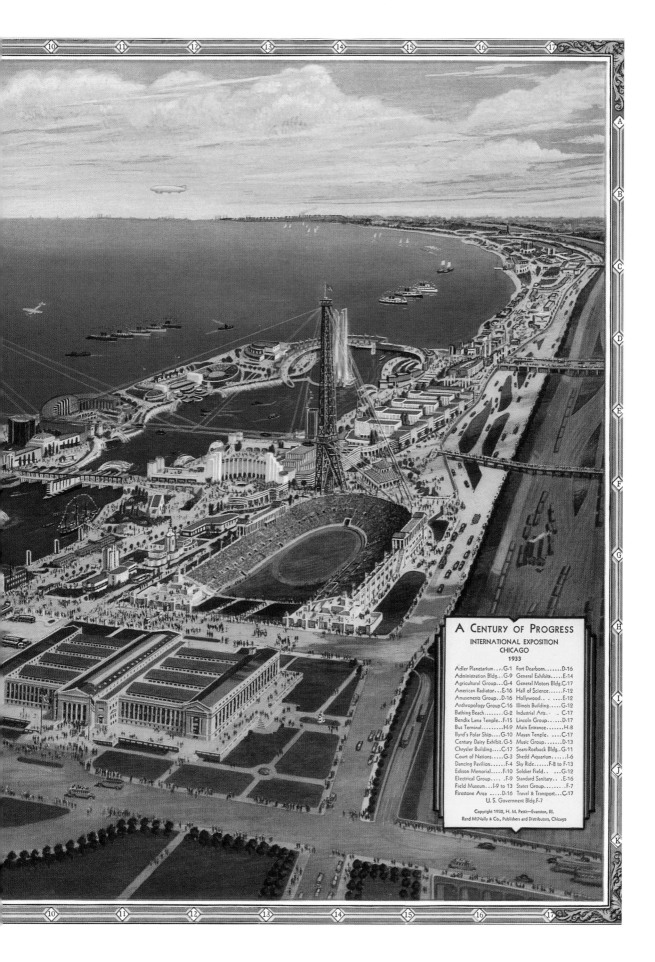

A CENTURY OF PROGRESS
INTERNATIONAL EXPOSITION
CHICAGO
1933

Adler Planetarium...G-1	Fort Dearborn.......D-16
Administration Bldg...G-9	General Exhibits....E-14
Agricultural Group...G-4	General Motors Bldg.C-17
American Radiator...E-16	Hall of Science......F-12
Amusements Group..D-16	Hollywood....E-12
Anthropology Group C-16	Illinois Building....G-12
Bathing Beach.......G-2	Industrial Arts.. C-17
Bendix Lama Temple..F-15	Lincoln Group...D-17
Bus Terminal.........H-9	Main Entrance......H-8
Byrd's Polar Ship....G-10	Mayan Temple. ...C-17
Century Dairy Exhibit..G-5	Music Group......D-13
Chrysler Building....C-17	Sears-Roebuck Bldg..G-11
Court of Nations.....G-3	Shedd Aquarium....I-6
Dancing Pavilion.....F-4	Sky Ride......F-8 to F-13
Edison Memorial.....F-10	Soldier Field. ...G-12
Electrical Group.... .F-9	Standard Sanitary. .E-16
Field Museum...I-9 to 13	States Group........F-7
Firestone Area D-16	Travel & Transport...C-17
U. S. Government Bldg.F-7	

SCIENCE HALL, CENTURY OF PROGRESS EXPOSITION—OLDSMOBILE STRAIGHT EIGHT AND SIX   3A-H546

PLATE 13 *(previous spread)*. Bird's-eye view of fairgrounds, by H. M. Pettit.
From *Chicago's Century of Progress* (Chicago: Rand McNally, 1933).

PLATE 14 *(top)*. Hiram Walker "Doodlebug" Pavilion. Postcard from
collection of author.

PLATE 15 *(bottom)*. North Court of the Hall of Science, with red and blue
Oldsmobiles. Postcard from collection of author.

COLOR KEY TO BUILDINGS ON FOLLOWING PAGES

PLATE 16 *(above)*. 16. Joseph Urban's color palette for the 1933 fair
season. From "A Century of Progress Colors Issued by the Textile
Color Card Association of the United States, Inc., with Permission
from A Century of Progress International Expositions, 1933,"
Textile Color Card Association of the United States, Inc., 1933.

PLATE 17 *(below)*. Color scheme for the Electrical Building. From
Museum of Science and Industry, Chicago.

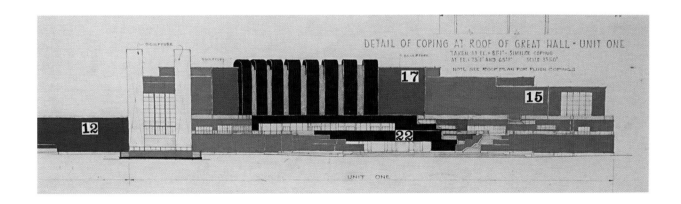

Interior view of the great hall showing the grand staircase and balcony.

PLATE 18 *(above).* An illustration of the color scheme of Great Hall of the Hall of
Science, which included white walls with battens in aluminum and light gray and
stair soffits in electric blue with trimmings in midnight blue and gold. From *Color
and Protection* (Cedar Rapids, Iowa: American Asphalt Paint Company, 1933), n.p.

PLATE 19 *(top facing).* Avenue of Flags in 1934 with red banners on a cool day. From
Hand Colored Views: A Century of Progress International Exposition, Chicago, 1933
(Chicago: Exposition Publications and Novelties, c. 1933), n.p.

PLATE 20 *(below facing).* Avenue of Flags in 1934 with blue banners on a hot day.
Kaufmann and Fabry, photographers.

GENERAL HOUSES INC. HOUSE

DESIGN FOR LIVING

PLATE 21 *(top facing)*. Living room of Vinylite House display in the Hall of Science. From Theodore C. Larson, "New Housing Designs and Construction Systems," *Architectural Record* 75 (January 1934): n.p.
PLATE 22 *(below facing)*. General Houses model house. Postcard from collection of author.
PLATE 23 *(above)*. Design for Living model house. Postcard from collection of author.
PLATE 24 *(left)*. Living area of the Florida Tropical House, A Century of Progress, 1933. From *The Florida Tropical Home at A Century of Progress, 1933* (New York: Kuhne Galleries, circa 1933), 15.

PLATE 25 (above).
Lighting nightscape.
From scrapbook in
collection of author.
PLATE 26 (right).
The Lagoon, painted
by Rudolph Ingerle,
showing the Triple
Fountain and lighting
of the sky over the
fairgrounds at night.
Courtesy of Aaron
Galleries.

proofing capability, workers placed a layer of fibrous insulation board under the metal panels in an attempt to reduce noise levels. The steel channels also provided some climate control. They formed flues allowing hot air to travel upward and escape through openings at the top, providing significant cooling on hot summer days.[120] In a contemporary article published in *Architectural Record,* Nathaniel Owings reported that a major disadvantage of steel walls was that many people mistook the metal panels for wood siding, so its use seemed dishonest.[121] Steel had other disadvantages, as well: Thin steel sheets dented easily and had to be treated to prevent corrosion, which made steel a relatively expensive building material when compared to other new wall products.[122]

Several model houses at A Century of Progress demonstrated potential uses of steel in residential construction. Howard T. Fisher built the General Houses home to demonstrate his system of mass-produced steel residential construction.[123] Two other steel model residences, the Armco-Ferro Enamel Frameless House and the Good Housekeeping Stran-Steel House, both constructed of porcelain-enameled wall panels, demonstrated the economic value of steel and the ease with which it could be adapted for applications in the building industry.[124] Promoters emphasized that exterior enameled surfaces never needed painting, as they could be cleaned using only water from a garden hose and, if damaged, could be replaced with relative ease.[125]

In 1932 Armco, the American Rolling Mill Company, built the first house sided in porcelain-enamel panels in Solon, Ohio.[126] The following

FIG. 4.15. Fairgoers tour the Armco-Ferro model residence. Kaufmann and Fabry, photographers.

year Armco built its model residence at the Chicago expositions. Designed by Robert Smith Jr. of Cleveland, the flat-roofed, four-bedroom house was covered in wide enamel strips with stainless steel liners. Like the General Houses design, the system of the Armco-Ferro Enamel House had no structural frame. The walls, assembled out of sixteen-gauge to twenty-gauge steel sheets, consisted of vertical Z sections welded together in the factory to form structural supports.[127] The company manufactured the resulting boxlike units, faced with porcelain enamel, in a variety of widths. Construction workers assembled the panels on site with "belyx" nails, and then filled the cores with rock wool for insulation.[128] This system of porcelain-enamel sheets allowed for quick construction; six men assembled the Armco-Ferro House within five days.[129]

While the Armco-Ferro House did not include a separate structural frame, the other steel house at the fair, the Good Housekeeping Stran-Steel House, did. Designed by H. Augustus O'Dell and Wirt C. Rowland of Detroit and sponsored by *Good Housekeeping* magazine, the house was specifically built to demonstrate a steel frame system designed to replace wood joists and two-by-fours. Leery of future public perception of modern building techniques, the company stressed the fact that the Stran-Steel House was not prefabricated. Trained carpenters could construct a house using their steel-frame product exactly as they would use wood.[130] In publicity materials, company spokesmen emphasized the benefits of structural steel framing over wood studs in regular residential construction, particularly the material's ability to resist fire and pests.

The Stran-Steel House was sided with panels of Glasiron Macotta, a porcelain enamel manufactured by the Maul Macotta Company. Each panel was two feet wide and two to eight feet long. Glasiron Macotta consisted of a layer of light-

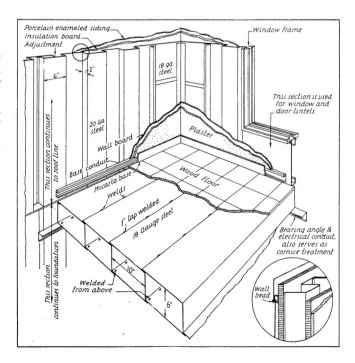

FIG. 4.16. Detail of the Armco-Ferro model residence showing floor and wall construction. From "The Modern Houses of the Century of Progress Exposition," *Architectural Forum* 59 (July 1933): 54.

FIG. 4.17. Good Housekeeping Stran-Steel model residence. From Dorothy Raley, *A Century of Progress Homes and Furnishings* (Chicago: M. A. Ring, 1934), 100.

weight Haydite aggregate covered with thin-gauge steel and a coating of Pemco architectural porcelain enamel fused to a layer of Toncan Iron.[131] Workmen attached two-ply half-inch sheets of overlapping Celotex fiberboard to the framing for insulation before attaching the Macotta panels to the structure with right-angle metal clips. Joints were then sealed with asphalt mastic. The product was available in a wide range of colors and color combinations. Among its other benefits, Macotta was relatively lightweight and fire resistant, and it had a high insulation value and could be erected quickly in the field.[132]

While neither sheet-steel panels nor porcelain-enamel panels became popular in residential construction, designers continued to use them for commercial building well into the 1960s. Porcelain enamel, in particular, found popular acceptance for exterior walls of small businesses. These included branches of successful restaurant chains, such as Stuckey's, White Castle, and A&W, as well as Standard Oil, Mobile, Shell, and Texaco gas stations.

While the benefits of wood and steel in construction were prominently featured in several of the modern houses at the fair, some of the neighboring model residences illustrated the potential of other exciting new building products, including innovative forms of stone and glass. One of the materials promoted at the event that clearly revealed the influence of the scientists' laboratory on the building industry was Rostone, a synthetic stone product. The Rostone Company of Lafayette, Indiana, promoted the material as "a new product resulting from the chemists' test tube and modern manufacturing methods."[133] It consisted of a mixture of pressurized shale, alkaline earth, water, and limestone waste from quarries located in southwestern Indiana.[134] Rostone, like its major competitor, Perma-Stone, came in a variety of colors and shapes in either polished or textured surfaces.[135] The shale was first dried, then pulverized and finely ground, and finally mixed with lime and water. Workers hand-formed the pliable mixture into specific shapes or placed it into molds, where it was compressed and allowed to harden. The absence of a high-temperature process prevented significant distortion of the product, allowing the material to meet precise specifications. According to the company, the mechanical processes of building and creating with Rostone closely followed those of natural stone. Builders could apply pieces of the material to existing wall surfaces with mortar or attach them to steel frames with special clips.[136] An announcement of the product in *Architectural Record* boasted that the material satisfactorily passed tests for "hardness, resistance to abrasion, toughness, freezing and thawing, and fire-resistance."[137] Rostone could be carved, cut, sandblasted, and polished just like natural stone.

FIG. 4.18. Rostone model residence. From Dorothy Raley, *A Century of Progress Homes and Furnishings* (Chicago: M. A. Ring, 1934), 118.

The Rostone Company initially promoted its product as being "advanced but not radical."[138] The company suggested it was suitable for both modern and traditional architecture. Like the Stran-Steel Corporation, the company questioned whether the public would accept modern building

materials and techniques and attempted to develop a market irrespective of future public taste. To generate a demand for residential use, it suggested Rostone as an ideal material for interior and exterior walls, floors, roofs, and decorative elements.[139]

The Rostone House at the Chicago fair, designed by Walter Scholer, represented the first use of the material outside Indiana. Although not considered a prefabricated design, the house did demonstrate a new structural system that used shop-fabricated materials. The exterior of the six-room dwelling consisted of slabs of cream-colored Rostone with a roughened texture connected with mastic in shiplap joints. Each piece measured eighteen inches by four feet by two inches. Blocks of Chinese-red Rostone trimmed with black and brown framed the entrance door, and red and brown roof slabs lined a paved deck. Inside, pieces of Rostone in colors similar to those on the exterior outlined the walls of the hall and the stairway. A large fireplace opposite a dining alcove of natural colored slabs was trimmed in flaming red.[140]

Although few of the largest buildings at the Chicago exposition included windows, several pavilions, including two model residences by George Frederick Keck, the House of Tomorrow and the Crystal House, exhibited innovative uses of plate glass.[141] The Owens-Illinois Glass Company of Toledo, Ohio, however, provided the most prominent example of a new glass product in its corporate pavilion, which was assembled in the housing exhibit area almost completely out of glass blocks—the first full-size building constructed of that product.[142]

The development of glass blocks (or glass bricks, as they were commonly known) grew out of the production of prismatic glass tiles, which had been created in the late nineteenth century for placement above storefronts to bring additional natural light into the rear areas of shops. Another predecessor of glass blocks were the heavy glass slabs placed in sidewalks or floors to allow light into basements or other underground areas in the late nineteenth century.[143] The first large wall surfaces of glass squares consisted of Luxfer Prismatic Tiles placed in concrete frames. These began appearing in progressive architectural designs in the early twentieth century, most notably at the 1914 Werkbund Exhibition in Cologne in Bruno Taut's Glass Pavilion (which, like the Owens-Illinois Glass-Block Building, included colored glass to create a memorable effect). Hollow glass bricks for use as a building material were probably first developed by Gustave Falconnier, a French engineer, who patented a molded, hexagonal prismatic glass block in 1886. Examples of his designs were exhibited in Chicago in 1893 at the World's Columbian Exposition. Falconnier's blocks, however, were unsuitable to building construction, as they often experienced condensation problems and were structurally unstable. In 1903 glass bricks were developed in Germany that contained one open side. While this resulted in less condensation, the blocks still had significant structural problems.[144]

FIG. 4.19. Interior of Bruno
Taut's Glass Pavilion
at the 1914 Werkbund
Exhibition, Cologne,
Germany. From Bildarchiv
Foto Marburg.

Owens-Illinois manufactured the first pressed glass blocks in 1932. Machines stamped out individual five-sided glass units. They were then hermetically sealed to a sixth side, thereby creating an airtight cavity inside the brick.[145] This method provided greater stability while it prevented moisture from seeping into the interior. Surfaces normally in contact with mortar were covered in the factory with a cement paint to ensure a solid bond after construction.[146] Although designed as a nonstructural material, the blocks were not easily broken and the company marketed them as ideal for curtain-wall construction.[147] Good insulators, the glass blocks helped keep severe heat or cold out of a building, while the translucent sides permitted diffused light to enter. An additional benefit was their relative strength and resistance to breakage in comparison to plate glass.

To add to the decorative qualities of its product, Owens-Illinois began producing colored blocks by mixing pigment into the cement coating. To achieve additional effects, designers specified the application of a vitreous layer of color to the outer surfaces. The layer was then fused to the glass during the manufacturing process. At the time of the Chicago exposition, the company advertised that its glass blocks were available in over 400 different colors.[148]

Marketed as being "strong enough for people who throw stones to live in," the Owens-Illinois Glass Company built its corporate pavilion at A Century of Progress to demonstrate the advantages of using glass blocks for wall construction.[149] The building consisted of a fifty-foot tower flanked by large projecting wings. Workers assembled walls of the glass blocks like masonry bricks. The ease of constructing with the material was illustrated to curious onlookers who visited the fairgrounds prior to opening day. They watched as five men built the walls of the pavilion (which contained 27,000 glass blocks) in only twelve days.[150] Although Owens-Illinois did not intend its glass block for load-bearing use, the company highlighted the fact that the walls of the pavilions, except for the tower, were self-supporting and did not need framing. The building also featured the wide range of colors available, as the hues of the glass ran from a pale yellow at the tower to a deep purple at the rear. Critics had predicted that the pavilion would be unbearably hot during the summer, but the air chambers in the individual bricks acted as insulation, moderating the temperature inside. The glass blocks did not need paint or plaster and could be kept clean with spray from a garden hose.[151]

In an article published in *World's Fair Weekly*, writer Joseph C. Folsom predicted that contemporary society was on the verge of a new glass age—an idea previously promoted by the German designers Bruno Taut and Paul Scheerbart in their treatise *Glasarchitektur* (1914).[152] Not only was it possible for modern people to live in glass houses by the early 1930s, but they could also fill them with new glass products. Exhibits in the Owens-Illinois Glass-Block Building displayed many of these, including air filters of Fiberglas (an insulation material developed in 1931) and glass containers for vacuum-packaged coffee, motor oil, and fruit preserves.[153]

The concept of a new, modern glass age was in part realized through the efforts of innovative scientists and engineers in the laboratories at Owens-Illinois and other corporations. The popular success of the Owens-Illinois pavilion helped stimulate further developments in the design of

FIG. 4.20. Owens-Illinois Glass-Block Building. Kaufmann and Fabry, photographers.

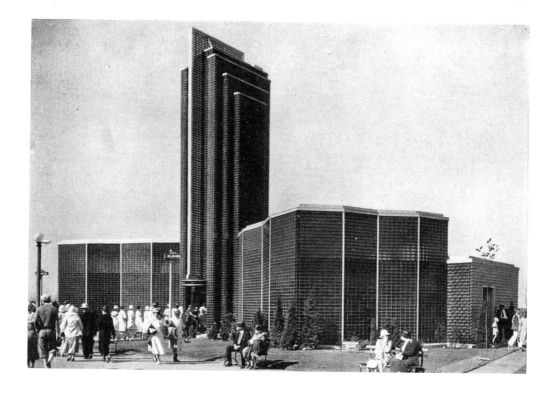

glass blocks. Insulux, a glass block sealed with lead, marketed by Owens-Illinois in 1935, became the first glass block widely available for exterior windows. About the same time, Pittsburgh-Corning (a joint venture of the Pittsburgh Plate Glass Company and the Corning Glass Works) began producing a heat-resistant glass block made of Pyrex. By the mid-1930s designers were specifying glass block in place of plate glass for the windows of factories and school buildings. In meeting growing industry demands, American glass companies had produced over 20 million glass blocks by 1940.[154]

Plastic also made its major debut as a modern building material at A Century of Progress. The marketers at Union Carbide and Carbon Corporation agreed that a new age had arrived, but they foresaw it as an era of plastics, not of glass. Union Carbide's scientists led the way with the development of Vinylite, the first vinyl floor covering, in 1931. The company initially presented its semiflexible vinyl asbestos tile product through the exhibition of the Vinylite House at the Chicago exposition. Sponsored in connection with the John B. Pierce Foundation, the Vinylite House was not a freestanding building but a display consisting of three rooms located on the main floor of the Hall of Science (Plate 21).[155]

An article in *Business Week* described Vinylite as a "colorless or colorful, odorless, tasteless, [and] non-inflammable" material that could "assume almost any shape from the cap on a toothpaste tube to the door of the bathroom itself."[156] Union Carbide's development of Vinylite grew out of laboratory discoveries by scientists in Europe and the United States beginning in the mid-nineteenth century.[157] In the 1920s scientists at chemical companies, including B. F. Goodrich, Union Carbide, and DuPont, were studying the wide range of textures and densities vinyl compounds could assume. By the time of the Chicago exposition, engineers at Union Carbide had produced numerous plastic products with various levels of success.[158]

The Vinylite apartment consisted of a living-dining room, a kitchen, and a bathroom. In addition to colorful checkerboard vinyl floor tiles, Union Carbide demonstrated the versatility of Vinylite by using it for almost everything in the dwelling.[159] The walls of the apartment consisted of twenty-four eight-by-two-and-a-half-foot modular panels of two-inch-thick Vinylite with aluminum coating.[160] Other plastic products included the doors, the translucent light panels, the moldings around the ceiling and baseboard, the doorknobs, the electric light plates, and even the transparent and translucent windows. In the bathroom, designers used the material for the towel racks and a grab bar, as well as for the toilet seat, toothbrushes, cosmetic and powder jars, and caps on the toothpaste and shaving cream tubes. The tableware in the kitchen, including cups, saucers, plates, tumblers, and trays, was also of Vinylite, while the refrigerator and kitchen table were finished with a Vinylite lacquer.[161]

While vinyl products, such as sun visors, raincoats, and linings of beer cans, began appearing on the market in the mid-1930s, many of the items on exhibit in the Vinylite House were not yet commercially viable.[162] Scientists had problems stabilizing the material, as early polyvinyl chloride compounds tended to become brittle over time or gummy when heated, and the designers of the Vinylite House could not forecast the future role of vinyl with total conviction.[163] Nevertheless, the exhibition of the model residence introduced millions of Americans to the potential of vinyl, thus helping pave the way for the public's embrace of plastics after the Second World War.

New plastic products also appeared in other exhibits at the fair. Most prominent were decorative laminates of phenol resin, such as Formica, Lamicoid, and Micarta, which began gaining in popularity during the late 1920s.[164] Leo Baekeland, who began impregnating fibrous sheets with a phenolformaldehyde resin in 1907, developed the process that led to the production of a decorative laminate.[165] Restrictions due to licensing policies on the patented Bakelite varnish (which initially was the binder for the laminate), however, severely limited early production of the material.[166] When the Bakelite patent expired in 1927, many other companies, including Westinghouse, began producing similar plastic laminates.[167] Progress in the development of laminated panels in the early 1930s was accelerated by greater availability of waterproof phenol resins as bonding adhesives.[168] In 1931 the Formica Corporation patented a process of incorporating a thin layer of aluminum

FIG. 4.21. Formica-walled entrance foyer of the Administration Building with drawings and models of fair pavilions on display. Models (from front to back) are the Administration Building, the Travel and Transport Building, and the Electrical Building. From "The Administration Building," *Architectural Forum* 55 (August 31): 138.

between the core and the actual laminate to improve its level of insulation. These early laminates, however, were available only in dark colors.[169]

The limited color range did not prevent the Formica Corporation from promoting its product at the Chicago fair. While no model house of the material was built at a major exposition until the New York World's Fair of 1964, Formica did appear at A Century of Progress in the interiors of several pavilions, including the Administration Building.[170] Workers covered the walls in the lobby of the building with laminated sheets of Formica wainscoting trimmed with bright metal. Designers also used the material on the interior of the porcelain-enamel Stran-Steel House.

PAINT AND LESS-VISIBLE INNOVATIVE BUILDING PRODUCTS

To take full advantage of many of the various modern materials used in the construction of the fair pavilions, other innovative products had to be incorporated into the designs. Most prominent were the gallons of brightly colored paint that provided a protective coating to the buildings' surfaces. The Chicago exposition saw the first major use of modern casein paint in the United States. Fair designers selected the cold-water-based material for its ability to maintain bright hues longer than other available paint products. Even other relatively new types of coatings, such as cement paints, phenol resin products, and rust inhibitors with a fish-oil base, tended to dust and fade significantly within three or four months when exposed to the elements.[171]

Valdura, the casein paint supplied to the fair by the American Asphalt Paint Company of Chicago, presented the most favorable choice of wall covering for the short-lived exposition buildings.[172] Developed in Germany, casein paint incorporates a binder of sour milk in emulsion in place of the traditional linseed oil and can accept a strong concentration of pigment in its base.[173] As a result, only one coat of casein paint, over a coat of aluminum primer, was necessary to cover the buildings' surfaces. The matte finish of the paint proved an ideal reflective surface for the exposition's spectacular lighting effects. The use of Valdura also significantly reduced labor costs, as the local painters' union allowed water-based paints, like casein, to be sprayed onto wall surfaces instead of being applied with three-inch brushes, as required for oil paints.[174] Valdura adhered well to a variety of surfaces, hardened quickly, and did not run or streak in the rain. Water did tend to dissolve thin layers of the paint, making the surface covering impractical for long-term exterior use. However, those responsible for painting the exposition viewed this as a self-cleaning process and considered it a positive characteristic, as rain would remove any accumulated dirt on the exposition pavilions without significantly reducing the intensity of most hues within the time span of a typical fair season.[175] As a result, the brilliantly painted pavilion facades always looked fresh.

The potential market for casein paint after the exposition was curtailed by the fact that it has a relatively short shelf life, after which it is unusable and smells like spoiled milk. Additionally, the paint's water solubility even after drying completely makes it undesirable for most permanent construction. However, Valdura became a predecessor for later vinyl polymers that provided better water-based alternatives for exterior surfaces.

Unlike the colorful casein paints or the various wall materials, not all new products used at A Century of Progress were visible to the fairgoers. Insulation boards and lubricants, though hidden behind the pavilion's facades, were important in the development of modern buildings. Celotex, for example, which became one of the most popular insulating materials in the mid-twentieth century, protected a number of buildings at the Chicago fair, including the Stran-Steel House.[176] Produced from sugar-cane waste, Celotex provided improved climate and noise control. When first produced in the 1920s, insulation board was such a new concept that the company's salesmen had to educate the building industry to its benefits.[177] Their promotional work paid off. By the 1930s a line of Celotex products had come to be widely used to insulate homes and commercial buildings, including the roof of the White House in Washington, D.C. Celotex's Cemesto-Board, a fire-resistant insulation product, was tested in 1931 at the exposition's Travel and Transport Building. When it was finally available for the general market in 1937, it came to be widely used in low-cost housing and service stations, as well as in partitions for offices and commercial buildings.[178] In the 1930s the company began to produce a surface material appropriate for the interiors of basements and attics and eventually developed products for use in more formal residential areas.

A second modern insulating material incorporated in several of the fair pavilion designs, including the House of Tomorrow, was aluminum foil. First used for insulation in 1925, it was promoted for its lack of measurable thickness.[179]

Another example of a new and less-obvious product at the Chicago exposition was a special type of lubricant developed specifically for the Travel and Transport Building. The designers of the building needed to ensure that the movable parts of the Breathing Dome receive proper lubrication during construction because once the structure was assembled, it would be exceedingly difficult to reach the bearings. Engineers realized that with the tremendous weight to be placed on the joints, regular oil or grease would eventually wear away, leading to potential structural failure. A new graphite paste that dried quickly, leaving a thick coating of hardened graphite on the bearings, provided an ideal solution.[180]

The wide range of modern building products at A Century of Progress illustrates the effect the rise of scientific technology and advanced manufacturing processes had on the building industry in the early 1930s. No longer did builders have to work around the imperfections found in natural materials. As a rule, man-made products offered greater consistency in quality, as well as uniform size. Modern manufactured materials tended to be stronger, less expensive, and easier to handle. In particular, panel products like plywood, Masonite, and Sheetrock lent themselves to innovative building processes that resulted in less costly and quicker construction techniques.

NEW CONSTRUCTION PROCESSES

The newly available factory-produced building materials highlighted at A Century of Progress were ideally suited to two major concepts in building construction gaining favor among progressive designers in the early 1930s: prefabrication and disposable architecture. Architects took advantage of the fair's impermanence and less-restrictive building code to test more-systematic construction techniques. In doing so they were able to keep construction costs affordable despite sharp increases in labor and material costs during the previous decade and a significant decrease in available funds as a result of the poor economy. Uniform lengths of steel framing, which arrived at the fairgrounds with equally spaced openings for fasteners already machine-punched in place, allowed workers to put together the various types of standardized wall panels in an assembly line. Screwing or bolting the panels of the pavilions together provided for easy disassembly and salvaging of the building parts after the close of the exposition. This led proponents of the concept of disposable architecture to highlight the Chicago fair in architectural journal discussions on the benefits of producing short-lived buildings.

An article on the exposition buildings published in *World's Fair Weekly* stated that one of the most significant aspects of the event's architecture was the almost-universal use—in all the major pavilions, in the ethnic villages, and in many of the houses—of prefabricated materials and construction techniques.[181] Several buildings, including a number of the model houses and a barn, were built specifically to demonstrate the benefits of prefabrication through the efficient assembly of standardized mass-produced building parts. The increased presence of manufacturing processes in architecture was also reflected at the exposition in the aesthetic form of the fair buildings, in particular the row after row of identical Quonset hut chicken coops located in the Poultry Farm display and in the assembly-line rhythm of matching entrance towers on the General Exhibits Building.

Howard T. Fisher built the General Houses model residence at the exposition specifically to generate interest in his system of prefabricated construction. Disillusioned by the academic architecture he studied while attending Harvard University, Fisher first investigated various building materials and methods while still a student in 1929. Three years later he founded General Houses, a company dedicated to the creation of well-designed prefabricated houses.[182] Prior to the company's incorporation, Fisher had attracted the backing of such major firms as the

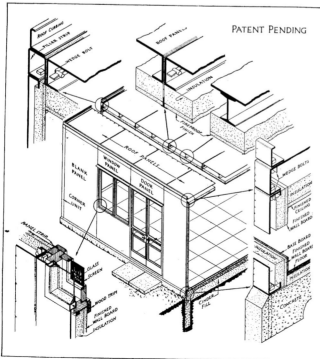

FIG. 4.22 *(above)*. Rows of identical Quonset hut chicken coops in the Poultry Farm exhibit. Kaufmann and Fabry, photographers.

FIG. 4.23 *(left)*. Detail of the prefabricated construction system of the General Houses 1933 model residence. From "The Modern Houses of the Century of Progress Exposition," *Architectural Forum* 59 (July 1933): 52.

Pullman Car and Manufacturing Company, which produced the steel wall and roof panels and the "battle deck" flooring for his houses.[183]

The General Houses' model residence at the Chicago exposition demonstrated one of the earliest prefabricated construction systems for modern houses in the United States.[184] Promotional literature referred to the one-story, two-bedroom, flat-roofed dwelling as the K_3H4DP house.[185] Setting the first number (which represented a subdivision of the basic house type) subscript suggested a chemical compound and gave the name a connotation clearly reflecting Fisher's modern scientific construction method.[186] The all-steel frameless dwelling was created from four interchangeable mass-produced exterior structural sections: three types of wall panels and a roof plate. The wall panels consisted of a solid section, a window section, and a door section. Each wall panel, four feet wide and approximately nine feet high, was constructed out of fourteen-gauge, rust-resistant, copper-bearing pressed sheet steel.[187] The roof panels, available in standardized lengths, fit together to form a watertight assembly that required neither an additional layer of roofing material nor flashing. The interior walls were built of insulation and steel, with partition panels constructed of sound-deadening insulation.[188] Unlike many other buildings at the exposition, the house integrated the walls as part of its structural system. The weight of the structure bore directly on the load-bearing panels.[189] Flanges, forming the sides of the wall panels, provided the rigidity necessary to support the weight of the roof.[190] Incorporating the structural system into the wall panels simplified construction, reducing on-site labor costs (Plate 22).

The assembly of Fisher's prefabricated steel exposition house required approximately 600 man-hours.[191] To construct the house, workers first set bolts into a concrete foundation to anchor the wall panels.[192] After bolting the sections to each other, they waterproofed the joints with mastic before covering them with small panel strips.[193] When the walls were completed, the roof sections were laid in place. A crew of four men with a crane (needed to lift the large panels) could assemble the basic shell of one of Fisher's small houses within two days.[194] In 1934 General Houses constructed a second house at A Century of Progress to demonstrate the use of open-web steel joists for supporting a roof. This framing system eliminated the need for a crane during construction, thereby simplifying the building process and reducing labor costs even further.[195]

In addition to its model house of porcelain-enamel steel, Armco sponsored the construction of a prefabricated steel goat barn located at the south end of the fairgrounds.[196] Armco, the first major industrial business to seriously enter the prefabricated housing market, developed the frameless barn in cooperation with three Chicago businesses: the Steelox Company, the Celotex Company, and Sears, Roebuck and Company. The designers created a prefabricated building system using twenty-gauge galvanized Armco iron, producing identical, standardized, interlocking steel panels, suitable for floors, roofs, and walls.[197] Influenced by the construction of the Travel and Transport Building, the individual units of Steelox also consisted of channel-shaped panels. But at sixteen inches across, they were much wider than those on the Railroad Hall. Shorter panels created openings for windows. As with the transportation building and the General Houses residence, flanges on the sides of the panels allowed the wall sections to interlock. Construction workers then sealed the joints with caulk. One-inch-wide panels of fiberboard inside the three-inch-wide channels helped insulate the building.

Promoters marketed this new method of steel construction as particularly applicable for low-cost buildings. They highlighted the fact that the standardized units could be stocked by building-materials suppliers. A farmer, they affirmed, could select one of the stock plans, buy the required number of units and fittings, then build his own "fire-, vermin- and rot-proof building" with relative ease.[198] If his needs changed over time, he could move or alter the building as necessary without significant waste or effort.

Although the Country Home Model Farm House, designed by the Chicago firm of Holsman and Holsman for the fair in 1934, was more traditional in style than those homes built by General Houses and Armco, it illustrated a dramatic new method of prefabricated construction. Sponsored by the Crowell Publishing Company (distributor of *The Country Home*, a national magazine for farmers), the Model Farm House was one of the exposition's two model residences constructed of brick. While the Common Brick Manufacturers' House was built specifically to promote the brick industry, Crowell's backers were more interested in demonstrating ideas for more efficient and affordable housing to potential rural homeowners. The publishing company stated that it sponsored the model house to illustrate "how the latest and most modern ideas in home planning, construction and equipment" could be applied to produce a comfortable, convenient, and practical farmhouse at a low cost.[199]

The house's exterior walls were built using one of the most innovative processes at the fair. The Model Farm House was the first residential prototype to incorporate brick precasting.[200] Instead of laying bricks in horizontal bands with mortar, as masons had done since Roman times, construction workers assembled the walls in large sections on the ground. To create these brick wall panels, they set up wood frames containing grids of reinforcing rods. They then filled the square openings with brick triads placed in alternating directions to form a basket-weave pattern on the wall surfaces. Cement mortar held the bricks and rods in place. The additional strength provided by the rods permitted the reduction of the walls' thickness from two bricks to one.

Promoters of the farmhouse believed that the precast would result in a "real boon to rural home building."[201] Not only did it reduce the cost, time, and materi-

FIG. 4.24. Assembly of the precast brick walls during construction of the Country Home Model Farm House. From *Country Home Model Farm House*, pamphlet produced by Crowell Publishing Company, 1934, from collection of author.

als needed to construct a brick house, but it also eliminated the need for highly skilled labor. Although workers cast the walls for the Model Farm House on site, promoters of precasting suggested that labor costs could be further reduced by constructing the brick panels in a factory and delivering the sections to the site ready for immediate assemblage.

In addition to promoting the benefits of prefabrication, a number of the exposition's designers and critics advocated a second, more controversial, modern building concept: disposable architecture. In keeping with the rise of modern manufacturing processes, as well as of a dominant consumer culture during the 1920s, which included creating artificial obsolescence at every level of consumption, architects began considering designing buildings to last a finite period, typically no more than a decade or two. A major impetus for this was a rise in the complexity of interior mechanical equipment. Continual improvements in ventilating, heating, and air-conditioning systems meant that workers had to make expensive alterations to existing structures. Changes in architectural styles and shifting land values resulting from changes in urban growth patterns led first critics and then the public to perceive many commercial and residential buildings as outdated shortly after construction. Disposable architecture seemed a logical solution to the problems of rapid obsolescence.

Louis Skidmore, chief of design for A Century of Progress, predicted that the construction of disposable buildings would have "an important effect on the economics of commercial building in the future."[202] He wrote:

> The structure of the 1933 World's Fair buildings offers a definite hope that a building practice will result that will produce commercial structures which will be designed to last no longer than their mechanical equipment and which will permit of [sic] economical demolition. By this means a marked savings in building cost would result which would bring the costs of production in the construction industry more in line with production costs in other industries.[203]

If builders could easily disassemble structures and then rebuild them every ten years—the typical life span of mechanical systems—the buildings could be constructed at a lower cost by using less-expensive materials.[204] Commercial building costs could then be kept in line with other business expenses.[205] Rebuilding would provide the opportunity for companies to keep up with architectural fashions, would allow the evolution of spatial and functional needs to be addressed as required, would avoid the difficult job of tearing out and installing new mechanical and electrical systems in existing structures, and would result in greater employment security for construction workers.[206]

Without a continuing need for dozens of large pavilions, most of the exhibition halls, like those of many earlier world's fairs, were to be demolished shortly after the close of the event. This prompted architects and organizers to promote the Chicago exposition as an example of the potential of temporary building design. The ability to be razed quickly was one of four basic requirements guiding the designs of the pavilions.[207] Almost all the architects considered both the value of salvageable parts and ease of demolition in their choice of building materials and construction methods.[208]

Architects did not limit the idea of disposable architecture to large commercial buildings. They also promoted the practice for residential construction. According to Howard Fisher, a major advantage of his General Houses prefabricated building system was the ease of adding to, altering, or disassembling a residence as a family's needs changed.[209] Daniel Burnham Jr., in the *New York Times Magazine,* stated that designing buildings to last "just as long as their interior mechanical equipment" would lead homeowners to buy a home the way they bought "a suit of clothes, with the intention of discarding it and buying another as soon as it grew shabby or out of date."[210] The general organizers of the Chicago exposition informed the public in *World's Fair Weekly* that soon architects would correct the old mistake of building one part of their houses to last a lifetime and the rest (the mechanical systems) to wear out in ten to fifteen years. Future housing, they predicted, would not only be constructed out of the new prefabricated materials but would also be designed for swift assemblage by "buttoning" the various sections together with bolts or clips, in techniques similar to those used in the construction of the Chicago fair buildings. As a result, altering walls would become as easy as changing the window dressings.[211]

FIG. 4.25. Visitors tour the Common Brick Manufacturers' model residence. From "The Modern Houses of the Century of Progress Exposition," *Architectural Forum* 59 (July 1933): 60.

In accordance with contracts signed prior to the construction of the fair pavilions, all the buildings at A Century of Progress, except those deemed worth saving by the South Park Commission, had to be removed from the site by 1 February 1935.[212] Earlier American world's fairs had left behind crumbled, worthless fragments; in contrast, the financiers of the 1933–34 event hoped to recoup a large portion of their initial investment

by selling used building materials from the pavilions for immediate reuse after the close of the event. Exposition organizers predicted a salvage value of 80 percent of the initial cost for the building materials, a figure 30 percent higher than that of previous world's fairs.[213]

The major exceptions to the practice of constructing pavilions of reusable materials were the Country Home Model Farm House, the Common Brick Manufacturers' House, and the Owens-Illinois Glass-Block Building. The sponsors of the last two buildings were more concerned with promoting the use of their specific building materials (which did not allow for easy demolition) than with efficient disassembly. The destruction of the glass-block and brick pavilions resulted in large quantities of debris with significantly lower salvage values than that of the steel-framed paneled buildings. The bolting and screwing together of the various types of prefabricated panels used in the construction of most of the other pavilions, however, allowed not only for easy demolition but also for reassembly at another location.[214]

Disposable architecture was promoted in the early 1930s in the pages of professional journals, major newspapers, and exposition publications. An article in the *New York Times Magazine* of 6 March 1932 quoted architectural commissioner Harvey Wiley Corbett as stating that disposable architecture was one of the "most important economic services" that the exposition offered.[215] The following year, in another *New York Times Magazine* article, celebrating opening day at the Chicago exposition, Daniel Burnham Jr. advocated adopting techniques used in the construction of the temporary exhibition pavilions to everyday building. The use of factory-made panels screwed or bolted to steel frames for easy disassembly, he forecast, would be "a means, intended or not, of abolishing long-established habits and conventions, [and] of making human society inconceivably more fluid. . . . Cities and towns may [now] change their shapes and even their locations like sandbars in the Missouri River."[216]

The author of an article on the exposition published in *Nation's Business* in June 1933 also supported designing buildings to last "only half as long as they are now."[217] He argued that disposable architecture was logical, as it would allow structures to keep up with the continual advancements in mechanical systems and at the same time would combat the often-rapid devaluation of a building in terms of location and function. Investment in foundations and structures built for permanence, he contended, prohibited economic demolition at the moment the building became obviously obsolete. By building disposable architecture, as exhibited at the Chicago exposition, he exclaimed, architects could immunize the world against the "deadly atrophy of obsolescence!"[218]

The reliance on prefabrication at A Century of Progress contributed significantly to the financial success of the event, despite the Great Depression, by greatly reducing material and labor costs. As the first extensive application of prefabrication in the United States using modern building materials, the fair illustrated to the American public practical methods for reducing construction costs. Builders began to rely heavily on prefabrication as manufacturers continued to standardize construction materials during the mid-twentieth century. Meanwhile, the concept of disposable buildings eventually found favor in more subtle ways in the building industry as designers began specifying new, more efficient, yet less durable, man-made materials, such as Sheetrock and Masonite, in place of more permanent, traditional natural building products, like stone and hardwoods. In particular, residential homes built after the Chicago exposition were designed to last not a century or more, as many of their predecessors had been, but often no longer than the standard thirty-year mortgage.

The use of the new materials, structural innovations, and assembly-line manufacturing processes, along with the rejection of historical forms, led progressive architects to develop new formal vocabularies for modern architecture. These included a significant reduction in applied decoration and the rise of new symbolic forms. Although as fair architecture the buildings produced for the Century of Progress International Exposition were set apart from everyday realities, the designs reflected important developments in the definition of modern architecture in America.

FIVE

EXPOSITION HOUSES OF TODAY AND TOMORROW

*The chief difference between the homes of
today and those of our forebears is that our
mothers and grandmothers "served" their
homes; whereas, the homes of us moderns
"serve" us! . . . The Machine Age has liberated
the world from the slavery of drudgery.*

DOROTHY RALEY, *A Century of
Progress Homes and Furnishings*

odel houses, like those discussed in
chapter 4, were among the most popular attractions at A Century of Progress. Well
over 1.5 million fairgoers toured the Home
and Industrial Arts Exhibit during the first
season of the exposition.[1] Situated in the center of the fairgrounds, this elaborate
domestic display offered homeowners the opportunity to inspect and evaluate new
ideas in modern architecture and living. Architects, building-products manufacturers, and other related businesses sponsored the individual model residences. The
designs clearly illustrated the dramatic impact a science-driven consumer culture
could have on future domestic environments by featuring mass-produced building
materials, novel methods of construction, progressive concepts for the organization of interior spaces, modern furnishings, and laborsaving devices. Nowhere else
at the exposition could visitors experience the potential of advances in science and
technology in a way that was so tangibly relevant to their daily lives.

Fair organizers promoted the houses' durability, convenience, livability, and
cost-efficiency.[2] In addition, the residences illustrated a number of modern design concepts being advocated by progressive architects in both the United States
and Europe.[3] Almost all the dwellings emphasized an efficient use of space and
had no cellars or attics. The inclusion of air-conditioning along with heating systems eliminated the need for windows that opened. Other new features included
attached garages and roof decks with solariums. The smooth wall surfaces and
clean-lined fixtures that appeared in many of the homes were marketed as a way
of reducing housekeeping chores by preventing dirt buildup in intricate joints and
crevices. While some exposition houses exhibited flat, unadorned facades recalling

progressive European designs (such as the houses built for the Weissenhofsiedlung in Stuttgart, Germany, and featured in the International Style Show), others incorporated art deco details. A few of the dwellings blended modern concepts with more traditional forms. Among the collection of model residences were a number of corporate pavilions, including the Owens-Illinois Glass-Block Building and the Crane Company Station.

The Home Planning Hall, designed by Ely Jacques Kahn, was a white building with an orange, zigzagging entrance facade. It provided a central thematic focus to the Home and Industrial Arts Exhibit area and contained exhibits that directly related to the "problems and wishes of modern home planning," including demonstrations of home equipment, household appliances, and building materials.[4] Three all-metal model kitchens illustrated the benefits of stainless-steel drain boards,

FIG. 5.1. Model houses at the Home and Industrial Arts Exhibit in 1933. From *Official Guide Book of the World's Fair of 1934* (Chicago: Cuneo Press, 1934), 126.

Lumber House
Brick House
Rostone House

House of Tomorrow
Florida Home
Armco-Ferro Enamel

Masonite House
Southern Cypress
Stransteel House

sinks, tabletops, and appliances. "Fact-finding research specialists" working in the pavilion carried out scientific tests of materials and household equipment, which ranged from enamelware to house paints to steel furniture, in front of large audiences.[5] Modern methods of refrigeration were also demonstrated. Like the caramel-wrapping machine at the 1930 exposition in Liège, a giant mixer for mayonnaise was in constant operation, to the amazement of onlooking fairgoers.[6] Various home appliances, including washing machines and plumbing fixtures, were also on display. While these exhibits attracted crowds of captivated visitors, what fascinated many of them even more was the surrounding neighborhood of full-scale model homes.

THE HOUSE OF TOMORROW

No other model residence generated greater interest among the general public than the House of Tomorrow.[7] Chicago designer George Frederick Keck, a major proponent of modern architecture in the United States, clearly realized the potential role a model home at A Century of Progress could play in advancing his pragmatic vision of progressive building design.[8] His primary objective was to make modern architecture more understandable and tangible to the public by focusing on the building type to which the average American could most easily relate.[9] In demonstrating the widespread benefits of modern design, he highlighted several characteristics shared by many progressive architects at the time. These included reliance on functional designs, an interest in new building technology, and a desire to eliminate historical forms. Keck realized that if his house was to hold its own in the carnival-like atmosphere of the exposition, it would have to radiate its own novel appeal. He achieved this by creating an unusual-looking glass-and-steel design that, although meeting the basic functional needs of a modern family, "entirely upset the conventional ideas of a home."[10] He believed that those who experienced his futuristic house would become more willing to forgo traditional historical forms in favor of functional, modern domestic designs.[11] In return, the architect hoped that by witnessing fairgoers' reactions as they toured his exposition house, he would acquire a better understanding of the public's general response to new design ideas.[12]

Keck combined the progressive tradition of midwestern architects, the language of European modernists, and the innovative applications of new building technology with his own keen sense of logic and practicality to produce a personal vision of modern architecture. As a native midwesterner, Keck was exposed to many underlying concepts of modern architecture during his schooling and early career through the writings and designs of Louis Sullivan, Frank Lloyd Wright, and other pioneering Chicago architects.[13] He fully embraced these older designers'

FIG. 5.4. Richards House, Watertown, Wisconsin. From *House of Tomorrow* (n.p.: B. R. Graham, 1933), brochure from collection of author.

though willing, were unable to obtain financing, Keck had begun searching for ways to promote modern residential designs as attractive financial investments. He thought that if bankers, who typically viewed nontraditional house designs as risky endeavors, could experience a well-designed, futuristic residence, they might become more willing to invest in less radical, modern-style houses.[22] This underlying agenda led Keck to make his exposition design appear as innovative as possible. As a result, the house became one of the most obvious realizations of a major theme of the exposition—the potential effect of recent advances in science and technology on everyday life.

According to a souvenir brochure on the House of Tomorrow given to those who toured the twelve-sided model dwelling, Keck had not attempted to give the building a specific style but rather had generated its eye-catching design by straightforwardly fulfilling the functional requirements of its program.[23] In addition, Keck borrowed formal characteristics and technical concepts from two earlier unusual residential designs. The first was the Richards House, an innovative octagonal brick dwelling built in Watertown, Wisconsin, in the mid-nineteenth century that the architect knew from childhood. Keck acknowledged that he had been strongly influenced not only by its basic plan but also by the inventive uses of gravity and convection to provide temperature control, ventilation, and running water in the house.[24] He even included a photograph of the Richards House in the souvenir pamphlet. Keck proclaimed in the caption of the illustration that if other basic tenets, in particular the belief that the functional requirements of a building should dictate its form. Like many of his progressive colleagues, he also felt strongly that applied ornament from past styles was neither appropriate nor acceptable for modern architectural designs.[14]

Although Keck remained in the Midwest for his formal education and through almost all of his career, he had a strong interest in architectural developments taking place elsewhere in the world. Like several of the other architects who produced residential designs for the exposition, he found the ideology of the European modernists especially intriguing and was influenced by the formal qualities of their architecture.[15] Keck particularly expressed an affinity for the ideas of Le Corbusier (he had purchased a copy of Le Corbusier's *Vers une architecture [Towards a New Architecture]* shortly after it became available in English).[16] As a result, his early designs often exhibited uses of materials, forms, and space similar to those of Le Corbusier and other modern European architects.[17] He also shared with the Europeans an unwavering desire to create better housing for the public. However, in contrast to the large social housing projects being designed for postwar Europe, Keck's work focused on the specific needs of individual clients. He thus produced distinctive residences that reflected the greater emphasis on the individual in the United States.

The ideas of Buckminster Fuller, the ingenious philosopher and inventor, also had a significant impact on Keck's early architecture.[18] Many of the architect's progressive ideas grew out of the inventor's groundbreaking Dymaxion designs. Fuller based many of his ideas on a profound belief that every social or industrial operation should be given the most efficient solution possible.[19] In attempting to reach their shared goal, Fuller and Keck each looked to new developments in technology for potential ways to improve the daily lives of average Americans by offering simpler and more comfortable home environments. Both men believed that new, less costly products and processes could produce more effective housing. The need to generate public acceptance for the unusual aesthetics and elements of their work played a major part in each of their decisions to produce model homes.

Keck's work for the Chicago World's Fair began in January 1933 when he applied for a permit to construct the House of Tomorrow in the Home and Industrial Arts Exhibit. On the application he stated that he wanted to build his model home to demonstrate newly available mechanical equipment and building materials.[20] According to his younger brother, William (who carried out some of the design work on the house), the older Keck specifically wanted to develop a model residence that visitors would find entertaining as well as educational in hopes of making them feel more at ease with modern architectural designs.[21] After having the plans of several of his forward-looking residences remain unrealized because clients,

FIG. 5.2 *(top f*
Demonstratic
mayonnaise n
Home Plannir
from collectic

FIG. 5.3 *(belo*
Fairgoers tou
Tomorrow in
and Fabry, ph

FIG. 5.2 *(top facing)*. Demonstration of the Kraft mayonnaise machine in the Home Planning Hall. Postcard from collection of author. FIG. 5.3 *(below facing)*. Fairgoers tour House of Tomorrow in 1933. Kaufmann and Fabry, photographers.

FIG. 5.4. Richards House, Watertown, Wisconsin. From *House of Tomorrow* (n.p.: B.R. Graham, 1933), brochure from collection of author.

though willing, were unable to obtain financing, Keck had begun searching for ways to promote modern residential designs as attractive financial investments. He thought that if bankers, who typically viewed nontradiptional house designs as risky endeavors, could experience a well-designed, futuristic residence, they might become more willing to invest in less radical, modern-style houses.[22] This underlying agenda led Keck to make his exposition design appear as innovative as possible. As a result, the house became one of the most obvious realizations of a major theme of the exposition—the potential effect of recent advances in science and technology on everyday life.

According to a souvenir brochure on the House of Tomorrow given to those who toured the twelve-sided model dwelling, Keck had not attempted to give the building a specific style but rather had generated its eye-catching design by straightforwardly fulfilling the functional requirements of its program.[23] In addition, Keck borrowed formal characteristics and technical concepts from two earlier unusual residential designs. The first was the Richards House, an innovative octagonal brick dwelling built in Watertown, Wisconsin, in the mid-nineteenth century that the architect knew from childhood. Keck acknowledged that he had been strongly influenced not only by its basic plan but also by the inventive uses of gravity and convection to provide temperature control, ventilation, and running water in the house.[24] He even included a photograph of the Richards House in the souvenir pamphlet. Keck proclaimed in the caption of the illustration that if other designers had duplicated the creative spirit and direct expression exemplified in the Richards House, America by the 1930s might have had an architectural technique comparable to the functional processes prevalent in its industries.[25]

The second precedent for Keck's glass duodecagon residence was the Dymaxion House, the unrealized experimental dwelling designed by Buckminster Fuller. This hexagonal house, with floors and a roof suspended from a central mast, was, according to its designer, to be built of yet-to-be-developed aluminum alloys and structurally stable transparent plastics.[26] Many of the novel ideas present in Keck's model home derived directly from the ideology behind the Dymaxion House. Included was an ardent commitment to efficiency through the application of new technological developments. Although Keck candidly recognized the influence the Richards House had on the design of his House of Tomorrow, he did not publicly acknowledge his much larger debt to Fuller's design.[27]

Heeding his own advice, Keck directly expressed the numerous inventive ideas incorporated in the House of Tomorrow by not hiding the innovations under historical forms, as was the case in the Italianate Richards House. Instead, he specified a continuous transparent facade for what became known as "America's first glass house."[28] The modern aesthetic of the exterior of the house was further emphasized by a flat roof. While horizontal roofs were often problematic in northern climates like that of Chicago, they were popular among progressive architects during this time. Designers (as well as clients) particularly liked the fact that flat roofs offered the

FIG. 5.5. Plans of the House of Tomorrow show an airplane hangar on the ground floor and a rooftop conservatory on the third floor. From *House of Tomorrow* (n.p.: B.R. Graham, 1933), brochure from collection of author.

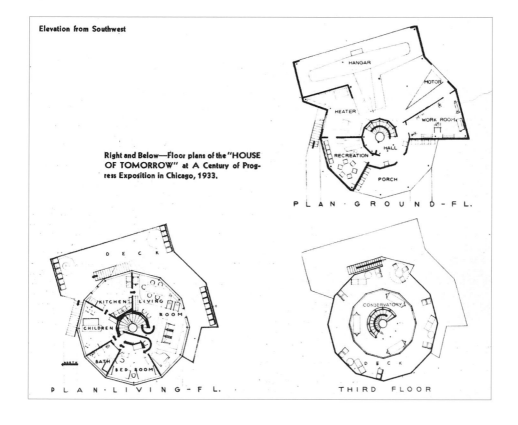

potential for additional living space at little extra cost. Keck limited decorative references in his design to the terraces, which were done in what a contemporary writer referred to as a "marine manner." This subtle style, derived from the design of ocean liners and typically limited to flat, neutral-colored walls, round porthole windows, and pipe railings, was favored by a number of modern designers, including Le Corbusier.[29]

The formal arrangement of major elements in the House of Tomorrow revealed a strong affinity to both the Richards and Dymaxion houses. All three house plans contained a series of rooms situated around a central stairwell. Keck adopted the basic polygonal design of the earlier multisided residences, but he increased the number of sides for his model dwelling to twelve. This decision was not made arbitrarily. In following a belief that the practical needs of a building should dictate its form, Keck took into consideration both the functional requirements of the project and the practical limitations of the construction materials to be used. In the case of the House of Tomorrow, twelve of the largest commercially available glass panels were needed to encircle the desired amount of interior space.[30]

FIG. 5.6. The House of Tomorrow under construction with the central structural core visible. From *House of Tomorrow* (n.p.: B. R. Graham, 1933), brochure from collection of author.

Keck adapted other forward-looking concepts featured in Fuller's Dymaxion design for the House of Tomorrow. Most significant were a structural system that consisted of floors cantilevering outward from a central core, and the use of newly available man-made building materials. While cables running from the top of the central tower to the edges of the outside walls provided additional support in the Dymaxion House, the three layers of structural steel framing and fiber-concrete floor slabs in the House

of Tomorrow received extra support from slender columns located at the edges of the exterior glass walls. As with the Dymaxion House, Keck placed the main living areas on the second floor. The ground level was reserved for mechanical equipment and family vehicles—a garage for an automobile and a hangar for a personal airplane.[31] Above the main living area, Keck incorporated additional living space by situating a small twelve-sided enclosed solarium in the center of his flat roof deck.

Fuller specified the use of materials with "standards higher than those currently on the market" for his Dymaxion House, but Keck was limited to existing products.[32] In addition to sheathing the upper levels of the House of Tomorrow in mass-produced tinted glass like that used in storefronts, he incorporated several recently developed products into his design. These included new types of phenoloid and insulated plasterboards that contained an interior layer of aluminum foil insulation in the opaque walls.[33] Function presented the most significant reason why Keck selected one material over another. For example, he wrote that he chose specific flooring materials for each room based on the intended use of the space. He floored main living areas in walnut or pine end-grain wood blocks for their elegant appearance, the recreation and children's rooms, as well as the bathroom, in rubber tiles for easy cleanup, and the garage and shop in cement for its durability.[34]

Influenced by contemporary ideas emanating from Europe, Keck, in the interior design of the house, presented a *machine à habiter* (machine for living) for future American families. He, like Fuller, strongly believed that the mechanization of a residence would lead to easier and more comfortable living. This meant going beyond the innovations of the Richards House and exercising complete control over interior environments by incorporating air-conditioning and passive solar heating. The result was an ability to maintain "fresh, odorless, dustless" air at optimal temperature and humidity levels throughout the year.[35]

A cooling system became a necessity since the windows could not be opened, thereby making natural temperature regulation impossible. Like the avoidance of windows in the major pavilions at the exposition, the use of fixed panes on the House of Tomorrow reflected a growing faith in man's potential to conquer nature through developments in science and technology. This belief is also illustrated in Keck's explorations into the benefits of passive solar heat in the home.[36] To control the light and solar energy that poured into the residence through the large glass walls on sunny days, the architect incorporated Venetian blinds, roller shades, and curtains.[37]

Keck further developed the concept of the house as a machine for living through the inclusion of a wide range of advanced appliances and gadgets; some, like a television set, were still in their initial phase of development.[38] The electrical kitchen contained an "iceless refrigerator" and other new time-saving appliances, including a mechanical dishwasher that both washed and dried the

dishes.[39] A photoelectric cell made it possible for the kitchen door to open and shut automatically when an invisible beam was interrupted.[40] Similar electronic technology allowed one to open and close the doors of the garage and the airplane hangar with only the push of a button. Keck's interest in electronic devices also led him to install an electric eye on the exterior of the home that could project an image of a person at the front door onto a small screen inside the residence.[41] These laborsaving devices provided a sense of wonderment to fairgoers and encouraged housewives to fantasize about the abundance of additional free time they would soon have to spend relaxing with their families.

To create an idealized environment for his radical new modern lifestyle of convenience, Keck incorporated into the design recent developments in room arrangements and furnishings. As in the Dymaxion House design, modern furniture contributed to the unconventional atmosphere of the House of Tomorrow. Interior designer Irene Kay Hyman created the modern interior room settings, while Keck and his chief draftsman, Leland Atwood, designed or selected most of the furniture and light fixtures.[42] Keck shared Fuller's distaste for unnecessary walls and, wherever possible, used furniture to divide the larger rooms into smaller spaces. He typically located more substantial pieces along the edges of rooms to preserve a sense of openness in the relatively small living areas. Keck favored movable over fixed pieces to allow for maximum flexibility in the floor plan.[43] Most of the furniture shared the clean lines of contemporary European designs. The sleek chrome-plated tubular dining room chairs and bedroom furniture, manufactured by W. H. Howell Company, for example, exhibited strong formal ties to contemporary designs produced by Ludwig Mies van der Rohe and Marcel Breuer.

Like many other modern architects, Keck believed that the natural beauty of the material should provide the basic aesthetic interest in modern designs. In the House of Tomorrow he specified individual pieces of exotic woods, polished metals, and luxurious fabrics. Influenced by Mies van der Rohe's use of elegant materials for large wall surfaces in buildings such as the German Pavilion at the 1929 Barcelona exposition, Keck positioned a soft-gray glass wall between the living room and kitchen, a polished black glass wall in the stair hall, and white glass walls around the bathroom.[44] In the main living area he placed tables of Macassar ebony, black walnut, and Hungarian ash. An ebony piano with chromium and glass legs and a white hand-woven Moroccan rug provided additional interest to the room. Keck wrote that he and Atwood had designed these individual pieces "to take a definite part in, [but also] be subservient to, the decorative scheme as a whole."[45] Together with the exterior form of the residence, the furnishings created a fantastic, yet harmonious, decorative scheme that led many fairgoers to believe that a better future was just around the corner.[46]

FIG. 5.8. Dining area of the House of Tomorrow in 1933, with tubular metal furniture. Hedrich-Blessing, photographers (HB-01670C). Courtesy of Chicago History Museum.

OTHER MODERN MODEL HOUSES

The House of Tomorrow became one of the most talked about highlights of the exposition. Despite having to pay a ten-cent entrance fee, over 1.25 million fairgoers toured the interior of the residence during the two seasons of the event.[47] While it may have been the most unusual model residence at A Century of Progress, it was not the only one to exhibit formal ties to the work of European modernists. One of the most distinctive of the exposition houses that evoked a European vocabulary was the six-sided, flat-roofed Brick House, also known as the Super-Safe Home, designed by Chicago architect Andrew Rebori. The Common Brick Manufacturers' Association sponsored the construction of the dwelling to increase public awareness of the continuing role common brick could play in a market that was increasingly being encroached on by new man-made materials. Rebori highlighted the ability of brick buildings constructed with modern techniques to stand up against the destructive effects of nature.[48] The incorporation of steel reinforcement bars between the layers of common bricks strengthened the structure and made possible large horizontal spans of the material in the house.[49]

The basic form of the Brick House closely recalled domestic designs produced by Le Corbusier in the 1920s, in particular his Citrohan House (1922). Rebori probably first became aware of the Citrohan House through its publication in Le Corbusier's treatise *Towards a New Architecture.* Both the Brick and Citrohan house designs placed the main living spaces on a second level that was partially supported on piers or *pilotis.* Covered parking for a family automobile was located below. A small ground floor tucked behind the parking area of each dwelling provided a place for utilities and other services. As with the House of Tomorrow, flat roofs and terraces offered outdoor living areas on the upper floors. Large sheets of industrial window panes, along with small, round, porthole windows, were also common to both Rebori's and Le Corbusier's designs. Cantilevered projections that protected interior rooms on the upper levels from excessive sunlight were common to the two houses. They differed dramatically, however, not only in their primary construction materials (brick versus

FIG. 5.9. Rendering of the Citrohan House project (1922) by Le Corbusier. Copyright 2006 Artists Rights Society (ARS), New York / ADAGP, Paris / FLC.

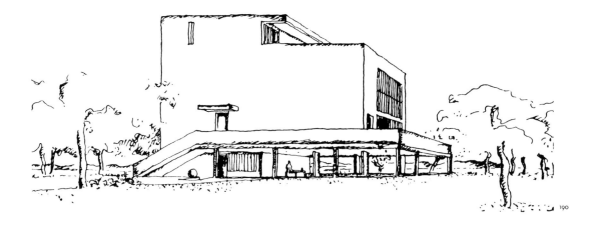

concrete) but also in the shape of their plans. Whereas Le Corbusier had relied on a traditional rectangular form, the footprint of the Brick House was an irregular hexagon, which resulted in unusually shaped interior rooms.[50]

Both of the designs united the dining and living areas, so the relatively small houses seemed significantly more spacious. A newspaper article in the *Chicago American* remarked that this practice was common to most of the model residences at the exposition. The author stated that a home built on a Century of Progress plan would probably have a roof deck, a recreation room, and an airplane hangar, but it would positively not have a dining room. Instead, meals would be served in a dining alcove located at one end of the living room that "may be shaped like the letter L or T or almost any other letter in the alphabet."[51]

The Brick Association specified that the walls of its house be left bare to clearly illustrate the use of brick for both interior and exterior surfaces. Most shocking to fairgoers were the brick ceilings that loomed heavily overhead in several of the rooms. The sparse furnishings in the house assured adequate space to allow large groups of fairgoers to parade though the dwelling. Much of the original furniture was of wood, which provided an agreeable contrast to the abundance of brick in

FIG. 5.10. Main living area of the Common Brick Manufacturers' model residence in 1933. From *Glass as an Architectural Medium in 9 Small Modern Houses at A Century of Progress 1933–4* (Toledo, Ohio: Libbey Owens Ford Glass Company, circa 1934), n.p.

the home. Carrara Glass walls offered additional relief from the masonry surfaces in the kitchen and bathroom.

Another model home that exhibited significant ties to the work of the European modernists was the Design for Living House by John C. B. Moore in association with S. Clements Horsley and Richard C. Wood (Plate 23). The exterior of the residence could have come directly from the drawing board of Le Corbusier. Its flat facades, ribbon windows, roof terraces, ground-floor garage, and entrance overhang were features common to several of the European architect's early houses, most closely resembling the Villa Stein.[52] The Design for Living House was built out of four-foot-wide vertical panels of yellow Homosote insulation board that were bolted to a traditional wood frame and a concrete foundation. In both the Villa Stein and the Design for Living House divorcing the wall surfaces from the structure allowed for flexibility in the composition of their facades. Window and door openings served as the primary decorative elements.[53] Two faint horizontal bands dividing the floor levels and a third near the roofline suggesting a cornice offered additional interest to the front and side elevations of the Design for Living House. The rear of the residence included a projecting ground-floor dining area and a porch covered by a large roof terrace. Rows of tall windows on both floors helped reduce the perceived division between interior and exterior living spaces, thereby encouraging people to take in what was then believed to be the healthful effects of extensive exposure to the sun.[54]

FIG. 5.11 *(below)*. Main living area of the Design for Living House, with aluminum fireplace and copper sheathing on walls. From "The Old Homestead Goes Modern," *World's Fair Weekly* (22 July 1933): 6. FIG. 5.12 *(top facing)*. Cover of *Sloane's House of Today at the Century of Progress Exposition*, pamphlet printed by William Edwin Rudge in 1933, from collection of author. FIG. 5.13 *(below facing)*. Living room of the House of Today, decorated with Regency furniture. From *Sloane's House of Today at the Century of Progress Exposition*, pamphlet printed by William Edwin Rudge in 1933, from collection of author.

SLOANE'S HOUSE OF TODAY

AT THE
CENTURY
OF
PROGRESS
EXPOSITION

Like many of the other model dwellings, the Design for Living House had no basement or attic. Heating and cooling equipment was located on the ground floor.[55] Additional characteristics the residence shared with other fair houses were fixed windowpanes and an open floor plan.[56] The interior rooms, designed by Gilbert Rohde, featured comfortable wood-and-upholstery furnishings and patterned wallpapers. The dining room furniture, for example, was of natural birch and deep brown African mahogany. Yellow and rust fabrics covered the chairs. Curtains were pale gray, a color also used in the bedrooms.[57] Reflective surfaces helped make the interior rooms appear larger. Portions of some walls were covered in Merimet, a thin copper sheathing that was polished and lacquered. The central focus of the living room was a large fireplace with a metal surround produced from a single sheet of aluminum with a semilustrous finish.[58] Large mirrored surfaces placed throughout the house further increased the sense of spaciousness.

Not all the model residences were so forward looking. Even the name of the House of Today model home suggested a more approachable and attainable design than some of the other exposition residences. Sponsored by the decorating company of W. & J. Sloane and designed by the firm of architectural commissioner Harvey Wiley Corbett (Corbett, Harrison, and MacMurray), the House of Today was not constructed to feature new building methods or materials, as were so many of the other model homes. Instead, it was built to display high-end furnishings.[59] The house presented a restrained art deco exterior with modernized Regency interiors. The white, scalloped facades, sided "in the fashion of flutes from a classical column," were detailed with stripped classical pilasters at the corners and a hint of a cornice near the roofline. The pilasters were edged in silver and topped by orange capitals. Aquamarine blue shutters framed the windows.[60] A garage attached to one side of the home balanced a roof deck and tower on the opposite end.

Most of the articles and pamphlets published on the house focused on its decor. Its opulence contrasted considerably with the more austere interiors of the Brick House and the House of Tomorrow. Fairgoers entered the House of Today through an octagonal entrance hall. The focal point of the foyer was a statue of the goddess Diana. According to one publication, a mirror located opposite the front door served a purpose "beyond the business of reminding incoming guests to powder their noses or straighten their ties," as it broke down the confines of the hall by "its soft reflection of the gallery beyond."[61] The grand thirty-two-foot-long gallery was elegantly decorated with dark sage-green walls and white taffeta curtains. A plum Biedermeier sofa and matching chairs rested on a black-and-white-checkered linoleum floor, and a mural depicting a romantic vision of life in the eighteenth century decorated an interior wall.

The most spectacular space in the house was a high-vaulted living room. A large chandelier hung from the center of its deep-blue ceiling. The walls were

painted a lemon color, which provided a striking background for the mahogany Regency furniture. It also contrasted sharply with a black Empire
fireplace. An exotic ambiance was created by the inclusion of a zebra-stripe
rug in the center of a conversation area at one end of the room. Blue and
white mirrored screens at the other end hid a semicircular dining alcove.[62]
To avoid disrupting the room's historical character, the telephone and the
radio equipment were concealed behind Regency-style bookcases.

In contrast to the traditionally decorated main living areas, the house's up-to-
date kitchen included sleek cabinets, a stainless-steel sink, and modern appliances.
Large windows amply lit the room. Factory-like fenestration, albeit framed by curtains, appropriately reflected the fact that modern kitchens were beginning to be
viewed as domestic scientific laboratories, with appliances arranged to enable the
housewife to move most efficiently through her daily chores.[63]

Another more conventional model house was designed by Ernest A. Grunsfeld

FIG. 5.14. Modern kitchen of the House of Today. From *Sloane's House of Today at the Century of Progress Exposition,* pamphlet printed by William Edwin Rudge in 1933, from collection of author.

FIG. 5.15. Wood-paneled living room of the Lumber Industries House. From Dorothy Raley, *A Century of Progress Homes and Furnishings* (Chicago: M. A. Ring, 1934), 83.

Jr. and was sponsored by the National Lumber Manufacturers' Association. Like the Common Brick Manufacturers' House, the Lumber Industries House promoted the use of a traditional building product at a time when steel and other competing man-made materials were becoming more prevalent in the market. The dwelling was specifically built to highlight the various types of wood available for residential use in the United States. Each of the five main rooms exhibited different types of wood. The spacious, vaulted-ceiling living room included elements of Appalachian walnut, and white oak in a herringbone pattern covered the floor. The dining room featured American walnut. Even the tableware was made of the wood.[64] Furnishings throughout the interior were also of different types of wood; they included walnut end tables, a cherry desk, and maple chairs. Patterned upholstery and area rugs provided contrast to the wood surfaces. The exterior of the house consisted of horizontal bands of California redwood attached to a lumber stud-and-joist frame. Vertical windows were located near each corner, allowing for cross-ventilation and greater variation in the arrangement of interior spaces.[65] Rounded corners of bent plywood that hid built-in downspouts hinted at streamlining. In the context of the other models in the Home and Industrial Arts Exhibit, the house's most unusual feature was a traditional pitched roof.

THE CRYSTAL HOUSE

The model houses proved so popular with fairgoers that several additional homes were built throughout the fairgrounds in time for the opening of the second fair season. Encouraged by both the economic and critical success of the House of Tomorrow, George Frederick Keck decided to use earnings from his first exposition house to design another experimental residence in 1934. While the House of Tomorrow had, to a large extent, fulfilled his goal of making more people aware of the potential benefits of progressive architectural designs, he felt that he could generate even more visibility for his ideas on modern architecture by constructing another, even more stunning, futuristic model home. The most significant difference between Keck's two residences (other than their basic forms) was that whereas the architect had created the House of Tomorrow to be a unique machine for living, he designed his Crystal House to highlight the potential benefits of prefabrication and mass production. Keck presupposed that adapting the assembly-line process used by the Ford Motor Company and many of the other corporations exhibiting at A Century of Progress would make modern residential architecture more affordable to the average American.[66]

In an essay discussing the interior furnishings of the Crystal House, Dorothy Raley laid out its major purposes:

FIG. 5.16. Glass-and-steel exterior of Keck's Crystal House built for the 1934 fair season. Hedrich-Blessing, photographers (HB-11078B). Courtesy of Chicago History Museum.

1. To provide the maximum interior living-area with the minimal use of space,—thereby effecting the first reform in a studied plan to reduce building costs;

2. To invent a new general design or a new pattern of Home where the Home serves the occupants, and not the occupants serve the home;

3. To provide a scientifically healthful, light, cheerful residence which capitalizes Nature's fickle moods to man's incessant advantage, night and day,—bringing the life-giving sunshine indoors, and excluding alike dry, hot, humid air in summer, and damp, raw, cold, biting winds in winter;

4. To design a house of such qualities in such a manner and of such materials that it lends itself to mass production, with abundant opportunity for individual expression in the matter of style,—in order that this ideal Home may be within the reach of the masses.[67]

In his desire to create a cost-efficient dwelling, Keck attempted to dramatically reduce the time required to build a single-family home. He admitted that the $15,000 cost of the initial Crystal House was excessive, but he predicted that in actual production the house could be built in as little as three weeks and both the price of materials and the cost of labor would drop significantly.[68] The short construction process, he claimed, would be made possible by preassembling elements for the house in a factory. Although it is unclear how Keck planned to actually put together the parts in the prefabricated version of his Crystal House, the walls and floors of the demonstration model, like those of most of the major exposition pavilions, were bolted together to allow for easy demolition after the close of the event.[69]

As with the House of Tomorrow, Keck relied on a dramatic formal composition to help attract attention to the Crystal House. His design overtly expressed the structure of the residence by projecting an exterior frame of steel columns and trusses beyond its glass walls. Additional steel columns on two sides of the tri-level glass box supported a large L-shaped terrace. Keck selected glass and steel as the major materials for the house because they could be assembled quickly and economically. He stated that he chose glass for the exterior facades not merely to bring attention to the house (which it did), but also because it symbolized "the type of material which goes into place readily and once in place is always finished[,] needing no upkeep."[70] Additionally, using transparent walls allowed the greatest possible light and sense of space inside the house.[71] The architect clearly expressed the various floor levels on the exterior through the use of different types of heavy plate glass for the walls, with translucent ripple-glass on the ground floor; sun-filtering, aqua-tinted glazing on the second level; and clear glass on the third floor.[72]

Keck once again consigned the main living areas to the second floor, locating the garage and utilities on the ground level. By placing the structural elements on the exterior, as had previously been done at the Travel and Transport Building, he produced an interior that allowed for maximum flexibility in the use of space. The only permanent divisions on the main floor were the walls enclosing the kitchen and another wall setting off the stair hall.[73] To help minimize sound levels in the open area, Acusti-Celotex was used for ceilings and interior partitions. Careful placement of furniture separated the remaining space into areas designated for living, dining, and study.[74]

The Crystal House shared many characteristics with earlier exposition homes. Keck again utilized fixed planes of glass and incorporated means to artificially cool and heat the residence. In an effort to improve the regulation of solar heat, he specified that aluminum Venetian blinds be installed on the exteriors of the windows to help cut down on the amount of heat trapped indoors between the glass and blinds.[75] Brown linen curtains on the south walls contributed to the reduction of bright sunlight entering the house on hot days.[76] All electric lighting came from plug-in fixtures with dimmers permitting precise control of artificial light levels.[77]

Keck also highlighted the natural characteristics of the exquisite materials used in the home's furnishings.[78] Leather seats accented chairs of Cuban mahogany. An unadorned wardrobe located in the man's bedroom also featured the elegant grain of mahogany. In the dining room, sea-green seat covers set off chairs and a table of light American ash.[79] The designer specified that only fabrics of solid hues be used in the house to avoid the distraction of eye-catching patterns. Many of the chairs and other furnishings designed by Atwood were close copies of works by progressive European modernists. Versions of Mies van der Rohe's Tugendhat chairs appeared in the living room, Le Corbusier's bentwood armchairs could be found in the lady's room, while chairs and other pieces based on designs by Walter Gropius and Marcel Breuer were located throughout the house.[80] The sparse placement of the modern furnishings and the large planes of different materials defining the walls and floors again created an atmosphere more like that of Mies van der Rohe's German Pavilion at the 1929 Barcelona exposition than like that of a middle-class American home.

Buckminster Fuller must have not objected to Keck's adopting some of his ideas

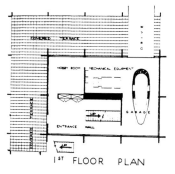

FIG. 5.17. Plans for the Crystal House with Buckminster Fuller's Dymaxion Car Number Three shown parked in the garage. From "Trends and Topics of the Times," *American Architect* 145 (July 1934): 40.

for the House of Tomorrow, since his Dymaxion Car Number Three was displayed as the family vehicle at the Crystal House.[81] The sleek, streamlined, three-wheeled automobile fit harmoniously with the experimental home and its furnishings. The inclusion of the futuristic car in the exhibit helped draw additional attention to the residence and helped present a more comprehensive vision of future housing to the public. Even with the Dymaxion Car on display, attendance figures at the Crystal House during the 1934 fair season did not come close to meeting projected numbers.[82] This unfortunate lack of visitors was almost solely due to the fact that exposition organizers had not allowed Keck to build his second design in the Home and Industrial Arts Exhibit area alongside the other model residences.[83] Instead, they relegated the house to a site behind the Electrical Building on Northerly Island, well hidden from the major streams of pedestrian traffic. Despite its poor location, the Crystal House did receive notice in architectural journals, trade publications, and popular newspapers.[84] As a result, the architect was able to present the prototype of his mass-produced futuristic home to the public, but mainly through secondary sources.

As in Keck's other modern designs, as well as in the work of prominent European architects, the aesthetic quality of the residence primarily derived from the natural beauty of its materials. Atwood stated that it was the aim of the designers "to bring out such values as beauty of surface and grain of fine woods, in combination with interesting textures of the materials—rather than to stress a superficial color scheme."[85] The last part was intended as a critique of Joseph Urban's chromatic design for the main fair pavilions. Keck covered the wall separating the stairs from the other living spaces in Macassar ebony. A handmade Moroccan carpet in a coffee color laid out on wall-to-wall Chinese matting helped define areas designated for different functions on the main floor. If desired, a hand-woven curtain in a natural color could be pulled to separate the study from the dining room.[86]

OTHER NEW HOUSES IN 1934

After realizing the extensive attention the modern exposition houses were attracting among members of the press and the general public, several corporations decided to sponsor their own model residences at A Century of Progress in 1934. One of the most intriguing was the Frigidaire Air-Conditioned House, which was designed to illustrate different ways homeowners could live in year-round comfort through the application of Frigidaire's air-conditioning equipment.[87] Like the Crystal House, the Frigidaire House was not part of the Home and Industrial Arts Exhibit. Instead, it was erected at the far south end of the fairgrounds next to the General Motors Building. While the location of a model house in the transportation section seemed odd to many

FIG. 5.18 *(top facing)*. Living room of the Crystal House, with modern furniture that clearly recalls works by progressive European designers. From Dorothy Raley, *A Century of Progress Homes and Furnishings* (Chicago: M. A. Ring, 1934), 37.
FIG. 5.19 *(below facing)*. The austerely furnished man's bedroom in the Crystal House. From Dorothy Raley, *A Century of Progress Homes and Furnishings* (Chicago: M. A. Ring, 1934), 41.

THE FRIGIDAIRE AIR CONDITIONED HOUSE

THE FRIGIDAIRE AIR CONDITIONED HOUSE

A CENTURY OF PROGRESS
CHICAGO·1934

A CENTURY OF PROGRESS
CHICAGO·1934

INTERESTING FEATURES

All rooms scientifically kept in the "Comfort Zone."

A dining room where it's never too hot to eat.

Aquarium showing amount of water taken out of the air each hour.

A kitchen that's cool in hot weather.

Bedrooms with the at-mosphere of a summer resort.

Windows that close when it rains.

Doors, windows, bed and Air Conditioner con-trolled by electric but-tons at the bedside.

A Buffet Model Frigidaire in the master bedroom.

Awnings that take orders from the sun.

THE DAY OF PRACTICAL AIR CONDITIONING FOR THE HOME IS HERE

ADJOINING GENERAL MOTORS BUILDING
OPPOSITE 31st STREET ENTRANCE TO EXPOSITION

FRIGIDAIRE CORPORATION · SUBSIDIARY OF
GENERAL MOTORS CORPORATION · DAYTON, OHIO

fairgoers, Frigidaire was a subsidiary of the General Motors Corporation, which sponsored the home's construction.

The exterior design of the Frigidaire House borrowed heavily from the modern residences exhibited the previous year. It featured plain walls, an attached garage, and a roof terrace with pipe railings, recalling the Florida Tropical House. A covered entrance and large awnings protected the interior from excessive sun and rain. While the rooms were more traditionally decorated than many of the earlier exposition houses (and more than the exterior would have suggested), the residence did incorporate a number of innovative features. Not surprisingly, the house was fully equipped with a variety of Frigidaire air-conditioning products: a central unit on the first floor and individual cabinet units on the second level. All rooms were designed to be "comfort zones," meaning that they were "never too hot or too cold, never too dry or too damp."[88] Doors, windows, and air-conditioners all could be controlled from bedside by a series of electric buttons. During inclement weather the windows automatically closed when sensors in the sills detected moisture. A solar sensor located on the roof controlled the awnings. When the sun was shining, the awnings automatically opened. When they were not needed, they magically rolled out of the way. A major highlight of the house was the leisure lounge, a small alcove off the master bedroom that contained an adjustable daybed. A brochure on the dwelling stated that the room offered a space where the wife could "thoroughly enjoy her afternoon siesta" and her husband could "completely relax after a hard day's work."[89] Some of the features in the home were designed to be both decorative and educational. A seven-gallon aquarium in the dining room, for example, not only served as a conversation piece but also, according to a brochure on the house, illustrated how much water the air-conditioning system removed from the air each hour on a typical Chicago summer day.[90]

Another new domestic exhibit, the Country Home Model Farm House (mentioned in chapter 4), attempted to appeal to rural homeowners by uniting popular modern features and building techniques with more conventional residential forms.[91] Its prefabricated brick walls sported cream-color exterior trim painted with Soya Bean Paint, which, as the name implies, was produced from soybeans.[92] Modern materials were also used throughout the inside of the house. Most of the walls consisted of various forms of Masonite wallboard, while floors were covered in easy-to-clean linoleum. The farm office located near the front door was walled in an Armstrong Linoleum product designed to look like pine paneling.

In reaction to the unusual futuristic domestic designs introduced the previous year, the architects stated that although they had attempted to make the farmhouse functionally modern, it was "absolutely devoid of freakishness."[93] The basic design was a traditional hipped-roofed

FIG. 5.20. Cover of *The Frigidaire Air Conditioned House, A Century of Progress, Chicago, 1934,* pamphlet produced by Frigidaire Corporation of Dayton, Ohio, 1934, from collection of author.

THE *Ideal* FARMHOUSE OF TODAY AND TOMORROW

Practical, comfortable, economical to build and *fireproof*—tells the story of the Model Farmhouse exhibited by The Country Home at A Century of Progress.

This house can be built anywhere in the United States at a cost of approximately $5,000.

It is constructed of brick, steel and concrete and introduces for the first time in this country many new ideas and methods of building.

The walls are not built brick by brick but are constructed in sections on the ground, the bricks reinforced by steel rods and the whole bound together with mortar. The walls are then set in place section by section. Roof and floors are also constructed in sections from steel "pans" which are bolted together and into which go concrete or insulating material. Walls, floors and roof lock together making the house not only fireproof but wind or cyclone proof as well.

There are thirteen rooms, including the garage, and there is a large sun deck or porch opening off the second floor.

This Model Farmhouse is exhibited by The Country Home as an added service to its readers and to rural people generally.

A complete description of the Model Farmhouse with photographs and floor plans is available in a booklet, "The Country Home Model Farmhouse." Price 10 cents.

ADDRESS

THE COUNTRY HOME
250 PARK AVENUE · NEW YORK, N. Y.

FIG. 5.21 *(above)*. The prefabricated brick *Country Home* Model Farm House. From *Country Home Model Farm House, A Century of Progress*, pamphlet from collection of author.

FIG. 5.22 *(facing)*. The traditional Sears Honor Bilt Home constructed next to the Sears-Roebuck Building in 1934. From *The Honor Bilt Home at A Century of Progress*, pamphlet produced by Sears, Roebuck and Company, 1934, from collection of author.

foursquare—a form common to many midwestern farmhouses—but with an attached garage to one side that was topped by a modern roof terrace complete with fashionable pipe railings. Corner windows on the second floor, like those on the Lumber Industries House, suggested that this was not a typical farmhouse. An L-shaped living and dining area, used in many of the other exposition houses, reflected the modern nature of the interior layout. The plan, however, clearly revealed that this was a rural residence. In addition to the farm office, the first floor included a workshop and an electrical milk room adjacent to the garage.

The most aesthetically traditional house at A Century of Progress in 1934 was the Honor Bilt Home, located at the north end of the fairgrounds in the backyard of the Sears-Roebuck Building. The air-conditioned house, based on a design from Sears's premier line of mail-order residences, presented a neocolonial style complete with shutters, clapboard, and a pitched roof that supported a lone dormer. Despite its conservative character, the house did include some innovative features. The split-level design had a flexible floor plan, so that as a family's needs grew, the square

The
HONOR BILT HOME
AT
A CENTURY OF PROGRESS

F6895—7.12.34

SEARS, ROEBUCK and CO. - CHICAGO - NEWARK, N. J.

footage of usable living space could be relatively easily increased by either expanding into the attic area or building an addition. Both traditional and new materials were used in the construction of the house. The exterior facades and details were of wood, brick, and a recently introduced Rostone product. Steel framing was chosen over wood to prevent unnecessary buckling or warping of the structure.

Members of the Modern Homes Department at Sears felt that their colonial-style exposition home presented a truly American design that was far more appropriate for a typical family living in the United States than any of the futuristic houses built at the Chicago fair. The sponsors claimed in a promotional pamphlet that while many architects had relied on flat roofs, steel panels, factory fabrication, and new and untried materials to cut housing costs, in reality they had had little or no success.[94] "The home is, after all," the brochure explained, "a thing of sentiment and tradition and people do not change within a few years their inherited ideas as to what is a proper home."[95] To reinforce the Honor Bilt Home's patriotic character, the walls of the main living areas were covered in knotty pine paneling of random widths, while reproductions of early American furnishings filled the rooms.

From the start, exposition architects knew that they were fighting an uphill battle in attempting to sell modern design forms and ideas to the general public. Most Americans continued to favor historical (particularly colonial) architectural designs because of their symbolic associations to the country's past.[96] For many fairgoers, the innovative exposition houses were too impersonal and odd looking. Especially in a time of depression, most American homeowners were searching for comfort in the familiar. The sleek and sparsely furnished futuristic houses were the antithesis of the desired domestic atmosphere, as the modern designs offered efficiency, not solace.

Several of the original modern houses received dramatic makeovers for the 1934 fair season that involved the incorporation of more traditional furnishings and decor. Even the House of Tomorrow, now out of Keck's creative control, was redecorated to appear less futuristic. Portions of the exterior phenoloid and plasterboard walls were replaced with sheets of copper. A new interior design by Mabel Schamberg "sought to achieve a 'quiet restful effect' by substituting calming tones of gray, brown, and beige and various shades of flamingo pink in place of the more intense colors of 1933."[97] Gone was the functionalist steel furniture in the living room and bedrooms. In its place were upholstered chairs selected for comfort and charm, giving the spaces cozier, more inviting atmospheres. In the bedrooms, more substantial beds and vanity sets, along with floral upholstery and curtains, contributed to an aesthetic that was more in keeping with the current day than the future.

Despite the presence of more traditional designs, millions of Americans were introduced to the potential of modern architecture through touring the House of Tomorrow and the other model residences at the exposition. The unusual formal qualities and novel mechanical devices filled the imaginations of fairgoers with

A CENTURY OF PROGRESS
1933 CHICAGO 1934

KAUFMANN · FABRY
OFFICIAL PHOTOGRAPHERS

a powerful glimpse of a future that was dramatically different from the world around them. Many visitors came away from A Century of Progress excited by the notion that easy, modern living would be waiting for them as soon as the economy recovered.[98] Others, however, were less receptive to the new technology and forms. In addition to finding the aesthetics of the austere, modern houses too different from the traditional notion of a home, some fairgoers reacted unfavorably because of a growing fear that people would become lost in the anonymity of the new machine-age world.

FIG. 5.23. The refaced House of Tomorrow in 1934. Kaufmann and Fabry, photographers (i26455aa). Courtesy of Chicago History Museum.

In building his two exposition houses, Keck did make modern architecture more familiar not only to the public but also to members of financial institutions. After the fair, homebuilders in the Midwest, including the architect's own clients, found it easier to obtain loans for nontraditional houses.[99] The banks' receptivity toward progressive designs, however, did not last long.[100] More enduring was the general acceptance by financial officers of new materials and methods that could be incorporated into traditional, as well as modern, residential designs.

Although even decades after the fair closed, most Americans continue to favor

FIG. 5.24. Living room of House of Tomorrow as refurnished in 1934. From Dorothy Raley, *A Century of Progress Homes and Furnishings* (Chicago: M. A. Ring, 1934), 74.

living in some form of traditionally styled dwelling, many of the innovative features highlighted in the model exposition houses were eventually incorporated into new homes. These included large open rooms, with furniture defining areas for conversing, dining, or studying; main living areas situated above ground level; and attached garages. Although few homes built since the exposition contain security systems with screens that project images of visitors at the front entry or interior doors that open with a wave of the hand, many houses are equipped with electronic security systems, motion-detector lights, and electric garage-door openers. Air-conditioning, television sets, dishwashers, and electric refrigerators lead a long list of available appliances and electronic gadgets that are now standard equipment in most American homes. While greater interest in passive solar heating has had only a limited impact on residential design, the concepts of prefabrication and mass production significantly altered home-construction practices. These developments made possible the appearance of whole new suburbs, such as the Levittowns and Greenbelt cities, built almost overnight of factory-made materials during the middle decades of the twentieth century.

SIX

UNBUILT VISIONS FOR A MODERN EXPOSITION

The omission of Frank Lloyd Wright [from the architectural commission] is serious. It is also very funny. As the years go on the joke will seem funnier and funnier. "Hamlet" without the Prince of Denmark could not be a more comical performance. Perhaps the largest claim that the distinguished architects now in charge of the Fair will have on the attention of posterity will be through this little omission.

LEWIS MUMFORD, "Two Chicago Fairs"

In addition to the built visions of modern architecture put forward at A Century of Progress, there were other designs produced for the event that were never realized. Some were developed solely as architectural exercises. Others did not see fruition for a variety of factors, most notably the unfavorable economic conditions during which the exposition was planned and built. The Great Depression, which had an impact on nations around the world, led to a significant decline in the number of foreign pavilions built at the fairgrounds in comparison to previous expositions.[1] While the event attracted extensive international participation, most countries did not feel that they could spare the resources to construct a freestanding building. Instead, many limited their involvement to sponsoring national exhibits in the Travel and Transport Building, the Hall of Science, or one of the other fair-owned pavilions.[2] France, for example, had initially planned to construct a major building designed by Paul Cret near the Hall of Science but changed its mind shortly before the fair opened, citing lack of funds.[3] Some proposed projects, such as Ralph Walker's mammoth Tower of Water, were eliminated from the exposition design for practical as well as financial reasons.

Two designers who used A Century of Progress to specifically promote their own progressive design ideologies by producing and then publicizing unrealized projects for the exposition were Frank Lloyd Wright and Norman Bel Geddes. Their designs present additional insight into the struggles that many American architects faced as they attempted to define for themselves an architecture appropriate for the United States in the early 1930s. Wright created dramatic, if not particularly realistic, conceptual schemes for the fair in an attempt to promote himself (then in his mid-sixties) as still a major player in American architecture. At the same time, industrial designer Norman Bel Geddes hoped to legitimize his own architectural career through the presentation of highly innovative theater and restaurant designs that he unsuccessfully marketed for the exposition. Examined alongside fair pavilions by the commissioners and by other progressive architects, such as George Frederick Keck, the designs produced by Wright and Geddes clearly illustrate the great plurality of forms in modern American architecture. At the same time, an exploration of these projects offers new perspectives on the ideas and debates prevalent among prominent designers regarding the direction of modern architecture.

FRANK LLOYD WRIGHT AND THE EXPOSITION

Wright used the exposition to promote his idiosyncratic vision of modern architecture by producing three conceptual schemes for A Century of Progress. These designs presented an important counterpoint to the overall plans created by the fair's architectural commission. While the committee members were busy designing an actual exposition for the modern age, Wright undertook a similar challenge, creating on paper his own utopian visions of a modern world's fair. Unlike the final exposition plans produced by the more traditional Beaux-Arts-trained commissioners, Wright's extraordinary fair schemes did not exhibit a stark contrast from his previous work. His quest to create an American architecture appropriate to the modern era began early in his career and continued throughout his long life. Greatly revered but with few significant built works to his name since the early 1920s, he was facing the growing opinion among critics that he was past his prime. The exposition presented an irresistible opportunity for Wright to illustrate that he still had relevant architectural ideas to impart to both his colleagues and the general public.[4] While the architect did not delineate many details on the drawings, his descriptions of the plans published elsewhere confirm his interest in incorporating innovative building materials and structural systems into the designs.

Wright's omission from the architectural commission, which created a tremendous outcry from the architect and his followers—including such prominent critics as Lewis Mumford, Douglas Haskell, and Henry Churchill—is what initially motivated him to produce designs for the Chicago exposition.[5] The fair offered a means through which he could promote himself and his ideas at a time when there were few realizable commissions on his drawing board. It also provided an opportunity for exploring new ideas without worrying about practical considerations, since he knew the projects would not be constructed. On a more personal level, Wright's exposition schemes presented a means of revenge for the perceived slight by the fair's architectural commission.

One of the earliest references to Wright's exclusion from the commission is in a letter to the architect, dated 8 October 1930, from close friend and former client Darwin D. Martin. Martin wrote that his brother William, also a previous client, had sent him an article from a Chicago paper reproaching the fair for not obtaining Wright's cooperation. Darwin Martin went on to suggest that Wright ask New York critic Alexander Woollcott to compose an even stronger statement that might result in lining up a building for the architect to design.[6] Articles protesting Wright's omission began appearing in the national press during the same month. The first, published by architect and critic Haskell in the *Nation,* likened the exposition's design commission without Wright to an anthology of American literature without Ralph Waldo Emerson. While Haskell correctly stated that the committee omitted Wright without so much as a consultation for "fear he would 'seek to dominate' and 'might not cooperate,'" the author downplayed the need for the committee members to work well together. He believed that the commission was making "too much of a minor trait."[7] The commission's worries were not unfounded, as Wright later arrogantly wrote in his autobiography that "surely it was better to have one architect out of employment in such parlous times than the 8 or 10 or 15 already employed at the Fair? Were I to come in they [the commissioners] would go out."[8]

The fair organizers' great concern about the potential for problems arising if Wright were to be added to the committee is clearly reflected in a letter from Raymond Hood to Wright dated 16 February 1931. In it Hood informed Wright that his name had been one of the first to be suggested by Paul Cret at an early selection meeting for the committee, but that it was Hood himself who had rejected the architect as temperamentally not fitting the commission. Hood wrote to Wright, "I felt that you were a strong individualist, and that if an attempt was made to harness you in with other architects, the result would be more apt to be a fight than a fair."[9] Those selecting the committee members clearly realized the importance of the members' being able to freely share ideas with each other and work together as a team.[10]

Allowing Wright to design a pavilion or group of buildings offered a potential compromise. Wright's son John, whose toy company sold Lincoln Logs and small statues of Lincoln and Fort Dearborn at the fair, suggested to commissioner Corbett that his father be allowed to design a major exhibit hall, much as Louis Sullivan had been given the Transportation Building at the 1893 World's Columbian Exposition. He wrote that "no doubt, the rest of the Fair Architecture may be badly 'shown up' by comparison with what he would do, but what of that. Wouldn't it be more appropriate to have it 'shown up' at the Fair than after the Fair."[11] The younger Wright then wrote to his father expressing his hope that if, "by any remote chance," the committee did call on the architect to design a building, he would decline the offer.[12]

Although no official record confirms it, according to Frank Lloyd Wright the architectural commission did eventually promise him a building at the exposition. However, following his son's advice, Wright stated that he declined the offer. In a letter to architect Rudolph Schindler dated 8 January 1931, Wright wrote that "the Fair is not worth worrying about. 'They' say I am to have a corner of it when 'They' get around to it. Probably one where I can't wiggle out very far. It would be better to refuse connection at this late day so far as the cause of an organic architecture goes."[13]

Despite the fact that Wright declared that he was unwilling to design a pavilion on the fairgrounds, he apparently did not totally dismiss the idea of constructing a building for fairgoers to view. In early 1933 the *Chicago Daily News* reported that the architect was planning to erect a steel-and-glass tower across from the fair entrance as a rival attraction to let people judge who had the better concept of modern architecture.[14] According to *Architectural Forum,* the plan called for various sections of the structure to illustrate different design treatments for office and apartment buildings. Other areas were to be devoted to "exhibitions of sketches and models of modern architecture and interior decoration" from Wright's new school of architecture, the Taliesin Fellowship.[15] The tower was to be financed by individual subscriptions of a dollar each. It is unclear whether this idea had been initiated by Wright or some of his supporters. However, when money began trickling in, Wright informed the Chicago newspaper that he had never had any intention of constructing a building near the fairgrounds.[16]

While Wright and his friends were creating a stir in the public press, the architectural commission for the exposition went on with the daily work of designing the fair. The complete absence of Wright's name in the minutes or any other record of the committee suggests that there was little, if any, formal communication between the commissioners and Wright. Personal correspondences and other public records, however, provide clues to the architect's relationship with the individual members of the commission and to his great desire to take advantage of a significant architectural event happening in his own adoptive city.

Although Wright neither officially contributed to A Century of Progress nor built a rival structure nearby, he did state that he was not in a position to criticize the fair's architecture unless he had something better to offer for comparison. He was adamant that he could produce much more appropriate designs for a modern world's fair than the members of the architecture commission, whom he branded a bunch of "skyscraper pilots."[17] To support his claim he produced three overall schemes for the exposition that he felt to be "genuine and practical as Modern Architecture."[18] Ironically, the first design presented his vision of a modern skyscraper. The other two plans consisted of a fair housed under a massive tent structure and one held on an elaborate series of floating barges. Wright introduced the designs at a meeting of the American Union of Decorative Artists and Craftsmen (AUDAC), held in New York City on 26 February 1931, where it had been decided ahead of time that the evening's discussion would revolve around the Chicago World's Fair.[19] Woollcott and Mumford, two of Wright's strongest allies, gave introductory remarks. In his statement, Mumford proclaimed his outrage over Wright's absence from the exposition's architectural commission. He then calmly blasted the official fair designs for not really being modern at all but "eclectic shams," illustrating only the latest fashion trend.[20]

Wright, the guest of honor for the evening, took this opportunity to continue Mumford's belittling of the architectural committee's designs. As Hood's letter to the architect explaining why fair organizers had declined to include him on the commission had been written only ten days prior to the AUDAC meeting, the unsettling words were probably fresh in Wright's mind when he arrived in New York. He took his exclusion from the commission both as a personal affront and as an attack on his architectural ideology. According to *Time* magazine, Wright exclaimed:

FIG. 6.1. Elevation of Wright's skyscraper design for A Century of Progress. Drawings of Frank Lloyd Wright copyright 2004 The Frank Lloyd Wright Foundation, Scottsdale, Arizona.

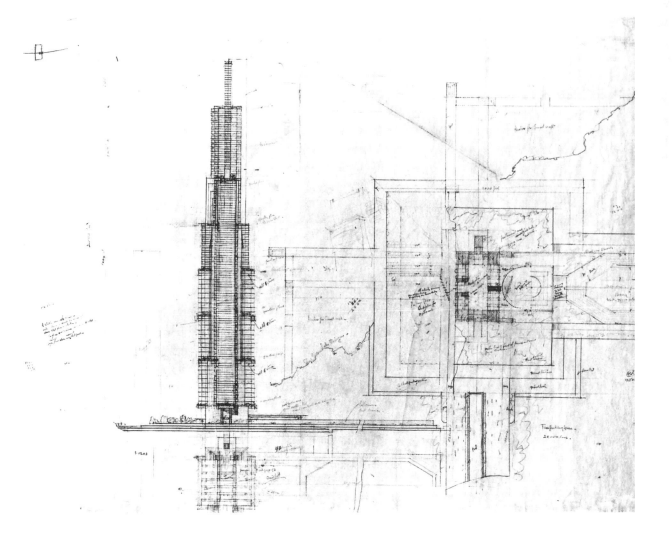

I'm trying to bring architecture back to America as something real to America. The proposed World's Fair in Chicago is a conspicuous example of modernism sprung up overnight, of superficiality, sham, [and] imitation. They are making a pretty cardboard picture of ancient wall masses.... They are specialists in spectacle. But the architecture for the Fair is only bad theater where theater does not belong. We want genuineness in our architecture—the genuine expression of American life.[21]

There is no mention of the presence at the meeting of Commissioner Corbett, who was also vice president of the hosting organization, but fellow committee member Hood did attend the event as an invited guest.[22] Hood, "perspiring with embarrassment," rebutted Mumford's and Wright's attacks by defending the fair organizers' process for selecting the members of the architectural commission. He then went on to substantiate the reason for Wright's exclusion by stating that the architect was too much of an individualist to be a productive committee member.[23]

Wright then proceeded to present his own schemes for the fair. He told the audience that he believed his designs to be, in contrast to the work of the exposition architects, "constructive criticism worth something to architecture," entertaining to himself and possibly, but not probably, fun for the commissioners.[24] He went on to proclaim that his first design, a 245-story, half-mile-high skyscraper, was a "genuine modern *construction*" (his emphasis), since it incorporated recent advances in both structure and materials.[25] As in his other skyscraper designs, from St. Mark's in the Bouwerie to the Price Tower, Wright planned the tower as a "stable concrete mass" with light concrete floor slabs on steel girders cantilevering out from a central core.[26] While the existing drawings of the exposition skyscraper indicate glass curtain walls, the architect later wrote in *An Autobiography* that the building was to be enclosed in "light, transparent glass substitutes."[27]

Wright located four levels of large terraces at the base of the tower. He extended one corner of the terraces into Lake Michigan to create an artificial harbor for watercraft.[28] The bottom three levels were to include parking for up to 30,000 cars.[29] A park on the top terrace would help abate fumes and noise from the parking area below.[30] Above the terraces and adjacent to the tower Wright located an auditorium that could seat 25,000 people. According to the architect, large fountains situated around the terraces, including in the lake to the north and east of the building, would offer interest at the base of the tower. These fountains, he wrote, were to be dramatically lit at night by a "modern light-projecting apparatus."[31]

Like the setback skyscrapers produced by the New York members of the architectural commission, Wright's tower was designed to step inward as it rose, creating places for roof gardens. Wright asserted that the highest stories would be reserved for garden observation decks and "pleasure places."[32] If no natural clouds were floating by the building, "aeroplanes would create colored ribbons to drift across it."[33] Sixty elevators, each with the potential capacity of fifty passengers and two operators, in a central core would provided access to the upper floors of the tower.

The second exposition design consisted of a massive canopy supported by a system of pylons and suspension cables. As with most of his architecture, Wright based this tent scheme on a modular unit.[34] Gigantic, 500-foot-wide, tented bays form the building blocks of the design. In his autobiography, he stated that bay after bay could be added to the design until enough land had been covered to accommodate all exhibitors.[35] An advantage of this concept, as with the final asymmetrical exposition layout by the commissioners, was that it allowed the fair to be built only as large as needed.

A rendering of the second scheme illustrates the astronomical scale of the tent design. The structure, as presented by Wright, would consist of a three-by-thirteen matrix of the immense bays. The massive complex was well over a mile long.[36] Although the pylons were labeled in the drawing

FIG. 6.2. Wright's tent design for A Century of Progress. Drawings of Frank Lloyd Wright copyright 2004 The Frank Lloyd Wright Foundation, Scottsdale, Arizona.

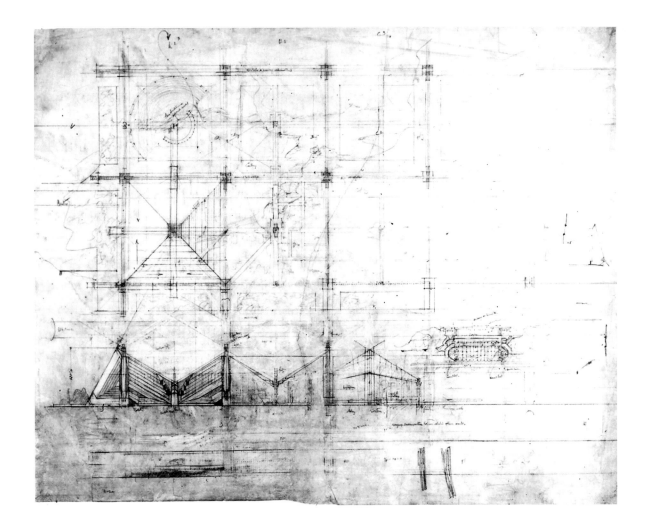

as being 275 feet tall, Wright wrote in his autobiography that the canopy supported by pylons could rise to 500 feet in height and fall to 150 feet between each unit.[37] Again, the architect planned to incorporate modern, man-made materials in his design. He stated that the tent, supported by a network of primary and secondary steel cables anchored to outside pylons, would be built out of "transparent fabrications, such as we have as modern glass substitutes in our day."[38]

In both the tent and skyscraper schemes, a large harbor to the east allowed access to the exposition by boat. Wright included a double-level parking garage running along the opposite side of the pavilions in the tent design to accommodate automobiles.[39] The architect planned to locate large circular performance halls in the gigantic semihexagonal end bays. He later incorporated similar round auditoriums in his designs for the Annunciation Greek Orthodox Church in Wauwatosa, Wisconsin, and the unbuilt Crescent Opera and Civic Auditorium, Baghdad (a design later reworked as the Gammage Memorial Theater in Tempe, Arizona).

FIG. 6.3. Wright's barge design for A Century of Progress. Drawings of Frank Lloyd Wright copyright 2004 The Frank Lloyd Wright Foundation, Scottsdale, Arizona.

Wright wrote that hanging screens would define individual exhibit areas as needed.[40] Patrons could observe the exposition activities while dining at restaurants located on suspended balconies around the structure. Along with moving sidewalks, waterways threaded through the parklike setting, leading visitors to individual exhibit sites. Rain or freshwater pumped to the tops of the massive pylons would periodically wash the canopy. This

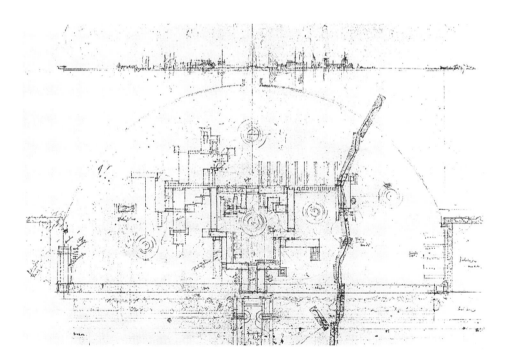

water, according to the architect, would pour through openings at low points in the covering creating immense waterfalls and filling an extensive system of artificial lagoons.[41]

FIG. 6.4. Wright's design for the Wolf Lake Amusement Park (not built). Drawings of Frank Lloyd Wright copyright 2004 The Frank Lloyd Wright Foundation, Scottsdale, Arizona.

Wright's third exposition design was less developed and even less practical than either his skyscraper or tent scheme. In this design, he imagined floating the entire exposition on an elaborate series of barges on Lake Michigan. Projecting an entertainment complex over a body of water was not an entirely new concept for Wright. He had explored the idea as early as the mid-1890s in his unrealized design for Wolf Lake Amusement Park. He went on to develop the concept further in his various schemes for Monona Terrace in Madison, Wisconsin. The idea to actually float the buildings on pontoons may have grown out of an earlier, unbuilt resort project he designed around 1922 that included small cabins floating on Lake Tahoe. In the case of the exposition design, Wright stated that lightly reinforced vacuum-sealed metal cylinders would support the barges or pontoons. The size and footprint of the pavilions would dictate the shape of the individual floating structures—large pontoons for large buildings, square pontoons for square ones, and so on. According to Wright, floating bridges and gardens would connect the individual barges together in a "continuous, varied, brilliant modern circumstance."[42] The result would be an organic assemblage of barges extending into the lake from a central area linked to nearby parking on the mainland.[43]

As in the exposition designs by the architectural commission, lighting played an important role in Wright's pontoon scheme. Thin, lightweight tubes of waterproof pulp or transparent synthetics, along with illuminated, transparent glass tubing, would, according to Wright, create "a sheer legitimate modern fabrication."[44] The glass tubes would form opalescent reeds reflecting in the water at night to create a "rhythmic sense of verticality."[45] Additional decorative effects could be produced by water pumps designed to shoot enormous arcs of water upward to great heights.

In all three schemes, Wright's images and descriptions reflect an approach to modern architecture much closer to that promoted by the commissioners than he would ever have admitted. He clearly looked to the use of innovative building materials and new ideas in construction for design inspiration. In both the skyscraper and tent designs, the newly available transparent materials he specified for the protective sheathing dictated the formal qualities of the exterior facades. Wright's pontoon scheme, with its use of glass tubing, also illustrated the incorporation of new products to achieve spectacular decorative effects.

The architect was intensely interested in pushing design technology to new limits. In the case of his exposition schemes, he did so in the safety of knowing that these designs would not be constructed. Wright was, however, soon able to fulfill his desire to explore the limits of several recent developments in building technology through details in some of his most original designs, constructed in the years immediately following the fair. Included were the concrete cantilevers for Fallingwater, his vacation house for Edgar Kaufmann in Bear Run, Pennsylvania, and the mushroom columns and Pyrex glass tubing used for the Johnson Wax Administration Building in Racine, Wisconsin.[46]

Wright shared with the architectural commissioners an interest in recycling the exposition buildings. Although the commissioners had to abide by the Chicago Park District's order that fair structures be removed from the site after the exposition closed, Wright discounted this fact in his plans. In all three schemes he envisioned the use of at least some elements of the designs at the site after the close of the event. For example, Wright foresaw the skyscraper being recycled for government offices and businesses.[47] Like the Eiffel Tower, which still remains standing from the 1889 Exposition Universelle in Paris, this permanent skyscraper, according to Wright, could serve as a reminder of the Chicago fair (as well as of his own architecture) for generations to come. Wright's tower, however, would have a more relevant purpose than a tourist attraction by becoming a vital civic center.[48] As for the tent scheme, although the canopy was to be built of a nonpermanent material, the enormous pylons were to remain in situ after the close of the event. Wright wrote that these massive towers could be transformed into decorative lighting fixtures for Chicago's lakefront park. From the third scheme, he envisioned the city transporting the individual pontoons to community parks along the lakeshore and reusing them as restaurants and "good time places."[49]

Time magazine reported that Wright "presided like a benign deity" over the

AUDAC meeting. The architect himself, in his own humbly arrogant fashion, re-called feeling that he had been forced into "an embarrassing, awkward position" in discussing the fair, because

> it would seem that I was present and spoke because I myself resented be-ing left out of the Fair. Whereas the truth was I resented only their quick turnover to my work and the pretentious scene-painting I knew coming of it as unworthy [of] the modern architecture I had myself given them. Only for this exploit? Standing there to speak, having no previous thought to the matter, several contrasting ideas of a fair that would be worthy [of] modern architecture[,] because [they were] square with our new structural resources[,] came into my mind. These ideas not unnaturally . . . developed as I talked. I had given the schemes no study. They were spontaneous.[50]

A letter from Wright to architect Henry Churchill written immediately prior to the event, however, suggests a different story. The designs were apparently pre-meditated, as he told Churchill that he was sending him a copy of his "Worlds Fair set-up" specifically in order that he would have something prepared to go on at the meeting.[51]

Wright wrote in *An Autobiography* that he could hear the eclectic members of the commission saying that they had thought of all his schemes themselves and rejected them as unrealistic. In reality, the commissioners were right—his exposi-tion designs were exceedingly impractical. Knowing his designs would never be re-alized, Wright ignored many of the more mundane requirements necessary for the successful realization of an actual exposition. For example, none of the schemes could have easily handled the size of a typical world's fair crowd, which in 1933 reached an average of over 125,000 visitors per day. One can easily imagine the chaos that would have resulted from large numbers of people attempting to reach a particular platform for a desired performance in his barge design or a certain floor level in his skyscraper scheme.[52] While Wright stated that there would be sixty large elevators in the skyscraper design, as illustrated in his drawings, the building was not physically large enough to house so many elevators and still maintain a reasonable amount of exhibit space on each floor. The immense scale of the tent scheme also raises questions about its constructability. In addition to basic design problems, the financial aspect of these fair projects was also problematic. Wright, not known for his fiscal responsibility, boldly proclaimed that all three of his de-signs could be built for the cost of the actual fair—improbable, especially consider-ing the budget for the constructed exposition was held to a minimum because of the economic instability of the time.[53]

Characteristics in Wright's schemes that were also found in earlier exposi-tion designs by the commission members suggest that any significant influence between Wright and the fair's designers probably traveled from the committee to the lone architect. Wright's interest in international expositions (he had visited at least three previous world's fairs and designed a building for a fourth) and his previous disparaging comments about the official exposition designs suggest that he was keenly aware of the commissioners' work.[54] Although Wright attempted to claim sole authorship of his concepts, both the basic premise of his tower form and the structural system of the tent design had been either considered or already implemented by the commission in the design of fair pavilions prior to the exhibition of his plans.[55]

While Wright did not further explore the use of floating pontoons in his later architecture, he did continue to experiment with other concepts found in his designs for A Century of Progress. The tent scheme, for example, was the first of several designs incorporating a cable or suspended structural system. Included were the Hanley Airplane Hangar, designed for Benton Harbor, Michigan, in 1954, and a tent pavilion for the Marin County Fair, designed in 1957.[56] Meanwhile, the skyscraper scheme was only one step in Wright's long investigation of tall-building design. His vertical fair building initially appears to contradict his general architectural preference for horizontal lines, as well as his often-expressed distaste for the skyscraper as a modern architectural form. The exposition tower design was similar in massing to an earlier project in which Wright had explored setback ordinances and other skyscraper regulations. The architect recycled this design again in the early 1930s for the skyscraper in his plan for an idealized community, Broadacre City. While he experimented with the design of tall towers in an urban context in his regulation exercise, Wright typically favored the construction of a single tower outside the congested core of the city or as the lone skyscraper in a smaller urban center, as with his only realized tall building, the Price Tower in Bartlesville, Oklahoma, built in 1952.[57] His desire to separate skyscrapers from dense metropolises was reflected not only in the design for Broadacre City but also in the skyscraper design for the world's fair. The tower would have been set apart from the rest of the Chicago skyline by both Grant Park and the Illinois Central Railway lines.[58]

Early in his career, Wright had witnessed firsthand the architectural

FIG. 6.5. Wright's suspended tent design for the Marin County Fair Pavilion (not built). Drawings of Frank Lloyd Wright copyright 2004 The Frank Lloyd Wright Foundation, Scottsdale, Arizona.

impact of the white, neoclassical exhibit halls of the 1893 World's Columbian Exposition. He fully understood the potential and influential power that a world's fair could have on architectural tastes. Offended by being excluded from the official architectural commission, Wright was able to promote himself and his architectural ideology at the expense of the committee by presenting his own ideas for a modern fair in a public forum. However, his conceptual ideas for creating a modern world's fair were not as different from those of the commission as he wanted people to believe. Both explored new building materials, forms, and construction techniques to create "modern" design solutions. A similar statement can be made in regard to another designer of unrealized plans for the Chicago fair—Norman Bel Geddes.

NORMAN BEL GEDDES, STREAMLINING, AND THE EXPOSITION

In an attempt to present A Century of Progress as a modern world's fair, the members of the architectural commission realized early on that it would be beneficial to receive advice from artists working in a variety of fields. A general feeling arose among the architects that while the value of painter as decorator had not diminished, that of sculptor, renderer, lighting engineer, civil engineer, plumbing engineer, and pageantry and dramatization expert had taken on additional importance in modern times.[59] The members felt that adding experts in these areas as consultants to the committee provided a logical means of acquiring the desired input. They thus invited designer Norman Bel Geddes, along with architectural renderer Hugh Ferriss, to join the committee under the title of "dramatization experts" with the task of assisting in the development of theatrical concepts that could enliven the atmosphere of the fair.[60]

Like Wright, Geddes produced a series of unbuilt schemes for A Century of Progress through which he promoted his own personal vision of modern architecture. The theater and restaurant projects he executed for the fair also reflected two additional developments in American architecture that took place at the beginning of the 1930s—the introduction of streamlining and the rise of the industrial designer.[61] In contrast to Wright and most of the other architects involved in the fair, Geddes created his exposition plans not as a professional architect but as a designer with a background in theatrical production.[62] Along with a group of other artists with formal training in areas outside architecture who came to be known as industrial designers, Geddes sought to improve the design of a wide variety of man-made items that ranged from grocery-counter scales to buildings. Not particularly interested in actively participating in the academic debates regarding the definition of modern architecture, Geddes strove to produce practical, yet aesthetically interesting, objects and buildings with commercial appeal. Common to many of his projects, including architectural designs, was an aerodynamic aesthetic highlighted by streamlined forms that reflected the rapidly increasing pace of modern life.

On 29 April 1929 Geddes completed his first major work for the architectural commission and submitted plans to Corbett (who was then serving as acting chairman of the committee) for an aquarium, two theaters (Number Six and Number Fourteen), and an Island Dance Restaurant.[63] Corbett tentatively approved the designs "on his own responsibility" and then personally gave Geddes approval to submit ten additional projects for the commission to examine at their meeting the following month.[64] These new designs included an aquarium restaurant (a transformation of his earlier aquatic project), a restaurant in the shape of an airplane, a Temple of Music, two more major theaters, one specifically designed for performances of the *Divine Comedy* and a Theatre Number Eight, and a Water Pageant Island Theatre. He also added two garden complexes and a series of puppet theaters.[65] Of these designs, Geddes told Albert, he did not believe there was one that would "not be a distinct contribution to the fair."[66] The commission discussed these unusual projects at a meeting in December 1929. At this time, they officially increased Geddes's responsibilities to include the illumination of all buildings and grounds. His first assignment was the lighting design for the Travel and Transport Building.[67]

In all of his work, including the fair pavilions, Geddes strove to create the most dramatic yet functionally (but, like Wright, not necessarily financially) practical solutions possible. He relied on his theatrical background to produce fantastic schemes that would offer new and exciting experiences to the fairgoers. His restaurant designs, for example, illustrated his exceptional ability to create spectacular environments for memorable dining experiences. These included the rotating Aërial Restaurant, where fair visitors could dine high above the fairgrounds surrounded by windows offering a continually changing bird's-eye view; the Seafood Restaurant, with underwater seating in a giant, triangular fish tank; and the Island Dance Restaurant, with dance platforms and tables located on a series of islands in the center of the lagoon.

Geddes's process for creating his architectural schemes began with a clear understanding of the programmatic requirements. He then gave careful attention to each component, from the basic form down to the smallest detail, to create a sense of unity in the design. At the same time, he completely avoided historical precedents. Instead, he found inspiration in ideas common to contemporary transportation vehicles and factory production. He felt they better reflected modern life than did traditional architectural sources. The result was a comprehensive design philosophy that often favored the use of smooth, geometrical forms without the inclusion of applied ornament.

Geddes was also deeply involved in advocating legitimate theater at a time when the public was increasingly turning its attention to new forms of entertain-

FIG. 6.6. Model of Norman Bel Geddes's Aërial Restaurant design. Courtesy of Estate of Norman Bel Geddes. The Harry Ransom Humanities Research Center, The University of Texas at Austin.

ment, including motion pictures and radio.[68] In attempting to give new life to the dramatic arts, those in theater looked for ways to free writers, actors, and even audiences from restrictions imposed by a traditional structure hundreds of years old.[69] Geddes, a leader in this struggle, saw the fair as an ideal avenue to use building design to promote innovative concepts in dramatic stage productions.[70] He was particularly interested in strengthening the relationship between the actors and the audience by creating more suitable architectural forms in which to house performances.[71] The designer also envisioned bringing some of the "outstanding theatrical talent of the world" to the Chicago exposition to stage productions "distinctly radical and free in their form and proportions."[72]

Previous innovations by Geddes in theater design included the introduction of a diagonal auditorium layout in 1915. This concept was first incorporated in his design for Theatre Number Six, published in 1922 and later incorporated into several of his exposition schemes. By placing the stage in a corner of the building, he not only provided more room for seating but also improved sightlines and created a deeper stage.[73] He continued to experiment with auditorium layouts, including the creation of thrust stages, which eventually led to the "theater-in-the-round" form.

Geddes also attempted to create additional unity between spectator and performer by designing complete environments in which the entire hall became

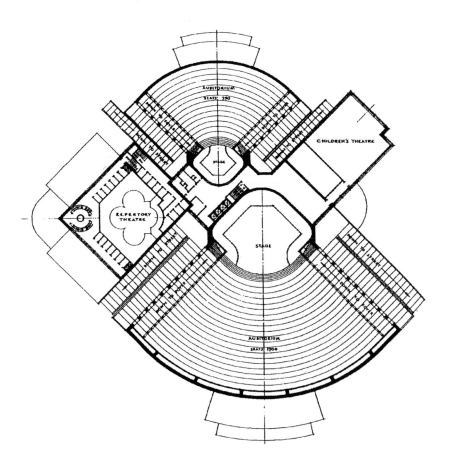

FIG. 6.7. Preliminary
plan of Geddes's Theatre
Number Six, which
included two auditoriums,
a cabaret, and a children's
theater. Courtesy of Estate
of Norman Bel Geddes.
The Harry Ransom
Humanities Research
Center, The University of
Texas at Austin.

visually linked to the stage, as in his Gothic cathedral auditorium set for Max Reinhardt's stage adaptation of *The Miracle*.[74] By the time Geddes began creating designs for A Century of Progress, however, he had begun to favor more neutral auditorium designs that neither added to nor detracted from the action on stage.[75]

In his exposition theaters Geddes diligently incorporated a lesson he had learned early on regarding the importance of unifying individual elements to the whole. In his Repertory Theatre, for example, he developed a coherent and efficient spatial organization for all departments needed to carry out a major production. In doing so, he clearly illustrated his ability to create a theater building for optimal functional efficiency. When designing the complex he took into consideration the specific needs of the actors, executives, and other personnel; the spatial needs for scenery, costumes, and storage; and the functional needs for social and recreational activities, including schooling and training.[76] This was not a simple task, as the Repertory Theatre incorporated four separate auditoriums into the design: large and small versions of his Theatre Number Six; a cabaret;

and a children's theater.[77] To allow for maximum efficiency, Geddes arranged the theaters around a nineteen-story tower. Each stage backed up to the central core to provide easy access to the offices, rehearsal rooms, workshops, scenery storage, and over 100 dressing rooms located inside. He also included movable platforms that could be raised or lowered on hydraulic lifts from the basement for rapid set changes. Public spaces, including smoking rooms, cafés, and other auxiliary areas, radiated outward. Broad foyers situated underneath the auditoriums of the two larger theaters provided space for people to promenade during intermissions.[78]

In addition to reusing concepts he had previously developed, Geddes created completely new theater designs with the Chicago exposition specifically in mind. These buildings, which ranged from a series of small puppet theaters, for presenting continuous free shows at different sites throughout the fairgrounds, to the Temple of Music, a theater that could easily be adapted to hold audiences ranging from 800 to over 10,000 people, demonstrate Geddes's tremendous creativity in architectural design.[79] Most of his exposition schemes, like the Temple of Music, which had movable walls and a roof that could roll back to transform the pavilion into an open-air auditorium, presented whimsical settings that were based on complex, but well

FIG. 6.8. Model of Geddes's Water Pageant Island Theatre, designed to be built in the fair's lagoon. Courtesy of Estate of Norman Bel Geddes. The Harry Ransom Humanities Research Center, The University of Texas at Austin.

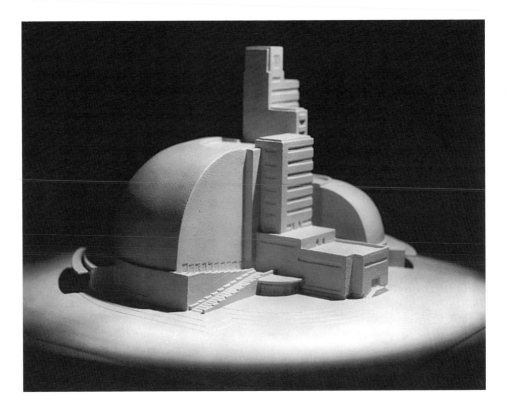

FIG. 6.9. Model of Geddes's Repertory Theatre design, showing rounded facades and setback tower. Courtesy of Estate of Norman Bel Geddes. The Harry Ransom Humanities Research Center, The University of Texas at Austin.

organized, design programs. His Water Pageant Island Theatre consisted of two groups of barges, one housing the stage and dressing rooms and the other, seventy-five feet away, forming the auditorium. Geddes designed the stage as an irregular series of angular platforms. The stacking forms served as a backdrop, thereby eliminating the need for most scenery.[80] To provide additional seating during performances, he included space for up to 500 canoes in the half-circle lagoon separating the stage from the auditorium. Docks for larger watercraft extended out from the seating area.[81]

The facades on Geddes's buildings achieved their decorative qualities not from applied ornament but instead from the presence of simple geometrical forms that reflected the functional needs of the spaces inside. The design of his Repertory Theatre illustrates this point. Two huge quarter segments of a sphere delineated the main theaters inside. Smaller rectangular auditoriums were situated in between. The form of the central tower, which echoed contemporary setback skyscraper designs, provided visual clues to its utilitarian functions. The vertical element also served as a symbolic marquee.

Although Geddes generated his building designs by first and foremost efficiently meeting functional needs, many of his theater projects for A Century of Progress included smooth, rounded shapes similar to the streamlined vehicles published in his book *Horizons.* For example, when viewed from above (as illustrated in the book) the design for Theatre Number Fourteen suggested a round bug skimming through water.[82] Geddes projected the entrance to the theater outward from the round body like an aerodynamic stern of a boat or plane. Steps, which encircled the theater, created the illusion of ripples radiating from the streamlined form. The Temple of Music also revealed Geddes's interest in the use of efficient shapes.[83] The rehearsal rooms located behind the main stage projected outward like the points of a star. The circular entrance foyers also pressed out away from a tall central tower to create four tapering teardrop units recalling Geddes's streamlined vehicular designs.[84]

GEDDES VERSUS ARCHITECTURAL COMMISSION

Geddes's immense creativity and longing for the extravagant led to major roadblocks in the realization of his exposition projects. Like Wright, Geddes had a strong personality and individualistic work style that quickly diminished the commissioners' desire to have him participate as an active member of the committee. They eventually rejected his designs. Geddes claimed that jealous, unemployed architects forced the cancellation of his pavilions on the grounds that, as a stage designer, he lacked professional credentials.[85] Letters and official documents, however, suggest that several other factors contributed to Geddes's projects not

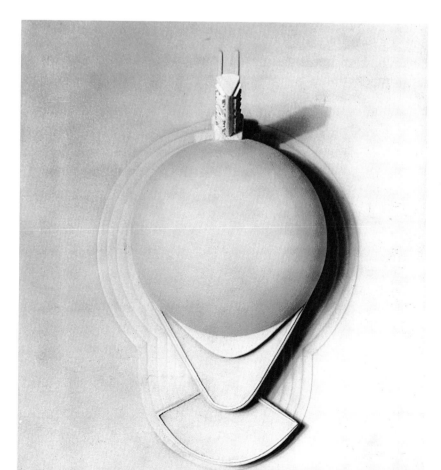

FIG. 6.10. Model of Geddes's Theatre Number Fourteen design, showing the streamlined form of the auditorium. Courtesy of Estate of Norman Bel Geddes. The Harry Ransom Humanities Research Center, The University of Texas at Austin.

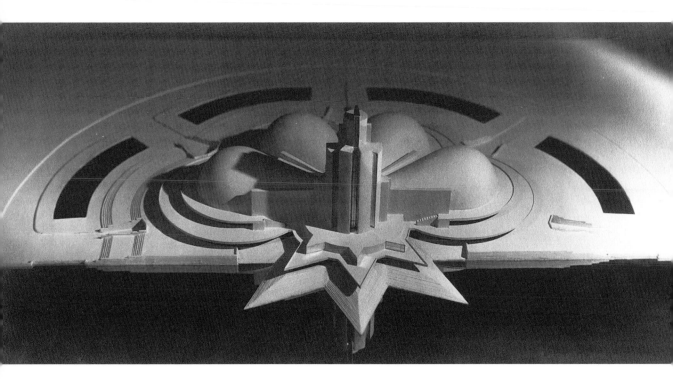

FIG. 6.11. Model of Geddes's Temple of Music design with projecting teardrop forms. Courtesy of Estate of Norman Bel Geddes. The Harry Ransom Humanities Research Center, The University of Texas at Austin.

being built. These included confusion over what work the designer was officially authorized to carry out, his "prima donna complex" and unwillingness to become a team player, and his preference for dramatic effect regardless of financial considerations.[86]

Almost from the start, the commissioners found Geddes's role as a consultant problematic. They were in part to blame, as they never clearly specified the parameters of his authority, and the designer was quick to capitalize on the ambiguity of his responsibilities. Instead of providing novel ideas for the exposition, as initially instructed, Geddes used the situation as an opportunity to design expensive and impractical entertainment pavilions that expressed his own ideas regarding both theater design and modern architecture.[87] Difficulties quickly arose between Geddes and the members of the commission over the disparity between what the designer created and what the committee thought was needed. Geddes produced over a dozen elaborate pavilion designs for the exposition; the architectural commission felt that two theaters, one seating 4,500 and one seating 1,000, and a temple of poetry were all that was necessary for presenting dramatic productions at the fair.[88]

Geddes's ego and strong idealism compounded the ill-fated situation. In July 1929 he wrote to Albert that he was only interested in contributing his services to the world's fair if the results approached his ideal of what the exposition should be. This demand for personal authority over individual designs conflicted with the harmonious working environment generated by the other members of the architectural commission.[89] The fact that Geddes pushed for more and more funding to carry out his pavilion designs only contributed to the growing friction between the designer and the commissioners.[90] This soon developed into a major issue, as he continued to create elaborate drawings after being told in writing not to incur any additional expenses unless specifically authorized.[91] Resentment among the committee members grew to the point where they no longer invited him to attend meetings or even sent him the minutes of their official gatherings.[92]

Difficulties reached a high enough level by March 1930 that the architectural committee reviewed images of Geddes's projects and discussed the value of his work to the design of the exposition at a commission meeting. While the meeting minutes do not reveal the details of this discussion, an apparently unfavorable review resulted in the formation of a New York subcommittee assigned to discuss with Geddes "his relationship to the commission and, if necessary, to recommend a successor."[93] The committee concluded that Geddes's services had been of little or no value to the exposition because he had focused on his pet projects while ignoring the other design work for the fair. The committee noted that some of the pavilions, such as his Divine Comedy Theatre, consisted of designs that he had already been working on for

FIG. 6.12. Plan and section of Geddes's Divine Comedy Theatre design. Courtesy of Estate of Norman Bel Geddes. The Harry Ransom Humanities Research Center, The University of Texas at Austin.

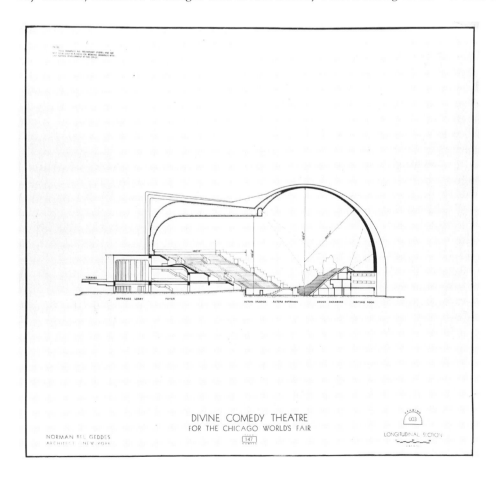

DIVINE COMEDY THEATRE
FOR THE CHICAGO WORLD'S FAIR

NORMAN BEL GEDDES

LONGITUDINAL SECTION

almost a decade.[94] Corbett, who observed Geddes's lack of interest in working in unison with the other commissioners, commented that the designer "apparently suffers from a prima donna complex, due to youth and a fear that he will not get full credit."[95]

Although Corbett had been a staunch supporter of the designer, he informed Albert that he feared the committee could do nothing further with Geddes.[96] On 19 May 1930 Geddes was listed as an "inactive consultant" in the minutes of the commission meeting. The committee, however, soon waffled on their opinion.[97] In June Corbett attended a performance of *Lysistrata* produced by Geddes. Inspired by the designer's ability to create eye-catching environments, Corbett suggested to fair organizers that Geddes be given another chance. The architect wrote to Albert that the New York members of the commission all felt that Geddes could still be of enormous value to the world's fair.[98] While the designer's role as a consultant continued to be discussed at committee meetings as late as September 1931, the commissioners never sought additional assistance from him. Even advisory work promised to him, including that of color consultant, was soon being carried out by others.[99]

The commissioners never bothered to officially inform Geddes that they no longer desired his contributions.[100] As late as six months before the opening of the exposition, the designer still assumed that he was an official consultant. By the time *Horizons* was published in 1932, Geddes had, however, all but given up hope of seeing any of his projects built at the fair. In his frustration, he began to sever the ties between his designs and the Chicago event. He proclaimed in *Horizons* that his Seafood Restaurant was suitable only for an exposition where expense is "no particular object, providing a unique result is obtained."[101] In an attempt to make some of the exposition pavilions more attractive to other potential clients, Geddes suggested ways they could be adapted for other conditions. For example, he stated that a smaller Island Dance Restaurant could be adapted for a roof garden. As with many of his architectural projects, he did not go into detail about how this could be carried out.[102]

IMPACT OF GEDDES'S IDEAS

Although Geddes's theater and restaurant schemes were restricted to paper, the influence of his artistic concepts could be found in both architectural and nonarchitectural designs that appeared at A Century of Progress. This was largely due to the publication of *Horizons.* While Geddes dedicated the first four chapters of the book to the potential role of streamlining in enhancing the efficiency of motor vehicles, he included photographs, models, and drawings of his exposition designs in the later chapters to illustrate his views on modern architecture. These projects also appeared in numerous articles published in general magazines, most notably

Time and *Popular Mechanics;* in design journals, such as *Theater Arts* and *Architectural Record;* and in newspapers across the country and in Europe, including the *New York Times* and the *München Illustrierte Presse.*[103] Geddes generated additional publicity for his ideas through a one-man show held at the Architectural League of New York in 1930 that featured some of his exposition schemes. Many prominent architects viewed the exhibit, including commission members Corbett and Hood.[104]

The promotion of his exposition designs significantly contributed both to the growth of streamlining in architecture and to the increasing presence of industrial designers in the creation of modern buildings during the 1930s. More specifically, Geddes's pavilion plans for the exposition led to innovations in architecture, including auditorium designs for legitimate theaters and novelty buildings, such as the rotating aerial restaurant. His ideas influenced designs not only at A Century of Progress but also at later expositions, in particular the 1939–40 New York World's Fair, for which industrial designers played a large role in the creation of many of the major pavilions.

While visitors to the Chicago exposition were unable to experience Geddes's pavilions firsthand, his basic design concepts appeared at the 1933–34 world's fair in the streamlining that was incorporated into the decoration and basic forms of exposition pavilions, individual exhibitor booths, and transportation vehicles on display. His innovative ideas also appeared in buildings other architects produced for the event.

FIG. 6.13. The Swift Bridge and Open Air Theatre, which recalled Geddes's design for his Water Pageant Island Theatre. From *The Swift Bridge of Service at A Century of Progress,* pamphlet produced by Swift and Company, 1934, from collection of author.

As a consultant to the architectural commission, Geddes provided a potential source of inspiration for the committee members. Even though the commissioners declined to use the designer's plans for the event, his work had a significant effect on the design of several of the smaller pavilions. In addition to the presence of streamlined forms, several theaters at the exposition clearly reflected the influence of Geddes's theater schemes. The Swift Bridge and Open Air Theatre (designed by E. A. Schiewe), for example, borrowed heavily from Geddes's unbuilt exposition pavilions.[105] The separation of the stage from the audience by a large basin of water, similar to Geddes's Water Pageant Island Theatre, provided the complex's most novel feature. In place of the individual angular elements of Geddes's water theater, Schiewe chose instead to incorporate the smooth, rounded, streamlined shapes common to many of the industrial designer's other projects, including Theatre Number Fourteen and the Divine Comedy Theatre. Nautical railings and the rounded ends of the flanking restaurants also reflect the increasing popularity of curving forms in architecture at this time, as did the backdrop of the stage, which consisted of a series of radiating arches.[106]

A second theater that exhibited similarities to Geddes's unbuilt projects was an outdoor stage that housed Gypsy dancing and marionette performances. Like Geddes's Island Dance Restaurant, the A&P Carnival Amphitheater featured a ro-

FIG. 6.14. A&P Carnival Amphitheater, which featured a rotating stage. Postcard from collection of author.

tating stage surrounded by a semicircular seating area. Whereas Geddes had designed his stage to turn continuously, the A&P stage did not rotate during productions. It only moved prior to show time and in the event of inclement weather. The ability to rotate the stage allowed spectators to

enjoy, when necessary, the protective covering of the colorful canopies that typically framed the stage.[107]

The emergence of Geddes's ideas in designs present at the exposition, along with the publication of his pavilion schemes and other building projects in *Horizons*, not only acquainted millions of people to new concepts in architecture but also introduced a new type of creative practitioner—the industrial designer—to the United States. By the end of the decade, this new profession had affected almost all areas of artistic production, including architecture. That industrial designers and their aerodynamic forms became prominent during the 1930s was in part due to Geddes's promotion of his exposition pavilions and the appearance of unadorned, streamlined forms at the Chicago fair. These designs played a contributing role in preparing the public to accept, and even welcome, the formal qualities of streamlining as one of a number of new aesthetic avenues in American modern architecture.

Although the exposition designs of Frank Lloyd Wright and Norman Bel Geddes, as well as those of George Frederick Keck, were distinctive, all three men based their design ideologies on views of modern architecture that were similar to those arrived at by the members of the fair's architectural commission. In contrast to the universal, aesthetically derived definition put forward by Henry-Russell Hitchcock and Philip Johnson, these designers (even Bel Geddes, with his favoring of aerodynamic forms) placed greater importance on using new construction materials, creative structural systems, and dramatic effects to meet the perceived needs of modern society and less importance on adhering to a specific formal vocabulary. As talented self-promoters, they all clearly understood the potential role the Chicago exposition could play in furthering their own architectural careers. Each, however, had a slightly different underlying reason for producing architectural designs for the event. Keck had hoped to sell the public (in particular those in the field of finance) on the benefits of modern residential design in order to increase the likelihood that his other progressive designs might be realized. Wright attempted to show his colleagues and critics that he was still a vital member of the profession with relevant ideas, while Bel Geddes promoted himself and his architectural ideas in order to bring new life to legitimate theater and to expand the scope of his career as an industrial designer. By producing innovative exposition designs, they all managed to attract a significant amount of publicity to their architectural ideas. Of these designers, Wright was the most successful in achieving his main goals. By taking full advantage of the New York critics' dismay over his exclusion from the architectural commission and promoting his own ideas through alternative schemes for the event, he managed to capitalize on what could have otherwise resulted in another major professional set back. Instead, the exposition contributed to the regeneration of his career during the mid-1930s.

The great creativity that these designers exhibited in their projects for the 1933–34 world's fair could be found in the work of other American architects at the time. A wide variety of buildings that were produced for the Chicago exposition by progressive designers, such as Albert Kahn, Andrew Rebori, Howard Fisher, and Ely Jacques Kahn, incorporated new ideas in building technology and design. The diversity of formal solutions in both the built and the unrealized architecture for the fair reflected the great plurality in the formal aesthetics of American architecture during these years. Unfortunately, commissions that allowed the freedom and had the budget for the personal experimentation offered by A Century of Progress were extremely rare in the years that followed the close of the event. The creative energy permeating the architecture of the fair was soon sapped as designers spent the rest of the decade struggling to obtain even the most mundane building projects.

SEVEN

THE CONTEMPORARY REACTION
AND IMPACT OF THE EXPOSITION

This Fair was erected as a carnival, employing the popular arts: the poster art for colour, the temporary construction method of Coney Island, the night-sign as a source for lighting, the arts of stage design for settings. It is therefore not interior to its nature to judge it as architecture in the school-book sense.

DOUGLAS HASKELL, "Mixed Metaphors at Chicago"

In contrast to the World's Columbian Exposition, which helped usher in a massive wave of neoclassical building throughout the United States, the second Chicago World's Fair played a less discernible role in the development of American architecture despite the immensity of its innovations and its tremendous public success. While it did contribute to a greater public acceptance of nonhistorical building forms, few architects looked to the fair as a significant source of aesthetic inspiration for their modern designs. As stated earlier, A Century of Progress's major contribution to the development of twentieth-century architecture lay instead in the introduction and promotion of innovative building products and processes adaptable to traditional, as well as progressive, designs.

Beyond the fact that the fair was not promoting a specific aesthetic vocabulary, a variety of factors contributed to the exposition's lack of direct formal influence on contemporary architecture. These ranged from the drastic reduction in all construction starts in the 1930s as a result of the depressed economy to the vast difference in functional needs between temporary exposition halls and most permanent buildings. The negative reaction to the selection of designers for the exposition's architectural commission and, later, to the basic formal qualities of its pavilions also contributed to the fair's failure to affect other types of architecture.

A writer from the *Saturday Evening Post* contended that the unfamiliar and arresting architecture of the Chicago fair was the "hottest controversial art topic of the hour."[1] Strong opinions regarding the aesthetic qualities of the exposition architecture appeared soon after the unusual forms began rising along the Chicago lakefront. While a number of harsh critiques of the fair's architecture appeared in literary magazines and architectural journals published on the East Coast, these views were not universal.[2] Members of the public, general reporters, and young architects tended to respond just as passionately but much more favorably to the festive designs.[3]

The initial responses from most architects, critics, and laypeople, whether positive or negative, focused primarily on how different the pavilions looked in comparison to more traditional architectural designs, particularly the neoclassical forms that had dominated the first Chicago World's Fair and that surrounded the Century of Progress fairgrounds. Almost everyone reacted especially ardently to the cylindrical Railroad Hall of the Travel and Transport Building with its prominent structural system. The pavilion was commonly described as daring, bizarre, original, and shocking. Arthur F. Woltersdorf, a fellow of the AIA, exclaimed in an *American Architecture* article, "What! Have they discovered oil in Burnham Park? Look at the derricks! No, gentle reader, there are no oil wells. What you see are the stanchions supporting the cables of the Travel and Transport Dome."[4]

It is not clear whether the Chicago members of the architectural commission intended to generate controversy as a means of publicizing the fair when they designed the transportation pavilion, or whether they were only taking advantage of the fact that the exposition provided an ideal opportunity to experiment with radical new design concepts. The designers' agenda notwithstanding, the building did bring significant early attention to the fair. Exposition organizers quickly capitalized on the pavilion's ability to attract public interest and used images of the Travel and Transport Building in articles and brochures promoting the event. Journalists also drew attention to the exposition by describing and often using illustrations of the spiderlike building. Most people who visited the fairgrounds accepted the startling design of the "glorified gas tank" as strange, yet intriguing. In contrast, many architects and critics viewed the complex as hideous or extravagant. Some viewed it as a sellout of good architectural principles for the sake of advertising.[5] These differing reactions to the formal design of the Travel and Transport Building reflect a significant division between recorded responses to the modern architecture of the exposition by general fairgoers and reporters, and reactions by vocal members of an elite intellectual class of architects and critics.

Laypeople typically reacted to the fact that the modern architectural forms were astonishingly different from what they were accustomed to seeing. Many, however, came to embrace the exposition as an exciting place where they could escape from the often-bleak realities of their everyday world.[6] In the process of experiencing the fair's architecture, they expressed a wide range of opinions. One visitor commented on how beautiful the exposition buildings appeared. A second felt that "all the damn nuts in the world" must have been involved in the design of the pavilions.[7] Another visitor expressed mixed feelings, observing that while "the buildings are crazy and the colors and lights even crazier," the "whole is a peep into a fairyland transcending in beauty any dream that could [only] be conjured up by the wildest imagination."[8] President Franklin D. Roosevelt declared that he liked the buildings so much that he "wanted to see every one of them." General John J. Pershing, who had commanded the Columbian Guards at the earlier Chicago exposition, was also charmed by the buildings. In contrasting the architecture of A Century of Progress with that of the first Chicago fair, he proclaimed that the buildings "far exceed the beauties of the Columbian Exposition."[9]

Joseph Urban's application of vivid hues to the facades of the pavilions provoked particularly intense reactions from many fairgoers. After the shock of the bright colors had dissipated, the visitors usually accepted the brilliantly painted buildings as appropriate to the festive environment of a world's fair. Both an advertiser from Chicago and a carpenter from New York attending the fair directly attributed the success of the event to the colors of the buildings.[10] Meanwhile, a housewife from suburban Oak Park, Illinois, exclaimed that while it took time to accustom oneself to the unusual buildings, the colors were indeed lovely.[11]

Most of the public's published responses to the architecture of the exposition focused on the group of model houses in the Home and Industrial Arts Exhibit. Homeowners, mesmerized by the new ideas and gadgets, often expressed positive comments regarding the modern dwellings, although many visitors wrote that they would not care to live in such unusual homes. Fairgoer Mrs. J. C. Lawrence told a writer for *Architectural Forum*

FIG. 7.1. Florida Tropical House. From Dorothy Raley, *A Century of Progress Homes and Furnishings* (Chicago: M. A. Ring, 1934), 52.

that both the brick and glass houses seemed too much like prisons, while a doctor from Dayton, Ohio, admitted that he was too scared even to enter the Common Brick Manufacturers' House, as it appeared "a bit too radical."[12] Other responses, however, were more complimentary, particularly in regard to the interior designs. Favorite models included the Rostone, Florida Tropical, and Masonite houses and the House of Today. Mrs. Frederick Foley, a housewife from St. Paul, Minnesota, exclaimed, "I think it's all quite beautiful, particularly at night. I am definitely and favorably impressed with the style. It hasn't been done very often, but I like it here as it is. Most of these model houses are lovely. My favorites are the Florida House and the Masonite House, and the green room in the Masonite House is the choice room in all the houses in my opinion."[13] Although it was typically received favorably, the modern architecture was viewed by many as something reserved for another time or place and not applicable to their own present lives (Plate 24).

Journalists, following their professional code, attempted to play down their personal opinions regarding the architecture of the exposition. Instead, they tended to use dramatic, picturesque terms to produce descriptive articles that were closely based on the constant stream of press releases issued by the fair's industrious public relations committee. One writer, for *Literary Digest*, proclaimed that the "modernistic towers of 'A Century of Progress' out-marvel the Arabian Nights with their varicolored splendor"; another, for *Popular Mechanics*, wrote of palaces with "glittering facades" and towers of "sparkling jewels."[14] Journalists employed particularly vivid adjectives to describe the color of the exposition. In discussing the event's lighting, the writer for *Literary Digest* declared that the "Rainbow City... flaunts to the sky the boldest hues of the spectrum, in audacious and sometimes cock-eyed forms."[15] Ben Hibbs, writing in *Country Gentleman*, stated that the "scintillating blues and greens, flaming scarlet, and a whole range of almost brutal yellows" employed by Urban were "so skillfully fused with architectural composition that the desperately bright pigmentation gives no offense."[16] With even more enthusiasm, a writer for *Popular Mechanics* proclaimed that whether one found the exposition "gaudy or gorgeous," the fact remained that it represented "the greatest spectacle of light and color ever achieved by man."[17]

A few reporters, such as S. J. Duncan Clark, did try to take a more sophisticated approach in describing the modern buildings to the general public, but they still focused their discussions on the pavilions' visual qualities. For instance, in a description of the Administration Building, published in the *Chicago Daily News*, Clark admitted to his readers that it was "a little difficult to get and hold the viewpoint needed to understand and evaluate what has been attempted in this structure of modernity."[18] However, in his own attempt to do so, he was immediately struck by the forthright simplicity of the building's lines and by the uncompromising horizontals and perpendiculars, the boxlike regularity, the absence of nonessentials,

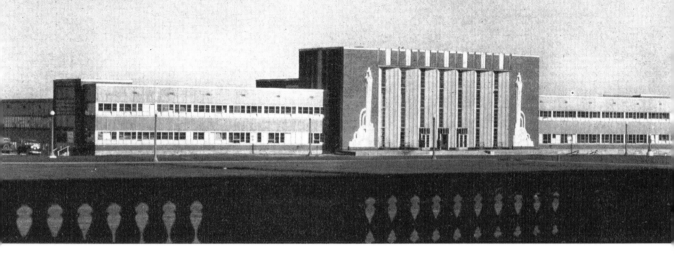

FIG. 7.2. Administration Building, showing its factory-like fenestration. Hedrich-Blessing, photographers. From Louis Skidmore, "Administration Building," *Architectural Forum* 55 (August 1931): 134.

and the uncluttered neatness of the pavilion. As a result, Clark believed that the building presented an "honest statement of function" dedicated to "energy, efficiency and economy," without absurd or irritating "ornamental excrescences."[19]

Even reactions to the aesthetic quality of the exposition architecture by those involved in the design of the event were mixed and often not as positive as one might expect. Commissioner Paul Cret was an especially harsh critic. He stated that "without its final coat of paint, its sculptural decorations, without the roads and plantings, and without the exhibits and crowds, the parasols and seats over the terraces," an exposition building is "reduced to the sad appearance of an unfinished apartment."[20] Of his own Hall of Science, he wrote that there was little "architecture" (as defined by John Ruskin) in the pavilion and that "the outside walls [of the building] shamelessly confess that they are built of thin veneer, and do not attempt to suggest the mass stability of masonry walls."[21]

Early in the planning process, the members of the architectural commission realized that their stage-set designs for the exposition were not likely to serve as formal sources for other buildings, as had the exhibition halls at the first Chicago World's Fair or the pavilions at the 1925 Paris exposition. They understood that by attempting to express more honestly the basic function (essentially that of a festive warehouse) and specific needs of large, temporary exhibition halls through the use of prefabricated panels, they could not expect their designs to serve as formal prototypes for more-permanent everyday architecture, especially during a period of declining building starts.[22] In following their chosen definition of modern architecture, the commissioners stated that they were less concerned with the final visual character of their pavilion designs than with meeting the specific functional needs of the buildings.[23] They believed that the exposition's most significant influence on the architectural profession would stem instead from their promotion of the concept of "disposable buildings" and their use of new construction materials and techniques.[24] Cret summed up the commissioners' pragmatic expectations regarding the aesthetic effect of the event when he stated that, because of its special program and its impermanence, "a world's fair building, whatever the talent of the architect, cannot hope to be one of the milestones of architecture."[25]

The commissioners knew almost from the start that the modern architectural designs they created were bound to attract a variety of responses from their colleagues. Corbett predicted that while conservatives and older designers would find the progressive forms shocking, younger members of the profession, already acquainted with modern ideas through their schooling, would accept the buildings as intriguing and possibly even inspiring.[26] Some architects, especially those with strong ties to Chicago, wrote favorably of the exhibition buildings. Other noted architects, such as Frank Lloyd Wright, criticized the pavilions while attempting to further their own design agendas.

Chicago architect and critic Thomas Tallmadge, like most people reacting to the exposition buildings, focused his remarks on the visual character of the pavilions. Prior to the event's opening, he predicted in *Vanity Fair* that the "Exposition will be the most beautiful thing man has created."[27] In his enlarged and revised edition of *The Story of Architecture in America*, published a few years after the close of the fair, Tallmadge stated that the Century of Progress International Exposition had to be regarded as "a vast proving ground for the New Architecture in all its aspects."[28] He contrasted the beautiful proportions of Cret's Hall of Science to the monstrous awkwardness of works by Le Corbusier. In a strange, yet graphic, descriptive fashion, Tallmadge favorably related several of the major exhibition halls to various species of insects. He saw the Travel and Transport Building as a spider, the Agriculture Building as a resplendent caterpillar, the Hall of Science as an Amazonian butterfly "slowly unfolding its iridescent wings," and the General Exhibits Building as a "battalion of devouring locusts."[29]

Alfred Granger, another Chicago architect and critic, agreed with Corbett and Tallmadge. He remarked in his book *Chicago Welcomes You* that he saw the exposition as a model that presented to future generations some of the design options made possible through architecture's recent release "from the shackles of ancient traditions."[30] He praised Cret's Hall of Science as a triumph in design, declaring it "intensely 'moderne,' while adhering to the fundamental principles of architectural design which have come down through the ages." Granger referred to the Administration Building as a wonderland of beauty and the Court of States as both beautifully landscaped and appropriately expressive of the dignity and power of the government. Looking beyond formal issues, he went on to reaffirm the architectural commissioners' belief that progressive designers would find significant inspiration not in the formal qualities of the modern pavilions but in "the discovery of new building materials and new methods of construction."[31]

Not all architects furnished such glowing reviews of the exposition designs. In the article "Fair Buildings Being Erected Cause Debates," the *Chicago Daily*

News published a particularly harsh letter by designer C. W. Taber in April 1931, a couple months after Wright had presented his alternative exposition schemes in New York City. Taber was exceptionally critical of the earliest fair buildings. Spurred on by a group of New York cultural critics responding caustically to the fair's architecture, Taber declared the Administration Building a disgrace to Chicago and the Travel and Transport Building a freak. He then asked women's clubs, art groups, and civic bodies to publicly protest and demand a change of architecture for the event.[32]

FIG. 7.3. The colorful Agriculture Building. Kaufmann and Fabry, photographers.

It is not clear how many, if any, women's clubs rose up against the design of the fair. However, in the same article, the newspaper also published several local architects' reactions to Tabor's comments. Ernest Grunsfeld, architect of the Adler Planetarium and the Lumber Industries House at the fair, believed that Tabor was jumping to too many conclusions without "analyzing the purpose of the fair."[33] He felt it would be an error to judge the pavilions too severely prior to their completion, assuming that once completed, with all their "appurtenances and lighting effects, and crowds of people," the buildings would be perceived as "magnificent, gay and festive."

Irving K. Pond, a noted Chicago architect and former president of the AIA, asserted that Tabor was taking the architecture of the fair far too seriously. He personally did not believe that the buildings would have a permanent effect on later architecture. Pond, in fact, did not even accept the exposition buildings as architecture but instead viewed them as "merely shelters for a fair, like a tent for a circus." Finding the commissioners' attempt to rely on applied color and lighting for building decoration unsuccessful, he went on to equate the exposition's modern pavilions to Caliban, the deformed monster in Shakespeare's *The Tempest*.[34]

In contrast, Walter S. Fraizer foresaw the potential of the fair pavilions to contribute to the development of progressive architecture. He believed that regardless of whether the buildings complied with "preconceived ideas of beauty they should be considered a radical move in architecture . . . the effect of which upon future architecture will be salutary." Fraizer went on to suggest that any controversy the buildings stirred up could only be beneficial to the profession and predicted that such debate might help "bring new trends into American architecture."[35]

Arthur F. Woltersdorf wrote one of the most comprehensive and balanced reviews, which appeared in *American Architect* two months after the exposition had opened.[36] He applauded the commissioners' decision to reject historical architectural forms, but he stated that they could not claim their designs as original, since they had derived many of the motifs from previous designs by progressive European architects. He observed that the style of the fair psychologically expressed the previous era through the use of architectural forms and coloration reminiscent of "lipstick, the hip flask and the cocktail shaker"—items symbolic of the Roaring Twenties.[37]

Woltersdorf greatly admired the automobile manufacturers' pavilions in particular. He proclaimed Albert Kahn's design of the General Motors Building "probably the best built, large structure in the Exposition" and commended Holabird and Root on their design for the Chrysler Building.[38] He referred to Ely Jacques Kahn's designs for Kohler and Johns-Manville as clever and applauded the Common Brick Manufacturers' House and other model residences on exhibit. However, he wasted no adulation on the Court of States located on the east side of Bennett's U.S. Government Building. He likened the pavilion's arrangement to that of a circus tent with a menagerie forecourt surrounded by lurid panels of sideshow attractions. In the case of the Court of States, the lurid panels consisted of paintings of state flags situated over individual state compartments that featured local achievements and products in place of human oddities.[39]

Woltersdorf also had little positive to say about the color scheme of the exposition. He referred to Urban as "the exterior color autocrat."[40] In contrast to the architects on the commission, who felt that the use of color united the buildings of the fair into a comprehensive program, Woltersdorf declared that Urban's treatment of color, which "cut in and out of the same building," led to further disintegration of the fair's overall design by emphasizing individual building planes. The writer found the Agriculture Building to be an interesting structure and well suited to exhibition purposes, but he admitted that the coloration of the pavilion, in particular the alternating stripes at the north end, was well beyond his understanding. He went on to describe the blacks, heavy reds, and dark blues of the Electrical Building as almost barbaric, and he contended that the coloration of the Court of Science, with its white-and-blue tower facades, blue bands, and bright yellow boxes placed against a wall of saffron, only managed further to disorganize the design.[41]

In contrast, Ely Jacques Kahn declared that the use of bright shades "whipped the whole scheme into a picture of sparkling color." Additional benefits of the color scheme, according to Kahn, included being able to hide several less-than-successful architectural experiments "through the judicious use of dark blues and blacks" and the ability to accent some objects, while downplaying others, to strengthen the "solidity of the buildings." Contemplating the impact of the exposition on future building, he declared in *Architectural Forum* that the color statement made at the fair was "by all odds the most vital contribution to a new architecture."[42]

The most acrimonious reactions to the aesthetics of the modern fair pavilions came from two prominent architects not directly involved in

FIG. 7.4. The Kohler Pavilion, by Ely Jacques Kahn. Kaufmann and Fabry, photographers.

Court of States
Federal Building
A Century of Progress

FIG. 7.5. The Court
of States at the U.S.
Government Building.
Postcard from
collection of author.

the event. The first, Ralph Adams Cram, was the leading neo-Gothicist in the United States during the early decades of the twentieth century. He severely criticized the fair's architecture in the *Boston Transcript* and in *Architectural Forum*, even though he admitted that he had not visited the exposition. Cram agreed with the commissioners that the influence of the modern halls would probably be limited to technological and scientific advances and that they would not serve as models for more permanent structures. He, however, did not attribute this to the fact that the fair buildings and more traditional structures addressed significantly different functional needs. Rather, he believed that the style adopted for the event was not modern at all. Cram declared that it was already old-fashioned, outmoded, and thus incorrigibly ugly. Unable to discern any progress in the pavilion designs, which he alleged were based on "a casual association of the gasometer, the freight yard and the grain elevator," Cram concluded that the "pasteboard containers" illustrated a "definite retrogression" in American architecture.[43]

The second, Frank Lloyd Wright, bitter about his exclusion from the architectural commission, went on a major campaign to denigrate the committee members' designs for the exposition. The introduction of his own three sketchy conceptual schemes for the event represented only one of the architect's tactics for promoting himself and his ideas at the expense of the commissioners. He wrote a number of damning articles in which he declared his omission from the exposition a "betrayal of an organic architecture."[44] As at the AUDAC meeting in New

York, Wright belittled the fair's designers and their work in these editorials without bothering to take into consideration the specific conditions by which the architects were limited and without making any attempt to fully understand the designs
or the larger goals that they were trying to achieve.[45] He labeled the architects a
bunch of eclectics and denounced their fair designs as "the product of the same
eclecticism that produced historical stylism from which the Exhibition claims to
break away."[46] Wright went on to allege that the Beaux-Arts-trained designers had
continued to rely on a "pseudo-classic plan-structure" with which they were familiar and that they had arrived at their modern elevations solely by "scraping off
capitals, cornices, pilasters and ornamental details."[47] The net results, according to
Wright, were false designs that were not to be considered architecture no matter
how gaily painted.

The exclusion of Wright from the architectural commission, more than any
other factor, led to the publication of a number of negative articles regarding the
architectural design of the exposition prior to the opening of the event. Much of
the unfavorable press appeared in East Coast current-events publications and was
written by nonarchitect critics, an occupation that was gaining greater influence in
dictating the direction of progressive architecture during these years.

Critics Douglas Haskell and Lewis Mumford initially led the loud outcry from
select members of New York architectural and intellectual circles against the designers of the Chicago exposition and, more specifically, against Wright's absence
from the event.[48] Criticism of the choice of designers and their exposition work
were major topics at professional meetings in New York and in articles in publications such as the *Nation* and the *New Republic.* In continuing his crusade to
have Wright included as a designer for the exposition, Haskell published an article
on the architect's behalf in the *Nation* and then encouraged Mumford to submit
a similar piece to the *New Republic.* The articles, written in the cynical tone often used by Wright, included obviously false and exaggerated statements. Haskell
expressed his trepidation that without Wright, the fair's architects would end up
presenting a fallacious modernism derived from the Paris exposition of 1925, much
as the World's Columbian Exposition had imposed the false classicism of the Beaux
Arts.[49] Mumford, meanwhile, worried that Wright's exclusion would result in an
exposition that was "dreadfully stagey."[50] At the AUDAC meeting in which Wright
presented his three fair designs, Mumford reiterated the architect's opinion that
the commissioners could not possibly contribute anything positive to the development of modern architecture. *Time* magazine reported that the critic pronounced
the new Chicago fair pavilions by the commissioners "merely pseudo-classical
buildings to which the architects have applied details of the new and at present
fashionable style exactly as they applied Gothic, Renaissance, [and] Georgian details to their steel frame skyscrapers."[51] The *New York Herald-Tribune* joined the

East Coast critics by inciting and then publishing a number of unfavorable opinions on the exposition that ranged from lukewarm to vehemently disapproving of the architectural designs for the event.[52]

In reaction to the uproar in the East, the *Chicagoan* published a brief summary by Wright in which he discussed his views regarding the exposition buildings. It also described the architect's schemes for the event. The *Chicagoan* then printed short rejoinders from a number of the midwestern architects working on the fair, including Louis Skidmore, Hubert Burnham, and Edward Bennett, as well as from C. W. Farrier and Shepard Vogelgesang. Instead of defending the aesthetic qualities of the pavilions or the selection of architects, these designers (taking a more politically neutral approach) presented general observations on the overall visual effect of the exposition; the specific problems of designing large, low-cost, temporary buildings; and the potential for future simplification of building practices through the adoption of the new materials and methods of construction used at the fair.[53]

When Wright made it known that, if ever asked, he would decline any role in the design of the fair, most of the nonarchitect critics dropped their campaign against the commissioners and turned their attention elsewhere.[54] Soon after the fair opened, however, Haskell rekindled his attack on the exposition architects and their designs. In August 1933 he published a major critique of the exposition in the *Architectural Review* titled "Mixed Metaphors at Chicago." In it he concluded that the exclusion of Wright had resulted in considerable damage to the design of the event. He then re-expressed his disdain for the work of the members of the architectural commission, proclaiming "eclectic once, eclectic always."[55]

Nevertheless, by opening day of the exposition's second season in May 1934, even Haskell's views had softened. Possibly influenced by criticism from New Jersey architect Arthur North and others on the superficial reactions to modern architecture offered by nonarchitect critics, Haskell began to look at the fair's architecture more comprehensively.[56] While still unable to let go of his belief that the commissioners had badly erred in their exclusion of Wright, he did finally begin to acknowledge the fair designers' substantial role in helping modern architecture gain popular recognition in the United States. Although he continued to find the formal elements of the pavilions chaotic, he admitted, "Architecturally, 1933 was the year of the Chicago Fair."[57]

In finally being able to look beyond the obvious formal issues, Haskell began to consider the special needs and goals of the short-lived exposition halls. He even began to view the bright colors of the buildings (which he had previously panned) as appropriate to a brief, festive event. He went as far as to admit that the concept of disposable buildings, which honestly reflected the ephemeral nature of the fair, could be adapted to serve the needs of an increasingly mobile modern society. As a result, Haskell wrote that the designs of the Century of Progress pavilions provided "a better promise for the succeeding decades" than the classical palaces of previous American expositions had done.[58] He additionally conceded that by consciously looking to the future for inspiration, as opposed to the past, as had Daniel Burnham Sr. and the other designers of the 1893 exposition, the commissioners opened the door to new developments in American architecture.

Although each group of fairgoers and critics responded somewhat differently to the buildings designed for A Century of Progress, they all contributed to the event's impact on the development of modern architecture in the United States. The descriptive articles written by reporters and published in the popular press helped generate great excitement for the fair. Their poetic characterizations of the exposition (along with special deals offered by the fair corporation and the major railways) drew millions of Americans to the fairgrounds. The pavilions' potential aesthetic impact on modern design was, however, tempered by the published remarks of several commissioners, who stated that they had never intended their experimental exhibition halls to serve as formal models for everyday buildings.

The influence of the pavilions was further diminished by the less-than-enthusiastic responses to the buildings' formal character by prominent architectural critics. Unfavorable comments regarding the architectural designs of the exposition did, however, influence the direction of contemporary architecture in the United States in two important ways. First, the controversy over the exclusion of Wright from the fair helped keep his name and his ideas regarding modern design before the public eye. Second, reviews of the exposition's pavilions by writers like Mumford and Haskell brought attention to the growing profession of nonarchitect design critics and helped increase their influence in the development of contemporary architectural design. As Robert Wojtowicz pointed out in his book *Lewis Mumford and American Modernism,* prior to the First World War architectural criticism by writers such as Montgomery Schuyler, Russell Sturgis, Mariana Griswold Van Rensselaer, and Claude Bragdon was confined mostly to professional publications.[59] Reviews published in architectural magazines, as Mumford later complained, amounted not to criticism but instead to "flattery, appreciation, [and] 'publicity.'"[60] Such adulation, along with the fact that by the 1920s Bragdon was the only one of these major critics still writing on building design, led Mumford to proclaim that the field of architectural criticism was all but dead.[61]

In an attempt to revive the occupation, Mumford became a leader of a new generation of critics whose formal training had typically taken place outside the architectural profession. These writers published their reviews primarily in elite current-events magazines. They thus had considerable freedom to criticize current architecture without worrying about repercussions while, at the same time, making their opinions available to a broader audience of readers. Although the aesthetic impact of the Century of Progress International Exposition on everyday architecture was limited, the event did have an influence on later modern architecture with similar functional needs. It also propelled a growing interest in and use of a number of popular, nonformal elements of building design.

THE IMPACT OF THE A CENTURY OF PROGRESS

While the fair's aesthetic impact on the development of mid-twentieth-century architecture was limited, many of the less obvious aspects of A Century of Progress's architecture significantly contributed to equally inconspicuous features of modern building design. These included new structural concepts, building materials, and construction processes. In some instances, the specific influences were limited or short-lived. In other cases, their impact continues to resonate in American architecture to this day.

The use or promotion of a building material or a construction concept at the exposition was never the sole reason for its widespread success or failure. The fair did, however, significantly contribute to people's awareness of new products and ideas. Early publicity about the exposition generated great public interest in the fair pavilions well before the event officially opened. The thousands of curious designers, builders, and potential clients drawn to the fairgrounds prior to opening day witnessed the first large-scale applications of prefabricated modern materials in the United States. After the exposition was under way, millions more experienced firsthand the brightly colored modern

FIG. 7.6. Some of the hundreds of publications that featured articles on the Century of Progress International Exposition. From "News of Fair in Pictures," *Progress* 2 (22 March 1933): n.p.

A few of the hundreds of magazines and trade journals which by means of words and photographs have told the story of A Century of Progress to millions of readers here and abroad.

All photographs by Photographic Division, 1

pavilions, as well as the numerous individual architectural exhibits, sponsored by building-related manufacturers and associations, located inside the pavilions.

For those unable to visit the Chicago exposition, secondary sources, including hundreds of articles, focused on its built environment. Almost all the major pavilions were the subject of lengthy, well-illustrated articles in *Architectural Forum* in which the authors meticulously described the designs of the buildings and included drawings of construction details. Scientific journals including *Engineering News-Record* and *Scientific American* highlighted the exciting new structural techniques exhibited at the fair, while more specialized building publications like *Concrete* and *Construction* published long analytical pieces on pavilion design issues that were directly relevant to their particular readerships. Articles on many of the most intriguing fair buildings, in particular the futuristic model houses, also appeared in popular home magazines, such as *Good Housekeeping* and *House and Garden*, as well as in other publications that ranged from *Fortune* to the *New York Times Magazine*. Even specialized trade journals with little or no direct connection to the exposition, like *Milk Plant Monthly* and *Florists' Review*, carried articles discussing the extraordinary architecture of the exposition.

IMPACT OF STRUCTURAL INNOVATIONS

The influence of the groundbreaking structural techniques introduced to Americans at A Century of Progress is primarily reflected in the designs of later specialty buildings with programmatic needs similar to those of the fair's pavilions, in particular temporary exposition halls and Olympic sports venues. Designers employed the structural techniques used in the catenary roof of the Travel and Transport Building and in the thin-shell concrete barrel-vaulted roof of the Brook Hill Farm Dairy for spanning large halls that required sizable areas of continuous space. Architects and engineers, however, favored the two systems for different types of buildings, preferring suspended roof structures for large, often temporary, festive buildings and thin-shell concrete roofs for structures with more permanent utilitarian purposes, such as airplane hangars and warehouses.

The Chicago architects who created the Travel and Transport Building incorporated a catenary roof into the design of the pavilion's Railroad Hall as a novelty and not as a potential prototype for future architecture.[62] In fact, at the time of construction they admitted their doubts as to its adaptability to more permanent architecture because of several major drawbacks with the structural form. Most significantly, the designers realized that over time, unprotected metal cables that were exposed to the elements had the potential to corrode.[63] Another problematic factor was the long-term wear on building joints and connectors caused by the shifting of individual parts of the structures with wind and temperature changes.

Construction workers also encountered difficulties in attempting to waterproof suspended roof structures, primarily because of problems with the seals between the movable building parts. The elimination of interior columns, meanwhile, not only forced vertical loads to travel farther to reach the ground but also dictated that the building had to be designed to resist wind forces without the benefit of the structural stiffness created by a columnar system.[64] The need to fireproof the pavilion created other challenges, in particular having to encase the flexible cables within a fire-resistant material.

While later designers only infrequently incorporate catenary structural systems into more permanent architecture, they do on occasion specify their use for exposition pavilions and sports arenas. The actual impact of the Travel and Transport Building even on these forms of architecture, however, is difficult to assess clearly. While the transportation pavilion received great attention in engineering and architectural publications, as well as from the popular press, during its construction and brief existence, after its demolition in 1935 the building was almost completely ignored by architects and engineers until the 1950s, in part because steel was unavailable for the construction of similar designs during the Second World War.

In 1954 the German engineer Frei Otto rekindled interest in catenary roofs with the publication of his Ph.D. dissertation, as *Das hängende Dach.* This work promoted Otto's conviction that suspended thin-membrane roofs provided the key to creating an appropriate architecture for modern times, much as the post-and-lintel had for the Greeks and the arch had for the Romans. He prominently featured a construction photograph of the

FIG. 7.7. Construction photograph of the Travel and Transport Building. From Frei Otto, *Däs hängende Dach* (Berlin: Ullstein A.G., 1954), 11.

Travel and Transport Building in a section on early post-and-tension structures in his book.[65] The distribution of Otto's treatise in the United States by Wittenborn and Company made his ideas, as well as the image of the long-demolished transportation pavilion, readily available to American designers. Additionally, Otto had promoted the use of post-and-tension structures during a trip to the United States in the early 1950s prior to completing his dissertation. On this journey, he had visited the New York offices of Severud-Elstad-Krueger, an engineering firm working at the time on the design of the Raleigh Arena (designed by Matthew Nowicki), one of the first buildings constructed in the United States after the Second World War to include a suspended roof structure in its design.[66]

The rise of interest in catenary structures during the mid-1950s is reflected in the design of fair buildings created for international expositions after the war. The basic post-and-tension technology of the Travel and Transport Building's structural system (as well as concrete shells) was used repeatedly at the Exposition Universelle et Internationale de Bruxelles in 1958, the first major international exposition held since the 1939–40 New York World's Fair. In Brussels the Soviet, U.S., and French pavilions, as well as several other buildings, all consisted of innovative designs that incorporated suspended roof structures.[67]

Architects continued to design buildings with catenary roofs for major international exhibitions held during the 1960s and at the start of the 1970s in New York, Montreal, and Osaka.[68] Promoters marketed the rotunda of the New York State Pavilion (designed by Philip Johnson) at the 1964–65 New York World's Fair as possessing the world's biggest suspended roof. Cables radiating out from sixteen columns over 100 feet tall supported a colorful Fiberglas roof that covered more area than a football field.[69] The initial scheme for the Transportation and Travel Building at the New York World's Fair (designed by Charles Luckman Associates) paid homage to its predecessor from the 1933–34 Chicago exposition by also including a suspended roof in its design. However, organizers rejected this scheme in favor of one that featured a truss system.[70]

Frei Otto continued to promote the concept of suspended roof structures into the 1970s.[71] With the rise of computers, designers and engineers could more easily carry out the difficult calculations required for more complex prestressed membranes. Built examples were still primarily limited to exhibition halls and major sports arenas, including Otto's own designs for the Federal Republic of Germany Pavilion at the international exhibition held in Montreal in 1967 and for the main sports stadium, along with two smaller adjacent buildings, at the 1972 Olympics in Munich.[72] Interest in suspended roof structures for exposition buildings continued through the end of the century. A number of the festive bridges and pavilions at Expo '92, held in Seville, Spain, and at Expo 2000, held in Hanover, Germany, relied on creative uses of catenary principles reminiscent of those found almost sixty years earlier at A Century of Progress.[73]

Local architects also employed the basic structural concept of the Travel and Transport Building in the design of several later buildings constructed in the Chicago area. Skidmore, Owings and Merrill (a firm whose two major founders had played significant roles in the design of A Century of Progress) incorporated suspended roofs into the designs of the Baxter Travenol Laboratories (1975) north of the city and the McCormick Place North Building (1984–86) constructed on the 1933–34 fairgrounds, immediately to the south of where Cret's Hall of Science once stood.[74] Toward the end of the century, the Chicago firm of Nagle Hartray and Associates produced a similar structural design for the city's main Greyhound–Trailways Bus Depot (1988–90), located about a mile west of the fairgrounds.

Like the catenary roof of the Travel and Transport Building, the multivaulted thin-shell concrete roof of the Brook Hill Farm Dairy served as an archetype for buildings whose functions also necessitated large unbroken spans of space. While Anton Tedesko had initially found it difficult to convince architects in the United States to incorporate thin shells into their designs, the Brook Hill Farm Dairy and the concrete dome of the Hayden Planetarium in New York City provided first-hand examples of thin-shell technology.[75] Designers in the United States learned about the Zeiss-Dywidag process for creating concrete shells primarily through articles in magazines and newspapers that featured the dairy and the planetarium

FIG. 7.8 *(facing)*. The New York Pavilion, New York World's Fair (1964–65), by Philip Johnson, with its suspended roof. Postcard from collection of author.
FIG. 7.9 *(above)*. The tented El Palenque, designed by José Miguel de Prada Poole, at Expo '92 in Seville, Spain. Photograph by author.

FIG. 7.10. Greyhound–Trailways Bus Depot, Chicago, Nagle Hartray and Associates, 1988–90. Photograph by author.

buildings. Tedesko authored many of these articles himself, including a lead article in the July 1934 issue of *Concrete* that presented a detailed description of the dairy's design and of the construction process for the roof.[76] The following year subscribers to *Engineering News-Record* read about the strong structural abilities of the dairy's thin-shell roof in an article that detailed the results of a special strength test made on the pavilion immediately prior to its demolition.[77]

The success of the roof of the Brook Hill Farm Dairy convinced Roberts and Schaefer, the building's engineering firm, of the practicality of thin-shell concrete. They continued to experiment with the material throughout the mid-twentieth century, using reinforced concrete shells for structures that required low-cost, large roof spans. Their ownership of the U.S. patent for the Z-D process made Roberts and Schaefer the sole designers of all major thin shells built in the country prior to the Second World War.

In addition to patent limitations, the excessive cost of creating the formwork necessary to erect thin-shell roofs presented a major initial stumbling block to the widespread construction of concrete shells. This was especially true in the United States, where labor costs were relatively high. The Brook Hill Farm Dairy was an important early experiment in developing a more cost-efficient construction method that consisted of an efficient reuse of formwork.[78] To reduce expenses, Roberts and Schaefer reused two of the three sets of barrel-shaped formwork to construct the last two of the dairy's five barrel vaults.[79] Further advances in reusable formwork took place several years later in their design for a sports arena (1936) in Hershey, Pennsylvania. The ice rink's roof, the largest concrete shell in the world at the time of its construction, consisted of a series of five separate segments of barrel vaults that were identical in cross section.[80] During construction, pieces of formwork traveled along the line of the vaulting allowing for multiple reuses of the forms.[81]

In the 1940s Roberts and Schaefer continued to make improvements to their roof designs as they produced thin shells for the U.S. military. In contrast to suspended roofs, which were rarely built during the war, concrete shells presented an ideal solution for roofing warehouses, factories, and airplane hangars. The ability of membrane structures to change their distribution of stress was noted as a major benefit of their use. This meant that partial destruction of the roof, or even of one of the supporting arches, during an attack would not be likely to cause complete collapse of the building.[82]

By 1941 Roberts and Schaefer had designed concrete-shell roofing to cover an area of almost 10 million square feet.[83] After the war, however, the company began facing competition from other design firms as patent rights opened up and articles in engineering journals and papers at

FIG. 7.11. Hayden Planetarium, New York City, 1934–35. Postcard from collection of author.

professional conferences began promoting the benefits of thin shells.[84] Interested designers included Eero Saarinen, who, by the mid-1950s, had joined a number of architects throughout the world in exploring the expressionistic potential of concrete shells.[85] His Kresge Auditorium at the Massachusetts Institute of Technology built in 1955 was one of the largest shell roofs to be constructed in the United States.[86] A few years later the architect received considerable publicity for his fluid, organic, bird-shaped shell roof of the TWA Terminal in New York (1961).[87]

Similar explorations in concrete-shell design also took place in other parts of the world. Some of the most aesthetically interesting included the dramatically cantilevered entrance canopy of the Ciba Plant in Churubusco, Mexico, by Felix Candela, in cooperation with Enrique de la Mora and Fernando Lopez Carmona (1955); the shallow lamella dome on Y-shaped piers of the Palazzetto dello Sport in Rome, by Pier Luigi Nervi (1957); the hyperbolic-paraboloidal-shell Phillips Pavilion, by Le Corbusier, and the birdlike form of the Civil Engineering Pavilion at the Exposition Universelle et Internationale de Bruxelles (1958); and the complexly curved sails of the Sydney Opera House, by Jörn Utzon (1957–73).

In the United States, the Roberts and Schaefer Company continued its involvement in reinforced concrete-shell roofs well after 1945. In addition to building a large number of barrel-vaulted commercial airplane hangars and sports halls, such as the Denver Coliseum (1954), they engineered the magnificent, groin-vaulted Lambert Airport in St. Louis (1953, 1955).[88]

FIG. 7.12 *(facing)*. Hershey Sports Arena, Hershey, Pennsylvania, 1936. From Anton Tedesko, "Large Concrete Shell Roof Covers Ice Arena," *Engineering News-Record* 118 (8 April 1937): 505. FIG. 7.13 *(below)*. The birdlike TWA Terminal, New York City, by Eero Saarinen (1961). Photograph by author.

FIG. 7.14. The dramatic birdlike concrete Civil Engineering Pavilion at the Exposition Universelle et Internationale, Brussels, 1958. Postcard from collection of author.

Along with other concrete-shell engineers, the firm began experimenting with more-complex roof forms in the late 1950s. Their May D&F Department Store in Denver, Colorado (1958), designed in collaboration with I. M. Pei, consisted of a thin-shell hyperbolic-paraboloid roof in the shape of four large back-to-back gables.[89]

While available sources offer some insight into the impact the Travel and Transport Building and Brook Hill Farm Dairy had on later roofing developments, the direct influence of the innovative pile-foundation system used at the exposition is harder to define. Records do show, however, that the structural system played a major role in the foundation designs for the buildings of the 1939–40 New York World's Fair. During the planning process, members of the board of design of the New York exposition specifically requested copies of foundation plans for Albert Kahn's Ford Building from the Chicago fair to use as a model for their major pavilions. As at Chicago, organizers situated the exposition on recently altered land; in the case of New York, workers at Flushing Meadows transformed a massive garbage dump into the site of the fair. After studying the design of the Ford Building, the architects and engineers concluded that a similar system could be used for pavilions located in almost all areas of the New York fairgrounds.[90]

BUILDING MATERIALS AND PROCESSES

The new construction products and processes exhibited at A Century of Progress came to be far more prevalent in modern American architecture than the new structural concepts highlighted at the exposition. Many of the innovative building products found at the fair, such as Celotex and Masonite, became common fixtures in modern construction. The rise in popularity of newly available forms of standardized wall panels revolutionized the building industry. In particular, they made possible an efficient construction process similar to the assembly-line methods used to manufacture other modern products, such as the various commercial objects, ranging from tin-can banks to automobiles, produced in the motion-filled corporate displays at the Chicago fair.

While 1933 may have been the "natal-year of pre-fabrication," the Century of Progress International Exposition was its coming-out party.[91] The demonstration of new materials and methods of mass production in the construction of the fair pavilions helped promote these new developments to the general public. Numerous individual designers and companies, as well as the U.S. government, became aware in these years of the benefits of prefabrication, in particular, for the creation of decent low-cost housing. During the Second World War, prefabrication went on to play a large role in the construction of rapidly assembled factories and housing to meet war-related needs. After the war, these modern building procedures and products allowed for the erection of thousands of new, single-family homes in suburbs across the country.

In addition to the new building concepts presented at the exposition, several other major factors contributed to the tremendous growth of interest in modern materials and prefabrication at the time of the fair. Many of these are discussed in Burnham Kelly's 1951 book *The Prefabrication of Houses.*[92] Most significant was the belief that prefabrication could provide an economic lift to industry, much as the construction of the exposition had contributed to the revival of Chicago's economy. Severely underutilized but well-established companies viewed the creation of mass-produced houses as a sure route to future financial success.[93] In the same vein, building product manufacturers felt that prefabrication provided the ideal means to regain their economic prosperity. Many individual investors, still reeling from the effects of the Great Depression, also regarded modern materials and construction processes as attractive investments with significant growth potential.[94]

Another major reason for the immense interest in new building products and prefabrication during and immediately after the Chicago exposition was the continually increasing need for adequate, affordable housing. The entry of the U.S. government into the production of low-cost housing in the mid-1930s provided confidence and support to those contemplating entering the residential construction market. The model residences at the fair demonstrated how the adoption of modern building materials and techniques could lead to more efficient housing. Articles in trade and popular publications that discussed the adaptability of standardized, man-made materials, such as gypsum board and steel framing, to prefabricated construction processes helped generate immense interest in mass-produced housing. A host of other institutions and companies interested in the application of more efficient construction processes soon joined the building-products manufacturers and trade organizations that had demonstrated prefabricated processes and materials at the Chicago exposition by building their own model residences. The August 1935 issue of *Architectural Record* featured a series of these test houses, including a steel-frame residence of precast reinforced Microporite (a composition of hydro-calcium silicate) slabs, sponsored by the John B. Pierce Foundation in New York; a house of stressed-skin plywood similar to that developed for airplanes, funded by the U.S. Forest Products Laboratory in Madison, Wisconsin; and a cellular, copper-bearing steel house by architect Richard Neutra in Altadena, California.[95]

Not all of these building innovations achieved significant financial success. Howard T. Fisher's General Houses, one of the best-known commercial providers of prefabricated residences, continued to manufacture mass-produced steel houses, like the model homes the firm exhibited at A Century of Progress, through the mid-1930s. In 1936 the company exchanged its load-bearing steel-panel designs for a steel-frame-and-panel system similar to those demonstrated by Armco-Ferro and Stran-Steel at the Chicago fair. By segregating the structure and wall surfaces, the company brought the product more in line with most of the other available forms of prefabricated systems. Despite this change and major efforts to publicize its residential designs, General Houses only managed to sell a total of several hundred modern steel houses, nowhere near the initial projected sales figures.[96] Other companies in the field realized similar dismal results. Between 1935 and 1940 fewer than 10,000 prefabricated, modern houses were constructed in the United States, totaling well under 1 percent of new single-family residences.[97]

A number of factors contributed to the tremendous difficulties many of those involved in prefabricated construction faced in the middle and late 1930s. In addition to a general lack of housing starts, growing opposition arose both inside and outside the building industry to prefabricated materials and forms. Even though designers tried to relate the cleaner lines common to prefabricated architecture with streamlining and the other new efficient concepts in modern living that had begun to gain public acceptance, most Americans still chose to live in a house that somewhat resembled, albeit often almost negligibly, a traditional design.

Adding to the situation was a dearth of public interest in the use of new materials that exhibited modern formal characteristics. According to a 1933 article in *Review of Reviews and World's Work*, advertisers and salesmen of new building products directed up to 50 percent of their efforts to overcoming consumers' sentimental feelings toward more traditional materials.[98] A 1934 random survey of *Time* magazine readers published in *Architectural Forum* reflected this belief. When asked what exterior material they would prefer using for a new home, an overwhelming majority of respondents replied "brick." Readers selected clapboard, stone, and stucco as the next three most-favored materials. Prefabricated units, concrete, and metal and glass all finished at the bottom of the list.[99] Over time the new products that proved most successful were those that were not limited to a specific modern aesthetic but instead could be easily adapted to more traditional styles.[100]

The concurrent financial, labor, real estate, and political situations also impeded immediate public acceptance of modern building products and prefabricated construction.[101] Economic factors, including the unstable financial market and, more specifically, the costs of developing and introducing a product, contributed to the failure of many building materials developed in the 1920s and early 1930s.[102] Some manufacturers, unrealistic in their projections for marketing their products, had believed that anything mass-produced was bound to be eventually made available at a lower cost.[103] This was not always the case. Start-up expenses often prevent any significant profit for years. Lacking a healthy market, many companies were unable to survive through their early lean years to see initial investments pay off. Another major obstacle was the relative backwardness of the building industry, both organizationally and technically. According to an article published in *Architectural Record* in 1939, "although competition among material manufacturers tends to stimulate development of new products, short-sightedness on the part of various establishments became a retarding influence."[104] For example, obsolete building codes and unyielding building inspectors often favored the continued use of costly and less efficient traditional materials. Union members and building suppliers also often balked at the use of new processes or products. They particularly denounced those advances that had the potential of reducing labor or materials, thereby threatening the workers' livelihood.[105]

Securing adequate financing also posed a major problem for those wanting to build a home of modern design. As mentioned earlier, architects, including George Frederick Keck and Frank Lloyd Wright, often faced major setbacks due to the conservative banking industry's unwillingness to lend capital to construct nontraditional buildings, especially those that were considered modern, hence unusual, in style. Even if banks were willing to provide the funding, clients often had a difficult time obtaining reasonable mortgage appraisals.[106] As a result, many designers felt reluctant to use unproven materials or processes, especially if they foresaw difficulties in seeing such designs realized.[107]

Compounding the situation was the fact that some of the new building products exhibited significant problems over the long term. Steel panels, for instance, tended to corrode when exposed to the elements. Bonding processes, developed to alleviate this problem, often made the material too expensive for use in the general housing market.[108] Despite these types of challenges, many new products, including Masonite, Celotex, and Formica, as well as gypsum boards and plywoods, became economically viable and went on to achieve significant commercial success.

The creation of defense housing programs sponsored by the U.S. government at the end of the decade saved from bankruptcy General Houses and many other companies that had ventured into prefabricated housing in the 1930s.[109] *Business Week* reported in 1941 that "Uncle Sam wants a lot of houses, he wants them in a hurry, and he wants them cheap."[110] To facilitate construction of large numbers of low-cost houses, the government sponsored a new method of "virtually risk-free" financing to investors and developers that required no down payment from the eventual owner.[111] In the same year, John M. Carmody, head of the Federal Works Administration, gathered together approximately 100 housing officials, including representatives from twenty-three prefabrication concerns, to discuss the development of policies that would allow for the use of assembly-line processes in constructing an enormous quantity of new residences.[112] This discussion led to the public funding of a series of large developments consisting of prefabricated housing. In January 1942 alone, funds were appropriated by the U.S. government for the initial construction of 42,000 "demountable" prefabricated units.[113] By mid-1942, over 300 construction projects had already been completed under government defense programs.[114]

After the close of the Second World War, the country's immediate need for low-cost, efficient, war-related buildings was replaced with just as urgent a need for adequate housing for returning soldiers and their quickly growing families. The enactment of the Veterans' Emergency Housing Program supported the construction of over a million units in 1946 and still more the following year.[115] The continuing American dream of owning a single-family home led to the use of prefabricated techniques and materials to construct massive suburban communities, such as the Levittowns. Bowing to the desires of homeowners and developers, these residences were typically not aesthetically modern, like most of the futuristic residences exhibited at the Chicago exposition. The designs, more in keeping with the traditionally styled Sears Honor Bilt Home at the exposition, were vaguely reminiscent of houses from America's colonial past.

The relatively low quality of many of these postwar houses reflects an underlying acceptance of the concept of disposable architecture promoted through the design of the Chicago fair. Excitement among progressive designers regarding this concept continued well beyond the early 1930s, as architects stressed the economic

and functional benefits of short-lived buildings. At a symposium on pre-fabrication sponsored by *House and Garden* in 1935, J. Andre Fouilhoux, a former partner of Raymond Hood and eventual codesigner of the Trylon and Perisphere at the 1939–40 New York World's Fair, proclaimed the senselessness of continuing to design houses to last 100 years.[116] He viewed cheaper, less durable construction as the ideal solution for buildings designed to best meet the needs of the rapidly changing modern world. Despite such rhetoric, most architects continued to market their buildings as permanent. The affordable materials and construction techniques they chose, however, resulted in less-durable structures becoming the norm across the country, a legacy that can still be seen decades later in both manufactured residential and commercial building. The lack of quality in much of this construction significantly contributed to the critical view of prefabricated housing prevalent in the United States during the second half of the twentieth century.

FIG. 7.15. Block after block of mass-produced housing in Levittown, Pennsylvania. Century #118. Courtesy of the National Archives.

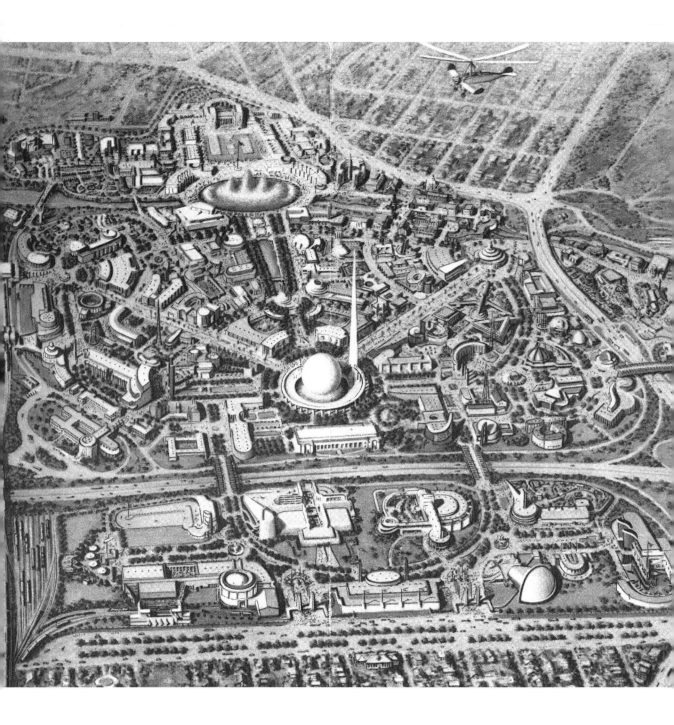

INFLUENCE OF A CENTURY OF PROGRESS
ON THE NEW YORK WORLD'S FAIR

While the formal qualities of the buildings at A Century of Progress did not have as significant an effect on architecture designed for the everyday world as did the products and processes used in their construction, the pavilions did serve as formal models for later buildings with similar functional, spatial, and economic needs— most significantly the temporary exhibition halls at later American expositions held during the 1930s in San Diego, Dallas, Cleveland, San Francisco, and New York.

Influenced by the success of the Chicago exposition, the organizers of the 1939–40 New York World's Fair hoped that by hosting a similar event they would improve their own city's dismal economic situation.[117] Like that of A Century of Progress, the corporation formed in 1935 to oversee the creation of the New York exposition consisted primarily of prominent business leaders who were more concerned with ensuring the financial success of the fair than with furthering a specific definition of modern architecture.[118] They looked back to the Chicago exposition as their primary source for information on how to build and operate a successful fair. Not only did they borrow ideas on how to organize and finance the event, what exhibition techniques to incorporate, and what types of entertainment venues to include, but they also looked to the low-cost, prefabricated, festive pavilions of the 1933–34 exposition as ideal prototypes for the architecture of their own upcoming event.[119]

Other New Yorkers, with vested interests in the direction of progressive architecture, expressed greater concern over the aesthetic character of the exposition than did the event's main organizers. The result was a new series of debates over the design of fair buildings and their role in guiding modern American architecture. An early heated dispute appeared in contemporary journals between designers who favored a modern exposition and those who believed that a traditional style would be more appealing to the masses. The modern functionalists, led by Lewis Mumford, took charge of the debate by assembling over sixty leading industrial designers and local architects, including several of the former Century of Progress architectural commissioners, for a meeting at the New York City Club in December 1935. Their goal for the gathering was to organize a united front from which to promote a modern style for the New York exposition.[120] According to an article published in the *New York Herald Tribune*, these progressive designers feared that reaction from "the bizarre modernism" of A Century of Progress might lead organizers to adopt the "retrogressive classical" style of the World's Columbian Exposition of 1893 (a style that continued to be favored by some of the conservative leaders of the

FIG. 7.16. Bird's-eye diagram of 1939–40 New York World's Fair. From *Official Guide Book of the New York World's Fair, 1939*, 2nd ed. (New York: World's Fair Publications, 1939), attachment to page 1.

AIA). The article went on to state, "Though the progressives would like to tone down Chicago's gaudy colors and bring about greater unity, they would not like to see 'the Parthenon rebuilt on the Flushing swamp.'"[121]

Several designers involved in the Chicago exposition spoke at the meeting. Harvey Wiley Corbett stated that "the scheme of the new fair should be contemporary and progressive in its architectural form." He felt that the inclusion of younger architects would help "counteract any 'archaeological' tendencies in style."[122] Surprisingly, former commissioner Ralph Walker suggested that, to guarantee a unified plan, the design be created not by a committee of architects, as at Chicago, but instead by an architectural dictator who would then be assisted by a group of design directors. Ely Jacques Kahn favored the use of architectural competitions to arrive at a modern style, a process that was currently being used to design some of the buildings for the Exposition Internationale des Arts et Techniques dans la Vie Moderne held in Paris in 1937.

Industrial designer Walter Dorwin Teague advocated the study of recent fairs and the incorporation of a functional approach in order to avoid the creation of "an aesthetic orgy." Mumford, believing that arguing over style was irrelevant, stated that "the very purpose and spirit of the project must dictate its architecture"—a view almost identical to that held by the architectural commissioners for the Chicago exposition, which he had earlier opposed.[123] Mumford also supported the creation of a new type of exposition that would not divorce scientific development from contemporary social issues, as he felt had happened at previous events. Instead, echoing the thematic goal of the Chicago fair, he called for an exposition that would closely relate developments in science with everyday life and, in doing so, would tell a story of "planned environment, planned industry, and planned civilization."[124]

Those present at the meeting selected a committee to further promote a modern design. Members included Mumford, Corbett, Walker, Teague, and several other New York designers.[125] Their work resulted in the creation of a detailed proposal for the event, titled "The Fair of the Future." It specifically called for a unified social theme and an architectural style derived from current functional needs and expressive of modern society's social order.[126] Grover A. Whalen, who had recently taken over as president of the New York Fair Corporation, adopted several of the key components of the proposal, including a plan to take the organization of individual exhibits a step beyond that at Chicago by dividing the exposition into seven thematic zones, each featuring a central pavilion housing a core exhibit.[127] In attempting to strike a compromise in the stylistic debate, he created a Theme Committee consisting of Teague and Robert Kohn, a former president of the AIA, whose main function was ensuring the creation of an exposition that would present a unified vision of all interrelated activities and interests of the "American way of life." The two men planned to accomplish this through a careful examination of the social consequences of new technology.[128]

The resulting New York World's Fair, like other international expositions, incorporated a wide assortment of building forms that ranged from historical replicas and ethnic villages to recent examples of progressive modernism. At least one building, the replica of the ornate Bendix Lama Temple (also known as the Golden Temple of Jehol), had been previously exhibited at A Century of Progress. While most of the New York pavilions did not directly derive their stylistic forms from Chicago, almost all shared important characteristics with exhibition halls at the earlier event. For example, the fair's Board of Design, which consisted of seven architects headed by Teague and Kohn, mandated that the buildings consist of steel-frame construction with walls of prefabricated gypsum board—the same materials used for most of the major exhibition halls at the Chicago fair.[129] Additional similarities included the presence of large spans of windowless wall surfaces, courtyards and changes in levels of elevations, and facades decorated with bright colors, bas-relief sculptures, and innovative night lighting.

Although organizers continually expressed the need to create a comprehensive design for the exposition in order to present a greater sense of

FIG. 7.17. The Bendix Lama Temple (also known as the Golden Temple of Jehol). Kaufmann and Fabry, photographers.

FIG. 7.18. Borden Building,
New York World's Fair,
1939–40. From Museum of
the City of New York.

unity than at A Century of Progress, the major pavilions built for
the New York fair exhibited an even broader variety of aesthetic
forms. With their flat surfaces and geometrical volumes, the Gas
Exhibits, Coty Cosmetics, and Borden buildings all could have easily blended into the Chicago fairgrounds.[130] However, the Administration Building,
the U.S. Federal Pavilion, and most of the focal exhibit halls, created by members
of the Board of Design, incorporated a form of modern or stripped classicism, with
fluted, capital-free piers, horizontal banding, and a traditional sense of balance and
symmetry. These characteristics recalled some of the major buildings at the 1937
Exposition Internationale, held two years earlier in Paris, especially the designs
of the prominent Soviet and German pavilions. Even though several members of
the Chicago architectural commission, in particular Paul Cret, had favored similar stripped, neoclassical forms for permanent civic buildings, the committee as a
whole had strongly rejected these forms for A Century of Progress. In contrast, to
help unify the fairgrounds, the Board of Design for the New York fair dictated the
use of one-story, stripped classical buildings, allowing occasional art deco motifs,
for all the thematic exhibition buildings.

The New York Board of Design, however, did not mandate that the architects
designing corporate or national pavilions follow a classical vocabulary. The great
popularity of "functional expressionism" at the Chicago exposition led designers

to create similar iconic buildings for the 1939–40 world's fair.[131] As at A Century of Progress, these pavilions either directly expressed the building's function or symbolically represented its purpose. Several buildings contained features clearly reminiscent of specific Chicago pavilions. For instance, large photographs towering over the entrance to the Eastman Kodak Building closely paralleled the colossal images of magazine covers on the earlier Time and Fortune Building.[132] A forty-foot-high cash register on the roof of the National Cash Register (NCR) Pavilion, meanwhile, was conceptually akin to the Havoline Thermometer in Chicago. It registered up-to-date attendance figures for the fair on its display, instead of the current temperature as recorded on the Havoline Building.[133] One popular example of a less literal iconic form at the New York fair was the Continental Bakery Pavilion, which sported a red-blue-and-yellow-polka-dotted facade reminiscent of a Wonder Bread wrapper.

Most of the more interpretive examples of functional expressionism at the New York World's Fair closely recalled the Italian Pavilion in Chicago by incorporating symbolic representations of transportation vehicles into their designs. The Marine Transportation Building included a pair of ocean-liner prows dramatically projecting from its facade, evoking the exterior of Chicago's Streets of Paris venue.[134] Next door the streamlined Aviation

FIG. 7.19. National Cash Register (NCR) Pavilion, recording the current attendance figure, New York World's Fair, 1939–40. Postcard from collection of author.

Firestone
Builds Today
THE TIRE OF TOMORROW

NEW YORK WORLD'S FAIR 1939

Building consisted of an aerodynamic form projecting out from a semicircular "airplane hangar" reminiscent of several of the unbuilt theater designs that Norman Bel Geddes had created for the Chicago exposition.[135] Architects, celebrating public excitement over developments in air transportation during these years, also incorporated aeronautical forms into the design of other pavilions with functions that tied less directly to the field of aviation. Examples included the streamlined Firestone Building, with its airplane-influenced silhouette, and the Electronic Products and the Sealtest buildings, each exhibiting forms resembling airplane fins. Even several of the entrance gates to the fair incorporated shapes evoking an aircraft empennage.[136] The iconic pavilions at Chicago and New York were both the predecessors of similar corporate pavilions at later fairs. They were also forerunners of a wave of commercial "ducks" built along America's highways during the mid-twentieth century. Hot dog–shaped refreshment stands, castle-shaped hamburger joints, and brontosaurus-shaped souvenir shops soon appeared across the country to draw attention to a variety of commercial ventures.[137]

Color and lighting played just as important roles in the design of the New York World's Fair as they had in Chicago. However, designers in New York organized the placement of color more rigorously. They assigned each of the seven thematic zones a different hue and arranged the sections prismatically. Only the Trylon and Perisphere at the center of the grounds

FIG. 7.20 *(below)*. The shiplike Marine Transportation Building, New York World's Fair, 1939–40. Harvey Cohn, New York. From Museum of the City of New York. FIG. 7.21 *(facing)*. The airplane-influenced silhouette of the Firestone Building, New York World's Fair, 1939–40. From *Firestone Builds Today the Tire of Tomorrow: New York World's Fair, 1939*, pamphlet produced by the Firestone Tire and Rubber Company, from collection of author.

were pure white. Buildings near the center were pale colors, with the dominant hues of the buildings becoming more and more intense the farther out from the center the pavilions were located.[138]

Once again critics took note of prominent architects missing from the list of participating designers for the New York fair. In fact, only a few of the leading American architects designed buildings for the event. Among them were William Lescaze, George Howe, and Harrison and Fouilhoux.[139] The editors of *Architectural Review* commented on the notable absence of progressive designers when they stated that while there were architects in the United States capable of producing fine modern designs, the "World of Tomorrow" was being designed by the "architects of yesterday."[140] Certainly the most notable architect missing from the event was Frank Lloyd Wright. In response, Lewis Mumford revived his campaign to publicize the architect through articles and letters in the mainstream press denouncing his absence. Mumford, along with his colleagues, in fact wrote little positive about the architecture of the New York fair, except in regard to a few modern foreign exhibits. The two that received the most

FIG. 7.22. Coney Island Hot Dog Stand, Conifer, Colorado. Photograph by author.

FIG. 7.23. Brazilian
Pavilion, New York
World's Fair, 1939–40.
From the Fay S. Lincoln
Photograph Collection.
Courtesy of Historical
Collections and Labor
Archives, Special
Collections Library,
The Pennsylvania
State University.

favorable comments were the elegant Finnish display by Alvar Aalto, with
its undulating wooden wall, and the Corbusian Brazilian Pavilion by Lucio
Costa and Oscar Niemeyer.

As at the Chicago exposition, the presence of a wide range of styles
(defended by New York Fair officials as a "reflection of our own day in its
complete lack of period style") was heavily criticized by reviewers as "superficial modernity." Talbot Hamlin referred to the fair designers' classical
pavilions as "packing-box" buildings. He wrote that while some buildings
included "domes or rotundas, breaks, extensive colonnades, cupolas, and
what not," in almost every case the additions had been disastrous, "having neither
monumentality nor gaiety, taking away from the simplicity, and producing confusion instead of interest."[141] Architect and writer Frederick Gutheim expressed
further outrage at the obvious ties exhibited between advertising and architecture.
He dubbed the forms of the exposition buildings a "Corporate Style," which he
defined as "a bastard dialect of architectural larceny and advertising."[142] As with
A Century of Progress, the New York World's Fair buildings' impact on more permanent architecture lay primarily in areas almost completely ignored by critics,
such as in the increased use of new forms of prefabricated building materials, the
application of more efficient construction methods, and the practice of designing buildings for shorter life spans—concepts of modern building still prevalent in
American architecture in the early twenty-first century.

THE CURTAIN FALLS

As night fell on 31 October 1934, the multicolored electrical extravaganza of the Century of Progress International Exposition flared and shimmered along the Chicago lakefront for one last time. The fair season had closed quietly the year before on a cold November evening with a nearly deserted park. In contrast, over 370,000 people converged on the fairgrounds on Halloween night 1934 to catch a final glimpse of the fair.[1] Even with record crowds and special activities, closing day for A Century of Progress was, in many respects, not unlike other days at the exposition.[2]

Thousands waited in long lines at the entrance gates as each visitor handed his or her admission ticket to an attendant before passing through the turnstile. Many headed directly to the base of the western Skyride tower to experience a final bird's-eye view of the colorful precinct from the vantage point of a streamlined rocket car. Others proceeded to one of the main pavilions to explore some of the hundreds of educational exhibits on display, such as the radio-controlled tractor in the Agriculture Building, or to marvel over a demonstration of a new advance in technology, such as wired television in the Electrical Building, or to catch a lecture presented by an expert, such as "The Human Eye and Its Care," by C. C. Darling in the Hall of Science. A variety of assembly lines in the corporate pavilions were busy pumping out their last consumer products, ranging from packaged bacon to Chevrolets, for the education and entertainment of fascinated viewers. Youngsters enjoyed attending the last episode of the *Buck Rogers Show,* a dramatization of the space-age comic strip, at Enchanted Island, while older fairgoers experienced their own thrill

FIG. P.I. Closing-night crowds at A Century of Progress in 1934. Courtesy of the *Chicago Tribune.*

by taking in a final ogle at Sally Rand, who was performing throughout the evening at the Italian Pavilion. Those interested in more family-oriented entertainment could catch a more wholesome show at one of the other ethnic venues: folk dances in the Dutch Village, ice skating in the Black Forest Village, or a Punch-and-Judy show in the Old English Village.[3]

As night fell and the crowds swelled, excitement among fairgoers grew as they realized that the end was growing near. At 10:00 p.m. the grand nightly spectacle, the Festival of Illumination, turned the lagoon into a glowing theater of light. Adding to the drama of the final performance were members of the Coast Artillery, the Field Artillery, the 108th Observatory Squadron, and other units of the armed services. The official closing ceremony, held in the Court of States, began upon the completion of the lighting festival at around 11:30 p.m. After a half hour of band and choral music and speeches by dignitaries including Illinois governor Henry Horner and Chicago mayor Edward J. Kelly, exposition president Rufus C. Dawes stepped to the front of the podium. In a move recalling the elaborate opening-night lighting ceremony, he pushed a button that unleashed "the most elaborate pyrotechnic display ever devised."[4] Within an instant the sky above the fairgrounds erupted in unbridled energy. Along the east side of the lagoon more than 2,000 giant rockets hurled upward and then exploded in space. Their glow covered the pavilions in magnificent coats of colored light for one last time.[5] By the close of the display an estimated half million aerial explosions had erupted, marking the exposition's passing into history.[6]

On a darker note, the start of the extravagant closing ceremony also served as a spontaneous signal for a growing crescendo of carnivalesque hysteria to spin out of control. Hordes of fairgoers began appropriating unique mementos of the magnificent event.[7] In the Halloween-night frenzy, people broke into many of the exhibition pavilions and walked away with furniture, light fixtures, signs, and decorative building details.[8] Not a shred of the sixty-five pennants that lined the Avenue of Flags that day survived. Even shrubs and trees were yanked out of the ground. Guards, many of whom ended the night requiring first aid, did their best to combat the full-scale pillaging. At the gates they stopped anyone with stolen goods, forcing the offenders to leave their illicit souvenirs behind before exiting the fairgrounds. The next morning fair officials awoke to an exposition hangover. Overturned park furniture, trampled landscaping, and broken light fixtures covered the fairgrounds as evidence of the tumultuous activities of revelers the night before.[9] Fortunately, most of the damage was to objects that were already scheduled for disposal as part of the planned demolition of the exposition.

Despite rumors that A Century of Progress might reopen its doors for a third season the following spring, procedures to erase the remarkable exposition from the lakefront went forward. Members of the event's Demolition Division worked efficiently, issuing almost all of the removal permits for fair buildings within two days of the exposition's close.[10] The actual destruction of the pavilions, however, dragged on significantly longer.

In accordance with an agreement between the Century of Progress Corporation and the Chicago Park District, the exposition was required to remove, by July 1935, all fair-owned buildings not slated for future use by the park district.[11] Concessionaires and exhibitors who had constructed their own buildings were under contract to remove those structures by February of that year. Many of these agreements were broken. It was not until

FIG. P.2. Carousing crowds on closing night at A Century of Progress in 1934. From scrapbook in collection of author.

Revelry;
Record;
rly Morn

Sign-ing Off!
Taking a Last
Remembrance
of the World's
Greatest Show

SOUVENIRS—Here's just one of the hundreds of visitors to the fair grounds last night who were successful in a mad search for something to carry away as a remembrance of the world's greatest exposition.

December that most of the major fair buildings were finally disassembled and the scrap materials handed over to a demolition contractor for resale.[12] The demolition was not fully completed until February 1936. The lone modern fair building remaining at the site after this time was the Administration Building, left behind to serve as the temporary headquarters of the Chicago Park District.[13]

The most dramatic events in the dismantling of the exposition were the toppling of the giant Skyride towers. Unlike their French counterpart, the Eiffel Tower, the dominating landmarks of the Chicago World's Fair were not destined to remain as prominent reminders of the once-marvelous exposition for future generations. On 8 June 1935, with "a shrieking, screaming chorus of rending steel," the west tower was pulled apart into two sections. Each massive segment plummeting to the ground with a thunderous crash.[14] Few people beyond the media witnessed the event, as the demolition of the tower was carried out at 5:52 a.m. under a shroud of secrecy due to its close location to Lake Shore Drive. Reacting to the public's disappointment in missing this momentous event, the fair corporation turned the felling of the east tower into the last grand spectacle of the exposition. Just as throngs of people had gathered at the grounds to witness the construction of the strange-looking modern pavilions during the months leading up to the opening of the fair, huge crowds of fair enthusiasts and thrill seekers congregated along the lakefront during the afternoon of 30 August 1935 to view the leveling of the second massive steel tower.[15] At 3:00 p.m. Rufus Dawes threw a switch, and within forty-two seconds the 1,600-ton tower had crumbled to the ground.[16] For many, the disappearance of the steel colossus was a clear sign that the rumors were false; there would be no 1935 fair season. A Century of Progress was indeed over.

While the majority of exposition pavilions were demolished on-site, a few of the buildings were given second lives in new locations. The Good Housekeeping Stran-Steel House was reconstructed in a Chicago suburb.[17] Six of the other model residences, including the House of Tomorrow, were shipped on barges across Lake Michigan to Beverly Shores, Indiana, to form the nucleus of a small summer community.[18] To help pay outstanding expenses relating to its construction and operation, the Crystal House, George Frederick Keck's second model home, like the majority of other fair pavilions, was dismantled after the close of the event and its materials were auctioned off.[19]

The financier of the Bendix Lama Temple boxed up the full-scale historical Chinese building in November 1934 for storage until the opening of the New York

FIG. P.3. Toppling of the east Skyride tower in August 1935. From A. H. Lubin, "The End of the Fair," *Commerce* (December 1935): 17.

World's Fair five years later.[20] Large segments of several of the major pavilions were also recycled after the exposition. The south half of the Travel and Transport Building reportedly became a dock warehouse in Muskegon, Michigan, while the northeast section of the Hall of Science was converted into an addition for the Empire Metal Products Company in suburban

FIG. P.4. The Rostone House is towed to its new location in Beverly Shores, Indiana. Courtesy of Jim Morrow.

Chicago.[21] Parts of some of the corporate buildings were also moved and reused. Ford, for example, reassembled the gear-shaped hall from its fair pavilion for a visitors' center at its River Rouge Plant in Michigan.[22]

When the Chicago Park District moved into more permanent head-quarters at the end of Soldier Field, the Administration Building was de-molished. All that was then left in situ to serve as a reminder of the magnificent fair was a single ancient column from Rome's port of Ostia, located at the former site of the Italian Pavilion. The column had been a gift from the fascist government to the City of Chicago to commemorate the momentous trans-Atlantic flight to the exposition by Italo Balbo and his air command.[23]

While A Century of Progress attracted the attention of a large number of prominent architects, building-materials manufacturers, and design critics, with the demolition of the pavilions the exposition's role in the rise of modern archi-tecture, like the fair itself, soon became a distant memory. Although it has been underappreciated by scholars, the short-lived exposition played a significant role in the development and acceptance of modern architecture in the United States. The fair presented an ideal venue for the exploration and promotion of a wide range of new ideas and design concepts. Event organizers gave designers the opportunity to respond to the evolving definition of modern architecture by allowing them to experiment without being limited by prohibitive codes, obstructive unions, restrictive clients, or, in the case of a number of conceptual designs, even the realities of a specific building program. The fact that only limited funds were available for the construction of the fair provided the necessary impetus for the more conservative designers of the architectural commission to move away from their classical training and experiment with modern materials to create less ornate but more innovative buildings. Forward-looking American designers, including Frank Lloyd Wright, Norman Bel Geddes, and George Frederick Keck, were also able to take advantage of the fair by developing and promoting their own innovative directions in modern architecture through both built and unrealized projects. The resulting designs produced by the architectural commissioners and others for the exposition were unified by a definition of modern architecture based on the use of new materials and processes to meet contemporary needs, visions that were much more in keeping with the larger developments in progressive architectural ideologies in the United States during the late 1920s and early 1930s than the more formal definition put forth in MoMA's International Style Show.

As the largest architectural program realized in the United States during the Great Depression, the variety of building forms at the Chicago exposition gave architect and nonarchitect critics something to react to and write about at a time when few other major building projects were under way. While people typically found the architecture of the exposition unusual, most eventually accepted it as appropriate for this type of event. However, a number of influential voices in the field of architecture panned the

FIG. P.5. The rotunda of the Ford Building was rebuilt as a visitors' center at Ford's River Rouge Plant in Michigan. Postcard from collection of author.

FIG. P.6. Balbo Monument with column from Ostia at the site of the Italian Pavilion. Courtesy of the Chicago Park District.

pavilions, often as part of an agenda to promote alternative directions in modern building design. These vociferous criticisms, along with the dramatic decline in the number of building starts in the years following the exposition due to the Great Depression and the Second World War, helped minimize the fair's direct aesthetic impact on later architecture. This lack of influence was compounded by the ephemeral nature of the event and its buildings. Unlike the permanent-looking pavilions of the first Chicago World's Fair, the buildings at A Century of Progress were designed to express more honestly their impermanence. The complete disappearance of the fair from the lakefront, which denied later designers and scholars the opportunity to experience the actual structures firsthand, further curtailed the exposition's visual influence. Additional factors—such as the fair designers' promotion of the pavilions as appropriate archetypes only for buildings with similar functional needs, the public's general preference for more traditional designs, the underlying attitude of cultural superiority of East Coast architects and critics (who continued to prefer to look east toward Europe for new ideas), and the transitional status of modern design during this period—all contributed to minimizing the event's direct aesthetic influence on future architecture in the United States.

Nevertheless, the Century of Progress International Exposition did have a significant, if less obvious, lasting impact on American architecture, most prominently through its role as a showcase for building materials and construction processes. Growing interest among architects and laypeople alike in the new, lighter, and more efficient man-made materials that were common throughout the fairgrounds contributed to an increase in the use of many of these products. Tied to the rise of the less costly modern materials was the concept of "disposable architecture," prominently illustrated by the short-lived fair pavilions. While only a few of the millions of fair visitors went on to commission their own "House of Tomorrow," many became much more willing to accept cheaper, less durable, manufactured building products in place of traditional materials for their new homes and businesses.

The underlying ideology behind the main exposition slogan, Science Finds —Industry Applies—Man Conforms, was a growing belief that developments in scientific technology would eventually allow man to conquer nature and that the corresponding consumption of mass-produced products would help lead to a more stable and homogenized society. By the end of the century, however, some of the negative impacts of this view had become clear. The production of an ever-increasing quantity of mass-produced commodities throughout the twentieth century contributed to considerable problems never envisioned by the organizers of A Century of Progress. These included substantial environmental consequences, ranging from a dramatic increase in air and water pollution to the disappearance of old-growth forests, farmland, and other natural resources. The discarding of convenient "disposable" products has led to the creation of massive landfills. Even more disturbing, a number of the exciting products featured at the Chicago fair, most significantly asbestos, were eventually discovered to have ominous toxic side effects.[24]

Many post–Second World War suburbs consist of block after block of homes and commercial buildings constructed out of the materials that seemed so promising at the 1933–34 exposition. Over time, as the modern, man-made products with limited life spans began deteriorating, many of those suburbs evolved from idealized bastions of cleanliness, uniformity, and safety to dilapidated areas of poverty. The primary benefits of disposable architecture quickly disappeared when the notion of rebuilding every decade or two, which was critical to the concept, was disregarded. By the end of the century, many of these neighborhoods had been abandoned by those who could afford to move elsewhere, as new rings of exurbs began to replace acre after acre of farmland on the edges of metropolitan areas. Compounding the situation was a dramatic increase in average house size, as families, attempting to achieve an idealized vision of American home life put forward by corporate marketers, began desiring more and more space to accommodate a growing quantity of requisite consumer goods, including electronic and home-improvement products that evoked the novel, laborsaving gadgets featured in exhibits, such as the House of Tomorrow, at A Century of Progress.

As in the years leading up to the Chicago exposition, people at the start of the twenty-first century question whether world's fairs have become passé. By focusing on the impact that advances in scientific technology had on humanity, fair organizers in the 1930s were able to show that international expositions did serve an important role in modern society. Similarly, those involved in the planning of world's fairs in the Internet age have demonstrated that international expositions continue to have an important educational purpose, now by focusing on issues of conservation and sustainability. These events project the same commitment to scientific technology in attempting to achieve a better tomorrow as did the 1933–34 exposition, but with recognition that there is a darker side to the modern culture that was so magnificently promised and promoted at A Century of Progress.

The theme of Expo 2000, held in Hanover, Germany, was Humankind—Nature—Technology: A New World Arising. Like the Chicago World's Fair, the event emphasized "humanity's vast potential for shaping its own future," but it also promoted the principle of sustainable development in hopes of achieving greater harmony between humanity, nature, and technology.[25] Exposition organizers specified that all pavilions not slated for permanent use at the site were to be assembled of renewable materials and rebuilt at a different location or were to be disassembled and their materials recycled after the close of the event.

Taking the concept of sustainability one step further, the theme of Expo 2005 in Aichi, Japan, was Nature's Wisdom. In contrast to the emphasis on mass consumption at A Century of Progress, the Aichi exposition was held to serve as a model of conservation for a global society. Exhibits suggested potential ways of resolving population and environmental problems through advances in scientific and information technologies. The modular pavilions and other features of the fairgrounds were built primarily of recycled PET bottles and recyclable timber provided by the exposition organization. The corporate and national pavilions were temporary structures and, as at Chicago, were designed for easy removal after the event closed, allowing the site to be transformed into a public park. With the recognition of the need to take better care of our world, these early twenty-first-century expositions have built upon the legacy of A Century of Progress by offering hope that with the help of advances in scientific technology the future will indeed be a better place, a belief that commenced with the spectacular modern vision of tomorrow that appeared along the lakefront in Chicago during the darkest days of the Great Depression.

FIG. P.7. *The Curtain Falls.* From *Chicago Herald and Examiner,* 31 October 1934.

The Curtain Falls

Copyright, 1934, by
The Chicago Herald and Examiner.

MAJOR BUILDINGS
AND ARCHITECTS OF
A CENTURY OF PROGRESS

MAIN EXHIBIT BUILDINGS

Administration Building	Bennett, Burnham, and Holabird
Agriculture Building	Arthur Brown and E. H. Bennett
Electrical Building	Raymond Hood
Foods and Agriculture Building	E. H. Bennett
General Exhibits Building	Harvey Wiley Corbett
Hall of Science	Paul Cret
Horticultural Building	L. F. Coleman
Hall of Social Science	Sculpture by Alfonso Iannelli and Leo Friedlander
Travel and Transport Building	Bennett, Burnham, and Holabird
U. S. Government Building	Arthur Brown and E. H. Bennett
Hall of Religion	Thielbar and Fugard
Home Planning Hall	Ely Jacques Kahn
Illinois Host Building	C. Herrick Hammond

COUNTRY PAVILIONS

Czechoslovakian Pavilion	Kamil Roskot with Bedrick Sirotek
Italian Pavilion	Mario de Renzi and Adalberto Libera
Swedish Pavilion	Robert G. Ostergren with Karl M. Bengtson
Japanese Pavilion	Iwakichi Miyamoto
Ukrainian Pavilion	Frederich B. Schmidt
Polish Pavilion (German-American Restaurant)	George L. Tucker and T. R. Lazarr Lazarewicz

OTHER PAVILIONS

American Radiator Building	Hood and Fouilhoux
Chrysler Building	Holabird and Root

General Motors Building — Albert Kahn
Johns-Manville Building — Ely Jacques Kahn
Kohler Building — Ely Jacques Kahn
Owens-Illinois Glass-Block Building — Elroy Ruiz
Sears-Roebuck Building — Nimmons, Carr, and Wright
Firestone Building — Burnham Brothers
Sinclair Refining Company Building — Burnham Brothers
Havoline Building — Alfonso Iannelli and Charles Pope
Dairy Building (Wonder Bakery Building) — Bennett, Parsons, and Frost

Edison Building — Carl Landefeld
Time and Fortune Building — Nicolai and Faro
Christian Science Monitor Building — Holmes and Finn

VILLAGES AND OTHER NOVELTY SITES

Belgian Village — Burnham Brothers with Alfons deRydt
Streets of Paris — Andrew Rebori and John W. Root
Skyride — D'Esposito, Robinson, and Steinman
Log Cabins — Heatherington, Architects
Golden Pavilion — Yuan-Hsi-Kuo (supervising architect)
Maya Temple — Franz Blom (chief researcher)
Fort Dearborn — John Whistler (delineator, 1804)
Enchanted Island — G. H. Buckley

MODEL HOUSES

Armco-Ferro Enamel Frameless House — Robert Smith Jr.
Good Housekeeping Stran-Steel House — H. Augustus O'Dell and Wirt C. Rowland
Common Brick Manufacturers' House — Andrew Rebori
Rostone House — Walter Scholer
House of Tomorrow — George Keck
Lumber Industries House — Ernest A. Grunsfeld Jr.
Masonite House — Frazier and Raftery

BUILDINGS ADDED IN 1934

Ford Building — Albert Kahn
Swift Bridge and Open Air Theatre (23rd Street Bridge) — E. A. Schiewe
Armour Building — Graham, Anderson, Probst and White
Brook Hill Farm Dairy — Richard Philipp
Wilson and Company Restaurant — Architectural Decorating Company
Colonial Village — Thomas E. Tallmadge

Black Forest Village	P. M. Fuller and Ray Cummins
Dutch Village	Burnham Brothers and C. Herrick Hammond
Irish Village	J. J. Murphy and William T. Hooper
Italian Village	Hugh Garden
Old English Village	D. H. Burnham Jr.
Spanish Village	D. H. Burnham Jr.
Tunisian Village	D. H. Burnham Jr.
Streets of Shanghai	Burnham Brothers and C. Herrick Hammond
Frigidaire House	Howard W. Germann
Crystal House	George Keck
General Houses, Inc. House	Howard Fisher
Stran-Steel House	George Loane Tucker

COLOR SCHEMES OF A CENTURY OF PROGRESS

AVENUE OF FLAGS

1933   Red-and-yellow flags; white bases

1934   Light blue or red flags; purple bases

TWELFTH STREET ENTRANCE

1933   Blue, red, black, white

1934   Purple piers with white exteriors

ADMINISTRATION BUILDING

1933   Central portion white; wings midnight blue; window trimmings royal blue and silver; ornament highlighted in gray and red; some yellow

1934   Central portion white; magenta wings with black trim

TRAVEL AND TRANSPORT BUILDING

1933   Upper part in green with blue recesses; lower area in yellow with blue; red pavilions

1934   White with blue supports; green pavilions with red and green supports

HALL OF SCIENCE

NORTH COURT

1933   White piers with blue recesses

1934   White with green wings; orange central bay

MAIN COURT

1933   Blue tower; orange-and-yellow rear wall; blue-and-white-striped lower level

1934   Green with white tower and orange highlights

WINGS

1933   Blue-and-white striped ground floor; yellow upper story

ELECTRICAL BUILDING

1933   Red with yellow, white, gray, and blue highlights; black verticals behind the neon cascade "fountain"; green bas-relief panels

1934   White piers; blue recessed areas

ILLINOIS HOST BUILDING

1933   White with yellow tower sides

1934   White; name and emblem in gold

GENERAL EXHIBITS BUILDING

1933   Towers in white, yellow, blue,
        light blue, dark blue, yellow,
        orange
1934   Towers in alternating yellow and
        white with blue centers; white
        buildings with blue highlights

U.S. GOVERNMENT BUILDING

1933   White piers; blue center; black
        wings; gold dome
1934   White with orange interior faces
        of piers; orange dome; magenta;
        red base

FOODS AND AGRICULTURE
BUILDING

1933   Yellow, blue, red, black,
        aluminum, and white
1934   Magenta-and-white-striped end
        with light yellow horizontals,
        orange horizontal top, and white
        and aluminum highlights

DAIRY BUILDING/
CONTINENTAL DAIRY
BUILDING

1933   Gray, black, and white
1934   White, magenta, and bright red

HALL OF SOCIAL SCIENCE

1934   White with magenta

HOME PLANNING HALL

1933   Green, white, orange, and black
1934   White building with orange
        center; accents of turquoise
        and yellow; blue flags

HALL OF RELIGION

1934   White with orange-red tower and
        light green awning; light yellow
        highlights

SEARS-ROEBUCK BUILDING

1934   Red tower with white corners;
        white with red streamlines;
        red columns at entrance

ITALIAN PAVILION

1934   White with blue tower and red
        interior of entrance; gray wings

GENERAL MOTORS BUILDING

1933   Orange tower with white piers,
        blue highlights
1934   White with red or orange
        highlights; green and turquoise
        at main entrance

CHRYSLER BUILDING

1934   White with yellow and lavender
        highlights

FORD BUILDING

1934   White with dark green, blue,
        and yellow accents

SKYRIDE TOWERS

1933   Gray structure with blue and
        white on the ground "houses"
1934   Green with orange top

NOTES

ARCHIVES

Art Institute of Chicago, Chicago: Department of Architecture, Chicago Architects
Oral History Project; Ryerson and Burnham Archives, Century of Progress Collec-
tion; Daniel H. Burnham Jr. and Hubert Burnham Papers; Edward H. Bennett
Collection; Voorhees, Gmelin, and Walker photographs (AIC)

Athenaeum, Philadelphia: Paul Philippe Cret Archive

Avery Architectural and Fine Arts Library, Columbia University, New York: Drawings
and Archives Collection (Avery)

Chicago History Museum (formerly Chicago Historical Society), Chicago: Holabird
and Root Papers; Century of Progress Records and Photographs (CHM)

Chicago Park District, Chicago (CPD)

Frank Lloyd Wright Building Trust (formerly Frank Lloyd Wright Home and Studio
Foundation), Oak Park, Illinois: Research Center Archives (FLWBT)

Frank Lloyd Wright Foundation, Taliesin West, Scottsdale, Arizona: Frank Lloyd
Wright Archives (TAL)

Harry Ransom Humanities Research Center, University of Texas, Austin, Texas:
Norman Bel Geddes Archive (NBG, HRC)

Masonite Corporation Archives, West Chicago, Illinois

Museum of Science and Industry, Chicago (MSI)

National Archives, Washington, D.C.: Prints and Photographs Division

New York Public Library, New York: New York World's Fair Collection (NYWF,
NYPL)

University of Chicago, Chicago: University of Chicago Library, Special Collections
Research Center, Cererar Collection (UofC)

University of Illinois at Chicago, Chicago: Department of Special Collections,
A Century of Progress International Exposition Papers (CofP, UIC); Lenox Lohr
Papers (Lohr, UIC)

University of Pennsylvania, Van Pelt-Dietrich Library, Philadelphia: Special
Collections, Paul Philippe Cret Archive; Architectural Drawings Collection,
Paul Philippe Cret Papers (Cret, UPenn); Lewis Mumford Papers

INTRODUCTION

1. Exposition organizers estimated that over 200,000 people attended the fair on opening day. Over 180,000 individual admission tickets were sold, and approximately 20,000 season passes were used to enter the fairgrounds. Avery, "258,000 See Fair in Two Days."

2. While the opening-night lighting spectacular was a fitting way to inaugurate an event that promoted the scientific advances of mankind, the scientists who organized the ceremony were significantly off in their calculations, as the distance from Arcturus to Earth is in actuality less than thirty-seven light years.

3. Lohr, *Fair Management*, 197.

4. Kinsley, "Arcturus' Light Miracle Thrills Evening Throngs."

5. Lohr, *Fair Management*, 197. Speaking was Professor Philip Fox, director of the Adler Planetarium.

6. The idea to use light from a star to open the exposition was first suggested by Edwin B. Frost, director emeritus of the University of Chicago's Yerkes Observatory, in 1930. The energy was transmitted to Chicago with the help of Western Union. The four observatories involved in the event were located at Williams Bay, Wisconsin; Cambridge, Massachusetts; Allegheny, New York; and Urbana, Illinois. "670 Million Miles an Hour," 10, 12.

7. Riley, *The International Style*, 83.

8. The Museum of Modern Art was founded in 1929.

9. The Weissenhofsiedlung, one of the most significant architectural exhibitions of the twentieth century, brought together the work of some of the most influential and progressive European designers, including Ludwig Mies van der Rohe, Peter Behrens, Le Corbusier, Walter Gropius, and J. J. P. Oud. For more information on the Weissenhofsiedlung, see Kirsch, *The Weissenhofsiedlung*, and Pommer and Otto, *Weissenhof 1927 and the Modern Movement in Architecture.*

10. Many of these letters are housed in the Century of Progress International Exposition Archive at the Daley Library Special Collections, the University of Illinois at Chicago.

11. The prefabricated translucent facades of the Crystal Palace consisted of thousands of twelve-by-forty-nine-inch mass-produced glass panels, standardized for rapid assembly. Hobhouse, *1851 and the Crystal Palace*, 50.

12. Josef Hoffmann created an exquisite room for the Vienna School of Applied Arts in the Austrian Pavilion at Paris, while Behrens, Olbrich, and Hoffmann all created designs for the St. Louis exposition. Friebe, *Buildings of the World Exhibitions*, 123; *Descriptive Catalogue of the German Arts and Crafts and the Universal Exposition, St. Louis*, passim.

13. For more information on the presence of ethnic villages at expositions in the 1930s, see Rydell, *World of Fairs*, and Morton, *Hybrid Modernities.*

14. For more information on the Exposition Internationale des Arts Décoratifs et Industriels Modernes, see the twelve-volume *Encyclopédie des arts décoratifs et industriels modernes au XXème siècle.*

15. The need for visual consistency prevented Rockefeller Center from embodying anywhere near the range of new developments in modern design as was seen in the architecture of the second Chicago World's Fair. Several historian have explained the

long and complex history of the design process of Rockefeller Center, including Robert Stern in *New York, 1930*, Jordy in *American Buildings and Their Architects*, Balfour in *Rockefeller Center*, and Krinsky in *Rockefeller Center*.

16. Alfred Barr, the first director of MoMA, was also involved in the creation of the exhibition. For more information on Hitchcock, Johnson, and Barr, see Riley, *The International Style*, 13, and Schulze, *Philip Johnson*.

17. Riley, *The International Style*, 66.

18. Social concerns were covered in the exhibit's housing section, which was organized separately by Clarence Stein, Henry Wright, and Catherine Bauer and curated by Lewis Mumford, as well as in a related essay "Housing," by Mumford published in the catalog.

19. Hitchcock and Johnson, *The International Style*, 13.

20. Hitchcock had praised these European designers in his earlier book *Modern Architecture* as the "new pioneers" responsible for initiating a European architectural movement based on lessons learned from engineers and the previous generation of progressive architects, including Wright, Behrens, Henry van de Velde, and Auguste Perret (designers Hitchcock considered only "half-modernists" and whom he labeled "the new traditionalists"). Hitchcock, *Modern Architecture*, passim; Hitchcock and Johnson, *The International Style*, 27.

21. Hitchcock and Johnson added other designers prior to the exhibition's opening when they realized that the architects originally selected for the show did not represent an extensive international assemblage. To validate their claim of the existence of an international style, the curators incorporated forty photographs to illustrate the extent of modern architecture in fifteen countries, ranging from Spain to Japan, that exemplified the aesthetic principles laid out in the exhibition. Wodehouse, *The Roots of the International Style*, 131; Riley, *The International Style*, 63.

22. In contrast, 186,000 people had attended MoMA's exhibit The Architect and the Industrial Arts in 1929. Riley, *The International Style*, 85–86.

23. No longer required to include a large number of designs by American architects, they eliminated all of Frank Lloyd Wright's work and the projects by the Bowman Brothers, whose preference for streamlined forms and whose lack of built commissions placed them outside of Hitchcock and Johnson's narrowing definition. Raymond Hood's designs, as well as those of several other American architects that did not quite fit the International Style idiom, however, were retained primarily so the authors could criticize specific design characteristics. With the elimination of Mumford's essay on housing, Hitchcock and Johnson focused solely on formal issues in the International Style book.

24. Deborah Frances Pokinski first discussed the evolving definition of modern architecture during this period in her work *The Development of the American Modern Style*, 51–72.

25. Moholy-Nagy, "The Diaspora," 24.

26. For designers' views on the state of American architecture around 1930, see Corbett, "The Meaning of Modernism," 268; Leonard, "What Is Modernism?" 22; and "Branding the Buildings at the Chicago Fair," 14.

27. For more information on the rise in popularity of machine-age forms, see Wilson et al., *The Machine Age in America*; Meikle, *Twentieth Century Limited*; and Banham, *Theory and Design in the First Machine Age*.

28. Farrier, "Exposition Buildings Unique in Form and Structure," 278.

29. The cost per cubic foot of most of the major pavilions at the exposition was $0.15 or less. One major exception was the Administration Building, which contained the required utilities of a permanent modern office building. Its final cost was close to $0.40 per cubic foot. Farrier, "Exposition Buildings Unique in Form and Structure," 278, 282.

30. Over 25,000 carpenters in the Chicago area, who had constructed over 100,000 bungalows in the city during the 1920s, were out of work in the early 1930s. Because of the lack of available employment, the construction bosses at the exposition had an easy time keeping approximately 2,600 of the best local construction workers busy building the fair. The lack of other major competing construction projects in town also meant that fair organizers did not have to battle Chicago's powerful labor unions. Stewart, "Construction Management Stressed over Technique," 291.

31. Bert M. Thorud, "Construction," press release, 10 May 1933, 1, CofP, UIC.

32. The lack of available work during the Great Depression meant that a number of research laboratories of large manufacturers in the United States had the time and resources to develop special products for the fair. Exposition designers also received data relating to new products from building associations and materials manufacturers, such as the American Institute of Steel Construction and various lumber organizations. This contributed to an increase in the use of low-cost products and inexpensive building processes. Thorud, "Construction," 2; Thorud, "Engineering Research and Building Construction," 65.

33. Crissey, "Why the Century of Progress Architecture?"; S. L. Tesone, memo to C. W. Farrier and J. Stewart, 16 October 1933, 65, CofP, UIC.

34. The state fire marshal, S. L. Legreid, and his representative, a Mr. Mattson, reviewed and approved individual pavilion plans for construction. Farrier, "Exposition Buildings Unique in Form and Structure," 278; Tesone, memo to Farrier and Stewart, 16 October 1933, 65.

35. Thorud, "Construction," 3. The building code for the exposition grounds went into effect on 21 December 1932. Before this, the Building Ordinance of the City of Chicago and the building code recommended by the National Board of Fire Underwriters had been used as guidelines. The new exposition code established basic requirements regarding exits and fire hazards; stress limits, classifications, and quality of materials; and light, ventilation, and sanitation. Thorud, "Engineering Research and Building Construction," 65; Tesone, memo to Farrier and Stewart, 16 October 1933, 65.

36. Thorud, "Engineering Research and Building Construction," 65; Thorud, "Construction," 3.

37. Condit, "The Century of Progress Exposition," 3.

38. Farrier, "Exposition Buildings Unique in Form and Structure," 282.

ONE: SCIENCE FINDS—INDUSTRY APPLIES—MAN CONFORMS

1. Those who held this view included several men important in the success of the second Chicago World's Fair, including Vice President Charles Dawes. Charles G. Dawes, "Statement of Charles G. Dawes, Vice President of the United States," 5. The Sesquicentennial Exposition, based on previous American world's fairs, concluded with a massive debt for Philadelphia to repay. The event's primary patriotic purposes, to cel-

ebrate the 150th anniversary of the signing of the Declaration of Independence and to rejuvenate American patriotism, failed to attract a significant international audience. Poor planning and bad weather compounded the problem. Attendance only reached 6,408,000, a fraction of the 21,480,000 visitors who had attended the 1893 Columbian Exposition. "Attendance at Previous Expositions," CofP, UIC. For more information on the Sesquicentennial Exposition, see Glassberg, "Philadelphia 1926 Sesquicentennial International Exposition," and Austin and Hauser, *The Sesqui-centennial International Exposition.*

2. Major Lenox Lohr, manager of the Chicago exposition, later reflecting on this fact wrote, "The universal advantages of the radio, the moving pictures and the automobile had produced a generation of sophistication that had no concern with expositions." Lohr, *Fair Management,* 9.

3. Farrier, "Exposition Buildings Unique in Form and Structure," 269–70. The need for a new type of exposition was clearly expressed in the congressional hearings held to authorize the president of the United States to invite the nations of the world to the Chicago fair. In his testimony before the House of Representatives, Vice President Dawes, brother of the exposition's president, Rufus Dawes, stated that the planners of the exposition realized that "unless a new idea could be found upon which to base an exposition of this sort, there was no reason to expect anything but the failure that has characterized almost every exposition of the kind that has been held since the world's fair modeled upon the old plan." Dawes, "Statement," 5.

4. The organizers' interest in the Deutsches Museum reflected the growing popularity of large scientific museums designed for the general public. Chicago's own Museum of Science and Industry was under development during the years that A Century of Progress was designed and under way. After the close of the exposition, the museum became the repository for many of the scientific exhibits from the event. William Allen Pusey, "Man's Conquest of Nature Is Theme of the Exposition," 3, CofP, UIC.

5. More people visited the 1927 B&O Railroad Exhibition in three weeks than had attended the Sesquicentennial Exposition in three months. Dawes, "Statement," 5.

6. On the concept of progress in various aspects of American culture during the early 1930s, see Beard, *A Century of Progress.*

7. Zunz, *Why the American Century?* xi, 74.

8. These included the Exposición International de Barcelona (1929); the Exposición Ibero-Americana in Seville (1929); the Exposition Internationale Coloniale Maritime et d'Art Flamand in Antwerp (1930); the Exposition Internationale de la Grande Industrie, Sciences, et Applications, Art Wallon Ancien in Liège (1930); and the Exposition Coloniale Internationale in Paris (1931), as well as other expositions in Stockholm (1930); Prague; Trondheim, Norway (1930); and Poznan, Poland (1929). Albert, "Learning from Other World's Fairs," 14, 22.

9. On the early history and planning of the Century of Progress Exposition, see Rydell, "The Fan Dance of Science," 525–42; Rydell, *World of Fairs.*

10. Myron E. Adams to Mayor [William] Dever, 17 August 1923, Folder 1-56, CofP, UIC. On Daniel Burnham's Plan of Chicago and the City Beautiful movement, see Draper, "Paris by the Lake," 106–19.

11. Adams to Dever, 17 August 1923.

12. "A Century of Progress Chronology of Early History," n.p., Folder 15-21, CofP, UIC.

13. Rufus C. Dawes, "Report of the Century of Progress Exposition," 139.

14. Lohr, *Fair Management*, 10.

15. *Official Guide Book of the Fair, 1933,* 16; Jackson, ed., *History of Centennials, Expositions, and World Fairs,* also, *The Fundamental Principles of Successful County and State Fairs,* n.p.

16. Dawes, "Report of the Century of Progress Exposition," 140.

17. In a memorandum to the trustees of the Century of Progress Exposition, Major Lohr informed the board members that the fair needed to restore "Chicago's wholesome status by a program of performance and house cleaning from within . . . followed by a world replacement of the hoodlum news with [a] sound, constructive selling of Chicago's realness and virtue." "Memorandum to the Trustees of the World's Fair," attached to the Minutes of the 29 October 1930 Board Meeting, Folder 11-12, CofP, UIC.

18. Trustees included Robert R. McCormick, editor and publisher of the *Chicago Tribune;* Julius Rosenwald, chief executive officer of Sears, Roebuck and Company; and Philip K. Wrigley, founder of the chewing gum company. Lohr, *Guides Memories,* 1; Paul T. Gilbert, "A Century of Progress Exposition: Herald of a New Age," *Chicago Progress,* n.d., 12. CofP, UIC.

19. Lohr, *Fair Management,* 12. The Dawes brothers were owners of the Pure Oil Company and directors of various utilities.

20. These officers became members of the exposition's executive committee and all except Burnham served the entire term of the event. Burnham resigned on 8 March 1934 and was succeeded by P. J. Byrne. *Official Guide Book of the Fair, 1933,* 16; Dawes, "Report of the Century of Progress Exposition," 141.

21. *A Century of Progress, Chicago International Exposition of 1933: A Statement of Its Plan and Purposes,* 4; Dawes, "Report of the Century of Progress Exposition," 151.

22. *A Century of Progress Chicago International Exposition of 1933: A Statement of Its Plan and Purposes,* 3.

23. Lohr, *Fair Management,* 7. By 1933 the Chicago metro area was growing at a rate of approximately 90,000 people a year and had reached a total population of close to 4 million people. Dawes, "Statement."

24. Dawes, "Report of the Century of Progress Exposition," 141.

25. *Official Guide Book of the Fair, 1933,* 18.

26. The slogan I Will appeared on a variety of sources publicizing the exposition, including political cartoons. Just prior to the opening of the exposition, I Will served as the symbol for Let's Go Chicago week, a publicity event for businesses to show their support for the fair and its host city.

27. Pusey, "Man's Conquest of Nature Is Theme of the Exposition," 4.

28. Dawes, "Report of the Century of Progress Exposition," 143.

29. The National Research Council was initially organized by the National Academy of Sciences. Dawes, "Report of the Century of Progress Exposition," 143–44.

30. Ibid.

31. George K. Burgess, letter to Rufus C. Dawes, 12 February 1929, Folder 5-254, CofP, UIC.

32. Crew, "The Exposition of Science," 237.

33. Dawes, "Report of the Century of Progress Exposition," 146.

34. Bell, "The Progress of Science," 281; Crew, "The Exposition of Science," 237–38.

35. Carey, *Medical Science Exhibits*, 35.

36. Lohr, *Fair Management*, 120.

37. *Official Handbook of Exhibits in the Division of Basic Sciences, Hall of Science, A Century of Progress, 1934*, 47.

38. *Official Guide Book of the Fair, 1933*, 60.

39. Zunz, *Why the American Century?* 83.

40. Ibid., xii.

41. Dawes, "Report of the Century of Progress Exposition," 143.

42. These books (like the fair) were designed to make the latest developments, advances, and hypotheses understandable to the general public. Horatio Hackett Newman, *Evolution Yesterday and Today*, vii.

43. Cole, *The Long Road from Savagery to Civilization*.

44. *Official Guide Book of the Fair, 1933*, 60.

45. Gifford Ernest, "Ways of Science Are Revealed in City Dump," 6.

46. Century of Progress International Exposition Publicity Department, "Social Science," press release, 25 June 1934, Folder 15-155, CofP, UIC; *Official Guide Book of the World's Fair of 1934*, 91–92.

47. Meikle, "Domesticating Modernity," 151–52.

48. *Official Guide Book of the Fair, 1933*, 14–15.

49. McDowell, "Masonite Inventor to Start Work on First Unit of Fair Home Group."

50. Berg, "First Television Theatre, Interesting Attraction at the World's Fair," 4, 6.

51. For more information on the housing exhibits, see chapter 5.

52. Malony, "Tomorrow's Housing"; Brown, "Chicago and Tomorrow's House?"; and "Beautiful Houses of Today and Tomorrow," in the *Official Guide Book of the Fair, 1933*, 67–72.

53. Up to 30,000 people a day paid ten cents to visit the fairgrounds prior to opening day. Dawes, "Statement," 121; Crissey, "Why the Century of Progress Architecture?" 16; Lohr, "Chicago Stages Its Second World's Fair," 271; "Fair Hums with New Activity as May 27 Nears, Roosevelt Regrets He Can't Open It."

54. For more information on the display of objects at expositions, see Giberti, *Designing the Centennial*, and Harris, "Museums, Merchandising, and Popular Taste."

55. Albert, "Learning from Other World's Fairs," 14, 22.

56. Quoted in Duffy, "Motion Key to Fair's Magic Lohr Says," 15.

57. "Suggestions for the Sales Force of the Exhibits Department," Folder 11-2, CofP UIC.

58. Van Zandt, "A Miracle in Cans," 54.

59. Ibid., 56–57.

60. The number of visitors to the exhibit far exceeded the company's expectations. Century of Progress International Exposition Publicity Department, "American Can Company," press release, 12 July 1934, Folder 1-385, CofP, UIC.

61. Van Zandt, "A Miracle in Cans," 54, 56–57.

62. Benjamin, "The Work of Art in the Age of Mechanical Reproduction," 550–57. For authenticity and world's fair souvenirs, see Gilbert, "World's Fairs as Historical Events," 23–24.

63. *Official Guide Book of the World's Fair of 1934*, 101.

64. "See Chevrolets Made."

65. Lohr, *Fair Management*, 137–38.

66. Ibid., 172; *Wings of a Century: The Romance of Transportation* (Chicago: A Century of Progress International Exposition, 1934), copy of brochure in collection of author.

67. The *Zephyr*'s trip from Denver to Chicago lasted thirteen hours and five minutes. The train achieved an average speed of 77.6 miles an hour and a top speed of 112.5 miles an hour. It took less than a second for the complete length of the streamlined train to pass by a stationary viewer. Meikle, *Twentieth Century Limited*, 160; Thayer, "Pioneer . . . a Wind from the West," 26.

68. Lohr, *Fair Management*, 158.

69. At the time of the exposition, only the recently completed George Washington Bridge across the Hudson River in New York City exceeded the Skyride in size.

70. Benevolo, *History of Modern Architecture*, 1:103.

71. Some of the most valuable displays in the Hall of Science were placed on permanent display in the Museum of Science and Industry at the close of the exposition. Dawes, "Report of the Century of Progress Exposition," 146–47.

72. Five major world expositions held between 1929 and 1931, however, did include at least one collective industry display. Albert, "Learning from Other World's Fairs," 14.

73. Dawes, "Report of the Century of Progress Exposition," 142.

74. Bell, "The Progress of Science," 281.

75. An exception was made when a display could be incorporated into a larger exhibit tied to the general theme of the fair. Ibid., 282.

76. The Ford Motor Company initially declined to build a corporate pavilion at A Century of Progress, but it went on to construct a large building for the 1934 fair season.

77. Carey, *Medical Science Exhibits*, 23. Several earlier expositions did, however, include individual medical exhibits.

78. Ibid., ix, 23.

79. Carey, "100 Years of Science in Medicine," 15.

80. Carey, *Medical Science Exhibits*, 23.

81. William Allen Pusey, memo, 18 September 1934, Folder 15-152, CofP, UIC.

82. Ibid.

83. Carey, *Medical Science Exhibits*, 35.

84. Carey, "100 Years of Science in Medicine," 14, 16.

85. Carey, *Medical Science Exhibits*, 32.

86. Constructed by technicians at the German Hygiene Museum in Dresden, the model was on loan from the Mayo Foundation of Rochester, Minnesota. Ibid., 40.

87. Lohr, *Fair Management*, 122. At the time of this writing, the human cross sections and series of human embryos and fetuses are still on display in Chicago at the Museum of Science and Industry.

88. John Holabird Jr., whose father was a member of the architectural commission, was thirteen and fourteen during the two seasons of the exposition. He recalls finding the Skyride boring and quickly losing interest in the other amusements. During his numerous visits to the fair (he estimates he made approximately fifty trips to the exposition over the two seasons), he spent most of his time exploring the exhibits in the Hall of Science and the Electrical Building. John Holabird Jr., conversation with author, Chicago, 8 November 1995.

89. *Official Guide Book of the Fair, 1933*, 40–41.

90. This became a significant underlying message in many of the medical exhibits. Carey, "100 Years of Science in Medicine," 16.

91. Carey, *Medical Science Exhibits*, 64.

92. Lohr, *Fair Management*, 122.

93. Carey, *Medical Science Exhibits*, 22.

94. Burnham [Jr.], "How Chicago Finances Its Exposition," 37.

95. The Columbian Exposition received $5,617,154.33 in funding, the Louisiana Purchase Exposition received $4,924,313.11 in support, and the Panama-Pacific Exposition received $5,716,320. Ibid.

96. The introduction of exhibitor fees was first suggested by Ernest T. Trigg, who felt that the exposition's corporation should take advantage of the fact that companies were now used to paying fees to exhibit at trade fairs and association meetings. For many companies, the value of being able to present their products to a large audience greatly outweighed the expense of exhibitor fees even during the depths of the Great Depression. Lohr, *Fair Management*, 34–35.

97. Dawes, "Statement," 1.

98. Dawes, "Report of the Century of Progress Exposition," 153.

99. Burnham [Jr.], "How Chicago Finances Its Exposition," 38; Dawes, "Report of the Century of Progress Exposition," 153; Condit, *Chicago 1930–70*, 5.

100. Lohr, *Fair Management*, 32.

101. *Official Guide Book of the Fair, 1933*, 19.

102. Burnham [Jr.], "How Chicago Finances Its Exposition," 38.

103. Dawes, "Report of the Century of Progress Exposition," 158.

104. *Official Guide Book of the Fair, 1933*, 19.

105. Dawes, "Report of the Century of Progress Exposition," 141.

106. Ibid., 150–51.

107. Ibid., 158.

108. Schnura, "Lenox Riley Lohr and a Century of Progress, 1933–34," 30.

109. Lohr, *Fair Management*, 35.

110. In 1929, when the likelihood of the exposition turning even a modest profit seemed highly improbable, the fair organizers decided that cultural and scientific institutions should become the primary beneficiaries of any remaining funds from the event. The South Park District received 25 percent of the profit, the Museum of Science and Industry 20 percent, the Chicago Art Institute 20 percent, and the Adler Planetarium 10 percent; the remaining funds were divided between the Yerkes Observatory, the Smithsonian Institution, the Chicago Regional Planning Commission, and associations created for the care and preservation of the Lama Temple of Jehol and Fort Dearborn. Ibid., 213.

111. Both the World's Columbian Exposition of 1893 in Chicago and the Panama-Pacific Exposition of 1915 in San Francisco succeeded in heightening public awareness without the expense of paid advertising. Dawes, "Report of the Century of Progress Exposition," 150.

112. According to Lohr, the exposition's corporation spent no money on advertisements in newspapers, newsreels, periodicals, or radio. *A Century of Progress Report of the President to the Board of Trustees, 14 March 1936*, 39.

113. Lohr, *Fair Management*, 213.

114. Dawes, "Report of the Century of Progress Exposition," 150.

115. "News of Fair in Pictures," 4.

116. Many fairgoers arrived in Chicago by special exposition trains. During Labor Day weekend in 1933, when Chicago played host to approximately 500,000 visitors, the Pennsylvania Railroad, the New York Central Railroad, and the Chicago and Northwestern Railroad brought a total of 65,000 extra riders to the city on supplementary trains. *Time Capsule/1933,* 89.

117. Ibid.; "Incidents of Opening Day."

TWO: DESIGNING THE CITY OF COLOR AND DELIGHT

1. Organizers of the Sesquicentennial International Exposition specified that its architecture be neocolonial, as the fair was held to "commemorate many events that were laid in Colonial settings." They also felt that the pavilions should harmonize with the buildings of Philadelphia, "where the precedents of what is known as the Colonial style abound." Austin and Hauser, *The Sesqui-centennial International Exposition,* 59.

2. For example, George Edgell, a professor at Harvard University, stated in 1928, "Modern American architecture includes all the architecture of America that has recently been built." Edgell, *The American Architecture of To-Day,* 3. Architectural historian Fiske Kimball reflected on the impermanence of what buildings the phrase *modern architecture* specifically referred to when he stated that "'modern' . . . is a relative term: its meaning changes from generation to generation. The creative nature of art itself determines that no single formula, however cogent, can long prevail." Fiske Kimball, "Louis Sullivan—an Old Master," 303.

3. A more extensive discussion of the use of the terms *modern, modernistic,* and *modernism* in the United States in the 1920s and early 1930s can be found in Pokinski's *The Development of the American Modern Style.*

4. Edgell, *The American Architecture of To-Day,* 83.

5. Mumford, *Sticks and Stones,* 148–49.

6. Ibid., 163.

7. All quoted in "Modernist and Traditionalist," 49–50.

8. Hood, "The Spirit of Modern Art," 445.

9. Ibid.

10. Leonard wrote in 1929, "When the materials of construction change, there is a continuity of the principles of architecture but not its form. Modern architecture is, therefore, only a restatement of the principles of architecture in new materials." Leonard, "What Is Modernism?" 24.

11. Harbeson, "Design in Modern Architecture: I—What Is Modern?" 3.

12. Arnaud, "The Evolution of a New Architecture," 50.

13. Ibid., 114.

14. According to an official resolution, the commission was to be a general advisory council to the president and board of trustees and was to devise a comprehensive general construction plan, which included adopting an architectural style. Chicago World's Fair Centennial Celebration of 1933 Board of Trustees, Resolution, 21 February 1928, CofP, UIC.

15. Sullivan made his prediction from the vantage point of thirty years after the close of the Columbian Exposition. On the last page of his autobiography he wrote,

"The damage wrought by the world's fair will last for half a century from its date, if not longer. It has penetrated deep into the constitution of the American mind, effecting there lesions significant of dementia." Sullivan, *An Autobiography of an Idea*, 325.

16. The *moderne* aesthetic popularized by the 1925 Paris exposition used zigzag forms and angular, stylized designs to reflect the vibrant energy and excitement of life in the United States and Europe during the 1920s.

17. Skidmore, "Planning and Planners," 29.

18. Paul Philippe Cret (1876–1945), born in France, attended the École des Beaux-Arts in 1903 before arriving in Philadelphia in the same year to begin teaching at the University of Pennsylvania.

19. For major commissions by Paul Cret, see White, *Paul Philippe Cret.*

20. Raymond Hood (1881–1934) took courses in architecture at the Massachusetts Institute of Technology and worked briefly in the office of Cram, Goodhue, and Furguson before attending the École des Beaux-Arts for approximately one year, ending in 1906. He returned to the United States and worked in Pittsburgh for Henry Hornbostel before returning to finish his *diplôme* at the École in 1910. For more information on Hood, see Kilham, *Raymond Hood, Architect*, and Robert A.M. Stern, *Raymond Hood.*

21. Hood, "Exterior Architecture of Office Buildings," 97–98.

22. Stern, *Raymond Hood*, 27n106.

23. Allen D. Albert to A.N. Rebori, 5 April 1928, CofP, UIC.

24. Skidmore, "Planning and Planners," 29. The lists of suggested architects do not appear to have survived.

25. Peterson, "The 1933 World's Fair," 124. The third qualification was probably added to help justify the exclusion of Frank Lloyd Wright, who was not known as a team player. The ability to work cooperatively, however, constituted an important factor in the planning process.

26. Arthur Brown Jr. (c. 1874–1957) had previously designed the Horticultural Building for the Panama-Pacific International Exposition in 1915. For more information on Brown, see "Arthur Brown Jr. Dies." Harvey Wiley Corbett (1873–1954) was a major participant in the promotion of tall office buildings, collaborating with architectural renderer Hugh Ferriss in exploring the design possibilities of the setback restrictions on skyscrapers in New York's 1916 zoning laws. For more information on Corbett, see Willis, "Harvey Wiley Corbett," 1:451.

27. Bennett had served as an assistant to Daniel H. Burnham Sr., director of works for the 1893 Columbian Exposition and the father of commissioner Hubert Burnham. John Holabird was the son of prominent Chicago architect William Holabird, a colleague of Daniel Burnham. William Holabird, with his partner Martin Roche, had designed several buildings, including the Stock Pavilion and the National Exposition Building of New South Wales, for the earlier Chicago World's Fair. For more information on Edward H. Bennett (1874–1954), see Draper, "Edward H. Bennett," 1:179. For more information on John Holabird (1886–1945), see Blanks, "Biographical Glossary," 464. For more information on Hubert Burnham (1882–1968), see "Biographical Sketch of Hubert Burnham," CofP, UIC.

28. Raymond Hood to Frank Lloyd Wright, 16 February 1931, TAL.

29. Norman Bel Geddes at the time was primarily working as a stage designer, while Hugh Ferriss was America's foremost architectural renderer. Albert, "The Archi-

tecture of the Chicago World's Fair of 1933," 430; Harvey Wiley Corbett to Dr. Allen D. Albert, 4 April 1930, CofP, UIC.

30. Skidmore, "Planning and Planners," 32. Neither Urban nor Vitale lived to see the realization of their designs for the fair. Alfred Geiffert Jr. replaced Ferruccio Vitale as the landscape consultant after the latter's untimely death in February 1933, while Shepard Vogelgesang replaced Joseph Urban, who died on 10 July 1933, as color consultant for the fair's 1934 season. Ibid., 61. For more information on Joseph Urban, see chapter 3.

31. The École des Beaux-Arts in Paris was the premier place to receive an architectural education in the nineteenth and early twentieth centuries. Architectural training there favored the creation of large projects, often for competitions, which incorporated axially symmetrical plans with elevations that often borrowed from classical antiquity; see Packard, "École des Beaux Arts," 269–71.

32. Raymond Hood to Paul Cret, 25 February 1928, Box 17, Paul Philippe Cret Archive, Special Collections, UPenn.

33. Ralph T. Walker (1889–1973) joined the New York office of McKenzie, Voorhees, and Gmelin in 1919 and later received acclaim for his art deco skyscrapers, including the Barclay-Vesey (1923–26) and the Irving Trust (1929–32) buildings, which incorporated setbacks in accordance with the 1916 New York zoning ordinance. For more information on Walker, see Willis, "Ralph Thomas Walker," 4:363.

34. Ralph T. Walker, "A New Architecture," 1.

35. Ibid.

36. Ibid., 4.

37. Cret, "Ten Years of Modernism."

38. Corbett, "The Meaning of Modernism," 268.

39. Wright et al., "All Fair," 12.

40. "Harvey Wiley Corbett Tells How Exposition Was Created," 25.

41. Granger, *Chicago Welcomes You*, 235.

42. Cret, response to Howard Lewis Shay. Cret, however, saw architecture as an art and wrote in 1927 that "an architecture which is deduced solely from the necessities of construction is not architecture, because it is not art,—it fails completely to evoke the emotional values latent in a mere manifold of mechanical factors. 'Architecture begins where the calculations end.'" Cret, "The Architect as Collaborator of the Engineer," 101.

43. Quoted in Vincent, "'Natura non facit saltus,'" 335.

44. Hood, foreword to *American Apartment Houses, Hotels, and Apartments*; R. W. Sexton, as quoted in Stern, *Raymond Hood*, 24.

45. John A. Holabird, for Harvey W. Corbett, to Rufus C. Dawes, 25 May 1928, CofP, UIC.

46. "World's Fair Plans Mapped by Architects," 4. Bennett had been chosen to create the initial schemes because of his previous experience in large planning projects. Chicago World's Fair Centennial Celebration of 1933, report labeled "W-1," n.d., 3, CofP, UIC.

47. "World's Fair Plans Mapped by Architects," 4; Skidmore, "Planning and Planners," 30.

48. Hubert Burnham, "Chicago's 1933 World's Fair," 127.

49. Designs by Walker and Cret also included forms of raised moving sidewalks.

Chicago World's Fair Centennial Celebration of 1933, Minutes of the Second Meeting of the Architectural Commission, 5 December 1928, 2–3, CofP, UIC.

50. When Bennett presented his designs to the Fifth National Conference on City Planning, he declared that "the most important consideration of the city plan, and one to which everything practically leads in the end, is the street system." Sennott, "'Forever Inadequate to the Rising Stream,'" 55. As consultant to the Chicago Planning Commission, he promoted wider avenues and elevated walkways and streets. Just prior to the planning of the exposition, a part of his design was realized in the construction of a bilevel road for Wacker Drive along the Chicago River on the north and west edges of the Loop in 1926, which allowed for the segregation of different types of traffic. Ibid., 57.

51. Corbett and Hugh Ferriss created visually seductive images suggesting how double-decker roads and elevated sidewalks could help alleviate traffic congestion in Manhattan. The designs offered potential solutions for moving large numbers of people and goods efficiently through the fairgrounds. Corbett declared that incorporating such features at the Chicago fair might even initiate a new type of exposition architecture. Krinsky, *Rockefeller Center,* 36; Corbett, "The Problem of Traffic," 204; Minutes of the Second Meeting of the Architectural Commission, 4.

52. The design of the gigantic office complex consisted of four massive towers and a series of smaller ones, taking advantage of the air rights above the Illinois Central Railroad yards north of Grant Park along Chicago's lakefront. Rau, "The Making of the Merchandise Mart, 1927–1931," 104, 107; Krinsky, "Chicago and New York: Plans and Parallels, 1889–1929," 232.

53. Benevolo, *History of Modern Architecture,* 1:109, 112; Goetz, *Up Down Across,* 14.

54. Architect Joseph Lyman Silsbee, best known for employing a young Frank Lloyd Wright, received an Edward Longstreet Medal from the Franklin Institute for coinventing the attraction, which consisted of a chain of 315 cars on a dumbbell-shaped track that could hold up to 5,610 people at one time. McCormick, "The Early Work of Joseph Lyman Silsbee," 172–73.

55. Minutes of the Second Meeting of the Architectural Commission, 9.

56. Frank Lloyd Wright later incorporated this idea into his design of the Guggenheim Museum in New York City.

57. Minutes of the Second Meeting of the Architectural Commission, 1.

58. Ibid., 5.

59. Albert, "The Architecture of the Chicago World's Fair of 1933," 421–30. Designs were published three months later in "Preliminary Studies for the Chicago World's Fairs."

60. According to Allen D. Albert, the architects at this point reluctantly admitted that "the architectural traditions of the past still held them." Crissey, "Why the Century of Progress Architecture?" 62.

61. Albert, "The Architecture of the Chicago World's Fair of 1933," 426–27.

62. "Preliminary Studies for the Chicago World's Fairs," 226.

63. Chicago World's Fair Centennial Celebration of 1933, Minutes of the Third Meeting of the Architectural Commission, 21 January 1929, 5, CofP, UIC.

64. This may have been a result of the commissioners' flight over the fairgrounds at the start of the planning process.

65. Airports appeared in both Bennett's and Walker's initial schemes.

66. Century of Progress International Exposition Publicity Department, "Architects," press release, 16 March 1929, CofP, UIC.

67. "Preliminary Studies for the Chicago World's Fairs," 217.

68. Albert, "The Architecture of the Chicago World's Fair of 1933," 428–30. The commission voted on each element of the *parti*. All passed unanimously, except for placing a monumental entrance at Sixteenth Street, which Ralph Walker opposed. Chicago World's Fair Centennial Celebration of 1933, Minutes of the Fourth Meeting of the Architectural Commission, 1 February 1929, 9, CofP, UIC.

69. These designs were published in "A Century of Progress," *Western Architect.*

70. While these historical site plans are not identical to those published in Hegemann and Peets, *The American Vitruvius,* their great similarity suggests that the commissioners probably used the book as a source for the historical plans. Similar comparative plans of earlier American expositions appear in George Edgell's book *The American Architecture of To-Day,* 52. The connection to Hegemann and Peets was first suggested to me by Richard Cleary.

71. In Ralph Walker's perspective it is unclear whether his tower represents the Hall of Science or the Tower of Water, his unrealized waterfall attraction.

72. Both Geddes and Ferriss promoted the use of dramatic theatrical effects in building design. Chicago World's Fair Centennial Celebration of 1933, Minutes of the Fifth Meeting of the Architectural Commission, 1 May 1929, 1, CofP, UIC.

73. Minutes of the Fifth Meeting of the Architectural Commission, 6.

74. "A Century of Progress," *Western Architect,* 93. Symmetry did prevail, however, in the individual elements of Hood's scheme.

75. Minutes of the Fifth Meeting of the Architectural Commission, 8.

76. Ibid. Hood may not have derived the informal layout from the Spanish expositions. Both fairs contained strong symmetrical axes that dominate the grounds, but they did include curved secondary streets. Louis Skidmore recalled that the idea for an informal layout was "brewing" in Hood's mind while he sailed to Europe. During a stop in Paris, Hood met two "Architectural Scholarship" men in the Café des deux Magots (probably Frank Roorda and Carl Landefeld) and told them of his idea. He sketched his new *parti* on the marble tabletop and asked the young architects to prepare a drawing quickly. When Hood returned to Paris several days later, the sketch was ready for him to take back to the United States. Skidmore, "Planning and Planners," 30; Bendiner, "Wild Gold Medal Winners I Have Known." In another version of this story, told by Walter H. Kilham Jr. in his biography of Hood, the architect came up with the idea while vacationing in Amalfi, Italy. He then traveled to Paris, where he had Skidmore, Roorda, and Landefeld draw up the design. Kilham, *Raymond Hood, Architect,* 108.

77. Paul Cret to Mr. Burnham, 1 July 1929, CofP, UIC; Minutes of the Fifth Meeting of the Architectural Commission, 8.

78. Minutes of the Fifth Meeting of the Architectural Commission, 12.

79. Comments made during the meeting and published in the minutes suggest that the commission members not in favor of an asymmetrical layout were Corbett, Brown, and Bennett. Minutes of the Fifth Meeting of the Architectural Commission, 13–14, 16.

80. Skidmore, "Planning and Planners," 31.

81. Cret was selected for the task because the commissioners believed he was the

one member who could take into consideration all the points raised at the meeting and create a successful final design. "A Century of Progress," *Western Architect*, 91; Minutes of the Fifth Meeting of the Architectural Commission, 16–17.

82. Chicago World's Fair Centennial Celebration of 1933, Minutes of the Sixth Meeting of the Architectural Commission, 28 October 1929, 13, CofP, UIC.

83. This decision probably resulted from a pragmatic concern over avoiding excessive costs, a concern that stemmed, in part, from the fair organizers' early decision not to rely on public funding to finance the event. Chicago World's Fair Centennial Celebration of 1933, Minutes of the Meeting of the Architectural Commission, 26 September 1929, CofP, UIC.

84. "A Century of Progress," *Western Architect*, 91.

85. In addition to cost, the noise and vibrations generated by rooftop vehicles were cited as major reasons for abandoning a proposed raised electrical "rapid" transportation system. Louis Skidmore, "Notes on Design Section—Department of Works, December 1929 to June 1932," 3, CofP, UIC.

86. Hood, not known for his delineating ability, often used clay models in his design process.

87. Hood eventually was assigned the Electrical Building on Northerly Island, and Walker was given the southern portion of the island. Cret, originally in charge of the General Exhibits Building, switched to the Hall of Science area, and Corbett took over the General Exhibits Building. The Chicago members codesigned the Administration Building, the Travel and Transport Building, and the entrances to the fairgrounds; Brown was placed in charge of the Dairy, Agriculture, and U.S. Government buildings. Architects who were not members of the commission designed many of the other fair pavilions. While the architectural committee had no jurisdiction over selecting architects for individual exhibitors, designs were subject to the exposition's authority and the commission's approval.

88. The Science Advisory Committee recommended to the architects that the focus of the fair be a "Temple of Pure Sciences" surrounded by exhibit halls devoted to the applied and social sciences. Rydell, "The Fan Dance of Science," 529.

89. The hall would have been a grand entrance for those arriving to the exposition by train on the Illinois Central Railway.

90. "A Century of Progress Exposition," *Construction*, 259.

91. Fair organizers decided to use plywood primarily because it was considerably less expensive, both in material and in construction costs, than the asbestos-cement wallboard used on the Administration Building. Additional benefits included the fact that plywood takes paint well and is adaptable to curved surfaces. Farrier, "Exposition Buildings Unique in Form and Structure," 280; Owings, "New Materials and Building Methods for Chicago Exposition," 286; Skidmore, "The Hall of Science, A Century of Progress Exposition," 362. For more information on the use of plywood at A Century of Progress, see chapter 4.

92. For example, Cret alternated full-size panels with smaller ones to create a tartan pattern on part of the south facade of the pavilion.

93. After the close of the exposition the artist donated *Science Advancing Mankind* to her alma mater, the Joliet Central Township High School in Joliet, Illinois. The school renamed it *Steelman* and adopted it as their mascot.

94. One major exception to this was the Time and Fortune Building, designed by

Nicolai and Faro, which had, in addition to huge reproductions of magazine covers, exterior facades completely covered in colorful, geometric surface decorations.

95. "Lighting Up for Fair," 13.

96. Chicago World's Fair Centennial Celebration of 1933, Minutes, Meeting of Illumination Committee, 9 May 1932, CofP, UIC.

97. "Lighting Up for Fair," 15.

THREE: PREFABRICATED PALACES

1. The groundbreaking for the first pavilion, the Administration Building, took place on 27 May 1930.

2. As at earlier world's fairs, the organizers of the Chicago exposition specified that a transportation pavilion be constructed in which they could highlight past and recent advances in various methods of travel. The enormous building housed everything from a weather-bleached Conestoga wagon to the pilothouse of a modern steamship, from a high-wheel bicycle of the 1880s to the world's "mightiest" electric locomotive. Daniel H. Burnham [Jr.], "Temples of Inspiration to Rise along Miles of Lake Shore," 22; *Official Guide Book of the World's Fair of 1934*, 147.

3. *Official Guide Book of the Fair, 1933*, 25.

4. The architectural critic Thomas Tallmadge, who designed the Colonial Village for the 1934 fair season, described the Travel and Transport Buildings as a "monstrous spider waiting in a web of steel." Quoted in "The Century of Progress Emphasis on Innovation," in Blaser, *Chicago Architecture*, 89.

5. Murchison, "Hors de Concours," 64. For more information on the Travel and Transport Building, see chapter 4.

6. "Harvey Wiley Corbett Tells How Exposition Was Created," 26–27.

7. This may reflect an influence of Hitchcock and Johnson's International Style Show on Corbett, who, as mentioned earlier, had presented a talk at the related symposium shortly after the MoMA exhibit opened in February 1932. Riley, *The International Style*, 83.

8. "Harvey Wiley Corbett Tells How Exposition Was Created," 13.

9. Ibid.

10. Skidmore, "Notes on Design Section—Department of Works, December 1929 to June 1932," 3. The reason the organizers hired a director of works separate from the architectural commission was to eliminate some of the confusion and conflict of authority over the construction of buildings that had plagued nearly all past American expositions. The one major exception to this was the Columbian Exposition in 1893, where Daniel Burnham Sr. served as director of works in addition to overseeing the fair's architects. Minutes of the Fourth Meeting of the Architectural Commission, 6–7.

Daniel Burnham Jr. was president of the Chicago Regional Planning Association and director of the National Bank of the Republic in Chicago. He was also a member of the Chicago Planning Commission and served as a trustee for the Chicago Symphony Orchestra. Farrier was associated with Bennett, Parsons, and Frost. From 1923 to 1929 he had worked for the Chicago Planning Commission. Century of Progress International Exposition Publicity Department, "Burnham," press release, 11 March 1930, CofP, UIC.

11. According to Nathaniel Owings, Skidmore received the position by separately

convincing Raymond Hood and Paul Cret to hire him. Skidmore had won the prized Rotch Traveling Fellowship, but at the time he still lacked practical experience. Owings, *The Space In Between*, 46.

Others hired to help oversee the construction work included F. H. McInerny as contract manager, Julius R. Hall as general superintendent of construction, E. T. Murchison as general superintendent of construction of roads, sewers, and water, and Colonel John Stewart as assistant to the director of works. The firm of Pearse, Greeley, and Hanson was employed to help design the water and sewer systems, and the firm of Sargent and Lundy served as consultants for electrical distribution. Lohr, *Fair Management*, 173.

12. In 1932 Skidmore changed titles to become the assistant director of exhibits in charge of design. The Exhibits Department quickly grew to approximately thirty employees, including designers, draftsmen, and supervisors. It functioned as the main contact point for exhibitors planning and installing their displays. After exhibitors signed space contracts, they received detailed drawings of their assigned areas. Even though exhibitors could choose their own designers, all plans had to be submitted to the Exhibits Department to be reviewed personally by Skidmore. Four department supervisors handled all problems regarding the construction and installation of displays; others in the office took care of issuing building and utility permits. Lohr, *Fair Management*, 114; Chicago World's Fair Centennial Celebration of 1933, Architectural Commission, "Design Section," report, CofP, UIC.

13. Skidmore, "Notes on Design Section—Department of Works, December 1929 to June 1932," 12. The Works Department designed exhibits for the Westinghouse Electric Company, the Federal Electric Company, Merck and Company, Texaco, the Safety Glass Company, the Kerr Glass Company, and the National Sugar Refining Company, among others. Chicago World's Fair Centennial Celebration of 1933, Architectural Commission, "Design Section," report, CofP, UIC.

14. Lohr, *Fair Management*, 114.

15. Haskell, "Frank L. Wright and the Chicago Fair," 605.

16. Daniel Burnham Jr. had attended most of these events. Notes, diaries, and photographs from his visits are located in the Daniel H. Burnham Jr. Collection at the Ryerson and Burnham Library, The Art Institute of Chicago.

17. John Holabird, one of the architects of the Administration Building, incorporated a similar undulating facade in his Research and Engineering Building design for the A. O. Smith Corporation in Milwaukee, Wisconsin, at approximately the same time the exposition building was under construction. "Research and Engineering Building of the A. O. Smith Corporation, Milwaukee, Wis.," 533.

18. In addition to experiencing foreign fair buildings firsthand, the exposition architects became aware of European pavilion designs through articles in American and foreign architectural journals. A contemporary issue of *Architectural Record*, for example, contained an extensive, well-illustrated article on the 1925 event, including a full-page illustration of the Pavillon de la Maîtrise. Paris, "The International Exposition of Modern Industrial and Decorative Art in Paris."

19. The patterned, perforated openings in the facade of the Hall of Science also paid homage to *art décoratifs* designs. The zigzag surfaces of the end walls of the building's inner hall, however, had a closer precedent in the Dutch Pavilion designed by Hendricus Theodorus Wijdveld for the Exposition Internationale, Coloniale, Maritime, et d'Art Flamand held in Antwerp, Belgium, which contained interior walls of a similar decorative design.

20. Below the herm figures, designed by Alvin Meyer, a zodiac wheel symbolized science, while wheels and gears represented industry. *Official Guide Book of the Fair, 1933,* 25.

21. Gaston LaChaise (1882–1935) was born in Paris. He studied at the École des Beaux-Arts in Paris before arriving in the United States in 1906. In addition to creating decorative sculpture for buildings, he also produced many portraits. Ricker, *Sculpture,* 18.

22. Ulric Ellerhusen (1879–1957) was born in Warren, Germany, and had studied art at the Art Institute of Chicago under Lorado Taft. Ibid., 12.

23. Tesone, "Symbolism in Fair Sculpture," 33.

24. Lee Lawrie (1877–1963) was born in Germany and schooled in Chicago and Baltimore. He worked in the studios of Augustus Saint-Gaudens and Philip Martiny and taught art at both Harvard and Yale universities. Lawrie's commissions include work on the Bok Tower in Lake Wales, Florida, and the main entrance to the RCA Building in New York City, which also incorporated figures of light and sound. Ricker, *Sculpture,* 16.

25. Ironically, supporters of both communism and fascism were also employing variations of classical vocabularies in their architecture, sculpture, and murals.

26. "The Hall of Science, A Century of Progress," 294.

27. The term *ducks* was first applied to these types of buildings by Robert Venturi and other postmodernists in the early 1960s.

28. In October 1932 Benito Mussolini personally approved funds to construct the building to house "only those matters relating to the Italian government, including tourism and general progress made during the present regime." "Italy," memo chronicling contact with the Italian government regarding its participation in A Century of Progress, CofP, UIC.

29. For more information on the Italian Pavilion, see Doordan, "Exhibition Progress," 219–31.

30. Meikle, *Twentieth Century Limited,* 153.

31. For more information on Geddes's role in the rise of streamlining in the United States, see chapter 6.

32. Speedlines, along with bas-relief sculpture, wrapped around the lower parts of the walls. Bell Systems, Clark Tractor, Western Union, International Harvester, and General Electric were among the many other companies sponsoring exhibit booths that contained streamline characteristics.

33. Flask is in the author's Century of Progress collection.

34. The Union Pacific introduced the first streamlined train when the *M-10,000* (later renamed the *City of Salina*) rolled out of the Pullman Car and Manufacturing Company shops on 12 February 1934. Meikle, *Twentieth Century Limited,* 160.

35. Caption of photograph, "Hiram Walker's Café Canadian Club," 26. Geddes was strongly influenced by Erich Mendelsohn, who believed that architecture expresses the will and spirit of a nation and its era. For Mendelsohn, machines, and in particular transportation vehicles, offered ideal alternatives to historical forms as sources for modern designs. He symbolized the rise of fast modern vehicles in the horizontal streamlining and rounded external form common to many of his building designs. He also believed that these forms made it easier for passing motorists to "read" individual building designs as they sped by. Mendelsohn, "Dynamics and Function," 72; Meikle, *Twentieth Century Limited,* 36, 49.

36. The great interest among architects in using color as a decorative feature is reflected in contemporary architectural publications. In an *Architectural Record* article, Leon Solon asserted, "There seems no doubt that polychromy will prove the logical solution of the decorative problem, and the uncompromising premises which must necessarily control the manner of its application will produce a technique without precedent." Solon, "Modernism in Architecture Illustrated with a Design by J. Beckening Vinckers for a Polytechnic School," 200.

37. Using color and lighting to decorate the buildings was first discussed shortly after the start of the planning process. Chicago architect and critic Alfred Granger suggested in January 1928 that "splendid color and Romanesque architecture" would be most appropriate for the lakeside site. Former prairie school architect Barry Byrne wrote to the World's Fair Commission that steel exposition buildings could be painted with aluminum paint of silver or gold and decorated with highlights in vermilion, ultramarine, emerald green, and black. Fogle, "Urge Rich Color at World's Fair," 6; Barry Byrne to Joseph Breen, 14 July 1928, CofP, UIC.

38. "Century of Progress Exposition," *Painters Magazine and Paint and Wall Paper Dealer*, 8.

39. "Urban's Use of Color Object Lesson to Industry," 13.

40. Urban had arrived in America in 1911 from Vienna bringing with him the ideas of the Wiener Werkstätte. In addition to his theater designs, he produced numerous interiors for nightclubs, hotel lounges, and private residences. Carter and Cole, *Joseph Urban: Architecture—Theater—Opera—Film*, cover jacket, 12.

41. Skidmore, "Planning and Planners," 32; Muschenheim, "The Color of the Exposition," 2.

42. The article went on to state that buildings painted from a "mass point of view" would have the same color on all four walls. In contrast, the anonymous writer pronounced that it was essential that buildings painted from a "volume point of view" have "some differentiation in color between the planes." "Century of Progress Exposition," *Painters Magazine and Paint and Wall Paper Dealer*, 8–9.

43. Kirsch, *The Weissenhofsiedlung*, 40–41.

44. "Urban's Use of Color Object Lesson to Industry." Earlier brightly colored plastics had tended to fade or discolor. For the development of color in plastics, see Meikle, *American Plastic*, 74–78.

45. "Color in Industry," 85–86, 88.

46. Miles, "A Color-Conscious Decade Ahead," 22.

47. *Color and Protection*, n.p.

48. Miles, "A Color-Conscious Decade Ahead," 22.

49. Fogle, "Urge Rich Color at World's Fair," 6.

50. "Color in Industry," 93.

51. "The Color Complex," 396–97. Several of the major skyscrapers that did incorporate prominent uses of color were designed by members of the fair's architectural commission. They included Raymond Hood's black-and-gold American Radiator Building (1924) and his greenish-blue McGraw-Hill Building (1931), both in New York, and the Burnham Brothers' green-and-gold Carbide and Carbon Building (1929) in Chicago.

52. Shepard Vogelgesang, "Lecture at Art Institute, Tuesday August 21, 1934," CofP, UIC.

53. "Color in Industry," 93.

54. Farrier, "Exposition Buildings Unique in Form and Structure," 282.

55. Urban incorporated over ninety colors throughout the whole design. Vogelgesang, "The New School for Social Research," 138, 143.

56. *Color and Protection;* Teegen, "Color Comes to the Fair," 19–20.

57. Teegen, "Color Comes to the Fair," 19–20.

58. Teegen, "Joseph Urban's Philosophy of Color," 271.

59. Muschenheim, "The Color of the Exposition," 3.

60. The percentages of the other colors were 20 percent, blue; 20 percent, orange; 15 percent, black; and the remaining 25 percent, shades of yellow, red, gray, and green. *Official Guide Book of the Fair, 1933,* 20.

61. "A Century of Progress," *Painters Magazine and Paint and Wall Paper Dealer,* 9.

62. Edward Bennett declared that "the wholesale use of red such as proposed in the Government area cannot I believe escape the criticism of association with ideas of government not acceptable in this country. . . . The proposed treatment in white and orange of the United States Government Building does not seem to me to be especially appropriate and I feel very strongly that the use of blue in both the Government and the States Buildings would be better, obviously cooler in appearance in summer and vastly more suitable." Edward Bennett to John Holabird, 26 March [1934], CofP, UIC.

63. Duffus, "The Fair: A World of Tomorrow," 2.

64. Vogelgesang, "Color Treatment of Exhibit Space," 371.

65. "Fair's Interior Decorations 95 Per Cent Completed."

66. Century of Progress Corporation, Publicity Office, "Buildings," press release, 18 May 1934, CofP, UIC.

67. Bennett, "A Color Palette for Your Mood," 44; "Painters Begin Task of Recoloring Fair Buildings."

68. Bennett, "A Color Palette for Your Mood," 44, 46.

69. The other percentages of color used at the 1934 fair were 14 percent, green; 11 percent, turquoise; 11 percent, purple-red; and the remaining 26 percent, "sprinkled through the new palette of eight colors." Ibid.

70. "A Century of Progress," *Architectural Forum,* 1.

71. Ibid.

72. "The Miracle of Light at the World's Fair," n.p.

73. Heyel, "A Century of Progress," 35.

74. "Permanent Impression of the Chicago Fair," 29.

75. Ryan, "Lighting 'A Century of Progress,'" 731.

76. Skidmore, "Planning and Planners," 32. Walter D'Arcy Ryan, director of General Electric's Illuminating Engineering Laboratory, had supervised the lighting of Niagara Falls in 1907 and had helped develop the innovative lighting designs for the Panama-Pacific Exposition in 1915.

77. McDowell, "Lighting Effects at Fair to Be Super-Spectacular."

78. Ryan, "Lighting 'A Century of Progress,'" 731.

79. Heyel, "A Century of Progress," 35.

80. Ryan, "Lighting the Exposition."

81. Ibid., 47.

82. Ibid.

83. Ryan, "Lighting 'A Century of Progress,'" 734.

84. Neon creates only red-orange gaseous lighting. Other colors were created by using different gases or by tinting the glass tubes. Borland, "Glass Pipe Magic," 24.

85. The first exhibition of a gaseous sign was at the Grand Palais in Paris in 1910.

In 1923 a Packard dealership in Los Angeles installed two signs using neon light. Rudi Stern, *Let There Be Neon*, passim.

86. Ryan, "Lighting the Exposition," 49. By contrast, only 5,000 feet of gaseous tube lighting had been at the 1931 exposition held in Paris. McDowell, "Neon Light as Seen at Fair Presages Architectural Use."

87. Ryan, "Lighting the Exposition," 49.

88. "A Story of Light and Color," n.p.

89. Borland, "Glass Pipe Magic," 24.

90. Ryan, "Lighting the Exposition," 49.

91. "A Story of Light and Color," n.p.

92. "A Century of Progress Exposition, Herald of a New Age," *Chicago Progress,* n.d., 15, CofP, UIC.

93. Ryan, "Lighting the Exposition," 50.

94. McConnell, "Lighting Heads the List of Special Facilities," 283.

95. Ryan, "Lighting the Exposition," 50.

96. "Aurora Borealis in the Westinghouse Century of Progress Exhibit," 17.

97. *The Magazine of Light* (General Electric), November 1933, 17.

98. C. M. Cutler, "New Lighting Features of the 1934 Century of Progress Exposition," paper presented to the Twenty-eighth Annual Meeting of the Illuminating Engineering Society, Baltimore, Maryland, 4 October 1934, 1, CofP, UIC.

99. Century of Progress International Exposition Publicity Department, untitled press release, 20 October [1934], CofP, UIC.

100. "Fair's Colorful Lighting Will Dazzle World," *Chicago Tribune,* circa Spring 1934, CofP, UIC.

101. Cutler, "New Lighting Features of the 1934 Century of Progress Exposition."

102. Century of Progress International Exposition Publicity Department, "Lighting 1934," press release, circa 1934.

103. This was nearly five times as much water as in the previous largest fountain in the world. Fair organizers boasted that this amount of water could service the current populations of Montana and Utah together. Ibid.

104. Ibid.

105. Cutler, "New Lighting Features of the 1934 Century of Progress Exposition."

106. Red lamps were 100 watts each; green, 150 watts; and blue, 200 watts. "Lighting 1934."

107. Westinghouse Technical Press Service, "'Daylight' Lighting for Ford Exhibit at Century of Progress," press release, circa 1934, CofP, UIC.

108. Century of Progress International Exposition Publicity Department, "Ultra-Violet," press release, n.d., CofP, UIC.

109. Century of Progress International Exposition Publicity Department, "Lighting 1934."

110. Century of Progress International Exposition Publicity Department, untitled press release, 20 October [1934].

111. McDowell, "Neon Light as Seen at Fair Presages Architectural Use."

FOUR: BUILDING INNOVATIONS AT THE EXPOSITION

1. Tomlan, "Building Modern America," 37–38.

2. "Contributions of Science and Technology to Building Design," 47.

3. Kocher and Frey, "New Materials and Improved Construction Methods," 282.

4. "Mass-Produced Houses in Review," 53.

5. Malony, "Tomorrow's Housing," 28. Even prior to the stock market crash, the housing market in the United States had been in a state of crisis. By the early 1930s, overproduction of large and expensive residences had flooded the market, and thus many new dwellings were left vacant. At the same time, at least half of the 30 million American households were living in substandard housing. Land values and labor costs alone made it impossible for the average builder to construct low-cost homes for even a minimal profit. The author of an article in *Collier's* saw mass-produced materials and prefabricated construction techniques as the only solution. Flynn, "Be It Ever So Prefabricated," 13; North, "Prefabricated Buildings Will Bring Lower Costs," 66.

6. Newman, "The Architect and New Materials," 404.

7. Kocher and Frey, "New Materials and Improved Construction Methods," 281.

8. Sherman, "New Materials and Methods in Country House Construction," 225–34.

9. Farrier and Thorud, "Design of the World's Fair Buildings," 386.

10. A preliminary drawing of the transportation pavilion, probably rendered by Hugh Ferriss (and which appears in the background of Figure 2.5), shows two massive round, domed halls connected to the main section of the building, representing wheels attached to an automobile frame or carriage. The second hall had been eliminated by the time working drawings were under way. The project's designers used a large circular hall for the railroad displays because "the natural habitat of the locomotive at rest is in a roundhouse." Farrier and Thorud, "Design of the World's Fair Buildings," 386.

11. Other domes built earlier in Europe were even larger. For example, the Great Market Hall at Leipzig had a diameter of 249 feet, and the Century Hall at Wrocław (formerly Breslau) spanned 213 feet at its diameter.

12. The first floor of the Railroad Hall continued out about fifty feet beyond the dome. Owings, "New Materials and Building Methods for Chicago Exposition," 288.

13. Lohr, *Fair Management*, 232; "Cable System to Support 200-Ft. Circular Roof," 74.

14. Concrete blocks, approximately thirty feet by twenty to thirty feet by up to eleven feet deep, provided the mass needed to withstand the tension from the roof. The columns were rigidly braced in four groups of three; each group worked together as a unit. The units were then tied together to form a cohesive structural network. Farrier and Thorud, "Design of the World's Fair Buildings," 392; S.L. Tesone, memo to C.W. Farrier and J. Stewart, 16 October 1933, 7, CofP, UIC; Lohr, *Fair Management*, 232; Owings, "New Materials and Building Methods for Chicago Exposition," 288, 40 advertising section; "Cable System to Support 200-Ft. Circular Roof," 74.

15. The design of the dome could withstand a dead load of fifteen pounds per square foot and a live load of twenty-five pounds with a horizontal wind pressure of twenty-five pounds. "Cable System to Support 200-Ft. Circular Roof," 74.

16. *Official Guide Book of the Fair, 1933*, 47.

17. Lohr, *Fair Management*, 232; *Official Guide Book of the Fair, 1933*, 47. Several adjustments in the structure contributed to that movement. For example, grouping the columns in threes ensured that not all were pulled directly inward when increased weight was applied to the roof. Instead, each middle tower moved directly toward the center while the two side towers traveled parallel with it. This allowed for a sag in the suspension cables that reduced the stress on the towers by providing more play in

the cables. Sliding radial expansion joints, placed around the dome, absorbed additional stress created by a reduction in the curve of the roof.

As each set of columns moved inward, the wall surface traveled with them. To avoid breaking glass, the walls that contained the four large sunburst windows were suspended on sliding bearings and had interlocking joints on the sides. Horizontal trusses at the top and bottom of these suspended walls took the wind stresses for each group of columns. Farrier and Thorud, "Design of the World's Fair Buildings," 390–91; Owings, "New Materials and Building Methods for Chicago Exposition," 40 advertising section.

18. L.H. Lohr, address to the Advertising Council of the Chicago Association of Commerce, 16 January 1930, UIC.

19. The first suspended roof on a permanent building in the United States was probably a shed-shaped roof for a corn granary in Albany, New York. The thirty-six-by-eighty-two-meter roof, constructed by J.K. Welding Company for the Cargill Grain Corporation, consisted of suspended strips of steel. Otto, *Das hängende Dach,* 23–24.

20. Farrier and Thorud, "Design of the World's Fair Buildings," 386.

21. Sears, *Roman Architecture,* 143–44.

22. The idea for using roofs suspended like tents at the exposition was introduced as early as the sixth meeting of the architectural commission. Minutes of the Sixth Meeting of the Architectural Commission, 6; Farrier and Thorud, "Design of the World's Fair Buildings," 386.

23. Otto, "Basic Concepts and Survey of Tensile Structures," 2:16.

24. Several early European designs were illustrated in the 1837 edition of Joseph-Mathieu Sganzin's *Cours de Construction,* an engineering text well known in the United States. "Large Roofs Suspended by Cables to Avoid Columns," 688–89; Kadlcák, *Statics of Suspension Cable Roofs,* 3–5.

25. Banister, "Bogardus Revisited, Part II," 11; Condit, *American Building,* 208. Architect Leopold Eidlitz proposed a second design for the 1853 New York Exposition that also included a suspended roof. Kihlstedt, "Formal and Structural Innovations in American Exposition Architecture," 211.

26. "The Architects of New York's World's Fair, 1939 Will Have a City Owned 1,003 Acre Site, a 40 Million Dollar Budget, and Attitude Aplenty," 33. According to architectural historian Turpin C. Banister, the building would have filled Reservoir Square (now Bryant Park) between Fortieth and Forty-second streets. Banister, "Bogardus Revisited, Part II," 11.

27. The entire structure was to have been constructed out of a multiple of three or four parts, "any one [of which] could afterwards be used for constructing an auditorium." "The Architects' of New York's World's Fair, 1939 Will Have a City Owned 1,003 Acre Site, a 40 Million Dollar Budget, and Attitude Aplenty," 33.

28. Harris, "Building an Illusion," 48.

29. "Some Contrasts with 1893," 295.

30. The house was exhibited as part of the store's advertising display for modern furniture from the 1925 Paris Exposition Internationale des Arts Décoratifs et Industriels Modernes. Horrigan, "The Home of Tomorrow, 1927–1945," 160n5; Fuller and Marks, *The Dymaxion World of Buckminster Fuller,* 21.

31. A model of the house was also exhibited at the Chicago Arts Club in 1930. Horrigan, "The Home of Tomorrow, 1927–1945," 141; Boyce, *Keck and Keck,* 44.

32. Drawings of the design for the hockey rink are in the collection of the Chicago

Historical Society Architectural Drawings Collection. Another unrealized design that incorporated a similar suspended system for its roof, Frank Lloyd Wright's massive tent scheme for the Chicago fair, is discussed in chapter 6.

33. In the spring of 1930, R. M. Hamilton, a Scotsman, put forward the first proposal for the construction of a gigantic suspension bridge for the fair. The actual Skyride was designed by Holton D. Robinson and David B. Steinman of New York, with the help of Joshua D'Esposito and I. F. Stern of Chicago. Other companies involved in the construction of the Skyride include the Great Lakes Dredge and Dock Company, which built the piers and anchorages; Inland Steel, which furnished the structural steel; and the Mississippi Valley Structural Steel Company, which fabricated and erected the steel. Grove, "Transporter Suspension Bridge to Thrill World's Fair Visitors," 172.

34. "Ford and A Century of Progress." This claim was a great exaggeration, as both the Chrysler and Empire State buildings in New York, built in 1929 and 1930, respectively, were over 1,000 feet tall.

The Skyride towers were served by the latest in "signal-control elevators" built by the Otis Elevator Company. Each tower included four elevators that could each hold up to thirty people. Two served the level of the cable cars while the other two continued upward to the observatories located at the top of each tower. In exhibits sponsored by Otis located in the observatories, the public could see the powerful lifting machinery and controlling devices for the elevators. "Towers," 91; Lohr, *Fair Management*, 173; Tesone, memo to Farrier and Stewart, 16 October 1933, 92.

35. Constructed by the Goodyear Zeppelin Company and furnished by the John A. Roebling and Sons Company, the rocket cars, which could hold thirty-six people each, were suspended from four one-and-a-half-inch-diameter cables. An automatic gripper engaged the car and moved it across the span at a rate of five miles per hour. Inside, car seats were arranged lengthwise so that passengers faced outward to enjoy bird's-eye views of the fairgrounds. Lohr, *Fair Management*, 173; *Official Guide Book of the World's Fair of 1934*, 24; Tesone, memo to Farrier and Stewart, 16 October 1933, 94; "Chicago's Sky-Ride," 41.

36. Tesone, memo to Farrier and Stewart, 16 October 1933, 92.

37. Lohr, *Fair Management*, 232–33. The Skyride became a symbol for A Century of Progress as the Eiffel Tower had in Paris in 1889 and the Ferris Wheel had for the World's Columbian Exposition in 1893.

38. Tesone, memo to Farrier and Stewart, 16 October 1933, 92.

39. *Official Guide Book of the World's Fair of 1934*, 24. Up to 3,000 fairgoers could travel on the Skyride in a single hour. An estimated 12 percent of all fairgoers went on the ride. Grove, "Transporter Suspension Bridge to Thrill World's Fair Visitors," 172; Lohr, *Fair Management*, 233.

40. The dairy was sponsored by the Brook Hill Farm of Genesee Depot, Wisconsin, in cooperation with Starline, Inc., of Harvard, Illinois. "Concrete Shell Roof Used on World's Fair Building," 775.

41. *Official Guide Book of the World's Fair of 1934*, 156.

42. The Continental Construction Company of Chicago built the pavilion. "Concrete Shell Roof Used on World's Fair Building," 775–76; Kalinka, "Design of Dome Structures," 163.

43. Century of Progress International Exposition Publicity Department, "Dairy," press release, CofP, UIC.

44. "Reinforced Concrete Shell Roof over Unobstructed Dairy Floor," 3.

45. Thus, the 1934 *Official Guidebook of the World's Fair* promoted the concrete building as "fire, vermin and rust proof." Century of Progress International Exposition Publicity Department, "Dairy"; *Official Guide Book of the World's Fair of 1934*, 156.

46. Century of Progress International Exposition Publicity Department, "Dairy."

47. "New Fair Buildings," 30.

48. The use of Haydite concrete also enhanced the insulation value of the roof. "Concrete Shell Roof Used on World's Fair Building," 776.

49. Ibid.; "New Fair Buildings," 30; Century of Progress International Exposition Publicity Department, "Dairy."

50. Not only did each barrel vault consist of a continuous longitudinal curve, but the vaults also curved upward along the length to allow for additional height across the center of the building. "Concrete Shell Roof Used on World's Fair Building," 775–76.

51. Dischinger first published a treatise on the mathematical formula for dome structures in 1928. Finsterwalder published the formula for barrel-vaulted forms in 1933. Billington, *Thin Shell Concrete Structures*, 173–74.

52. Joedicke, *A History of Modern Architecture*, 140. The first nonreinforced shell vault, according to architectural historian Carl Condit, was built in 1910 at the Bercy Railway Station in suburban Paris. Better known were the well-publicized airship hangars at Orly, designed by Eugène Freyssinet in 1924, which incorporated two rows of parabolic arches. Condit, *American Building*, 276–77.

53. Eugene W. Stern, "Spiderweb Concrete in Europe," 114.

54. Elliott, *Technics and Architecture*, 196.

55. The Frankfurt dome rose only eleven feet from an octagonal frame supported by eight columns. Stern, "Spiderweb Concrete in Europe," 114; "Shell Concrete for Spanning Large Areas," 91.

56. Stern, "Spiderweb Concrete in Europe," 115.

57. The Leipzig Market Hall domes were formed by four elliptical shells three and nine-sixteenths inches thick. Radial ribs on the exterior of the dome stiffened the roof to prevent transverse bending. Cowan, *Science and Building*, 152; "Thin Concrete Shells for Domes and Barrel-Vault Roofs," 538.

58. By way of comparison, the dome of the Roman Pantheon is approximately 143 feet in diameter, and the domes of both the Florence Cathedral and St. Peter's at the Vatican are around 137 feet in diameter.

59. Anton Tedesko (1903–94) developed an interest in construction engineering while studying at the Institute of Technology in Vienna, where he graduated in 1926. The following year he traveled to the United States and worked briefly for the Mississippi Valley Structural Steel Company in Illinois. After returning to Europe for further schooling, Tedesko received an engineering degree in 1930 from the Technischen Hochschule of Berlin. Upon graduation, he began working for Dyckerhoff-Widmann. Boeckl, *Visionäre und Vertriebene*, 345; Pace, "Anton Tedesko, 90, an Expert in Uses of Reinforced Concrete"; Billington, *Thin Shell Concrete Structures*, 15; "Development of Shell Construction," 107.

60. In these positions, he continued to advocate the use of thin shells, a campaign that he carried on throughout his long career. Tedesko, "Low-Cost Repairs Restore Concrete Hanger to Design Strength," 9; "Special Facilities for Painting Air Force Planes Provided in Long Span Prestressed-Concrete Hanger," 7.

61. The Hayden Planetarium was still in the planning stage in June 1934 but was completed about a year later. "Illustrated News," 468; Pape, "Thin Concrete Shell Dome for New York Planetarium," 105.

62. Earlier innovations in foundation designs in Chicago included the first use of isolated footings in the Bordon Block (1880); the first isolated footing in pyramidal form in the Montauk Block (1882); the first use of wood piles for a building other than a grain elevator in the Hiram Sibley and Company Warehouse (1883); and the first use of "Chicago" caissons, or cylindrical concrete piers, in the west party wall of the Chicago Stock Exchange, which adjoined the Herald Building (1894). By the time of the second Chicago World's Fair, the use of caissons was widespread in the city because of the comparatively low load-carrying capacity of the upper soil level along the lakefront. Randall, *The Development of Chicago Building Construction*, 18–19.

63. Articles include "New Materials and Building Methods," by Nathaniel A. Owings in the April 1932 issue of *Architectural Record*, and "Engineering Research and Building Construction," by Bert Thorud in the July 1933 issues of *Architectural Forum*.

64. "How Chicago Went Fishing and Landed the Fair Grounds," 7.

65. Ibid.; Skidmore, "The Hall of Science, A Century of Progress Exposition," 362.

66. Farrier, "Exposition Buildings Unique in Form and Structure," 280.

67. Ibid.

68. Ibid.

69. Skidmore, "The Hall of Science, A Century of Progress Exposition," 362.

70. Thorud, "Engineering Research and Building Construction," 66.

71. Ibid.; Farrier, "Exposition Buildings Unique in Form and Structure," 280, 282.

72. Sherman, "New Materials and Methods in Country House Construction," 226.

73. Tomlan, "Building Modern America," 37–38.

74. Regardless of the major focus of the individual model residences, each suggested ways construction costs could be reduced while providing better and more efficient designs. Together, the dwellings made up the first major modern housing exhibition with full-scale models geared specifically for American homeowners. While earlier European exhibits, including the Weissenhofsiedlung in Stuttgart and the Werkbundsiedlung, held outside Vienna in 1932, served as models for the Home and Industrial Arts Exhibit, the fair's demonstration houses presented distinctively American designs that exhibited much greater variety in forms. The inclusion of houses by builders and building manufacturers, in addition to architects, contributed to this pluralistic vision.

75. Century of Progress International Exposition Publicity Department, "Houses," press release, [1934], CofP, UIC.

76. "New Age—New Materials—New Architecture," 7.

77. G. E. Swenson to Daniel H. Burnham, 11 June 1931, CofP, UIC.

78. Thorud, "Engineering Research and Building Construction," 68.

79. A major advantage of steel framing is its lack of structural defects, such as those, like cross-grain shrinkage, found in wood. Another benefit is that steel framing can be fabricated with rigid, standardized openings for the attachment of walls and other building elements. Sherman, "New Materials and Methods in Country House Construction," 229; Burchard, "The Role of Materials in Modern Housing," 345.

80. The Administration Building, however, was the only major pavilion intended

to remain standing after the close of the event. The decision to construct the building in the first place was made when fair organizers realized that it would cost less to build their own offices at the exposition's site than to rent space nearby. Construction took place from May to November 1930. Bruegmann, *Holabird and Roche, Holabird and Root*, 147.

81. "A Century of Progress Exposition," *Construction*, 259. The Johns-Manville Company, producers of Transite, placed a 28,000-pound rock of asbestos in front of its own corporate pavilion. Exhibits demonstrating the use of asbestos in home remodeling were located inside the building. "Asbestos Carries Appeal to Visitors to Fair Show"; *Official Guide Book of the World's Fair of 1934*, 134–35.

82. The Maizewood panels were half an inch thick. Benefits of the material included fire-resistance and its strong bonding strength with plaster. The manufacturer produced Maizewood by weaving the fibers of cornstalk into large continuous boards that could be cut with a saw to specified size. Farrier, "Exposition Buildings Unique in Form and Structure," 279; "The Forum of Events: Products and Practices," 40.

83. "The Administration Building—A Century of Progress Exposition," 213, 215.

84. *Official Guide Book of the Fair, 1933*, 25. A mural on the wall of the Trustees' Dining Room depicting industry, designed by Davis Leavitt, was constructed of the recently developed Flexwood veneer in different types of wood, including Australian lacewood, American walnut, primavera, oak, sugar maple, teakwood, holly, birch, mahogany, ayous, and ebony. *Chicago and the World's Fair, 1933*, 78.

85. Swenson to Burnham, 11 June 1931.

86. Thorud, "Engineering Research and Building Construction," 67.

87. Gypsum board was also used on the Electrical Building, the Communications Building, the Agriculture Building, the Dairy Building, the U.S. Government Building and Court of States, and the Maya Temple. Willoughby, "Buildings Tell the Story of Progress," 24.

88. Owings, "New Materials and Building Methods for Chicago Exposition," 286.

89. Konrad and Tomlan, "Gypsum Board," 269–70.

90. "Extract from Specifications for the General Contract for the General Exhibits Group," CofP, UIC.

91. Similar interplays of planes and surfaces could be found on a number of designs by European modernists in these years, including the Tourist Pavilion by Robert Mallet-Steves for the 1925 Paris exposition.

92. "Extract from Specifications for the General Contract for the General Exhibits Group."

93. Interior floor surfaces in the General Exhibits Building included wood, Masonite, magnesite, and composition tile. Terraces, meanwhile, were floored with various types of asphalt composition plank. Thorud, "Engineering Research and Building Construction," 68–69.

94. Owings, "New Materials and Building Methods for Chicago Exposition," 286.

95. The process of sandwiching thin pieces of wood together had been carried out as far back as ancient Egypt. Wood, *Plywoods*, 1.

96. Jester, "Plywood," 132.

97. Wood, *Plywoods*, 5–6.

98. While plywood made with casein and blood-albumin glues was considered water resistant, the adhesives did not stand up well when immersed in water, and over time

the panels had a tendency to rot. Phenol resins provided a much better alternative. By 1933 they were being used for boat hulls and for the pontoons of seaplanes, as well as to bond wood to insulation materials, such as in the Transite used on the Administration Building. "Technical News and Research, New Products," 295; Lowenthal, "Trends in the Development of Building Materials," 81; Burchard, "The Role of Materials in Modern Housing," 341–42, 344; Sherman, "New Materials and Methods in Country House Construction," 229; Jester, "Plywood," 132.

99. "Contributions of Science and Technology to Building Design," 47.

100. Asbestos-cement board needed half-inch spaces between joints to allow for expansion and contraction. The material was also brittle, relatively heavy, and difficult to paint. Owings, "New Materials and Building Methods for Chicago Exposition," 285–86.

101. Skidmore, "The Hall of Science, A Century of Progress Exposition," 363. To prepare the plywood surfaces for painting, the boards were first primed with hot linseed oil at the mill. Owings, "New Materials and Building Methods for Chicago Exposition," 286.

102. Other benefits of plywood included that the material was slow burning, could serve as a subflooring for exhibit space, permitted greater latitude of finishes for exhibitors, and had greater insulation value than the metal decking. Workmen constructed the floors of the Hall of Science of three-by-eight-foot panels of five-ply five-eighths-inch plywood. The panels were connected with tongue-and-groove joints bonded with water-resistant glues. Owings, "New Materials and Building Methods for Chicago Exposition," 283.

103. "Large Panel Units Outstanding Advance at the Fair," *American Builder*, 26.

104. *Official Guide Book of the Fair, 1933*, 25.

105. "Facts and Figures Relative to the Production of Masonite Products," article in the Masonite Corporation Archives, West Chicago, Illinois; *Masonite Corporation*, 4–5.

106. "Technical News and Research, New Products," 296. Presdwood was a hard flooring material with a built-in core of the less-dense Quartrboard, which made the surfaces more resilient and quieter. The Masonite Corporation had previously demonstrated the potential use of its products for temporary structures with the construction of a cylindrical Presdwood newspaper stand at the international exposition in Stockholm, Sweden, in 1930. A photograph of this stand is in the Masonite Corporation Archives.

107. "The Modern Houses of the Century of Progress Exposition," 56.

108. *Masonite Presents This Interesting Home*, pamphlet 5(31), Cererar Collection, UofC.

109. "The Modern Houses of the Century of Progress Exposition," 56.

110. McDowell, "Masonite Inventor to Start Work on First Unit of Fair Home Group"; Raley, *A Century of Progress Homes and Furnishings*, 91–92.

111. "The Modern Houses of the Century of Progress Exposition," 56.

112. Masonite Corporation, *Masonite: A Souvenir of the 1934 World's Fair*, 1934, brochure in collection of author.

113. A.N. Consior to Dowse Sash and Door Co., 16 February 1934, CofP, UIC; Louis Skidmore to Masonite Corporation, 27 February 1935, CofP, UIC.

114. Skidmore to Masonite Corporation, 27 February 1935.

115. Malony, "Tomorrow's Housing," 28.

116. Editors of *Fortune, Housing America*, 123. The practice of rolling metal plates

dates to 1615, when lead sheets were rolled by hand. The invention of the continuous steel-rolling machine, with tremendous production capacity, allowed large enough quantities of steel sheets to be available for mass-produced items, such as prefabricated steel buildings. "Contributions of Science and Technology to Building Design," 45.

117. The material was also used on the curved walls of the Electrical Building and the Hall of Science. Owings, "New Materials and Building Methods for Chicago Exposition," 285.

118. The size of the panels made it easier to construct curving walls than it would have been with other available materials.

119. "The Travel and Transport Building," 501.

120. Farrier, "Exposition Buildings Unique in Form and Structure," 280.

121. Owings, "New Materials and Building Methods for Chicago Exposition," 285. The widespread belief among practitioners of modern architecture that presenting one material to look like another was both dishonest and inappropriate to proper building design grew out of the ideas of prominent eighteenth- and nineteenth-century architectural theorists, including Abbé Laugier, Augustus Welby Pugin, and John Ruskin.

122. For example, steel cost approximately twice as much as gypsum board. Ibid., 283.

123. "The Modern Houses of the Century of Progress Exposition," 52.

124. Chapple, "Opportunities for Contractors and Dealers," 23. Also known as vitreous enamel, porcelain enamel consists of a thin layer of glass fused to a metal surface. First incorporated in the design of jewelry and other art objects, porcelain enamel was beginning to be used for appliances and bathroom fixtures by the early 1930s. See Jester, "Porcelain Enamel," 255–57.

125. "Steel Houses," 330; Folsom, "Farewell to the Paint Can," 34.

126. "Steel Houses," 330.

127. "Homes and Housing Materials to Be Exhibited," 293.

128. *Official Guide Book of the Fair, 1933,* 68.

129. "The Modern Houses of the Century of Progress Exposition," 54; "The Old Homestead Goes Modern," 5.

130. *Stran-Steel House at A Century of Progress, Exhibited in Co-operation with Good Housekeeping,* pamphlet 7(36), Cererar Collection, UofC.

131. The Porcelain Enamel Manufacturing Company manufactured Pemco architectural porcelain enamel. The Republic Steel Company produced Toncan Iron (a rust-resistant brand). Larson, "New Housing Designs and Construction Systems," 14; *Stran-Steel House at A Century of Progress, Exhibited in Co-operation with Good Housekeeping.*

132. "The Modern Houses of the Century of Progress Exposition," 54–55; *Stran-Steel House at A Century of Progress, Exhibited in Co-operation with Good Housekeeping.*

133. Century of Progress International Exposition Publicity Department, untitled press release, 29 March [circa 1933], CofP, UIC.

134. Brown, "Chicago and Tomorrow's House?" 248; Larson, "New Housing Designs and Construction Systems," 24; "Rostone—a New Processed Stone," 28.

135. "Rostone—a New Processed Stone," 28. The Perma-Stone Company, which marketed itself as the "originator of moulded stone wall-facing," was founded in 1929 in Columbus, Ohio. McKee, "Simulated Masonry," 175.

136. McKee, "Simulated Masonry," 177.

137. "Rostone—a New Processed Stone," 28.

138. *Rostone—a Colorful Synthetic Stone of Entirely New Chemical Composition,* pamphlet, CofP, UIC.

139. McKee, "Simulated Masonry," 177.

140. Larson, "New Housing Designs and Construction Systems," 24.

141. Keck's model houses for the exposition are discussed in chapter 5.

142. "New Exhibits in Fair's Glass Block Building" [1934], CofP, UIC.

143. Neumann et al., "Glass Block," 196.

144. Ibid., "Glass Block," 194.

145. "Glass Block—New Building Material," 128.

146. "New Exhibits in Fair's Glass Block Building."

147. "Glass Block—New Building Material," 128.

148. Folsom, "The Eighth Wonder of the World," 34.

149. "Glass Block Building," 24; "Glass Houses," *Business Week,* 18.

150. "Glass Houses," *Architectural Forum,* 50.

151. Folsom, "The Eighth Wonder of the World," 34; "Glass Block—New Building Material," 128; "Glass Houses," *Architectural Forum,* 50.

152. Scheerbart wrote in *Glasarchitektur* that the use of glass in architecture would "completely transform mankind" and "help contribute to the rise of a modern culture." He promoted the use of double-glazed walls, glass block, wired glass, and glass towers in urban centers, where cars, motorboats, trains, and aircraft would also be crafted in colored glass. Bruno Taut realized some of Scheerbart's ideas in his Glass Pavilion at the 1914 Werkbund Exhibition in Cologne. The interior of the Glass Pavilion was like a giant kaleidoscope of color, and at night the exterior shone like a giant crystal jewel. The designers (and clients) were promoting the positive social qualities of using glass. To emphasize them, mottoes, like Colored Glass Destroys Hatred, were inscribed on the sides of the building. Scheerbart and Taut, *Glass Architecture—Alpine Architecture,* passim.

153. "Fiberglas: A Fabulous Infant," 20; Folsom, "The Eighth Wonder of the World," 34.

154. Neumann et al., "Glass Block," 197.

155. The John B. Pierce Foundation was founded by businessmen interested in adapting the concept of prefabrication and new technology to the construction of affordable housing. Meikle, *American Plastic,* 85.

156. "Vinylite," 8.

157. Henri Victor Regnault, a French chemist, first produced vinyl resin in 1838, while E. Bauman, a German chemist, developed its solid polymer, polyvinyl chloride (PVC or vinyl), in 1872. Irwin Ostromislensky went on to patent the first rubber-like vinyl products in 1912. DuBois, *Plastics History U.S.A.,* 280; Meikle, *American Plastic,* 83.

158. Meikle, *American Plastic,* 83; *Giants of the New Age,* pamphlet produced in 1933 by the Union Carbide and Carbon Corporation in connection with A Century of Progress, copy in collection of author.

159. *Giants of the New Age.*

160. Singer, *Plastics in Building,* 26–27.

161. About the only objects in the display not of vinyl were the plumbing fixtures, the gas range, the bathtub, and upholstered furniture and draperies. *Giants of the New Age;* "Vinylite," 8. For more information on the materials of the products in the Vinylite House, see Meikle, *American Plastic,* 84.

162. DuBois, *Plastics History U.S.A.*, 283.

163. Meikle, *American Plastic*, 83–84.

164. *Official Guide Book of the Fair, 1933*, 25.

165. Walker et al., "Decorative Plastic Laminates," 127.

166. DuBois, *Plastics History U.S.A.*, 375.

167. In 1912 Daniel J. O'Connor, a young Westinghouse engineer, covered a section of rolled phenol paper tubing with a Bakelite varnish and slit it in half. By heating the tube and then pressing it flat, he created Micarta, the first phenol laminated sheet. Ibid., 374–75; Walker, "Decorative Plastic Laminates," 127.

168. Burchard, "The Role of Materials in Modern Housing," 344.

169. Light-colored and wood-grained laminates were not available until the end of the 1930s, when John D. Cochrane Jr., a scientist at the Formica Corporation, developed a method that made their production possible. Walker, "Decorative Plastic Laminates," 127–28.

170. The company did sponsor the construction of an experimental house of the material in the late 1930s in Cincinnati. Ibid., 128–29.

171. Some of the earliest pavilions, which initially received coats of oil paint, faded as much as 75 percent. Teegen, "Painting the Exposition Buildings," 366–68.

172. Valdura was the only paint consultants found that provided the desired brilliance, intensity, and permanence, and it gave a matte finish adaptable to artificial illumination. Otto Teegen to Albert Kahn, 8 December 1932, CofP, UIC.

173. "'Fast' Colors for Buildings at Fair."

174. Teegen to Kahn, 8 December 1932.

175. Color stability tests of casein paint took place on the south facade of the Electrical Building, which received the winds off Lake Michigan and the harsh south sun during most of the day during late summer. After eight months only two shades of blue exhibited any noticeable reduction in intensity. Teegen, "Painting the Exposition Buildings," 366, 368.

176. Brown, "Chicago and Tomorrow's House?" 248.

177. "Celotex: Houses from Sugar Cane," 80.

178. Gould et al., "Fiberboard," 124.

179. "Contributions of Science and Technology to Building Design," 47; Larson, "New Housing Designs and Construction Systems," 29.

180. Lohr, *Fair Management*, 232–33.

181. "New Age—New Materials—New Architecture," 7.

182. "Steel Houses," 330.

183. Other companies that supplied parts included the American Radiator and Standard Plumbing Corporation (heating and plumbing), Thomas A. Edison, Inc. (concrete), the Container Corporation (insulation), the Curtis Corporation (windows, cabinets, and millwork), the General Electric Company (wiring and appliances), the Pittsburgh Plate Glass Company (glass and paint), and the Concrete Engineering Company (design of the concrete foundation). Jandl, *Yesterday's Houses of Tomorrow*, 162.

184. The first General Houses residence was built for Ruth Page, Fisher's sister-in-law, in 1929 in Winnetka, Illinois. Larson, "New Housing Designs and Construction Systems," 18.

185. "The Modern Houses of the Century of Progress Exposition," 52.

186. For those less scientifically inclined, Fisher also named the design the Elmhurst. Jandl, *Yesterday's Houses of Tomorrow*, 158. Fisher may have borrowed the idea

for a letter-number labeling system from the Architects' Small House Service Bureau, which had created a similar system a decade earlier to encode the sizes of its houses and where their designs originated. For more information on the Architects' Small House Service Bureau, see Schrenk, *Your Future Home.*

187. "A Product of General Houses," 70.

188. Brown, "Chicago and Tomorrow's House?" 248.

189. Editors of *Fortune, Housing America,* 123.

190. The flanges also served as narrow mullions on the window and door panels. "A Product of General Houses," 70.

191. Larson, "New Housing Designs and Construction Systems," 18.

192. Jandl, *Yesterday's Houses of Tomorrow,* 163.

193. Larson, "New Housing Designs and Construction Systems," 19.

194. Jandl, *Yesterday's Houses of Tomorrow,* 163.

195. With bolts and a socket wrench, the entire house, except for furnishings and interior equipment, was assembled on its foundation within 200 hours. Ibid., 164.

196. "Frameless Steel Houses," 337.

197. "Steel Barn," 9.

198. Ibid.

199. *The Country Home Model Farm House,* 2.

200. Ibid., 6.

201. Ibid., 7.

202. Louis Skidmore, untitled press release, 11 March 1932, 1, CofP, UIC.

203. Skidmore, "Expositions Always Influence Architecture," 80.

204. "A Century of Progress Exposition," *Construction,* 259.

205. Just prior to the opening of the fair, C. W. Farrier, then assistant director of maintenance and operation for A Century of Progress, wrote that the exposition could provide a solution to the housing shortage though the concept of short-term buildings. He believed that if houses could be erected so that costs could be amortized over only fifteen years, "the people of America would be better served than if it were necessary for some of them to accept substandard housing conditions." Farrier, "Exposition Buildings Unique in Form and Structure," 282.

206. Skidmore, untitled press release, 11 March 1932.

207. The other requirements were that the buildings be of sound construction, economical, and of good appearance. "Chicago Exposition Buildings Exemplify Sound Construction for Short Service," 20.

208. A Century of Progress International Exposition Publicity Department, "Architecture," press release, 21 March 1933, 2, CofP, UIC.

209. Larson, "New Housing Designs and Construction Systems," 18.

210. Quoted in Duffus, "The Fair: A World of Tomorrow," 3.

211. "New Age—New Materials—New Architecture," 7.

212. The two major exceptions were Fort Dearborn and the Administration Building. The demolition of buildings continued into 1936. Lohr, *Fair Management,* 262, 265–66.

213. Grey, "Bizarre Patterns for Chicago's Fair," 11.

214. Several sponsors of pavilions took advantage of this and relocated their buildings to other sites after the close of the fair. For more information on the relocation of fair pavilions, see the postscript. The dismantling of exposition buildings to be reassem-

bled elsewhere was not a new concept. The Crystal Palace was disassembled and then rebuilt in another location after the close of the 1851 Great Exposition in London.

215. Grey, "Bizarre Patterns for Chicago's Fair," 11.

216. Duffus, "The Fair: A World of Tomorrow," 3.

217. Willoughby, "Building Tells the Story of Progress," 24.

218. Ibid.

FIVE: EXPOSITION HOUSES OF TODAY AND TOMORROW

1. Approximately 1,636,000 visitors toured the Common Brick Manufacturers' House in 1933. Ibid., 27.

2. Boyce, *Keck and Keck*, 51.

3. Industrial designer Norman Bel Geddes introduced many of these potential characteristics of future housing to the general public in a 1931 *Ladies Home Journal* article. He wrote, "Synthetic materials will replace the products of Nature in buildings.... Every roof will be a garden.... Exterior walls will be of thinner materials to effect economy of space. Houses, in all climates, will have flat roofs. Every floor will have one or more terraces. . . . The garage will be part of the house and will be placed on the street front. Service quarters will be at the front of the house; living rooms at the back. All metal used in house construction will be so alloyed or treated as to render it noncorrosive. In small houses the dining room, as a separate chamber, will be eliminated. Houses, in the main, will tend to be smaller, but the fewer rooms they contain will be larger. . . . Windows, while admitting [ultra]violet rays, will not open. All dwellings will be ventilated by artificial means; washed air, heated or cooled according to season, will be delivered from a central plant. The home will become so mechanized that handwork will be reduced to a minimum. Mechanical devices, controlled by the photo-electric cell, will open doors, serve meals, and remove dirty dishes and clothes to the appropriate department of the building." Geddes, "Ten Years from Now," 3.

4. *Official Guide Book of the Fair, 1933*, 67–68.

5. *Official Guide Book of the World's Fair of 1934*, 133.

6. Kraft Miracle Whip salad dressing, a variation of mayonnaise made with a cooked base, was developed by National Dairy Products and introduced at A Century of Progress in 1933.

7. For more information on the House of Tomorrow, see Schrenk, "George Keck and His House of Tomorrow."

8. For additional information on Keck's architectural career, see Boyce, *Keck and Keck*, and Menocal, *Keck and Keck, Architects*.

9. William Keck, conversation with author, 16 March 1993.

10. "Building Speed to Be Feature of Glass House," *Chicago Tribune* [circa 1934], CofP, UIC.

11. Beardsley, "House of Future to Be a Feature at World's Fair."

12. "Building Speed to Be Feature of Glass House."

13. For more information on Keck's early exposure to the modern ideas of Sullivan, Wright, and other progressive midwestern architects, see Menocal, *Keck and Keck, Architects*.

14. In 1933 Keck wrote, "The chief concern of the architect was not to give a

specific form to his buildings, but rather to find a solution to the many and varied new requirements of a residence in a simple and direct manner. The causes were considered first, the effects later." *House of Tomorrow*, 1, copy in collection of author. (The author is grateful for the gift of this pamphlet from the late William Keck.)

15. Menocal, *Keck and Keck, Architects*, 15.

16. In his treatise Le Corbusier proclaims that designers should look to recent engineering feats, such as grain elevators, ocean liners, and motor vehicles, for inspiration in creating modern architecture—a concept greatly favored by Keck. Le Corbusier, *Towards a New Architecture*.

17. For example, an unrealized concrete house design that Keck, with Vale Faro, created in 1927 for S. P. Bradley of Watertown, Wisconsin, includes a simplification of building forms, an emphasis on surface planes, and open volumes similar to those of contemporary European designs.

18. One way Keck learned about Fuller's ideas was through other designers. Keck's employee Leland Atwood, who made significant contributions to the designs for both the House of Tomorrow and later the Crystal House, was a friend of Fuller's. Another potential tie was Robert Paul Schweikher, Atwood's employer prior to entering Keck's office, who, as a draftsman, had worked for Fuller on the design of the Dymaxion House. Jandl, *Yesterday's Houses of Tomorrow*, 84; *Sixty Years on the Arts Club Stage*, 8–9; Boyce, *Keck and Keck*, 47, 54–55n11.

19. Fuller and Marks, *The Dymaxion World of Buckminster Fuller*, 4.

20. "Application for Permit for Exhibition of Building Materials: The Housing Group, A Century of Progress," submitted 10 January 1933, CofP, UIC.

21. William Keck, "The Perspective of a Modern Architect in the 1930s," Frank Lloyd Wright Home and Studio Foundation Volunteer Retreat, 2 November 1991, copy, Research Center Archives, FLWBT, Oak Park, Illinois.

22. Keck, conversation with author, 16 March 1993.

23. *House of Tomorrow*, n.p.

24. Rainwater, collected in a basin on the Richards House's flat roof, flowed into a cistern in the basement, providing running water for a kitchen located there. A brick-enclosed furnace, which burned four-foot-long pieces of cordwood, heated the water. Additional heat traveled upward through ductwork, hollow walls, and a central stairwell providing radiant heat to the major rooms of the house. A small cabinet in one wall held a pitcher of warmed water for washing faces on cold days, while a pan of heated water raised the humidity level in the house during the dry winter months. During the summer the house was naturally ventilated by opening windows in the cupola and on the southwest side of the dwelling, which created a natural draft. Keck, "The Perspective of a Modern Architect in the 1930s."

25. *House of Tomorrow*, n.p. The Richards House was just one of over 1,000 octagonal houses to be built across the country in the mid-1850s after the publication of Orson S. Fowler's 1853 treatise *A Home for All, or The Gravel Wall and Octagon Mode of Building*, which promoted the construction of eight-sided houses. Fowler, *The Octagon House*, back cover.

26. While industry was able to produce some of these innovative materials by the early 1930s, it had not yet advanced far enough to be able to actually build a Dymaxion House. This fact became apparent when, according to Fuller in an unsubstantiated story, fair president Rufus Dawes asked how much it would cost to construct a full-

scale working model of the Dymaxion House at the Chicago exposition. Fuller's response of a hundred million dollars stunned Dawes. Included in this cost, however, was the expense of the research necessary to develop all the as-yet unrealizable elements in his design. Moreover, scientific developments during the previous five years, according to Fuller, had dropped this figure significantly from the billion dollars he had quoted in 1928. With the construction of a Dymaxion House at the exposition still a financial impossibility, the House of Tomorrow became the next closest thing to the realization of Fuller's design. Fuller and Marks, *The Dymaxion World of Buckminster Fuller*, 22–23.

27. It is unclear whether Keck intentionally avoided mention of Fuller in his *House of Tomorrow* pamphlet. The architectural press picked up on the similarity of the House of Tomorrow to the Dymaxion House. An article on the Home and Industrial Arts Exhibit in the July 1933 issue of *Architectural Forum*, for example, pointed out that Keck's design had a unique appearance similar only to the Dymaxion House by Fuller. *House of Tomorrow*, n.p.; "The Modern Houses of the Century of Progress Exposition," 61.

28. Duffy, "House of Glass Rising at the Fair."

29. "Now You Can Actually Live in a House of Glass," 20.

30. Keck, conversation with author, 16 March 1993.

31. During the exposition the garage housed a Pierce-Arrow Silver Arrow car, and the airplane hangar sheltered a facsimile of a Curtiss-Wright biplane owned by Charles Lindbergh. Keck, "The Perspective of a Modern Architect in the 1930s."

32. Many of the products included in Fuller's futuristic house were also significantly more advanced than what was currently available on the market. For example, no obtainable product came close to the transparent plastic vacuum plates that he specified for the walls. A product similar to Duralumin, a high-strength, heat-treated aluminum alloy, to be used for the nontransparent walls, the structural mast, and the sheltering hood on the roof of the house, only came onto the market four years after Fuller obtained the patent for his Dymaxion House design. Fuller and Marks, *The Dymaxion World of Buckminster Fuller*, 22.

33. Duffy, "House of Glass Rising at the Fair."

34. *House of Tomorrow*, n.p.

35. While a few office buildings were air-conditioned, cooled interiors were still an unknown luxury for most people prior to the fair. The presence of the air-conditioning system in the House of Tomorrow helped draw large crowds to the dwelling on hot summer days. Ibid; Banham, *The Architecture of a Well Tempered Environment*, 178.

36. According to William Keck, his brother first realized the tremendous potential of solar heat in glass buildings during the construction of the exposition house when he witnessed carpenters in their shirtsleeves working on the interior of the unheated residence on a cold early spring day. Keck, conversation with author, 16 March 1993.

37. *House of Tomorrow*, n.p. Keck continued to explore passive solar heating in his later residential designs, including the B. Lamar Johnson House (1938) and the Hugh Duncan House (1941). For more information on his later passive solar designs, see Boyce, *Keck and Keck*.

38. *House of Tomorrow*, n.p.

39. The dishwasher was an addition to the house in 1934. At the same time gas appliances replaced the electrical stove and refrigerator. Raley, *A Century of Progress Homes and Furnishings*, 71.

Fuller incorporated most of his futuristic gadgets in the food-preparation area, which was located in the utility room of the Dymaxion House design. Included was an automatic dish-washing machine that he claimed could not only wash and dry dishes, like Keck's, but also return them to their storage shelves. Fuller and Marks, *The Dymaxion World of Buckminster Fuller*, 91.

40. "The Modern Houses of the Century of Progress Exposition," 61.

41. Beardsley, "House of Future to Be a Feature at World's Fair."

42. Local firms then fabricated the furniture and light fixtures. *House of Tomorrow*, n.p.

43. Built-in furniture in the Dymaxion House design included a fifteen-foot-long pneumatic couch and an even longer hanging dining table in the main living areas. Other rooms contained built-in maps, tables, and a radio-television receiver. Even the circular wardrobes, which provided space for up to fifty dresses on rotating racks, were stationary. Fuller and Marks, *The Dymaxion World of Buckminster Fuller*, 89, 91.

44. *House of Tomorrow*, n.p. Mies van der Rohe's use of pure, unadorned slabs of glass, travertine, and green Tinian and golden onyx dorée marbles brought out the immense natural beauty of the materials. Functional, yet decorative, elements in the pavilion included thin, chrome-plated X-shaped columns; a black area rug; reflection pools; *Evening,* a bronze figure of a woman; and a pair of Mies van der Rohe's Barcelona chairs.

45. *House of Tomorrow*, n.p.

46. Unity was also created through the always-present curtains and glass walls, as well as through the use of color.

47. Jandl, *Yesterday's Houses of Tomorrow,* 136.

48. Raley, *A Century of Progress Homes and Furnishings,* 27.

49. "More Than a Million Have Already Visited the Super-Safe Home," 6–7; *Official Guide Book of the World's Fair of 1934,* 129.

50. Rebori may have been influenced by Fuller's Dymaxion design when he chose to use a hexagonal plan. Another major difference between the two designs was the fact that Rebori limited his main living space to one level, whereas the Citrohan House featured a two-story living room.

51. MacDonald, "You Like Glass Houses? Go to Fair."

52. For more information on the 1920s houses of Le Corbusier, see *Le Corbusier Œuvre Complète,* as well as Curtis, *Le Corbusier,* and Gans, *The Le Corbusier Guide.*

53. *Glass as an Architectural Medium in 9 Small Modern Houses at A Century of Progress 1933–4,* n.p.

54. "The Century of Progress Has Its Own Design for Living," 16.

55. Ibid.

56. *Glass as an Architectural Medium in 9 Small Modern Houses at A Century of Progress 1933–4,* n.p.

57. One of the bedrooms featured salmon and gray in the curtains and rugs. Wallpaper in a tartan design of the same colors covered the walls. The other bedroom combined gray with blue and white, with violet-blue and grey wallpaper and a deep blue ceiling balanced by a deep blue rug on the floor. Wool fabrics in gray and white were used for the curtains and in violet-blue and gray for the bedspread. "The Century of Progress Has Its Own Design for Living," 16.

58. Ibid., 60.

59. *Official Guide Book of the Fair, 1933,* 72.

60. "On View at the Century of Progress," 53.

61. The angled walls to each side of the mirror were decorated with panels of black and green onyx paper. Images of lyres filled the center panels. *Glass as an Architectural Medium in 9 Small Modern Houses at A Century of Progress 1933–4*, n.p.

62. *Sloan's House of Today.*

63. Raley, *A Century of Progress Homes and Furnishings*, 13.

64. Ibid.

65. Lohr, *Fair Management*, 132.

66. "Building Speed to Be Feature of Glass House."

67. Raley, *A Century of Progress Homes and Furnishings*, 35.

68. "This Year's Glass House," 6. Work slated for week one included pouring the concrete base and footings for the steel columns and installing pipes for water, gas, and sewer. Week two involved constructing the exterior, including the assembly of the walls and roof. Week three included applying the interior finishes. Century of Progress International Exposition Publicity Department, "Glass House," press release, 5 May 1934, CofP, UIC; "Glass and Steel . . ."

69. The individual floor elements consisted of one-eighth-inch-thick metal plates separated by five-inch channels that were welded to the sides with stiffening bars at three-foot intervals. This type of sandwich construction provided space between floor levels for the mechanical equipment, including the air-conditioning and a gas-fired heating system. Century of Progress International Exposition Publicity Department, "Model Home Group," press release, [1934], CofP, UIC; Slade, "'The Crystal House' of 1934," 351.

70. While Keck selected glass for the walls of the house, he stated, "Any other suitable material could be used, if such were available. For instance, if a new substance with the qualities of glass, but either opaque or semi-opaque, is developed, it might be substituted for portions of the outer wall." Quoted in "This Year's Glass House," 6.

71. Raley, *A Century of Progress Homes and Furnishings*, 35.

72. Century of Progress International Exposition Publicity Department, "Model Home Group."

73. Boyce, *Keck and Keck*, 50.

74. Atwood, "The Crystal House," 36.

75. Slade, "'The Crystal House' of 1934," 352.

76. Atwood, "The Crystal House," 36.

77. Bargelt, "Glass and Steel House of Future Erected at Fair"; Century of Progress International Exposition Publicity Department, "Glass House."

78. Furnishings designed by both Keck and Atwood were fabricated by the Chicago Workshops. Marianne Willish, an associate of the workshops, selected and coordinated the decorative schemes for each room. Slade, "'The Crystal House' of 1934," 352.

79. Atwood, "The Crystal House," 36.

80. Slade, "'The Crystal House' of 1934," 352.

81. Fuller's Dymaxion Car was also featured as the last episode in the Century of Progress's elaborate transportation show, *Wings of a Century*. Fuller and Marks, *The Dymaxion World of Buckminster Fuller*, 112.

82. The lack of income from admission fees resulted in a financial disaster for Keck and others who had invested in the construction of the Crystal House. Boyce, *Keck and Keck*, 52.

83. The reason for the remote location of the Crystal House is not entirely clear.

Keck's application to build the glass-and-steel dwelling on a site along Leif Erikson Drive near the House of Tomorrow was turned down at least three times in the late winter of 1934. Fair organizers stated on the rejected application that they felt the architect would not be able to keep the large area properly landscaped and that a dwelling better for the site could be found. Ironically, investors of the House of Tomorrow (Keck had sold his interest in the house after the 1933 season) may also have objected to having a new, competing futuristic house that also charged an entrance fee located so close by. Keck finally received approval to construct the Crystal House at the less desirable Northerly Island site on 10 April, less than seven weeks before the start of the exposition's 1934 season. "Summary of Proposal—Application for a Concession," 3 February 1934, CofP, UIC; Robert Boyce, *Keck and Keck*, 47; Keck, conversation with author, 16 March 1993.

84. It was mentioned in articles in *Architectural Forum, Pencil Points, Welding Engineer, Celotex News, Christian Science Monitor, Chicago Tribune,* and *Chicago Daily News.*

85. Atwood, "The Crystal House," 37.

86. Ibid., 36.

87. *The Frigidaire Air Conditioned House, A Century of Progress, Chicago, 1934.*

88. Ibid.

89. Ibid.

90. Ibid.

91. *The Country Home Model Farm House,* 11.

92. The versatility of soybeans was demonstrated at A Century of Progress in 1934 in exhibits sponsored by the Ford Motor Company, including a small plot of soybeans and a soybean-processing machine. At the time Henry Ford was deeply involved in the development of a wide range of soybean products for potential use in the automobile industry. Ibid., 9.

93. Ibid., 2.

94. *The Honor Bilt Home at A Century of Progress,* n.p.

95. Ibid.

96. Both builders and bankers favored the construction of colonial residential designs. The Architects' Small House Service Bureau, the only plan service to be endorsed by the American Institute of Architects, tried to adhere to traditional revival styles for their small-home designs in the 1920s and 1930s. They proclaimed that using an authentic style, meaning Spanish, Dutch, or New England Colonial or English Tudor, added between 10 and 20 percent to the resale value of a house. The majority of their plans were colonial, a style that they promoted as a model of "good taste, logic and strength." Schrenk, *Your Future Home,* xi.

97. The repeal of Prohibition between the two fair seasons led Schamberg to replace the ground-floor workroom with a cocktail room, which she promoted as a "necessary adjunct to the well equipped home." Schamberg, "The House of Tomorrow, Interiors," 73.

98. Visitors found the model houses both intriguing and bemusing. A collection of reactions to the architecture of the exposition was published in "The Lay Critics Speak," 28.

99. Keck, conversation with author, 16 March 1993.

100. An article published in *Architectural Record* in 1937 reported that because

of Americans' increased mobility, the measurement of the mortgage risk on a specific house had shifted away from the borrower's ability to repay the loan and toward the perceived physical security of the residence itself. As a result, bankers became increasingly concerned about the resale potential of houses. The desirability of the dwelling, not only to the initial homeowner but also to the population at large, became a major factor in banks' willingness to approve home loans. Vermilya, "Houses of Modern Design Do Receive Mortgage Loans," 62.

SIX: UNBUILT VISIONS FOR A MODERN EXPOSITION

1. High tariffs, which made selling foreign products in the United States difficult, was another factor that had a negative impact on foreign participation. Most nations concluded that it was only practical to promote traditional handicrafts and luxury goods to the American market because of prohibitive import duties. Lohr, *Fair Management*, 154.

2. Countries that had initially planned to exhibit at A Century of Progress but later declined to participate included Argentina, Colombia, Cuba, France, Great Britain, Hungary, Lithuania, the Netherlands, Norway, Persia, Poland, Romania, Turkey, and Yugoslavia. Poland, and connected Polish American organizations, withdrew from the fair after construction on its national pavilion had already begun. The building was later used as the German-American Restaurant. India also considered participating, and a preliminary design for an Indian pavilion by architect John Donald Tuttle was published in the *Chicago American* in 1932. At least four nations went on to exhibit in the Travel and Transport Building: Brazil, Canada, Luxembourg, and the Irish Free State. Denmark exhibited in the Hall of Science, and Costa Rica sponsored exhibits in the Agriculture Building. Lohr, *Fair Management*, 155–56; "India Contribution to the Fair."

3. The French government scaled down its initial design for a large national pavilion before completely abandoning plans to construct a building in March 1933 because of "a continuing financial crisis." Duffy, "France Out as World Fair Exhibitor"; "France," memo chronicling contact with the French government regarding France's participation in A Century of Progress, CofP, UIC.

4. At the time of the exposition's opening Wright was sixty-five years old, an age when many workers consider retirement. Several years earlier, Henry-Russell Hitchcock had proclaimed Wright to be the "greatest architect and perhaps the greatest American of the early twentieth century." Wright refuted Hitchcock's comment, stating that not only did he intend to be the "greatest architect who has yet lived—but the greatest American who will ever live." In 1928 Fiske Kimball placed Wright in a chapter titled "Counter-Currents" in his book *American Architecture*, to which Wright, rarely without a comeback, responded, "I am heartily sick of the historical falsifying of the real course of ideas in the Architecture of our Country. . . . I am still smarting from Fiske Kimball's well-meant obituary." Even noted architectural critic Lewis Mumford, who was one of Wright's staunchest supporters, discussed the architect in the past tense in his prominent book *The Brown Decades*, originally published in 1931. Hitchcock, *Frank Lloyd Wright*; Kimball, *American Architecture*, 192–200, quoted in Johnson, *Frank Lloyd Wright versus America*, 33–34; Mumford, *The Brown Decades*, 79.

Other avenues through which Wright promoted his ideas during this period include his Kahn Lectures at Princeton University; an exhibit at the Architectural League headquarters in New York; his autobiography, *An Autobiography*; his new school, the Taliesin Fellowship; and his utopian vision, Broadacre City.

5. Architectural critic Douglas Haskell, a journalist by profession, served as the secretary of the American Union of Decorative Artists and Craftsmen (AUDAC) and was the associate editor of *Architectural Record* from 1929 to 1930 and the architectural critic for the *Nation* from 1930 to 1942. Lewis Mumford, a prolific writer, was the architectural critic for the *New Yorker* from 1931 to 1963 and authored its "Skyline" column. Henry Churchill was a progressive New York architect who had designed the Lowell Apartment Hotel, in association with Herbert Lippmann, and a shop for bookseller and art dealer E. Weyhe.

6. Darwin D. Martin to Frank Lloyd Wright, 8 October 1930, TAL.

7. Haskell, "Frank L. Wright and the Chicago Fair," 605.

8. Wright, *An Autobiography*, 352.

9. Raymond Hood to Frank Lloyd Wright, 16 February 1931, TAL.

10. The only documented friction among the members of the commission during the planning process for the fair was reflected in a letter from Cret to Corbett. Cret complained that Corbett's design for the General Exhibits Building ignored decisions made earlier that affected Cret's Hall of Science. Paul Philippe Cret to Harvey Wiley Corbett, 10 October 1931, CofP, UIC.

11. John Lloyd Wright to Harvey W. Corbett, no date, TAL.

12. John Lloyd Wright to Frank Lloyd Wright, 18 May 1931, TAL.

13. Frank Lloyd Wright to Rudolph Schindler, 8 January 1931, TAL.

14. "Wright Plans Rival Display for World's Fair."

15. "Wright Rival Fair."

16. Two letters from Wright to Harry Beardsley at the *Chicago Daily News*, located in the Taliesin Archives, discussed the fact that the architect had no intention of constructing a competing building near the fairgrounds. Both letters, however, have the words "not sent" scrawled across them. Frank Lloyd Wright to Mr. Harry Beardsley, 23 February 1933, TAL; Frank Lloyd Wright to Mr. Harry Beardsley, 28 February 1933, TAL.

17. Wright et al., "All Fair: As the Architects View the Lake Front," 12.

18. Wright, *An Autobiography*, 357.

19. The fact that the topic was pre-selected is revealed in a letter Wright's secretary K.E. Jensen wrote to Don Glassman on 18 February 1931 suggesting that he might be interested in the fact that Wright would be at the 26 February meeting of AUDAC, to which the press was invited, and where the topic was going to revolve around the Chicago world's fair. K.E. Jensen to Don Glassman, 18 February 1931, TAL.

20. "Wrightites vs. Chicago," 63.

21. Ibid., 63–64.

22. Kilham, *Raymond Hood, Architect*, 112.

23. "Wrightites vs. Chicago," 63.

24. Wright, *An Autobiography*, 352–53.

25. Ibid., 354.

26. Drawing #3103.003, TAL.

27. Wright, *An Autobiography*, 354; Drawing #3103.003.

28. Wright, *An Autobiography*, 354.

29. Drawing #3103.002, TAL.

30. Drawing #3103.003.

31. Wright, *An Autobiography*, 354.

32. Ibid. Notations on two drawings of the skyscraper scheme in the collection of the Taliesin Archives provide clues as to how the building was to be constructed and the functional uses of specific parts of the tower. Comments regarding circulation of automobiles to the site and parking facilities for large numbers of vehicles are also located on the drawings. Drawing #3103.003; Drawing #3103.005, TAL.

33. Wright, *An Autobiography*, 354.

34. Wright's use of a unit system dates back to his early prairie-house period. He continued to design using a similar method throughout his career, as illustrated by his later Usonian houses.

35. Wright, *An Autobiography*, 355.

36. It appears to be well over 6,500 feet long. Drawing #3103.001, TAL.

37. Ibid.; Wright, *An Autobiography*, 355.

38. Wright, *An Autobiography*, 355.

39. Drawing #3103.001.

40. Wright, *An Autobiography*, 355.

41. Ibid. Wright had previously explored the aesthetic design potential of allowing water to pour through openings in roof structures by placing open drains in the eaves of many of his early commissions, including the Robie House in Chicago, through which rainwater could drain creating miniature waterfalls.

42. Wright, *An Autobiography*, 356–57.

43. Drawing #3103.004.

44. Wright, *An Autobiography*, 356.

45. Ibid.

46. These well-publicized commissions significantly contributed to the renaissance of his architectural career, which continued until his death in 1959.

47. Wright, *An Autobiography*, 354.

48. That Wright was thinking about the Eiffel Tower in relation to his skyscraper design is reflected in the presence of an outline of the tower, along with one of the Empire State Building, on his drawing of the skyscraper scheme. He included the historic buildings to illustrate relative building heights. The outlines of the Eiffel Tower and the Empire State Building also appeared on later drawings of other skyscraper designs by Wright, including on an elevation of his mile-high building.

49. Wright, *An Autobiography*, 356–57.

50. "Wrightites vs. Chicago," 63–64; Wright, *An Autobiography*, 353.

51. Frank Lloyd Wright to Henry Churchill, 17 February 1931, TAL.

52. Wright nonsensically projected that "if elevators could handle the population of New York, they could handle the crowds at the Fair." Wright, *An Autobiography*, 354.

53. Wright et al., "All Fair: As the Architects View the Lake Front," 12.

54. Wright stated that he had attended the 1876 Centennial International Exposition in Philadelphia with his mother. As a young architect he visited the 1893 Columbian Exposition and later the 1904 Louisiana Purchase Exposition in St. Louis. Additionally, he designed a pavilion for the Larkin Company at the 1901 Pan-American Exposition in Buffalo, New York.

55. Wright must have been familiar with the early preliminary schemes for the exposition by the architectural commissioners that included tall towers, as they were

widely published in major American architectural journals. He also undoubtedly was aware of the well-publicized suspended roof structure of the Travel and Transport Building's Railroad Hall, which was fully constructed by the time he presented his exposition schemes at the February 1931 meeting of AUDAC in New York.

56. Other examples of designs by Wright that included the use of a cable structural system were a self-service garage project in 1949 for New York City and the New Sports Pavilion for Belmont Park, New York, in 1956. Neither of these designs was ever built.

57. I thank Dana Hutt for sharing this insight.

58. Wright investigated the potential of the skyscraper throughout his career. His exploration of rotated tower forms first appeared two years prior to his world's fair plans in the design for a series of towers for St. Mark's in the Bouwerie in New York City. The concept was finally realized with the construction of the Price Tower. One of Wright's last major skyscraper designs was the mile-high skyscraper of 1956, intended for Chicago.

59. Minutes of the Third Meeting of the Architectural Commission, 2–3.

60. Report labeled "W-1," ND, 3; Corbett to Albert, 4 April 1930. Other artists initially suggested as potential consultant committee members were architectural renderer Jacques Lambert and illuminator Jacob Ozzi, whose work included the original lighting design for the Eiffel Tower. Minutes of the Third Meeting of the Architectural Commission, 2–3.

61. For background on the term *industrial design* and the early history of the field, see Wilson et al., *The Machine Age in America*, 85. In their attempt to restyle products for the modern era, Geddes and many other industrial designers looked to the machine, in particular to the aerodynamic forms of airplanes, submarines, and dirigibles, for design inspiration. They understood the benefits of aerodynamic shapes, which involved merging extraneous details into unified wholes that typically could be more economically produced. Streamlined designs feature smooth, curving forms and prominent horizontal lines, usually grouped in threes. Both elements reflect the rapid linear motion of modern motor vehicles. For more information on the early developments of aerodynamic forms, see Bush, *The Streamlined Decade,* and Heskett, *Industrial Design.*

62. Geddes had little formal artistic training beyond a brief period in the studio of Norwegian painter Henrik Lund, who advised his pupil to stay away from schools and "allow his thoughts to develop in their own way." Geddes began his involvement in theater during the mid-1910s. This background contributed greatly to his ability to create innovative and dramatic environments. His earliest architectural designs were small experimental performance spaces for members of the Little Theatre movement in Los Angeles. Willis, "Norman Bel Geddes," 2:182; Bliven, "Norman-Bel Geddes," 182; Geddes, *Miracle in the Evening,* 155–58, 163–64.

63. Norman Bel Geddes, personal minutes of meeting with [Harvey Wiley] Corbett, 29 April 1929, NBG, HRC.

64. Geddes received additional encouragement to proceed with the designs from Allen D. Albert and Daniel Burnham Jr. before and after apparently securing official sanction from the commission at their meeting on 1 May 1929. Norman Bel Geddes, personal minutes of meeting with Mr. [Harvey Wiley] Corbett, Dr. [Allen D.] Albert, and other members of the Architectural Commission, 1 May 1929, NBG, HRC; Minutes of the Fifth Meeting of the Architectural Commission, 18; Norman Bel Geddes,

Personal minutes of meeting with Dr. [Allen D.] Albert and Miss Mary Coggeshard, 22 July 1929, NBG, HRC.

65. Norman Bel Geddes, Personal minutes of meeting with Mr. [Harvey Wiley] Corbett, 3 May 1929, NBG, HRC; Norman Bel Geddes, Personal minutes of meeting with [Harvey Wiley] Corbett, [Raymond] Hood, [Ralph] Walker, and [Paul] Cret, 21 January 1930, NBG, HRC.

66. Norman Bel Geddes to Dr. A[llen] D. Albert, 2 July 1929, CofP, UIC.

67. According to Geddes, on 30 December 1929 Corbett had selected him to produce the illumination design for the exposition's buildings and grounds. Corbett, however, instructed the designer not to proceed on that work until he had received written authorization from either the commission or the board of directors. Desired work from Geddes included a half dozen "airplane view perspectives of various lighting effects of the complete ensemble of the Exposition." Norman Bel Geddes, personal minutes of meeting with Dr. [Allen D.] Albert and [Harvey Wiley] Corbett, 30 December 1929, NBG, HRC; Geddes, *Horizons,* 161.

68. Geddes wrote to Albert that he hoped to "revise drama on the basis of lasting things, such as poetry, architecture, painting, and music, and establish something that is not merely temporary, popular, and vogue" but that would make "drama as everlasting as it has been." Norman Bel Geddes to Dr. A[llen] D. Albert, 23 July 1929, CofP, UIC.

69. Bragdon, "Towards a New Theatre," 171. Many new ideas in theater during this period grew out of the work of German director Max Reinhardt, with whom Geddes had worked, and the experimental productions of the Little Theatre movement in the United States.

70. Geddes's widely publicized fair projects presented some of the most experimental developments in stagecraft during these years. Their streamlined forms and innovative space arrangements contrasted sharply with the typical, more conservative theaters of the 1920s, which featured elaborate niches, sculpted figures, columns, and fanciful murals. R. W. Sexton and B. F. Betts highlighted many of these more traditional theaters in the first volume of their work *American Theatres of Today.*

71. Geddes's emphasis on creating a closer relationship between the audience and the action on stage was shared by other designers of auditoriums in the 1930s. For example, architect Barry Byrne, the designer of a series of Catholic churches in these years, began to project the main altar toward the center of the sanctuary so that ceremonies could be performed closer to the parishioners. Byrne, "Christ King Church—Cork, Ireland," 176.

72. Geddes especially wanted to encourage fresh ideas in theatrical writing by inviting prominent dramatists to produce new, noncommercial, pieces specifically for the Chicago exposition. These works, he hoped, would bring forward "the untouched possibilities of the theatre as an independent form of expression." In his effort to reach this goal, Geddes wrote letters seeking input from leading designers in various artistic fields, including Pablo Picasso, Igor Stravinski, Eugene O'Neill, and Frank Lloyd Wright. While Geddes recalled that he received, with only two exceptions, ten to twenty pages of constructive comments from each of these men, existing letters in the Norman Bel Geddes Archive at the Harry Ransom Humanities Research Center (NBG, HRC) suggest that in reality he received much shorter and less detailed replies. Norman Bel Geddes to Dr. A[llen] D. Albert, 23 October 1929, CofP, UIC.

73. In addition to rotating the theater house, Geddes created an even more spacious feel to the auditorium by eliminating balconies and boxes (except for a single row of loges located immediately behind the outer row of tiered seating).

74. For information on his setting for *The Miracle*, see Innes, "Theatre after Two World Wars," 401.

75. Geddes, *Horizons*, 143–44.

76. Ibid., 142.

77. According to Geddes, the Large Musical Comedy Theatre was to seat 2,000, and the Intimate Theatre for Drama, 500; the cabaret was to provide table seating for 400. (A plan of the complex includes figures of 1,700 seats for the larger auditorium and 750 seats for the smaller one.) The children's theater auditorium was designed to seat 200 youth on the main floor and 60 adults above in a balcony. Geddes to Albert, 2 July 1929; Roberts, *Norman Bel Geddes*, 19.

78. Geddes, *Horizons*, 151.

79. Geddes included parking for 1,720 automobiles under the Temple of Music. According to the designer, double lanes would allow up to 100 cars per minute to load or unload passengers. Patrons arriving by watercraft would be accommodated by three separate docks. Ibid., 166; "Six Theater Projects," 774.

80. "Six Theater Projects," 773.

81. Geddes to Albert, 2 July 1929; "Six Theater Projects," 773.

82. Geddes, *Horizons*, 160.

83. Ibid., 166.

84. As with Theatre Number Fourteen, overhangs and radiating stairs producing symbolic motion ripples around the building. "Six Theater Projects," 774.

85. "Geddes Explanation of Architectural Registration Difficulty," 4 December 1940, NBG, HRC.

86. Many of these letters and documents are housed in NBG, HRC.

87. Geddes wrote to Albert acknowledging that his theater designs for the exposition were quite apart from his position as "Advisory Council to the Architectural Commission" since his designs were much broader in scope. Geddes, to Albert 2 July 1929; report labeled "W-1," ND, 3.

88. Arthur Brown Jr. to Dr. Allen D. Albert, 14 January 1930, CofP, UIC.

89. Geddes's egotistical attitude is reflected in a July 1929 letter he wrote to Albert. In it he stressed his interest in completing his designs for the event as quickly as possible so that they would be ready for the commissioners to incorporate when arriving at a solution from their *parti*, since several of his projects covered such a wide area of the fairgrounds that they would significantly impact the overall scheme of the event. Geddes to Albert, 2 July 1929.

Similar attempts to achieve a high level of personal control throughout his career led critics to proclaim that Geddes wasted more of industry's money than anyone or anything else. Heskett, *Industrial Design*, 111.

90. In one case, even though Albert had specifically told Geddes that he would receive no remuneration for any future work until the former returned from a trip to Europe, the designer continued to badger him and eventually received permission to continue to work on designs for the event to the amount of $2,500 or $3,000 to be billed at a later date. Geddes, personal minutes of meeting with Albert and Coggeshard, 22 July 1929.

91. D[aniel] H. B.[urnham] to Nat A. Owings, 13 September 1933, CofP, UIC. Ged-

des received a telegram from the Chicago members of the architectural commission dated 28 December 1929 specifically indicating that he was to do no further work for the fair without written authorization. Corbett and Albert reiterated this requirement two days later in a meeting with Geddes. Geddes, personal minutes of meeting with Albert and Corbett, 30 December 1929.

92. Norman Bel Geddes, to Dr. A[llen] D. Albert, 27 October 1932, CofP, UIC; Brown to Albert, 14 January 1930. The last meeting of the commission that Geddes was invited to attend was on 3 May 1929. In a letter to Corbett in March 1930, Geddes wrote that on at least three or four occasions he had been promised copies of various meeting minutes but had yet to receive them. Norman Bel Geddes to Harvey Corbett 14 March 1930, CofP, UIC.

93. The committee was composed of Hood, Corbett, and Walker. After Walker left on a trip to Europe, the task fell to the other two architects. Chicago World's Fair Centennial Celebration of 1933, Minutes of the Eighth Meeting of the Architectural Commission, 17 March 1930, 3, CofP, UIC; Corbett to Albert, 4 April 1930.

94. Geddes had begun working on his Divine Comedy Theatre as early as 1922. The auditorium, specifically designed for the production of Dante's classic, consists of a layout similar to a Greek theater. Its huge, unornamented domed ceiling helped unify the stage and seating areas. Corbett to Albert, 4 April 1930; Geddes, *Horizons*, 156–57.

95. Corbett to Albert, 4 April 1930.

96. It appears that even as early as March 1929 Corbett was playing games with Geddes regarding the designer's role on the commission. In a letter written to Albert that month, Geddes complained that Corbett had informed him that his advisory position had not yet been confirmed, yet the next day a newspaper announcement released by Albert stated that the designer was indeed a consultant to the committee. Geddes believed that his recent honest critique of Corbett's preliminary design and favoring of Holabird's led Corbett to not be up front with him. Norman Bel Geddes to Dr. Allen D. Albert, 8 March 1929, CofP, UIC.

97. Chicago World's Fair Centennial Celebration of 1933, Minutes of the Meeting of the Architectural Commission, 19 May to 21 May 1930, 5, CofP, UIC. Geddes had been completely left out of the decision-making process for the exposition. In March 1930 he informed Corbett that he was unable to contribute anything significant as he had been absent from meetings and had had no opportunity to comment. Geddes to Corbett, 14 March 1930.

98. Harvey Wiley Corbett to Dr. Allen D. Albert, 19 June 1930, CofP, UIC.

99. Geddes to Albert, 27 October 1932.

100. Chicago World's Fair Centennial Celebration of 1933, Minutes of the Meeting of the Architectural Commission, 29 September 1929, 3, CofP, UIC.

101. Geddes, *Horizons*, 193.

102. He did, however, state that the water in the "lagoon" of the restaurant could be eliminated or reduced in size. Ibid., 191.

103. Articles also appeared in *Theater Arts Magazine, American Magazine, Creative Art*, and *Every Week Magazine*, as well as in the *Christian Scientist Monitor*, the *Chicago Daily News*, and the *Philadelphia Public Ledger*. Copies of these articles are housed in NBG, HRC.

104. "Geddes Explanation of Architectural Registration Difficulty"; "Application of Norman Bel Geddes for Certificate as Registered Architect," NBG, HRC.

105. The Swift Bridge and Open Air Theatre, with seating for 1,700, was specifi-

cally built for daily performances of the Chicago Symphony Orchestra. *Official Guide Book of the World's Fair of 1934*, 111.

106. The basic form of the stage, with its rounded stepping arches, was repeated in the design of many other outdoor performance venues throughout the United States in the 1930s, including in Grant Park just north of the fairgrounds in Chicago; for the Hollywood Bowl in Los Angeles, California; at the 1936 Texas Centennial Exposition in Dallas, Texas; and the 1936–37 Great Lakes Exposition in Cleveland, Ohio.

107. *Official Guide Book of the Fair, 1933,* 101.

SEVEN: THE CONTEMPORARY REACTION AND IMPACT OF THE EXPOSITION

1. Crissey, "Why the Century of Progress Architecture?"

2. Negative opinions usually focused on the designers' choice of forms, the absence of windows on the main pavilions, and the decorative use of color and illumination.

3. While critics were referring to the architecture of the fair as atrocious, crazy, and "a mess of modernistic succotash," younger designers defended it as "good architecture and good art" because it was original and daring and because it spoke "the language of the new liberty in art." Crissey, "Why the Century of Progress Architecture?" 16.

4. Woltersdorf, "Carnival Architecture," 18.

5. "Bizarre Patterns for Chicago's Fair," 10; Haskell, "Mixed Metaphors at Chicago," 49; Woltersdorf, "Carnival Architecture," 18.

6. "The Lay Critics Speak," 28.

7. "All Roads Lead to Chicago's Rainbow City," 29. A visitor from St. Paul, Minnesota, agreed, stating that the architecture was all crazy. He was sure that if Harry K. Thaw (the millionaire murderer of the prominent American architect Stanford White in 1906) had driven though the fairgrounds, he would have clearly realized that he had killed the wrong architect! "The Lay Critics Speak," 28.

8. "The Miracle of Light at the World's Fair," n.p.

9. Both quoted in "All Roads Lead to Chicago's Rainbow City," 29.

10. Evans, "Exposition Architecture," 17–21.

11. "The Lay Critics Speak," 28.

12. Ibid.

13. Ibid.

14. "All Roads Lead to Chicago's Rainbow City," 29; Magee, "Building with Light," 8.

15. "All Roads Lead to Chicago's Rainbow City," 29.

16. As quoted in ibid.

17. "The Miracle of Light at the World's Fair," n.p.

18. S. J. Duncan Clark, "Beauty of Balance: The Prophetic in Mass and Line at A Century of Progress Exposition," reprint from the *Chicago Daily News*, CofP, UIC.

19. Ibid.

20. Paul Cret, as quoted in Vincent, "'Natura non facit saltus,'" 344.

21. Ibid.

22. Cret wrote, "The architecture of a World's Fair is primarily a stage set. Built for a few months, it ought not to attempt, with plaster and cardboard, an imitation of permanent buildings, but should accept with good grace to be a midsummer dream, or

nightmare! Its principal function, after that of being a form of warehouse, is to create a festive atmosphere, a sort of unreal world to take us away from the daily humdrum." "Paul P. Cret, Symposium on the '33 Fair: Title?" manuscript, Paul Philippe Cret Papers, UPenn; Cret, "The Festive Stage Setting," 4.

Albert Kahn shared Cret's view, stating in the July 1933 issue of *Architectural Forum*, "Admirable as is much of the building at the Chicago Fair, it can hardly be called 'architecture.' Indeed, the problem must necessarily be one of stage-setting, festive, gay, colorful, and joyous, in which anything savoring of permanent architecture would be quite out of place." Kahn, "A Pageant of Beauty," 26.

23. Harvey Wiley Corbett wrote in the *Journal of the Royal Architectural Institute of Canada* that the architectural commission was not "thinking in terms of modernism but only in terms of functionalism, and [only] when they had finally evolved a *programme* of requirements, conditions of site, type of construction, and convinced the management of the advisability of at least two stories of exposition space" did they proceed to focus on how the space was to be enclosed. Corbett, "The Architecture of the World's Fair," 102.

24. Louis Skidmore pointed out the benefit of using the new products and processes exemplified in the major exhibition halls, and he avoided specific mention of the buildings' formal qualities. He also highlighted the economic benefits of adopting practices used in the construction of the temporary exposition pavilions for more traditional, permanent commercial building. Louis Skidmore, "A Century of Progress," CofP, UIC.

25. Cret, "The Festive Stage Setting," 5.

26. Corbett, "The Significance of the Exposition," 1.

27. Thomas Tallmadge, as quoted in Granger, *Chicago Welcomes You*, 250.

28. Tallmadge, *The Story of Architecture in America*, 309–11.

29. Ibid.

30. Granger, *Chicago Welcomes You*, 231.

31. Ibid., 237, 240, 245.

32. "Fair Buildings Being Erected Cause Debates."

33. Ibid.

34. Ibid.

35. Ibid.

36. Woltersdorf, "Carnival Architecture."

37. Ibid., 20.

38. Ibid., 15, 18.

39. Ibid., 13–14.

40. Ibid., 10.

41. Ibid., 13.

42. Ely Jacques Kahn, "Close-Up Comments on the Fair," 23.

43. Woltersdorf, "Carnival Architecture," 13; Cram, "Retrogression, Ugliness," 24.

44. Wright, "At the Chicago World's Fair," 46.

45. In the article Wright wrote for the *Architects' Journal*, he attempted to defame the commissioners: "Let's forgive the expediency of these shallow architects for their exploitation of appearances belonging by nature to work deeper than their understanding. Let's say these men did the best they knew how to do with their newest eclecticism." Wright, "At the Chicago World's Fair," 46.

46. Ibid.

47. Ibid.

48. Even though several prominent East Coast architects led the commission, the verbal backlash against A Century of Progress emanating from New York reveals another chapter in the continual rivalry between the two major urban architectural centers in the United States. This competitive design battle initially flared up when Chicago, an up-and-coming city on the prairie, won the right to host the World's Columbian Exposition over New York and several other prominent American cities.

49. Haskell, "Frank L. Wright and the Chicago Fair," 605.

50. Mumford, "Two Chicago Fairs," 271.

51. "Wrightites vs. Chicago," 63.

52. "Branding the Buildings at the Chicago Fair," 14.

53. The specific emphases of several of the designers' responses reflect their backgrounds and roles in the design of the event. For example, Vogelgesang discussed use of color in architecture and the importance of protecting the prefabricated building panels of the pavilions with paint. Farrier (who assisted Skidmore in overseeing the daily activities of designing the Chicago exposition) focused on the commissioners' success in addressing the need for "short lived, economically constructed buildings." Bennett, meanwhile, still deeply involved in issues of city planning, predicted that the unity of the fair buildings and the inclusion of a "symphony of color and light" would greatly "contribute to ideas of permanent Civic development." Wright et al., "All Fair as the Architects View the Lake Front," 27.

54. Wright wrote to Raymond Hood just days before the AUDAC meeting that he now preferred to be "on the outside. . . . I feel I can be more useful to Architecture in our country—definitely as well as politically free from any connection with the Fair." Frank Lloyd Wright to Raymond Hood, 18 February 1931, Douglas Haskell Archive, Avery Architectural and Fine Arts Library.

55. Haskell went on to suggest that the commissioners' inability to break completely from their classical training resulted in the presentation of "mixed metaphors" at the fair. To illustrate his point, he singled out the Hall of Science. The pavilion of "'cardboard' construction," the critic wrote, contained forms at the entrance more appropriate to Cret's designs for permanent stone buildings than to the large, prefabricated plywood exhibition hall. Haskell personally found the "schizophrenic result" greatly offensive, as it reduced "the pleasure, for a perceptive man, in displays intended for light-hearted moods." While he wrote favorably about the illumination of the buildings at night and the design of the exhibits inside the pavilions, as well as about the potential influence of the model residences, Haskell found significant fault in the lack of harmony in the overall composition of the fairgrounds. He felt that Urban's color scheme (which he erroneously stated was adopted in an emergency to help tie together the chaotic composition of the haphazardly placed buildings) also greatly contributed to the jumbled effect. He sharply criticized Urban's "poster principle," stating that instead of unifying the disjointed buildings, the use of different colors on individual facades further visually decomposed the pavilion designs. To further emphasize his distaste for the colors of the pavilions, Haskell poked fun at the brightness of the buildings' colors, suggesting that hawkers at the gates of the fair did a thriving business selling dark glasses to protect fairgoers' eyes not only against the summer sun but also against the buildings. Haskell, "Mixed Metaphors at Chicago," 47.

56. For more information on architects' reactions to design critics, see North, "Committing Mayhem on Architecture," and Ely Jacques Kahn, "This Modernism."

57. Haskell, "Architecture, 1933," 109–10.

58. Ibid., 110.

59. Wojtowicz, *Lewis Mumford and American Modernism*, 75.

60. Lewis Mumford, introduction to TS, "Houses, Machines, Cities," Lewis Mumford Papers, UPenn, quoted in Wojtowicz, *Lewis Mumford and American Modernism*, 75.

61. Mumford, introduction to TS, quoted in Wojtowicz, *Lewis Mumford and American Modernism*, 75.

62. Farrier and Thorud, "Design of the World's Fair Buildings," 387; Minutes of the Sixth Meeting of the Architectural Commission, 8.

63. This problem, however, had been solved decades earlier for bridge construction. Farrier and Thorud, "Design of the World's Fair Buildings," 387.

64. Howard, "Suspension Structure," 230.

65. Otto, *Das hängende Dach*, 11, 158.

66. Pehnt, ed., *Encyclopedia of Modern Architecture*, 278–79. The structural design of the Raleigh Arena incorporates two parabolic crisscrossing arches to form a saddle-shaped roof. Severud, "Hung Roofs," 102.

67. Friebe, *Buildings of the World Exhibitions*, 180–81; "Architecture at Brussels," 164. Other buildings that incorporated suspended structural systems at the 1958 exposition in Brussels included the "Marie Thomas" Pavilion, the European Coal and Steel Community Pavilion, and a large snack bar. Le Corbusier's Phillips Pavilion and the Civil Engineering Pavilion were roofed with concrete shells. "Bruxelles 58," 38, 41, 42, 46.

68. These included the New York World's Fair of 1964–65; the Universal and International Exhibition: Man and His World, held in 1967 in Montreal; and the Japan World Exhibition, held in 1970 in Osaka.

69. Initially, transparent panels in the roof flooded the interior with color. The use of Fiberglas prevented the panes from shattering with movement caused by changes in the roof load. *Official Guide New York World's Fair, 1964/65*, 107, 192. While the building remains standing at the start of the twenty-first century (and was featured in the 1997 movie *Men in Black*), the roof structure no longer exists.

70. Cables from eight pylons that projected through the building supported the structure. The first floor was set back and sheathed in transparent glass, making the second and third stories visually heavier, so the building looked like a large rectangular version of Fuller's Dymaxion House. "That Fair Again," 66; *Official Guide New York World's Fair, 1964/65*, 212.

71. Otto further promoted the concept in the second volume of *Tensile Structures*, published in 1973. Articles in architectural periodicals and an exhibit of his work at MoMA in 1972 brought even greater attention to these forms. Otto et al., *Tensile Structures*.

72. The netting of the Federal Republic of Germany Pavilion in Montreal stretched to cover 8,000 square meters. Three large masts (the tallest at thirty-five meters) and several smaller ones introduced great variety into the form. Thirty cables attached to the edges of the netting were anchored in bedrock to provide the needed tension for the structure. Five years later Otto designed a series of linear organic tent structures to cover part of the seating, as well as a sports hall and a small natatorium, in the main stadium complex for the Munich Olympics. Friebe, *Buildings of the World Exhibitions*, 190, 196; "Ein Zeit aus Staht und Plexiglas," 55.

73. These included the Alamillo Bridge and Viaduct, the covered Avenida de Europa (a street surrounded by twelve pavilions of European nations), the German Pavilion (with a precariously hung massive, circular roof), and El Palenque at Expo '92 in Seville and Hall 8/9, the Stage Canopy, and the modular Umbrella Canopies at Expo 2000 in Hanover. *Expo '92 Seville Architecture and Design*, 137, 324; "Popular Mechanics," 55; Flamme-Jaspers, *Expo 2000 Hannover*, 42, 239, 252.

74. When the original convention center on the site, the Metropolitan Fair and Exposition Building (1960), burned to the ground in 1967, a cable-suspended roof paying homage to the earlier transportation building was presented as the initial design for a replacement hall. This scheme was dropped in favor of a design, produced by C. Murphy and Associates in 1971, that included a massive truss system and clear glass curtain walls. The design recalled an earlier unrealized scheme for a convention hall for the same site by Mies van der Rohe. "Chicago Had Suspended Roof Once Before"; Davidson-Powers, "McCormick Place North Pays Homage to Mies and Modernism," 45–46.

75. Roberts and Schaefer, the engineers of the Brook Hill Farm Dairy at A Century of Progress, were also the engineers on the Hayden Planetarium. "Form Swallows Function," 107. The Hayden Planetarium was completed soon after July 1935. Pape, "Thin Concrete Shell Dome for New York Planetarium," 105.

76. These included articles in the *Journal of the American Concrete Institute, Engineering News-Record,* and *Popular Mechanics.*

77. According to a report by the Portland Cement Association, the building showed "good elastic behavior." Up to 200 extra pounds per square foot (ten times the live load for which the dairy had been designed) were loaded onto the roof; when it was removed, the structure recovered with only a few hairline cracks. "Thin Concrete Shell Roof Tested under Large Unsymmetrical Load," 635–36.

78. "Shell Concrete for Spanning Large Areas," 105.

79. "Reinforced Concrete Shell Roof over Unobstructed Dairy Floor," 3.

80. Tedesko, "Large Concrete Shell Roof Covers Ice Arena," 505–6.

81. Tedesko, "Z-D Shell Roof at Hershey," 7; Witmer, "Sports Palace for Chocolate Town," 3.

82. Thin-shell roofed buildings built during the Second World War included a massive warehouse complex in Columbus, Ohio, and airplane hangars at air force bases in Limestone, Maine, and Rapid City, South Dakota, and at the U.S. Bureau of Yards and Docks in San Diego, California. "Shell Concrete for Spanning Large Areas," 104.

83. Some of the later buildings with thin-shell barrel vaults designed by Roberts and Schaefer are the Philadelphia Skating Club and Humane Society, in Ardmore, Pennsylvania, with a clear span of 105 feet; a building for the New York Fire Department on Long Island, designed in 1947 with a span of 121 feet; and a hockey stadium in Quebec, designed in 1949 with a span of 240 feet. Ibid.

84. For example, in the early 1950s the American Society of Civil Engineers (ASCE) formed the Committee on Masonry and Reinforced Masonry to examine the potential of thin shells. A 177-page manual, written primarily by committee member Alfred L. Parme and produced by the ASCE, helped simplify the complex mathematical formulas needed for designing thin concrete shells, thereby making their use less intimidating for engineers.

A second conference, held at the Massachusetts Institute of Technology in 1954, brought 450 architects, engineers, and builders together to discuss how to use concrete more efficiently through the use of thin shells. In addition to the publication of the conference proceedings, other designers became aware of the possibilities of this type of roofing through an article in *Architectural Forum* that presented some of the highlights of the M.I.T. event. Whitney, "Shell Design Adaptable to Many Uses," 90; Billington, *Thin Shell Concrete Structures*, 21; "Shell Concrete Today," 157–67.

85. One of his first experiments with thin shells was a domed auditorium for the General Motors Center at Warren, Michigan, in 1955. Melaragno, *An Introduction to Shell Structures*, 149.

86. The design, a curved equilateral triangle with sides 150 feet in length, contained its natural outward thrust by linking the three corners together underground. Ibid., 152; Temko, *Eero Saarinen*, 29.

87. Saarinen's TWA Terminal reflected a trend in concrete-shell roofs to create more aesthetically interesting forms, a practice that began in Europe in the mid-1930s. As a result of patent limitations and the Second World War, this practice did not reach the United States until the beginning of the 1950s.

88. The architectural firm of Lorimar and Rose designed the Denver Coliseum to incorporate a 253-foot clear span. "Shell Concrete Today," 160; Tedesko, "Thin-Shell Arch Selected for Denver Coliseum," 448–52. Designed by Hellmuth, Leinweber, and Yamasaki and engineered by William C.E. Becker and Tedesko, the vaults of the St. Louis airport, four and a half to eight inches thick, span 122 feet in each direction. The design was one of the earliest to explore the creative formal possibilities of thin shells. Pehnt, *Encyclopedia of Modern Architecture*, 258; Condit, *American Building Art*, 181.

89. Melaragno, *An Introduction to Shell Structures*, 157–59.

90. Many of the records from the New York World's Fair are located at the main branch of the New York Public Library in New York City.

91. "Mass-Produced Houses in Review," 53.

92. Kelly, *The Prefabrication of Houses*.

93. "Mass-Produced Houses in Review," 53.

94. Kelly, *The Prefabrication of Houses*, 29.

95. Like the John B. Pierce Foundation, the U.S. Forest Products Laboratory became a leader in the exploration of prefabricated construction processes. U.S. Forest Products went on to cosponsor a large, widely publicized housing experiment in Fort Wayne, Indiana, which included fifty single-family houses built of a stressed-skin plywood-panel system similar to that used in its Madison, Wisconsin, design. "Moderate-Cost House Construction and Equipment," 116; "Fifty Plywood-Panel Houses Built at Rate of One a Day," 38.

96. Jandl, *Yesterday's Houses of Tomorrow*, 166.

97. Kelly, *The Prefabrication of Houses*, 50.

98. Malony, "Tomorrow's Housing," 30.

99. The question read: "What material would you specify for the exterior walls? Shingles; clapboard; brick; stucco; concrete; stone; metal and glass; pre-fabricated units[?]" Brick received 184 votes; clapboard, 81; stone, 57; stucco, 32; concrete, 16; prefabricated units, 11; shingles, 10; metal and glass, 8; and logs (not a given option), 1. "A Quiz in Taste," 473.

100. Lowenthal, "Trends in the Development of Building Materials," 78. Masonite

Presdwood, for example, did not initially catch on as an exterior wall material because of its nontraditional appearance and lack of permanence. The product initially found its niche as a construction product for temporary buildings, such as exhibition pavilions and Quonset huts. Toward the end of the twentieth century, an improved version of Masonite, visually identical to the clapboard siding of early American colonial homes, appeared on the market as an alternative to vinyl siding.

101. Malony, "Tomorrow's Housing," 29.

102. Lowenthal, "Trends in the Development of Building Materials," 79.

103. For example, with the exceptions of sugar cane and licorice fibers, most vegetable fibers, such as corn, tried for building products like fiberboards and insulation were not economically viable. Burchard, "The Role of Materials in Modern Housing," 344.

104. Lowenthal, "Trends in the Development of Building Materials," 78–79.

105. Ibid., 78; Malony, "Tomorrow's Housing," 29.

106. Kelly, *Prefabrication of Houses*, 40.

107. Lowenthal, "Trends in the Development of Building Materials," 78.

108. Burchard, "The Role of Materials in Modern Housing," 345.

109. General Houses became one of the first firms to join the war effort and provide housing and other types of low-cost, prefabricated buildings for the military and war industries. Kelly, *Prefabrication of Houses*, 40.

110. "Housing Cycles," 42.

111. Albrecht, ed., *World War II and the American Dream*, 20.

112. "Housing Cycles," 42; Hoyt, "Prefab Conference Held," 16.

113. The U.S. government built many of these houses at industrial plant sites, such as Avion Village, located near an airplane factory in Grand Prairie, Texas. Over 11,000 workers and their families descended on the small town, which had a prewar population of only 1,595. To help meet the housing needs of these new residents, the government gave Central Contracting Company of Dallas 100 days to construct 300 new homes. The company employed Dallas architect Roscoe P. DeWitt and Los Angeles architects Richard Neutra and David R. Williams to create the designs. To demonstrate how rapidly the prefabricated houses could be constructed, the government sponsored a timed competition. A group of fifty workers assembled one of the manufactured houses in less than an hour to win the event. Haskell, "The Revolution in House-Building," 47–50; Colean, "Prefabrication Needs the Architect," 65.

114. Haskell, "The Revolution in House-Building," 47.

115. Albrecht, *World War II and the American Dream*, 25.

116. "A Symposium of Prefabrication," 70.

117. New York World's Fair, Department of Press, News Release Number 61, 9 December 1936, NYWF, NYPL.

118. The Fair Corporation, created in September 1935, consisted of 108 representatives from both the public and private sectors of the city. Cusker, "The World of Tomorrow," 3.

119. "Tomorrow, Inc.," 6.

120. Robert A. M. Stern, *New York, 1930*, 729.

121. "World Fair Friends Rally to Keep 'Parthenon off Flushing Swamp.'"

122. Ibid.

123. Ibid.

124. Stern, *New York, 1930*, 729.

125. Other members were I. Woodner Silverman, a designer of the 1931 Paris Exposition Coloniale Internationale; Philip Youtz, director of the Brooklyn Museum; Gilbert Rohde, director of the Works Progress Administration Design Laboratory; Michael M. Hare, secretary of the Municipal Art League and the organizer of the City Club meeting; and Henry Wright. "World Fair Friends Rally to Keep 'Parthenon off Flushing Swamp,'" 26.

126. "The Fair of the Future 1939: A Proposal Submitted by the Committee formed at the Dinner at the City Club, Wednesday, December 11, 1935," amended 10 February 1936, 13 May 1936, NYWF, NYPL.

127. The debate over style for the New York World's Fair not only briefly delayed the start of designing the event but also led to the resignation of the first fair president, George McAneny. The seven thematic zones were community interests, medicine and public health, science and education, production and distribution, communications and business systems, transportation, and food. Stern, *New York, 1930*, 729–30.

128. Cusker, "The World of Tomorrow," 4.

129. In addition to Teague and Kohn, other members of the committee included Stephen Voorhees (a partner of Ralph Walker), New York architects Richmond H. Shreve and William Delano, landscape architect Gilmore Clarke, and engineer Jay Downer. Additionally, both Paul Cret and Eero Saarinen served as consultants. As at the Chicago exposition, the committee oversaw all design aspects of the fair, including the appointment of architects and final plan approval. They also designed approximately a third of the major exhibition halls. Santomasso, "The Age of Reason," 35; New York World's Fair Corporation, Minutes of the Board of Design, 16 May 1936, NYWF, NYPL.

130. The Gas Exhibits Building was designed by Skidmore and Owings with John Moss, the Coty Cosmetics Building was by Morris Sanders, and the Borden Building was by Voorhees, Walker, Foley, and Smith.

131. In order to guarantee unity in the exterior expressions of all the buildings, the Board of Design initially passed a resolution stating that neither gigantic enlargements of product forms nor the use of walls as outdoor advertisements would be permitted—a rule that obviously was not closely followed. New York World's Fair Corporation, Minutes of the Board of Design, 8 October 1937, NYWF, NYPL.

132. The Eastman Kodak Building was designed by Eugene Gerbereux with help from Walter Dorwin Teague.

133. The NCR Pavilion was designed by Ely Jacques Kahn along with Walter Dorwin Teague. *Official Guide Book of the New York World's Fair, 1939*, 60.

134. The Marine Transportation Building was designed by Ely Jacques Kahn in connection with Muschenheim and Brounn.

135. Santomasso, "The Age of Reason," 35–36. The Aviation Building was designed by William Lescaze and J. Gordon Carr.

136. The Firestone Building was designed by George W. McLaughlin of Wilbur Watson and Associates, the Electronic Products Building by A. Stewart Walker and Leon N. Gillette, and the Sealtest Building by De Witt Clinton Pond.

137. Nowhere else has the ability to reduce cultural meaning architecturally through the construction of minimal iconic forms, as demonstrated in the ethnic villages at world's fairs, been so skillfully honed as in the Walt Disney amusement properties. At the World Heritage Showcase located in Epcot Center, Walt Disney's permanent world's fair in Orlando, Florida, in the space of an afternoon, visitors can travel from

"Mexico" to "China" to "Morocco" without having to cover vast distances or deal with climatic differences between the various countries. With cultures reduced to their "minimal negotiable signifiers," visitors to Epcot can enjoy eating ethnic specialty foods, watching traditional dances, and buying "authentic" souvenirs from the many sanitized venues without having to deal with the realities of dirt, crime, or language difficulties. Sorkin, "See You in Disneyland," 216.

138. *Official Guide Book of the New York World's Fair, 1939*, 37–38.

139. As mentioned earlier, Lescaze designed the Aviation Building with J. Gordon Carr; George Howe participated in the design of the Children's World Amusement Area; and Harrison and Fouilhoux designed a pavilion for the Consolidated Edison Company of New York, as well as the centerpieces of the fair, the Trylon and the Perisphere. Stern, *New York, 1930*, 730, 740.

140. "The New York World's Fair," 62.

141. Hamlin, "World's Fair 1939 Model," 675.

142. Gutheim, "Buildings at the Fair," 286.

POSTSCRIPT

1. Later estimates put the attendance figure at closer to a half million, but the official figure for closing day was 372,127 visitors, the highest recorded daily attendance figure for the 1934 fair season. Lohr, *Fair Management*, 260; "Assure Payment in Full to All Fair's Backers."

2. Although busy, the fairgrounds were not overly packed during the first part of the day. Only 195,577 of the record crowd had entered the fairgrounds by 6:00 p.m. Shinnick, "Crowd Sets Record for Attendance during 1934."

3. "Final Day's Program at Fair."

4. Ibid.

5. Mullin, "Late Throngs Jam Fair; End Two Days Away"; Mullin, "Exposition Ends in Thrilling Burst of Fireworks."

6. Mullin, "Late Throngs Jam Fair; End Two Days Away."

7. Lohr, *Fair Management*, 261.

8. Shinnick, "Crowds Sets Record for Attendance during 1934."

9. Piles of battered greenery surrounded each gate, where fairgoers had been forced to abandon their plunder. Lohr, *Fair Management*, 261.

10. Ibid., 262.

11. Ibid., 262–63, 265.

12. A. H. Lubin was the winning contractor on the demolition bid. He paid $28,000 for what was believed to have been well over a million dollars' worth of building materials. "Fair Profit Is Made by Lubin in Wrecking of World's Fair."

13. Although it was on the initial list of buildings to be removed after the close of the exposition, Fort Dearborn also remained on the fairgrounds until it burned several years later. Louis Skidmore, "A Century of Progress Notice of Removal of Exposition Structures," n.d., copy in the collection of the Chicago Park District; Lohr, *Fair Management*, 266.

14. Lohr, *Fair Management*, 265.

15. Several hundred thousand people gathered to witness the event. Lubin, "The End of the Fair," 56.

16. Ibid.

17. Unfortunately, the house rebuilt in Palos Height, Illinois, was torn down in 1992. Other versions of the Good Housekeeping Stran-Steel House were built after the close of the exposition at 2105 Chestnut Avenue in Wilmette, Illinois; at the corner of Golf View and Wagner roads in Glenview, Illinois; and in Philadelphia, Pennsylvania.

18. The houses, along with ten structures from the Colonial Village, were bought and moved by real estate developer Robert Bartlett to Beverly Shores to bring attention to his fledgling lakeshore resort. Five of the houses were still extant in 2006: the House of Tomorrow, the Rostone House, the Cypress House, the Florida Tropical House, and the Armco-Ferro Enamel House. Kerch, "Futuristic Homes of '30s Survive in Indiana"; Busk, "Homes of Future Past."

19. Boyce, *Keck and Keck*, 52.

20. Lohr, *Fair Management*, 263.

21. Lubin, "The End of the Fair," 20.

22. Lohr, *Fair Management*, 263.

23. Ibid., 266.

24. The first case of death caused by exposure to asbestos was documented in the 1920s. By the time of the Chicago fair, many manufacturers of asbestos products knew of the serious health issues surrounding the material but avoided publicizing this information. "Asbestos Dangers Were Often Concealed," http://www.asbestosnetwork .com/asbestos/de_history_medical.htm (accessed 26 April 2005).

25. Flamme-Jaspers, *Expo 2000 Hannover*, 8.

BIBLIOGRAPHY

"The Administration Building." *Architectural Forum* 55 (August 1931): 133–42.

Albert, Allen D. "The Architecture of the Chicago World's Fair of 1933." *American Architect* 135 (5 April 1929): 421–30.

———. "Learning from Other World's Fairs: The Collective Exhibit Marks a New Mode to Replace Older Conceptions." *Chicago Commerce*, 22 November 1930, 13–14, 22–23.

Albrecht, Donald, ed. *World War II and the American Dream.* Cambridge: M.I.T. Press, 1995.

"All Roads Lead to Chicago's Rainbow City." *Literary Digest*, 3 June 1933, 29–30.

Allen, John E. "Construction of Long-Span Concrete Arch Hanger at Limestone Air Force Base." *Journal of the American Concrete Institute* 46 (January 1950): 405–14.

"American Architect." *New Republic*, 11 March 1931, 358.

Applebaum, Stanley. *The Chicago World's Fair of 1893: A Photographic Record.* New York: Dover, 1980.

"Architect Harvey Wiley Corbett Dies at 81." *Architectural Forum* 100 (May 1954): 44, 46.

"Architects of New York's World's Fair, 1939 Will Have a City Owned 1,003 Acre Site, a 40 Million Dollar Budget, and Attitude Aplenty." *American Architect* 147 (October 1935): 32–34.

"Architecture at Brussels: Festival of Structure." *Architectural Record* 123 (June 1958): 163–70.

Arnaud, Leopold. "The Evolution of a New Architecture." *American Architect* 141 (May 1932): 49–53, 114.

"Arthur Brown Jr. Dies." *Architectural Forum* 107 (September 1957): 103.

"Asbestos Carries Appeal to Visitors to Fair Show." *Chicago Daily News*, 20 July 1933.

"Assure Payment in Full to All Fair's Backers." *Chicago Daily Tribune*, 2 November 1934.

Atwood, Leland. "The Crystal House." In *A Century of Progress Homes and Furnishings*, ed. Dorothy Raley. Chicago: M. A. Ring, 1934.

"Aurora Borealis in the Westinghouse Century of Progress Exhibit." *Display World*, May 1933, 17, 25.

Austin, Erastus Long, and Odell Hauser. *The Sesqui-centennial International Exposition: 150 Years of American Independence.* Philadelphia: Current, 1929.

Avery, Delos. "258,000 See Fair in Two Days: Star Again Lights Wonders; Fireworks Thrill Thousands." *Chicago Herald and Examiner*, 29 May 1933.

Balfour, Alan. *Rockefeller Center: Architecture as Theater.* New York: McGraw-Hill, 1978.

Banham, Reyner. *The Architecture of a Well Tempered Environment.* Chicago: University of Chicago Press, 1969.

———. *Theory and Design in the First Machine Age.* London: Architectural Press, 1967.

Banister, Turpin C. "Bogardus Revisited, Part II: The Iron Towers." *Journal of the Society of Architectural Historians* 16 (March 1957): 11–19.

Bargelt, Louise. "Glass and Steel House of Future Erected at Fair." *Chicago Tribune*, 8 July 1934.

Beard, Charles. *A Century of Progress.* New York: Harper and Brothers, 1932.

Beardsley, Harry M. "House of Future to Be a Feature at World's Fair." *Chicago Daily News*, 8 April 1933.

Bedford, Steven McLeod. "Louis Ayres." In *The Macmillan Encyclopedia of Architects*, ed. Adolf K. Placzek. New York: Free Press, 1982.

Bell, J. Franklin. "The Progress of Science: Applied Science and Industry at 'A Century of Progress Exposition.'" *Scientific Monthly* 36 (March 1933): 281–83.

Bendiner, Alfred. "Wild Gold Medal Winners I Have Known." *AIA Journal* 28 (May 1957): 24–25.

Benevolo, Leonardo. *History of Modern Architecture.* Vol. 1 of 2. Translated from *Storia dell' architettura moderna* (1960). Cambridge: M.I.T. Press, 1971.

Benjamin, Walter. "The Work of Art in the Age of Mechanical Reproduction." In *Marxism and Art: Essays Classic and Contemporary*, ed. Maynard Solomon. New York: Random House, 1973.

Bennett, Wade Ware. "A Color Palette for Your Mood." *Commerce*, June 1934, 44–46.

Berg, Bert. "First Television Theatre, Interesting Attraction at the World's Fair." *Radio Industries*, August–September 1934, 6.

Billington, David P. *Thin Shell Concrete Structures.* 2nd ed. New York: McGraw-Hill, 1982.

"Bizarre Patterns for Chicago's Fair." *New York Times Magazine*, 6 March 1932, 10.

Blanks, Maurice. "Biographical Glossary." In *Chicago Architecture and Design, 1923– 1993: Reconfiguration of an American Metropolis*, ed. John Zukowsky. Munich: Pretel-Verlag, for the Art Institute of Chicago, 1993.

Blaser, Werner, ed. *Chicago Architecture: Holabird and Root, 1880–1992.* Boston: Birkhäuser, 1992.

Bliven, Bruce. "Norman-Bel Geddes: His Art and Ideas." *Theater Arts Magazine* 3 (1919): 179–90.

Boeckl, Matthias, ed. *Visionäre und Vertriebene: Österreichische Spuren in der modernen amerikanischen Architektur.* Berlin: Ernst and Sohn, 1995.

Borland, Charles. "Glass Pipe Magic." *Commerce*, December 1933, 23–25, 32.

Boyce, Robert. *Keck and Keck.* Princeton, N.J.: Princeton Architectural Press, 1993.

Bragdon, Claude. "Towards a New Theatre." *Architectural Record* 52 (September 1922): 170–82.

"Branding the Buildings at the Chicago Fair." *Literary Digest,* August 1933, 14.

Brown, Frank Chouteau. "Chicago and Tomorrow's House?" *Pencil Points* 14 (June 1933): 245–51.

Brown, John Russell, ed. *The Oxford Illustrated History of Theatre.* New York: Oxford University Press, 1995.

Bruegmann, Robert, ed. *Holabird and Roche, Holabird and Root: An Illustrated Catalog of Works, 1880–1940.* 3 vols. New York: Garland, 1991.

"Bruxelles 58." *Architecture d'aujourd'hui* (1958): 1–47.

Burchard, John Ely. "The Role of Materials in Modern Housing." *Architectural Record* 78 (November 1935): 341–46.

Burnham, Daniel H. [Jr.]. "How Chicago Finances Its Exposition." *Review of Reviews and World's Work* 86 (October 1932): 37–38.

———. "Temples of Inspiration to Rise along Miles of Lake Shore." *Chicago Commerce,* 18 October 1930, 21–23.

Burnham, Hubert. "Chicago's 1933 World's Fair." In *Living Architecture,* ed. Arthur Woltersdorf. Chicago: A. Kroch, 1930.

Bush, Donald J. *The Streamlined Decade.* New York: George Braziller, 1975.

Busk, Celeste. "Homes of Future Past." *Chicago Sun-Times,* 23 December 1983.

Byrne, Barry. "Christ King Church—Cork, Ireland." *Western Architect* 39 (October 1929): 175–77. Reprinted in *Prairie School Architecture: Studies from "The Western Architect,"* ed. H. Allen Brooks. New York: Van Nostrand Reinhold, 1983.

"Cable System to Support 200-Ft. Circular Roof." *Engineering News-Record* 106 (8 January 1931): 73–75.

Carey, Eben J. *Medical Science Exhibits: A Century of Progress.* Chicago: A Century of Progress, 1936.

———. "100 Years of Science in Medicine." *Chicago Commerce,* March 1933, 14–17.

Carter, Randolph, and Robert Reed Cole. *Joseph Urban: Architecture—Theater—Opera—Film.* New York: Abbeville Press, 1992.

"Celotex: Houses from Sugar Cane." *Fortune,* February 1939, 80–84, 120.

"A Century of Progress." *Architectural Forum* 61 (July 1934): 1–32.

"A Century of Progress." *Architectural Record* 73 (May 1933): 342–53.

"A Century of Progress." *Western Architect* 38 (June 1929): 91–98.

A Century of Progress, Chicago International Exposition of 1933: A Statement of Its Plan and Purposes and of the Relation of States and Foreign Governments to Them. Chicago: A Century of Progress, 1932.

"The Century of Progress Emphasis on Innovation." In *Chicago Architecture: Holabird and Root, 1880–1992,* ed. Werner Blaser. Boston: Birkhäuser, 1992.

"A Century of Progress Exposition." *Construction,* November 1932, 259–62.

"Century of Progress Exposition." *Painters Magazine and Paint and Wall Paper Dealer,* June 1932, 8–10.

"A Century of Progress Exposition, Herald of a New Age." *Chicago Progress,* n.d., 9–18+.

"The Century of Progress Has Its Own Design for Living." *House and Garden,* August 1933, 16–17, 60.

A Century of Progress International Exposition Papers (CofP, UIC). Department of Special Collections. University of Illinois at Chicago.

A Century of Progress Report of the President to the Board of Trustees, 14 March 1936. Chicago, 1936.

Chapple, Bennett. "Opportunities for Contractors and Dealers." *American Builder* 55 (August 1933): 23.

Chicago and the World's Fair, 1933. Chicago: F. Husum, circa 1933.

"Chicago Exposition Buildings Exemplify Sound Construction for Short Service." *Construction Methods* 14 (May 1932): 20–23.

"Chicago Had Suspended Roof Once Before." *Chicago Daily News,* 16 October 1967.

Chicago's Century of Progress. Chicago: Rand McNally, 1933.

"Chicago's Sky-Ride." *Scientific American,* January 1933, 41.

Cole, Fay-Cooper. *The Long Road from Savagery to Civilization.* Baltimore, Md.: Williams and Wilkins, in Connection with the Century of Progress Exposition, 1933.

Colean, Miles L. "Prefabrication Needs the Architect." *Architectural Record* 90 (September 1941): 64–68.

Color and Protection. Cedar Rapids, Iowa: American Asphalt Paint Company, 1933.

Color Beauties of A Century of Progress, Chicago, 1933. Chicago: Exposition Publications and Novelties, 1933.

"The Color Complex." *Architect* 11 (January 1929): 396–97.

"Color in Industry." *Fortune,* February 1930, 85–94.

"Concrete Shell Roof Used on World's Fair Building." *Engineering News-Record* 112 (14 June 1934): 775–76.

Condit, Carl W. *American Building: Materials and Techniques from the First Colonial Settlement to the Present.* Chicago: University of Chicago Press, 1968.

———. *American Building Art: The Twentieth Century.* New York: Oxford University Press, 1961.

———. "The Century of Progress Exposition: An Outline of Its Contributions to the Building Arts." In *1992 World's Fair Forum Papers,* vol. 1, *Legacies from Chicago's World's Fairs: A Background for Fair Planning.* Evanston, Ill.: Center for Urban Affairs and Policy Research, Northwestern University, 1984.

———. *Chicago, 1930–70: Building, Planning, and Urban Technology.* Chicago: University of Chicago Press, 1974.

"Contributions of Science and Technology to Building Design: 1891–1941." *Architectural Record* 89 (January 1941): 42–47.

Corbett, Harvey Wiley. "The Architecture of the World's Fair." *Journal of the Royal Architectural Institute of Canada* 11 (June 1934): 100–102.

———. "The Meaning of Modernism." *Architect* 12 (June 1929): 268–72.

———. "The Problem of Traffic." *Architectural Forum* 46 (March 1927): 201–8.

———. "The Significance of the Exposition." *Architectural Forum* 59 (July 1933): 1.

The Country Home Model Farm House. New York: Crowell, 1934.

Cowan, Henry J. *Science and Building: Structural and Environmental Design in the Nineteenth and Twentieth Centuries.* New York: John Wiley and Sons, 1978.

Cram, Ralph Adams. "Retrogression, Ugliness." *Architectural Forum* 59 (July 1933): 24–25.

Cret, Paul Philippe. "The Architect as Collaborator of the Engineer." *Architectural Forum* 49 (July 1928): 97–104.

———. "The Festive Stage Setting." *Architectural Forum* 59 (July 1933): 4–5.

———. Response to Howard Lewis Shay. *T-Square Club Journal* 1 (February 1931): 14.

———. "Ten Years of Modernism." *Architectural Forum* 59 (August 1933): 91–94.

Crew, Henry. "The Exposition of Science." *Scientific Monthly* 35 (September 1932): 228–38.

Crissey, Forrest. "Why the Century of Progress Architecture? An Interview with Allen D. Albert." *Saturday Evening Post*, 10 June 1933, 16–17, 60, 62–64.

Culhane, John. *The American Circus: An Illustrated History.* New York: Henry Holt, 1990.

Curtis, William J. R. *Le Corbusier: Ideas and Forms.* New York: Rizzoli, 1992.

Cusker, Joseph P. "The World of Tomorrow: Science, Culture, and Community at the New York World's Fair." In *Dawn of a New Day: The New York World's Fair, 1939/40,* ed. Helen A. Harrison and Joseph P. Cusker. New York: Queens Museum and New York University Press, 1980.

Davidson-Powers, Cynthia. "McCormick Place North Pays Homage to Mies and Modernism: An Unconventional Tribute." *Inland Architect* 32 (September–October 1988): 43–46.

Dawes, Charles G. "Statement of Charles G. Dawes, Vice President of the United States." *Hearings before the Committee on Ways and Means, House of Representatives, on H. J. Res. 365, A Resolution Authorizing the President of the United States, under Certain Conditions, to Invite the Participation of Other Nations in the Chicago World's Fair, Providing for the Admission of Their Exhibits and for Other Purposes.* 70th Cong., 2nd sess. 5 January 1929. Washington, D.C.: U.S. Government Printing Office, 1929.

Dawes, Rufus C. "Report of the Century of Progress Exposition." In *History of Centennials, Expositions, and World Fairs, also The Fundamental Principles of Successful County and State Fairs,* ed. George Jackson. Lincoln, Neb.: Wekesser-Brinkman, 1939.

Descriptive Catalogue of the German Arts and Crafts and the Universal Exposition, St. Louis. St. Louis, Mo.: Imperial German Commission, 1904.

"Development of Shell Construction." *Progressive Architecture* 72 (May 1992): 107.

Doordan, Dennis P. "Exhibition Progress: Italy's Contribution to the Century of Progress Exposition." In *Chicago Architecture and Design, 1923–1993: Reconfiguration of an American Metropolis,* ed. John Zukowsky. Munich: Pretel-Verlag for the Art Institute of Chicago, 1993.

Draper, Joan E. "Edward H. Bennett." In *The Macmillan Encyclopedia of Architects,* ed. Adolf K. Placzek. New York: Free Press, 1982.

———. "Paris by the Lake: Sources of Burnham's Plan of Chicago." In *Chicago Architecture, 1872–1922,* ed. John Zukowsky. Munich: Pretel-Verlag for the Art Institute of Chicago, 1987.

DuBois, J. Harry. *Plastics History U.S.A.* Boston: Cahners Books, 1972.

Duffus, R. L. "The Fair: A World of Tomorrow; Blithely Chicago's Century of Progress Calls Man to Embark upon a Great Adventure, Painting for Him in a Glory of Light and Color the Promise of Life That Science Makes Possible." *New York Times Magazine,* 28 May 1933, 1–3.

Duffy, Sherman R. "France Out as World Fair Exhibitor." *Chicago American,* 3 March 1933.

———. "House of Glass Rising at the Fair." *Chicago American,* 8 April 1933.

———. "Motion Key to Fair's Magic Lohr Says." *Chicago American,* 27 May 1933.

Edgell, George. *The American Architecture of To-Day*. New York: Charles Scribner's Sons, 1928.

Editors of *Fortune. Housing America*. New York: Harcourt, Brace, 1932.

"Ein Zeit aus Staht und Plexiglas." *Baumeister* 68 (January 1961): 55.

Elliott, Cecil D. *Technics and Architecture: The Development of Materials and Systems for Buildings*. Cambridge: M.I.T. Press, 1992.

Encyclopédie des arts décoratifs et industriels modernes au XXème siècle (1925). Reprint, 12 vols. New York: Garland, 1977.

Ernest, Gifford. "Ways of Science Are Revealed in City Dump." *Chicago Daily News*, 4 August 1933.

Evans, Almus Pratt. "Exposition Architecture: 1893 versus 1933." *Parnassus* 5 (May 1933): 17–21.

Expo '92 Seville Architecture and Design. New York: Abbeville Press, 1992.

"Fair Buildings Being Erected Cause Debates." *Chicago Daily News*, 17 April 1931.

"Fair Hums with New Activity as May 27 Nears, Roosevelt Regrets He Can't Open It." *Chicago Daily Tribune*, 17 May 1933.

"Fair Profit Is Made by Lubin in Wrecking of World's Fair." *Chicago Daily News*, 5 December 1935.

"Fair's Interior Decorations 95 Per Cent Completed." *Chicago American*, 15 May 1933.

Farrier, Clarence W. "Exposition Buildings Unique in Form and Structure." *Engineering News-Record* 110 (2 March 1933): 278–82.

Farrier, Clarence W., and Bert M. Thorud. "Design of the World's Fair Buildings." *Western Society of Engineers* 35 (October 1930): 384–94.

"'Fast' Colors for Buildings at Fair." *Chicago American*, 4 April 1933.

"Fiberglas: A Fabulous Infant." *Business Week*, 16 September 1939, 20–22.

"Fifty Plywood-Panel Houses Built at Rate of One a Day." *Architectural Record* 86 (September 1939): 37–40.

"Final Day's Program at Fair." *Chicago American*, 31 October 1934.

Findling, John. *Chicago's Great World's Fairs*. New York: Manchester University Press, 1994.

Findling, John, and Kimberly D. Pells, eds. *Historical Dictionary of World Fairs and Expositions*. Westport, Conn.: Greenwood Press, 1990.

Flamme-Jaspers, Martina, ed. *Expo 2000 Hannover: Architecture*. Ostfildern, Germany: Hatje Cantz, 2000.

Flynn, John T. "Be It Ever So Prefabricated." *Collier's*, 13 July 1935, 12–13, 50.

Fogle, Dan. "Urge Rich Color at World's Fair." *Chicago Daily News*, 18 January 1928.

Folsom, Joseph C. "The Eighth Wonder of the World." *World's Fair Weekly*, 4 November 1933, 34.

———. "Farewell to the Paint Can." *World's Fair Weekly*, 7 October 1933, 34.

"Ford and a Century of Progress." *World's Fair Archival Video*. Vol. 1. Videotape, 29 minutes. Corrales, N.M.: New Deal Films, n.d.

"Form Swallows Function." *Progressive Architecture* 72 (May 1992): 106–9.

"Formica Walls at A Century of Progress." Advertisement in *Architectural Forum* 61 (July 1934): 12.

"The Forum of Events: Products and Practices." *Architectural Forum* 58 (March 1933): 40.

Fowler, Orson S. *The Octagon House.* N.p.: Fowlers and Wells, 1853. Reprint, New York: Dover, 1973. Page references are to the reprint edition.

"Frameless Steel Houses." *Scientific American,* December 1932, 337.

"Frei Otto at Work." *Architectural Design* 41 (March 1971): 137–67.

Friebe, Wolfgang, ed. *Buildings of the World Expositions.* Leipzig: Druckerei Volksstimme Magdeburg, 1985.

The Frigidaire Air Conditioned House, A Century of Progress, Chicago, 1934. Dayton, Ohio: Frigidaire Corporation, Subsidiary of General Motors Corporation, circa 1934.

Fuller, R. Buckminster, and Robert Marks. *The Dymaxion World of Buckminster Fuller.* Carbondale and Edwardsville: Southern Illinois University Press, 1960.

Gans, Deborah. *The Le Corbusier Guide.* Princeton, N.J.: Princeton Architectural Press, 1987.

Geddes, Norman Bel. *Horizons.* Boston: Little, Brown, 1932.

———. *Miracle in the Evening.* Garden City, N.Y.: Doubleday, 1960.

———. "Ten Years from Now." *Ladies Home Journal,* January 1931, 3.

Giberti, Bruno. *Designing the Centennial: A History of the 1876 International Exhibition in Philadelphia.* Lexington: University of Kentucky Press, 2002.

Gilbert, James. "World's Fairs as Historical Events." In *Fair Representations: World's Fairs and the Modern World,* ed. Robert W. Rydell and Nancy E. Gwind. Amsterdam: VU University Press, 1994.

Gilbert, Paul T. "A Century of Progress Exposition: Herald of a New Age." *Chicago Progress,* n.d., 9–19.

"Glass and Steel . . ." *Chicago Tribune,* 8 June 1934.

Glass as an Architectural Medium in 9 Small Modern Houses at A Century of Progress, 1933–4. Toledo, Ohio: Libbey Owens Ford Glass Company, circa 1934.

"Glass Block Building." *Architectural Record* 74 (July 1933): 24.

"Glass Block—New Building Material." *Scientific American,* September 1933, 128.

"Glass Houses." *Architectural Forum* 59 (September 1933): 50.

"Glass Houses." *Business Week,* 4 January 1933, 18.

Glassberg, David. "Philadelphia 1926 Sesqui-centennial International Exposition." In *Historical Dictionary of World Fairs and Expositions,* ed. John E. Findling. Westport, Conn.: Greenwood Press, 1990.

Goetz, Alisa, ed. *Up Down Across: Elevators, Escalators, and Moving Sidewalks.* New York: Merrell, 2003.

Gould, Carol S., Kimberly A. Konrad, Kathleen Catalano Milley, and Rebecca Gallagher. "Fiberboard." In *Twentieth Century Materials,* ed. Thomas C. Jester. New York: McGraw-Hill, 1995.

Granger, Alfred. *Chicago Welcomes You.* Chicago: A. Kroch, 1933.

Grey, George W. "Bizarre Patterns for Chicago's Fair." *New York Times Magazine,* 6 March 1932, 10–11.

Grove, William G. "Transporter Suspension Bridge to Thrill World's Fair Visitors." *Engineering News-Record* 109 (11 August 1932): 172–73.

Gutheim, Frederick. "Buildings at the Fair." *Magazine of Art,* May 1939, 286–89+.

"The Hall of Science, A Century of Progress Exposition." *Architectural Forum* 57 (October 1932): 293–96; 305–10.

Hamlin, Talbot. "World's Fair 1939 Model." *Pencil Points* 19 (November 1938): 672–86.

Hand Colored Views: A Century of Progress International Exposition, Chicago, 1933. Chicago: Exposition Publications and Novelties, 1933.

Harbeson, John F. "Design in Modern Architecture: I—What Is Modern?" *Pencil Points* 11 (January 1930): 3–10.

Harris, Neil. "Building an Illusion: The Design of the World's Columbian Exposition." In *Grand Illusions: Chicago's World's Fair of 1893,* ed. Neil Harris. Chicago: Chicago Historical Society, 1993.

———. "Museums, Merchandising, and Popular Taste: The Struggle for Influence." In *Material Culture and the Study of American Life,* ed. Ian M. G. Quimby. New York: Published for the Henry Francis du Pont Winterthur Museum, Winterthur, Delaware, by W. W. Norton, 1978.

"Harvey Wiley Corbett Tells How Exposition Was Created." *Architect and Engineer* 113 (June 1933): 25–29.

Haskell, Douglas. "Architecture, 1933: Looking Forward at Chicago." *Nation,* 24 January 1934, 109–10.

———. "Frank L. Wright and the Chicago Fair." *Nation,* 3 December 1930, 605.

———. "Mixed Metaphors at Chicago." *Architectural Review* 74 (August 1933): 47–49.

———. "The Revolution in House-Building." *Harper's Magazine,* June 1942, 47–54.

Hegemann, Werner, and Elbert Peets. *The American Vitruvius: An Architects' Handbook of Civic Art.* New York: B. Blom, 1922.

Heskett, John. *Industrial Design.* New York: Oxford University Press, 1980.

Heyel, Carl. "A Century of Progress." *Co-operative Engineer,* October 1931, 20–23, 35, 37.

Hines, Thomas S. *Burnham of Chicago: Architect and Planner.* Chicago: University of Chicago Press, 1974.

"Hiram Walker's Café Canadian Club." *Architectural Forum* 61 (July 1934): 26.

Hitchcock, Henry-Russell. *Frank Lloyd Wright.* Paris: Cahiers d'Art, 1928.

———. *Modern Architecture: Romanticism and Reintegration.* New York: Payson and Clarke, 1929.

Hitchcock, Henry-Russell, and Philip Johnson. *The International Style.* 1932. Reprint, New York: W. W. Norton, 1966. Page references are to the reprint edition.

Hobhouse, Christopher. *1851 and the Crystal Palace.* New York: E. P. Dutton, 1937.

"Homes and Housing Materials to Be Exhibited." *Engineering News-Record* 110 (2 March 1933): 293.

The Honor Bilt Home at A Century of Progress. Newark, N.J.: Sears, Roebuck and Co., circa 1934.

Hood, Raymond M. "Exterior Architecture of Office Buildings." *Architectural Forum* 41, no. 3 (September 1924): 97–98.

———. "The Spirit of Modern Art." *Architectural Forum* 51 (November 1929): 445–48.

Horrigan, Brian. "The Home of Tomorrow, 1927–1945." In *Imagining Tomorrow: History, Technology, and the American Future,* ed. Joseph J. Corn. Cambridge: M.I.T. Press, 1986.

House of Tomorrow. N.p.: B. R. Graham, 1933.

"Housing Cycles." *Business Week,* 16 August 1941, 42–46.

"How Chicago Went Fishing and Landed the Fair Grounds." *World's Fair Weekly,* 6 May 1933, 7.

Howard, Seymour. "Suspension Structure." *Architectural Record* 128 (September 1960): 230–37.

Hoyt, Kendall K. "Prefab Conference Held." *Architectural Record* 89 (March 1941): 16.

"Illustrated News." *Architectural Record* 75 (June 1934): 468.

"Impulse from Star Captured by Powerful Telescopes to Turn on Lighting System of the World Fair." *Chicago Tribune*, 27 May 1933.

"Incidents of Opening Day." *Chicago Tribune*, 28 May 1933.

"India Contribution to the Fair." *Chicago American*, 19 October 1932.

Innes, Christopher. "Theatre after Two World Wars." In *The Oxford Illustrated History of Theatre*, ed. John Russell Brown. New York: Oxford University Press, 1995.

Jackson, George, ed. *History of Centennials, Expositions, and World Fairs, also The Fundamental Principles of Successful County and State Fairs.* Lincoln, Neb.: Wekesser-Brinkman, 1939.

Jandl, H. Ward. *Yesterday's Houses of Tomorrow: Innovative American Homes, 1850–1950.* Washington, D.C.: Preservation Press, 1991.

Jester, Thomas C. "Plywood." In *Twentieth Century Materials*, ed. Thomas C. Jester. New York: McGraw-Hill, 1995.

———. "Porcelain Enamel." In *Twentieth Century Materials*, ed. Thomas C. Jester. New York: McGraw-Hill, 1995.

Joedicke, Jürgen. *A History of Modern Architecture.* New York: Praeger, 1959.

Johnson, Donald Leslie. *Frank Lloyd Wright versus America: The 1930s.* Cambridge: M.I.T. Press, 1990.

Jordy, William. *American Buildings and Their Architects: The Impact of European Modernism in the Mid-Twentieth Century.* Garden City, N.Y.: Anchor Books, 1976.

Kadlcák, Jaroslav. *Statics of Suspension Cable Roofs.* Brookfield, Vt.: A. A. Balkema, 1994.

Kahn, Albert. "A Pageant of Beauty." *Architectural Forum* 59 (July 1933): 26.

Kahn, Ely Jacques. "Close-Up Comments on the Fair." *Architectural Forum* 59 (July 1933): 23–24.

———. "This Modernism." *T-Square Club Journal* 1 (September 1931): 5.

Kalinka, J. E. "Design of Dome Structures." *Engineering News-Record* 115 (1 August 1935): 163.

Keck, William. "The Perspective of a Modern Architect in the 1930s." Frank Lloyd Wright Home and Studio Foundation Volunteer Retreat, 2 November 1991. Videotape. FLWBT.

Kelly, Burnham. *The Prefabrication of Houses: A Study of the Albert Farwell Bemis Foundation of the Prefabrication Industry in the United States.* Cambridge: Technology Press of the M.I.T. Press, 1951.

Kerch, Steve. "Futuristic Homes of '30s Survive in Indiana." *Chicago Tribune*, 3 August 1985.

Kihlstedt, Folke Tyko. "Formal and Structural Innovations in American Exposition Architecture: 1901–1939." Ph.D. diss., Northwestern University, 1973.

Kilham, Walter H., Jr. *Raymond Hood, Architect: Form through Function in the American Skyscraper.* New York: Architectural Book Publishing Company, 1974.

Kimball, Fiske. *American Architecture.* New York: Bobbs-Merrill, 1928.

———. "Louis Sullivan—an Old Master." *Architectural Record* 57 (April 1925): 289–304.

Kinsley, Philip. "Arcturus' Light Miracle Thrills Evening Throngs." *Chicago Sunday Tribune*, 28 May 1933.

Kirsch, Karin. *The Weissenhofsiedlung: Experimental Housing Built for the Deutscher Werkbund, Stuttgart 1927*. Stuttgart: Deutsche Verlags-Anstalt, 1992.

Kocher, A. Lawrence, and Albert Frey. "New Materials and Improved Construction Methods." *Architectural Record* 73 (April 1933): 281–93.

Konrad, Kimberley A., and Michael A. Tomlan. "Gypsum Board." In *Twentieth Century Materials*, ed. Thomas C. Jester. New York: McGraw-Hill, 1995.

Krinsky, Carol Herselle. "Chicago and New York: Plans and Parallels, 1889–1929." *Museum Studies* 10 (1983): 232.

———. *Rockefeller Center*. New York: Oxford University Press, 1978.

"Large Panel Units Outstanding Advance at the Fair." *American Builder* 55 (August 1933): 26–27.

"Large Roofs Suspended by Cables to Avoid Columns." *Engineering News-Record* 87 (27 October 1921): 688–89.

Larson, C. Theodore. "New Housing Designs and Construction Systems." *Architectural Record* 75 (January 1934): 1–36.

"The Lay Critics Speak: Random Reactions from Chance Conversations." *Architectural Forum* 59 (July 1933): 28.

Le Corbusier. *Le Corbusier Œuvre Complète*. Vol. 1, *1910–1929*. Zurich: Les Editions d'Architecture (Artemis), 1964.

———. *Towards a New Architecture*. Translated by Frederick Etchells from 13th edition of *Vers une architecture*. New York: Payson and Clarke, 1927.

Leonard, Louis. "What Is Modernism?" *American Architect* 136 (November 1929): 22–25, 112.

"Lighting Up for Fair." *World's Fair Weekly*, 3 June 1933, 13–15.

Lohr, Lenox R. "Chicago Stages Its Second World's Fair." *Engineering News-Record* 110 (2 March 1933): 269–77.

———. *Fair Management*. Chicago: Cuneo Press, 1952.

———. *Guides Memories: A Century of Progress*. Chicago: A Century of Progress, circa 1935.

Lowenthal, Milton. "Trends in the Development of Building Materials." *Architectural Record* 85 (May 1939): 78–83.

Lubin, A. H. "The End of the Fair." *Commerce*, December 1935, 17–21, 56.

MacDonald, Hazel. "You Like Glass Houses? Go to Fair." *Chicago American*, 30 May 1933.

The Magazine of Light (General Electric), November 1933.

Magee, H. W. "Building with Light." *Popular Mechanics*, July 1933, 8.

Malony, T. J. "Tomorrow's Housing." *Review of Reviews and World's Work* 88 (November 1933): 28–31.

Masonite Corporation: The First Fifty Years. Chicago: Masonite Corporation, 1975.

"Mass-Produced Houses in Review." *Fortune*, April 1933, 52–57.

McConnell, J. L. "Lighting Heads the List of Special Facilities." *Engineering News-Record* 110 (2 March 1933): 283–85.

McCormick, Thomas J. "The Early Work of Joseph Lyman Silsbee." In *In Search of Modern Architecture: A Tribute to Henry Russell-Hitchcock*, ed. Helen Searing. Cambridge: M.I.T. Press, 1982.

McDowell, Malcolm. "Lighting Effects at Fair to Be Super-Spectacular." [*Chicago Daily News*], 29 March 1934. CofP, UIC.

———. "Masonite Inventor to Start Work on First Unit of Fair Home Group." *Chicago Daily News*, 14 October 1932.

———. "Neon Light as Seen at Fair Presages Architectural Use." *Chicago Daily News*, 1 August 1933.

McKee, Ann Milkovich. "Simulated Masonry." In *Twentieth Century Materials*, ed. Thomas C. Jester. New York: McGraw-Hill, 1995.

Meikle, Jeffrey. *American Plastic.* New Brunswick, N.J.: Rutgers University Press, 1995.

———. "Domesticating Modernity: Ambivalence and Appropriation, 1920–1940." In *Designing Modernity: The Arts of Reform and Persuasion, 1885–1945*, ed. Wendy Kaplan. New York: Thames and Hudson, 1995.

———. *Twentieth Century Limited: Industrial Design in America, 1925–1939.* Philadelphia: Temple University Press, 1979.

Melaragno, Michele. *An Introduction to Shell Structures: The Art and Science of Vaulting.* New York: Van Nostrand Reinhold, 1991.

Mendelsohn, Erich. "Dynamics and Function" (1923). In *Programs and Manifestoes on Twentieth-Century Architecture*, ed. Ulrich Conrads. Cambridge: M.I.T. Press, 1964.

Menocal, Narciso G. *Keck and Keck, Architects.* Madison, Wisc.: Elvehjem Museum of Art, 1980.

Miles, Maud Maple. "A Color-Conscious Decade Ahead." *Commerce*, March 1933, 22.

"The Miracle of Light at the World's Fair." *Popular Mechanics*, October 1934, 497–512+.

"Moderate-Cost House Construction and Equipment." *Architectural Record* 78 (August 1935): 104–23.

"Modern Architecture." *Architecture* 58 (October 1928): 209.

"The Modern Houses of the Century of Progress Exposition." *Architectural Forum* 59 (July 1933): 51–62.

"Modernist and Traditionalist." *Architectural Forum* 53 (July 1930): 49–50.

Moholy-Nagy, Sibyl. "The Diaspora." *Journal of the Society of Architectural Historians* 24 (March 1965): 24–26.

"More Than a Million Have Already Visited the Super-Safe Home." *Building Economy*, July–August–September–October 1933, 6–8.

Morton, Patricia A. *Hybrid Modernities: Architecture and Representation at the 1931 Colonial Exposition, Paris.* Cambridge: M.I.T. Press, 2000.

Mullin, Earl. "Exposition Ends in Thrilling Burst of Fireworks." *Chicago Daily Tribune*, 1 November 1934.

———. "Late Throngs Jam Fair; End Two Days Away." *Chicago Daily Tribune*, 30 October 1934.

Mumford, Lewis. *The Brown Decades.* 1931. Reprint, New York: Dover, 1971. Page references are to the reprint edition.

———. "Housing." In *Modern Architecture*. New York: Museum of Modern Art, 1932.

———. *Sticks and Stones.* Boni and Liveright, 1924. Reprint, New York: Dover, 1954. Page references are to the reprint edition.

———. "Two Chicago Fairs." *New Republic*, 21 January 1931, 271–72.

Murchison, Kenneth. "Hors de Concours." *Architectural Forum* 59 (July 1933): 63–64.

Muschenheim, William. "The Color of the Exposition." *Architectural Forum* 59 (July 1933): 2–5.

"Navy Builds Concrete Hangers at San Diego." *Engineering News-Record* 127 (4 December 1941): 786–88.

Neumann, Dietrich, Jerry G. Stockbridge, and Bruce S. Kaskel. "Glass Block." In *Twentieth Century Materials*, ed. Thomas C. Jester. New York: McGraw-Hill, 1995.

"New Age—New Materials—New Architecture." *World's Fair Weekly*, 20 May 1933, 5–7.

"New Fair Buildings." *Architectural Forum* 61 (July 1934): 11–30.

"The New York World's Fair: The Buildings." *Architectural Review* 86 (August 1939): 55–94.

Newman, Horatio Hackett. *Evolution Yesterday and Today*. Baltimore, Md.: Williams and Wilkins, in Connection with the Century of Progress Exposition, 1932.

Newman, James B. "The Architect and New Materials." *Architectural Forum* 60 (June 1934): 404.

"News of Fair in Pictures." *Progress* 2 (22 March 1933): 4.

"Nine Major Buildings, A Century of Progress, Chicago 1933." *Architectural Forum* 59 (July 1933): 7–22.

North, Arthur Tappin. "Committing Mayhem on Architecture." *T-Square Club Journal* 1 (July 1931): 11–13.

———. "Prefabricated Buildings Will Bring Lower Costs." *American Architect* 141 (May 1932): 66–67, 90.

"Now You Can Actually Live in a House of Glass." *House and Garden*, September 1933, 20–21.

Official Guide Book of the Fair, 1933. Chicago: Cuneo Press, 1933.

Official Guide Book of the New York World's Fair, 1939. 2nd ed. New York: World's Fair Publications, 1939.

Official Guide Book of the World's Fair of 1934. Chicago: Cuneo Press, 1934.

Official Guide New York World's Fair, 1964/65. New York: Time, 1964.

Official Handbook of Exhibits in the Division of Basic Sciences, Hall of Science, A Century of Progress, 1934. Chicago: A Century of Progress, 1934.

Official World's Fair in Pictures: Chicago, 1933. Chicago: Reuben H. Donnelley, 1933.

"The Old Homestead Goes Modern." *World's Fair Weekly*, 22 July 1933, 5–8.

"On View at the Century of Progress." *House and Garden*, July 1933, 52–53.

Otto, Frei. "Basic Concepts and Survey of Tensile Structures." In *Tensile Structures: Design, Structure, and Calculation of Buildings of Cables, Nets, and Membranes*, ed. Frei Otto, 2 vols. Cambridge: M.I.T. Press, 1969.

———. *Das hängende Dach*. Berlin: Ullstein AG, 1954.

Otto, Frei, Rudolf Trostel, and Friedrich Karl Schleyer. *Tensile Structures: Design, Structure, and Calculation of Buildings of Cables, Nets, and Membranes*, ed. Frei Otto, 2 vols. Cambridge: M.I.T. Press, 1967, 1969, 1973. Originally published as *Zugbeanspruchte Konstrucktionen* (1962).

Owings, Nathaniel A. "New Materials and Building Methods for Chicago Exposition." *Architectural Record* 71 (April 1932): 279–88, 40 advertising section.

———. *The Space In Between: An Architect's Journey.* Boston: Houghton Mifflin, 1973.

Pace, Eric. "Anton Tedesko, 90, an Expert in Uses of Reinforced Concrete." Obituaries. *New York Times,* 3 April 1994.

Packard, Robert T. "École des Beaux Arts." In *The Encyclopedia of Architecture, Design, Engineering, and Construction,* ed. Joseph A. Wilkes and Robert T. Packard. New York: John Wiley and Sons, 1988.

"Painters Begin Task of Recoloring Fair Buildings." *Chicago Daily News,* 12 April 1934.

Pape, Paul. F. "Thin Concrete Shell Dome for New York Planetarium." *Engineering News-Record* 115 (25 July 1935): 105–9.

Paris, Francklyn. "The International Exposition of Modern Industrial and Decorative Art in Paris." *Architectural Record* 58 (October 1925): 365–85.

The Parisian Dream City: A Portfolio of Photographic Views of the World's Exposition at Paris. St. Louis, Mo.: Thompson, 1900.

Pehnt, Wolfgang, ed. *Encyclopedia of Modern Architecture.* New York: Abrams, 1964.

"Permanent Impression of the Chicago Fair." *Literary Digest,* 25 November 1933, 29.

Peterson, Charles S. "The 1933 World's Fair." *Pencil Points* 10 (February 1929): 124.

Pokinski, Deborah Frances. *The Development of the American Modern Style.* Ann Arbor, Mich.: UMI Research Press, 1984.

Pommer, Richard, and Christian F. Otto. *Weissenhof 1927 and the Modern Movement in Architecture.* Chicago: University of Chicago Press, 1991.

"Popular Mechanics." *Architectural Review* 190 (June 1992): 55–58.

"Preliminary Studies for the Chicago World's Fairs." *Pencil Points* 10 (April 1929): 217–28.

"A Product of General Houses." *Architectural Forum* 57 (July 1932): 65–72.

"A Quiz in Taste." *Architectural Forum* 60 (June 1934): 472–74.

Raley, Dorothy. *A Century of Progress Homes and Furnishings.* Chicago: M. A. Ring, 1934.

Randall, Frank A. *The Development of Chicago Building Construction.* Urbana: University of Illinois Press, 1949.

Rau, Deborah Fulton. "The Making of the Merchandise Mart, 1927–1931: Air Rights and the Plan of Chicago." In *Chicago Architecture and Design, 1923–1993: Reconfiguration of an American Metropolis,* ed. John Zukowsky. Munich: Pretel-Verlag, for the Art Institute of Chicago, 1993.

"Reinforced Concrete Shell Roof over Unobstructed Dairy Floor." *Concrete* 42 (July 1934): 3–4.

"Research and Engineering Building of the A. O. Smith Corporation, Milwaukee, Wis." *Architectural Forum* 55 (November 1931): 533–40.

Rice, Norman N. "Small House Construction: A Problem to Be Solved." *Architectural Forum* 55 (August 1931): 217–22.

Ricker, Jewett E., ed. *Sculpture: A Century of Progress, Chicago, 1933.* Chicago, 1933.

Riley, Terence. *The International Style: Exhibition 15 and the Museum of Modern Art.* New York: Rizzoli, 1992.

Roberts, Jennifer Davis. *Norman Bel Geddes: An Exhibition of Theatrical and Industrial Designs.* Austin: University of Texas at Austin, 1979.

"Rostone—a New Processed Stone." *Architectural Record* 73 (May 1933): 28.

Ryan, W. D'Arcy. "Lighting 'A Century of Progress.'" *Electrical Engineering* 53 (May 1934): 731–36, plates.

———. "Lighting the Exposition." *Architectural Forum* 59 (July 1933): 47–50.

Rydell, Robert W. "The Fan Dance of Science: American World's Fairs in the Great Depression." *Isis* 76 (1985): 525–42.

———. *World of Fairs: The Century of Progress Expositions.* Chicago: University of Chicago Press, 1993.

Santomasso, Eugene A. "The Age of Reason: Architecture and Planning at the 1939/1940 New York World's Fair." In *Dawn of a New Day: The New York World's Fair, 1939/40,* ed. Helen A. Harrison and Joseph P. Cusker. New York: Queens Museum and New York University Press, 1980.

Schamberg, Mabel. "The House of Tomorrow, Interiors." In *A Century of Progress Homes and Furnishings,* ed. Dorothy Raley. Chicago: M. A. Ring, 1934.

Scheerbart, Paul, and Bruno Taut. *Glass Architecture—Alpine Architecture.* Ed. Dennis Sharp. New York: Praeger, 1972.

Schnura, Shelia Ford. "Lenox Riley Lohr and A Century of Progress, 1933–34: Management and Moxie Create a Unique Fair." M.A. thesis, Chicago State University, 1982.

Schrenk, Lisa D. "George Keck and His House of Tomorrow." *Chicago Architectural Journal* 9 (2000): 62–65.

———. *Your Future Home.* Washington, D.C.: A.I.A. Press, 1992.

Schulze, Franz. *Philip Johnson: Life and Work.* New York: A. A. Knopf, 1994.

Schwarz, Charles. "Light Rays from Arcturus Beam Brightly." *Chicago Daily News,* 22 May 1933.

Sears, Frank. *Roman Architecture.* Rev. ed. 1982. Bath, U.K.: Bath Press, 1989.

"See Chevrolets Made." General Motors advertisement. *World's Fair Weekly,* 26 August 1933, n.p.

Sennott, R. Stephen. "'Forever Inadequate to the Rising Stream': Dream Cities, Automobiles, and Urban Street Mobility in Central Chicago." In *Chicago Architecture and Design, 1923–1993: Reconfiguration of an American Metropolis,* ed. John Zukowsky. Munich: Pretel-Verlag for the Art Institute of Chicago, 1993.

Severud, Fred. "Hung Roofs." *Progressive Architecture* 37 (March 1956): 99–107.

Sexton, R. W., and B. F. Betts, eds. *American Theatres of Today: Illustrated with Plans, Sections, and Photographs of Exterior and Interior Details of Modern Motion Picture and Legitimate Theatres throughout the United States.* 2 vols. New York: Architectural Book Publishing Company, 1927.

"Shell Concrete for Spanning Large Areas." *Architectural Forum* 91 (December 1949): 101–5.

"Shell Concrete Today." *Architectural Forum* 101 (August 1954): 157–67.

Sherman, Roger W. "New Materials and Methods in Country House Construction." *Architectural Forum* 58 (March 1933): 225–35.

Shinnick, William. "Crowd Sets Record for Attendance during 1934." *Chicago Daily Tribune,* 1 November 1934.

Silliman, Benjamin Jr., and C. R. Goodrich. *The World of Science, Art, and Industry, Illustrated from Examples in the New-York Exhibition, 1853–54.* New York: G. P. Putnam, 1854.

Singer, Joseph B. *Plastics in Building.* London: Architectural Press, 1952.

"670 Million Miles an Hour." *World's Fair Weekly,* 3 June 1933, 10–12.

"Six Theater Projects." *Theater Arts Magazine,* September 1930, 762–79.

Sixty Years on the Arts Club Stage: Sixtieth Anniversary Catalogue. Chicago: The Club [Arts Club of Chicago], 1975.

Skidmore, Louis. "The Administration Building." *Architectural Forum* 55 (August 1931): 213–16.

———. "Expositions Always Influence Architecture." *American Architect* 141 (May 1932): 26–29, 79, 80.

———. "The Hall of Science, A Century of Progress Exposition: Details of Structure and Equipment." *Architectural Forum* 57 (October 1932): 361–66.

———. "Planning and Planners." *Architectural Forum* 59 (July 1933): 29–32.

Slade, Thomas M. "'The Crystal House' of 1934." *Journal of the Society of Architectural Historians* 29 (1970): 350–53.

Sloan's House of Today. New York: Ch. W. and J. Sloane, 1934.

Solon, Leon V. "Modernism in Architecture Illustrated with a Design by J. Beckening Vinckers for a Polytechnic School." *Architectural Record* 60 (September 1926): 193–200.

"Some Contrasts with 1893." *Engineering News-Record* 110 (2 March 1933): 295.

Sorkin, Michael. "See You in Disneyland." In *Variations on a Theme Park,* ed. Michael Sorkin. New York: Noon Day Press, 1992.

"A Special Advertising Section for A Century of Progress." *Architectural Forum* 59 (July 1933): 17–30.

"Special Facilities for Painting Air Force Planes Provided in Long Span Prestressed-Concrete Hanger." *Civil Engineering* 29 (January 1959): 6–9.

Stearns, Wallace N. "The Colosseum Revisited." *Art and Archaeology* 15 (February 1923): 59–64.

"Steel Barn." *Business Week,* 28 July 1934, 9.

"Steel Houses." *Architectural Forum* 58 (April 1933): 327–31.

Stern, Eugene W. "Spiderweb Concrete in Europe." *Architectural Forum* 55 (July 1931): 113–20.

Stern, Robert A. M. *New York, 1930: Architecture and Urbanism between the Two World Wars.* New York: Rizzoli, 1994.

———. *Raymond Hood.* New York: Rizolli, 1982.

Stern, Rudi. *Let There Be Neon.* New York: Abrams, 1979.

Stewart, John. "Construction Management Stressed over Technique." *Engineering News-Record* 110 (2 March 1933): 289–92.

"A Story of Light and Color." *World's Fair Weekly,* 23 September 1933.

Sullivan, Louis. *An Autobiography of an Idea.* New York: American Institute of Architects, 1922, 1924. Reprint, New York: Peter Smith, 1949. Page references are to the reprint edition.

Swales, Francis S. "Draftsmanship and Architecture as Exemplified by the Work of Ralph T. Walker." *Pencil Points* 11 (August 1930): 613–15.

"A Symposium of Prefabrication." *House and Garden,* December 1935, 65–72.

Tallmadge, Thomas E. *The Story of Architecture in America.* Rev. ed. New York: W. W. Norton, 1936.

"Technical News and Research, New Products: Wood, Textiles, Paper." *Architectural Record* 73 (April 1933): 295–306.

Tedesko, Anton. "Large Concrete Shell Roof Covers Ice Arena." *Engineering News-Record* 118 (8 April 1937): 505–10.

———. "Low-Cost Repairs Restore Concrete Hanger to Design Strength." *Civil Engineering* 17 (January 1947): 9–12.

———. "Thin-Shell Arch Selected for Denver Coliseum." *Civil Engineering* 24 (July 1954): 448–52.

———. "Wide-Span Hangers for the U.S. Navy." *Civil Engineering* 11 (December 1941): 697–700.

———. "Z-D Shell Roof at Hershey." *Architectural Concrete* 3 (1, 1937): 7–11.

Teegen, Otto. "Color Comes to the Fair." *World's Fair Weekly,* 6 May 1933, 19–20.

———. "Joseph Urban's Philosophy of Color." *Architect* 69 (May 1934): 257–71.

———. "Painting the Exposition Buildings." *Architectural Record* 73 (May 1933): 366–69.

Temko, Allen. *Eero Saarinen.* New York: George Braziller, 1962.

Tesone, S. L. "Symbolism in Fair Sculpture." *World's Fair Weekly,* 21 October 1933, 33.

"That Fair Again." *Progressive Architecture* 43 (January 1962): 66.

Thayer, Marshall. "Pioneer . . . a Wind from the West." *Railroad Model Craftsman,* February 1971, 24–26.

"Thin Concrete Shell Roof Tested under Large Unsymmetrical Load." *Engineering News-Record* 115 (7 November 1935): 635–36.

"Thin Concrete Shells for Domes and Barrel-Vault Roofs." *Engineering News-Record* 108 (14 April 1932): 537–38.

"This Year's Glass House." *Christian Science Monitor,* 8 September 1934, 6.

Thorud, Bert M. "Engineering Research and Building Construction." *Architectural Forum* 59 (July 1933): 65–69.

Time Capsule/1933. New York: Time, 1967.

Tomlan, Michael A. "Building Modern America: An Era of Standardization and Experimentation." In *Twentieth Century Building Materials,* ed. Thomas C. Jester. New York: McGraw-Hill, 1995.

"Tomorrow, Inc." *Parnassus* 9 (5 October 1937): 6.

"Towers." Advertisement for the Otis Elevator Company. *Fortune,* September 1933, 91.

"The Travel and Transport Building: A Century of Progress Exposition." *Architectural Forum* 55 (October 1931): 449–56, 501–6.

"The Trend of Progress in House Design." *American Architect* 143 (July 1933): 22–29.

"Urban's Use of Color Object Lesson to Industry." *Business Week,* 31 May 1933, 12–13.

Van Zandt, J. Parker. "A Miracle in Cans." *Review of Reviews and World's Work* 90 (October 1934): 54–57.

Vermilya, Howard P. "Houses of Modern Design Do Receive Mortgage Loans." *Architectural Record* 82 (July 1937): 62–64.

Vincent, Marc. "'Natura non facit saltus': The Evolution of Paul Cret's Architectural Theory." Ph.D. diss., University of Pennsylvania, 1994.

"Vinylite." *Business Week,* 8 July 1933, 8.

Vogelgesang, Shepard. "Color Treatment of Exhibit Space." *Architectural Record* 73 (May 1933): 370–74.

———. "The New School for Social Research." *Architectural Record* 69 (February 1931): 138–45.

Walker, Anthony J. T., Kimberly A. Konrad, and Nicole L. Stull. "Decorative Plastic

Laminates." In *Twentieth Century Materials,* ed. Thomas C. Jester. New York: McGraw-Hill, 1995.

Walker, Ralph T. "A New Architecture." *Architectural Forum* 48 (January 1928): 1–4.

White, Theo B., ed. *Paul Philippe Cret: Architect and Teacher.* Philadelphia: Art Alliance, 1973.

Whitney, Charles S. "Shell Design Adaptable to Many Uses." *Civil Engineering* 23 (February 1953): 89–91.

Willis, Carol. "Harvey Wiley Corbett." In *The Macmillan Encyclopedia of Architects,* ed. Adolf K. Placzek. New York: Free Press, 1982.

———. "Norman Bel Geddes." In *The Macmillan Encyclopedia of Architects,* ed. Adolf K. Placzek. New York: Free Press, 1982.

———. "Ralph Thomas Walker." In *The Macmillan Encyclopedia of Architects,* ed. Adolf K. Placzek. New York: Free Press, 1982.

Willoughby, Raymond. "Building Tells the Story of Progress." *Nation's Business* 21 (June 1933): 22–24.

Wilson, Richard Guy. "International Style: The MOMA Exhibition." *Progressive Architecture* 63 (February 1982): 92–105.

Wilson, Richard Guy, Dianne H. Pilgrim, and Dickran Tashjian. *The Machine Age in America, 1918–1941.* New York: Abrams, 1986.

Witmer, D. Paul. "Sports Palace for Chocolate Town." *Architectural Concrete* 3, no. 1 (1937): 3–6.

Wodehouse, Lawrence. *The Roots of the International Style.* West Cornwall, Conn.: Locus Hill Press, 1991.

Wojtowicz, Robert. *Lewis Mumford and American Modernism.* New York: Cambridge University Press, 1996.

Woltersdorf, Arthur F. "Carnival Architecture." *American Architect* 143 (July 1933): 10–21.

Wood, Andrew Dick. *Plywoods: Their Development, Manufacture, and Application.* Brooklyn, N.Y.: Chemical Publishing Company, 1943.

"World Fair Friends Rally to Keep 'Parthenon off Flushing Swamp.'" *New York Herald Tribune,* 12 December 1935.

"World's Fair Plans Mapped by Architects." *Chicago Herald and Examiner,* 24 May 1928.

Wright, Frank Lloyd. "At the Chicago World's Fair." *Architects' Journal* 78 (15 July 1933): 45–47.

———. *An Autobiography.* 2nd ed. New York: Duell, Sloan and Pearce, 1943.

Wright, Frank Lloyd, C. W. Farrier, Shepard Vogelgesang, Louis Skidmore, Hubert Burnham, and E. H. Bennett. "All Fair: As the Architects View the Lake Front." *Chicagoan* 11 (23 May 1931): 12–13, 27.

"Wright Plans Rival Display for World's Fair." *Chicago Daily News,* 18 February 1933.

"Wright Rival Fair." *Architectural Forum* 58 (April 1933): sup. 32.

"Wrightites vs. Chicago." *Time,* 9 March 1931, 63–64.

Zukowsky, John, ed. *Chicago Architecture and Design, 1923–1993: Reconfiguration of an American Metropolis.* Munich: Pretel-Verlag for the Art Institute of Chicago, 1993.

Zunz, Olivier. *Why the American Century?* Chicago: University of Chicago Press, 1998.

INDEX

LISA D. SCHRENK

is associate professor of architecture
and art history at Norwich University in
Northfield, Vermont. She was formerly the
education director for the Frank Lloyd Wright
Home and Studio Foundation in Oak Park, Illinois.